CW00919802

THE ART OF FRENCH PIANO MUSIC

DEBUSSY, RAVEL, FAURÉ, CHABRIER

THE ART OF FRENCH PIANO MUSIC

DEBUSSY, RAVEL, FAURÉ, CHABRIER

ROY HOWAT

YALE UNIVERSITY PRESS
NEW HAVEN AND LONDON

Copyright © 2009 by Roy Howat

All rights reserved. This book may not be reproduced in whole or in part, in any form (beyond that copying permitted by Sections 107 and 108 of the U.S. Copyright Law and except by reviewers for the public press), without written permission from the publishers.

For information about this and other Yale University Press publications please contact:

U.S. Office: sales.press@yale.edu   yalebooks.com
Europe Office: sales@yaleup.co.uk   yalebooks.co.uk

Set in Minion by J&L Composition Ltd, Filey, North Yorkshire

Library of Congress Control Number: 2009920775

ISBN 978-0-300-21305-8

A catalogue record for this book is available from the British Library

10 9 8 7 6 5 4 3 2 1

CONTENTS

ILLUSTRATIONS

. . . je sçauray toûjours gré à ceux qui, par un art infini soutenu par le goût, pouront ariver à rendre cet instrument susceptible d'expression . . .

– François Couperin (1er Livre de *Pièces de clavecin*)

ACKNOWLEDGMENTS

To list all those who helped make this book happen could fill a book in itself, and I beg forgiveness for any inadvertent omissions. Inspiring teachers whose insights have indelibly marked me – only a few of them are still among us – include Ken Hetherington, Frank Spedding, Sir David Willcocks, Philip Radcliffe, Ian Kemp, Wight Henderson, Michael Gough Matthews, Jacques Février, Vlado Perlemuter, Nina Walker, Brigitte Wild, and Igor Hmelnitsky. To these last three in particular, along with the late Jean Gibson, I owe much of my freedom and technique at the piano; to Ian Kemp I am grateful for the scholarly guidance that helped shape my first book, *Debussy in Proportion*; to George Caird, Sarah Verney Caird and Mary Verney I am ever-thankful for directing me to Perlemuter. As a chamber music coach, the late Miles Coverdale left an unforgettable imprint of the wit, élan and sophistication of Fauré's music; only now does it strike me what a role this played in prompting the present Chapter 18. Unforgettable stimulus came from my time working with the late Peter Platt at the University of Sydney; never will I forget the animation and focus of our many musical sessions and conversations. And how lucky I was to grow up with music-loving parents and my tolerant sister Helen, with all of whom I enjoyed playing duets. My francophile mother had me chirping a few words of French even before I tried my first notes on the piano; she later started me on the violin, setting off many years of string playing that make me automatically think orchestrally at the piano.

Sympathetic fellow-researchers have made French music a doubly enjoyable field of work, in which special gratitude goes to an informal *club des franco-philes* across the world (and their many publications), including Kenneth van Barthold, Joan Booth, Sidney Buckland, Jessica Duchen, Katharine Ellis, Neil Heyde, Robin Holloway, Barbara Kelly, Hugh Macdonald, Deborah Mawer,

Roger Nichols (who, with Philip Radcliffe, first spurred my Chabriophilia), Robert Orledge, Caroline Potter, Caroline Rae, John Rink, Paul Roberts, Lucy Robinson, Jim Samson, John Sidgwick, Jeremy Siepmann, Nigel Simeone (who, along with Charles Timbrell and Donald Dixon, talked me into writing this book), Richard Langham Smith, Simon Trezise, John York; Elliott Antokoletz, James Briscoe, Bruce Brubaker, Carlo Caballero, Tim Carter, Annegret Fauser, Gail and Jacques Delente and many participants at the French Piano Institute, Mark DeVoto, David Grayson, Julia Hennig, Ken Johansen, Sylvia Kahan, Cathy Kautsky, David Korevaar, Philip Lasser, Bennett Lerner, Robert Levin, Ralph Locke, Mark McFarland, Julian Martin, Scott McCarrey, Gwendolyn Mok, Nancy Nicholson, Arbie Orenstein, Jann Pasler, Tom Plaunt, Sabina Ratner, Marie Rolf, Anat Sharon, J.-Y. Song, Arthur Wenk, Marianne Wheeldon, Lesley Wright; Michael Christoforidis, Roger Covell, Deborah Crisp, Terence Dennis, Helen Kasztelan, Elizabeth Kertesz, Heath Lees, Julia Lu, Kerry Murphy, Deborah Priest, Nicholas Routley, Shirley Trembath, Tamás Vesmas and David Tunley, along with others listed in particular contexts below; and the late Felix Aprahamian, William Austin, Elaine Brody, Douglass Green, Paul Jacobs and Grant Johannesen. Several of us from that musical list were first brought together by Margaret G. Cobb, doyenne of Debussy research and founding *animatrice* in the early 1970s of the Centre de Documentation Claude Debussy, who continues to inspire us all. Keith and Frances Moffat have my gratitude for their hospitality during many research visits to New York.

In continental Europe encouragement, information and practical help have come from Jean-François Antonioli, Régis and Catherine d'Avezac, Marcel Bitsch, Thierry and Pierrette Bodin, Narcis Bonet, Pierre Boulez, Antony and Sheila Brown, Graham Buckland, Marie-France Calas, Philippe Cassard, Núria Cunillera Salas, Jean Claude Darcey, Micheline and the late Roger Delage; Michel Denis, Philippe Dinkel, Sylvie Douche, Jean-Jacques Eigeldinger, Henri Garus, Judith Gentil, Jay Gottlieb, Nina Gubisch-Viñes (for access to the diaries of her great-uncle Ricardo), Carles Guinovart, Charles Guy, Nancy Harper, Eric Heidsieck, Denis Herlin, Philippe Junod, Cyprien Katsaris, Henri-Louis de La Grange, Joe Laredo, Claire Launchbury, Eric Van Lauwe, Cécile Leblanc, Noël Lee, Edmond Lemaître, Anik Lesure-Devriès and the late François Lesure; Alain Louvier, Marcel Marnat, Glade Masselot, Olivier Mazal, Dominique Merlet, Rachel Moore, Jean-Michel Nectoux, Albert Nieto, Bertrand and Jacqueline Ott, Alain Planès, Gerald Pointon, Alain Poirier, Sébastien Risler, Michel, Sylvie and Solène Romieu, Jane Schmidt, Georges Starobinski, Jacques Tchamkerten, Cecilio Tieles Ferrer, Julian and Margie Todd, Damien Top, Myriam Chimènes and Alexandra Laederich of the Centre de Documentation Claude Debussy in Paris, and Rémi Copin of the Musée Claude Debussy at Saint Germain-en-Laye; and the late Marcel Ciampi, Marius Flothuis, Isabelle

Gouïn, Claude Helffer, Arthur Hoérée, Eugene Kurtz and Manuel Rosenthal. To the late Germaine Inghelbrecht (widow of 'D.-E.') I am ever-grateful for introducing me to Debussy's stepdaughter Mme Gaston de Tinan, the 'Dolly' of Fauré's duet suite. I was lucky to spend many afternoons hearing Mme de Tinan's recollections of how her stepfather played his music, and indeed of a whole epoch. For the privilege of playing on Debussy's, Ravel's and Fauré's still-beautiful pianos I am thankful to Claire Moser (Musée Labenche, Brive), Mme Claude Moreau (Musée Maurice Ravel, Montfort l'Amaury) and Thierry Maniguet (Musée de la musique, Paris). Expertise on reproducing rolls and pianos came with limitless friendliness and enthusiasm from Denis Hall and Rex Lawson (London), Denis Condon and Robert Mitchell (Sydney) and Ken Caswell (Austin), as well as from Richard Cole of The Musical Museum, Brentford.

Librarians worldwide have facilitated my access to sources, often ingeniously tracking down rare material and spontaneously supplying invaluable leads: in particular I thank the library staff at the Royal College of Music and Royal Academy of Music, London, Richard Andrewes and the Cambridge University and Music Faculty Libraries, Margaret Cranmer and the Rowe Library at King's College, the British Library, the Bibliothèque nationale de France (under its music curator Catherine Massip) and the Médiathèque Mahler in Paris, the Médiathèque Hector Berlioz at the Paris Conservatoire, the Abbaye de Royaumont (Marie-Christine Daudy and the late Isabelle Gouïn), the Conservatoire de Genève, J. Rigbie Turner and the Pierpont Morgan Library and Museum, New York, the Harry Ransom Center at the University of Texas, Austin (and the late Carlton Lake), and librarians at other universities and conservatoires around the USA, Australia and New Zealand. The insights obtained from musical editing prompt me to acknowledge my many helpful colleagues at Peters Edition and Editions Durand, along with the late Ronald Herder of Dover Publications; extracts from Ravel's music are reproduced here by kind permission of Editions Durand.

Radio producers who helped or encouraged me to explore some of the present book's themes include David Dorward, Nigel Wilkinson and Edward Blakeman (BBC Radio), Jean-Pierre Derrien, François Hudry, Martine Kaufmann, David Mechtry, Jean-Luc Rieder and Philippe Zibung (Radio France Musique and Radio Suisse Romande), John Aielli (KUT Radio, Austin), and Philip Carrick, Andrew Ford, Ralph Lane, Kevin Roper and Charles Southwood (ABC Classic FM and Radio National, Australia). Wendy Hiscocks has my warm gratitude for years of enjoyable piano duo partnership and for all she has taught me about hearing music and reading its notation through a composer's ears and eyes.

For other information, insights, encouragement and enlightening discussions I thank Richard Abram, Peter Adamson, Nicholas Bannan, Joseph

Banowetz, Michael Beckerman, Alban Beikircher, Michel Bellavance, Malcolm Bilson, Nefra Canning, Roderick Chadwick, Michael Coupe, Ward Davenny, Shaun Dillon, Daniel Dorff, Jonathan Dunsby, Stephen Emmerson, Diane Enget, Allan Evans, Malcolm Gillies, Richard Goode, Velma Guyer, Christopher Hogwood, Raymond Holden, J. Barrie Jones, Jeffrey Kallberg, Vincent Lenti, Alys Lewis, Oliver Lewis, Glyn Marillier, Peter Martin, Rosalind Martin and Peter Tonkin, Gerard McBurney, Ian Munro, Denes Nagy, Brian Newbould, Angela Newport and Roy Cox, Michael Noone, Peter Norris, Robert Philip, Bernard Roberts, Henry Roche, Hugh and Rowena Rosenbaum, Carl Schachter, Roderick Shaw (to whom I am specially indebted for some structural and thematic ideas developed in Chapters 2 and 4), Aaron Shorr, Peter Sheppard-Skærved, Janet Snowman, Gil Sullivan, Jonathan Summers, Joan Thackray, Susan Tomes, Erzsébet Tusa, Stephen Walsh, William Whitehead, Graham Williams, Cheryl and the late Dennis Stoll, and the late Cath Ellis, Numa Libin, Brian Michell, Bunty Newport and Stanley Sadie; plus Anne Boyd, David Bromfield, Kimi Coaldrake, Mervyn Cooke, Reis Flora, Hakiem van Lohuizen, William Malm, Inge van Rij, A. M. G. Rutten, Mrs H. Teunissen, and the members of the University of Western Australia gamelan (regarding Chapter 8), Anastasia Belina, Simon Perry, Nicholas Walker, Hannah Wallace, Mei-Huei Wei and the late Bill Tawse (regarding Chapter 9), Olivier Baumont, Rosalind Halton, Kimiko Okamoto, Nicholas Parle, Elena Vorotko and the late Scott Ross (regarding Chapter 10), Leslie Howard, John Phillips and Alan Walker (regarding Chapter 11), Maria Metaxaki (regarding Chapter 19), and Geoffrey Walker for Lisztian and many other insights. Angela Turner has my thanks for her work on musical examples and for many stimulating musical conversations, David Kilpatrick for his elegant diagrams, and Alistair Mills, Robin Mills and Benjamin Fallows for help with computing matters.

Several chapters develop material from earlier articles and chapters: for kindly permitting me to reuse this material I am grateful to Ashgate Books (*French Music since Berlioz*), Cambridge University Press (*The Cambridge Companion to Chopin*, *The Cambridge Companion to Ravel*, *Debussy in Proportion* and *Debussy studies*), Harwood Academic Publishers (*Recovering the Orient*), the *New Grove Dictionary of Music & Musicians* ('Claude Debussy', section 10), and the journals *Musicology Australia*, *Cahiers Debussy* and *Studies in Music*. Belinda Webster of Tall Poppies Records not only provided the golden opportunity to record all Debussy's solo piano music on compact disc (TP 094, 123, 164 and 165), but also generously allowed the reproduction of excerpts on the internet pages that supplement this book; Éditions Stil (Alain Villain) and ABC Classics (Lyle Chan and Martin Buzacott) I thank for the equivalent with my recordings of Chabrier and Fauré. For the same purpose EMI Classics kindly allowed reproduction of two songs performed by Mary Garden and Claude Debussy (from the CD collection including *Pelléas et Mélisande* conducted by Roger Désormière, 3 45770 2); I thank Duncan Moore for arranging this.

At Yale University Press, Malcolm Gerratt, Stephen Kent and Harry Haskill and my copy-editor Polly Fallows have my heartfelt gratitude for their encouragement, guidance and patience. Nigel Simeone and Roger Nichols read this book in early draft and provided invaluable feedback; Carlo Caballero, Michael Christoforidis, Jean-Jacques Eigeldinger, Denis Herlin, Neil Heyde, Denis Hall, Rex Lawson, Lucy Robinson, Richard Langham Smith and Rob Young did the same with individual chapters. Emily Kilpatrick I thank with special warmth and happiness for a multitude of musical and literary insights, and for her enormous help and loving support in the book's later stages of preparation, including the compilation of the Index. The initial research for Chapter 8 was enabled by a Visiting Fellowship in 1987 at the Humanities Research Centre of the Australian National University, Canberra. An Arts and Humanities Research Board Fellowship in Creative Arts at the Royal College of Music (2000–2003) made preparation of the book a practical reality; grateful acknowledgement is expressed to both these institutions (and to Paul Banks and Dame Janet Ritterman at the latter) for their support. My gratitude extends to the support given by the Royal Academy of Music (and in particular Amanda Glauert) where a subsequent post as Keyboard Research Fellow helped me bring the book to completion.

INTRODUCTION

Mᴏʀᴇ than thirty years of playing, editing, teaching and talking about French piano music have left me ever fonder and more admiring of it. Yet I often see it pose problems to listeners and performers, even in conservatoires where it can make the most fluent students lose confidence. What's the secret of playing French music, I'm often asked? The only secret I can think of is that there is, or should be, no secret. The composers did all they could to make themselves clear on the page and, as much as any music, this repertoire demands straightforward and unaffected performance, letting its emotional frankness and expressive structural logic speak for themselves. We just need to ensure the evocative surfaces don't mask that underlying strength and coherence. (Maybe that's the secret.) In particular, the idea of playing French music in a haze of rubato is contradicted by virtually everything the composers said, up to and including Poulenc. What they did repeatedly ask for was suppleness of colour and dynamics within firm rhythm. These relationships reflect the intrinsic plasticity of the French language in combination with its historical and philosophical rigour.

All that said, dots on a page are not music *per se*: for us to sense what inspired the composers to write the dots in the first place demands familiarity on our part with the sounding idiom and the writing. The following chapters study this from varied angles and are aimed at performers, scholars, students and amateurs for whatever help they may provide in evoking the composer's world of sound and feeling, and in the hope that we can hear and play the music with something of the inner fire that made the composers want to write it.

Composers famously tend to be suspicious of letting others analyse their music, doubtless because it too easily isolates or petrifies elements which in reality work in constant relation and motion. The analyses offered here aim at observing these interactions, following as much as possible the technical norms of the composers' own era and training. If we can read the music's notation and structure in the ways the composers did, we're more likely to hear it as they did. This is doubtless why Chopin – like Alfred Cortot a century later – insisted on his piano students analysing their repertoire in terms of key relationships, themes, paragraphs and punctuation – the sort of analytic perception that keeps us oriented within the structure, broadening not narrowing our view. If a refrain emerges to avoid gratuitous liberties (for which we have the composers' repeated word), the aim is far from puritanical – our composers were hardly puritans in everyday life – but rather to make the most of the skilful ways in which they focus the music's expression on the page for our benefit.

Good editions are thus indispensable. Regardless of price, the best edition will always end up being most economical for us, for the simple reason that inferior ones waste our time and energy with corrupt instructions that we later have to unlearn. When bar numbers are absent from even a critical edition, numbering them ourselves is a useful tool for grasping musical structures; it led me to one of the most interesting finds I ever made, documented here in Chapter 5.

Finally, the book ventures some practical information at the keyboard. Without spoonfeeding, the aim is to help readers find their own informed solutions, addressing questions that regularly arise in lessons and classes.

In focusing on four composers, the intention is to combine breadth of view without spreading matters too thin. The two chapters on Chabrier explain his high profile here. Several chapters deliberately view composers together rather than one by one, on the basis that each makes best sense in the context of his fellows, rather than in glass jars out of their native soil. Nor does any of them need such quarantine: all are strong enough to stand up in one another's company. Most of our composers also had at least passing acquaintance with one another: it's quite a thought that the elderly Fauré and the aged Saint-Saëns were still composing after Debussy died and after the much younger Ravel had written his last solo piano music. Poulenc just missed a boat by being born five years after the death of his hero Chabrier; nor did he manage to meet Debussy, though as a teenager he cheekily wheedled an autograph letter from him (by sending him a mock-official questionnaire about César Franck).

In Chapters 6–11 the aim is not so much to prove influences (a perennially slippery pursuit) but rather to trace shared language and gestures for whatever musical insights they can offer, including the constant fascination of sensing through the fingers or ear when any particular piece can be felt tapping into a vaster, often international reservoir of shared gestures, syntax, even formal archetypes. Nor do the present chapters need to be read in printed order, even if the order is designed (rather like that of Debussy's Preludes) for optimum coherence.

Translations from French sources are my own unless otherwise indicated; for reasons of space the original French is not given but is always identified by published source. Bibliographic references in the text or footnotes are usually given in abbreviated form, with full details in the Bibliography. Volumes of the Durand *Œuvres complètes de Claude Debussy* are identified by series and volume numbers (for example 1/5 for the Preludes which constitute Series 1 Volume 5). The other regularly used abbreviation is *F-Pn* musique (following the New Grove reference system) for the music department of the Bibliothèque nationale de France, Paris.

A selection of recordings related to this book can be accessed via www.yalebooks.co.uk or www.royhowat.com

PART 1

THE EXACTITUDE OF MUSICAL 'IMPRESSIONISM'

CHAPTER 1

PAINTING IN SOUND

For me there is only one art, not several – Maurice Ravel

Like it or not, the word 'impressionism', originally coined as an insult, is probably here to stay, for both painting and music. Rather than resist, we can benefit from a look at how exactly some techniques in painting are reflected in this music. Numerous structural elements are involved, as well as skilful use of surface sonority and modal colour. French habits are traditionally visual – Parisian concerts are still normally advertised and listed under the heading *spectacles* – and it can fairly be said that a French composer uninterested in painting would be rather like one uninterested in cuisine. Debussy is reported more than once as saying he would have liked to be a painter,[1] reflecting a life-long passion ranging from Watteau, Titian and Velázquez via Turner, Goya, Japanese prints, the Pre-Raphaelites and Impressionists, Whistler, Gustave Moreau and the illustrator Arthur Rackham, to his painter friends Maurice Denis, Henry Lerolle, Alfred Stevens, Odilon Redon, Frits Thaulow, Henry de Groux, Jacques-Émile Blanche, the figurative artist Alexandre Charpentier and the sculptress Camille Claudel. This preoccupation embraces literature through one of Debussy's literary idols, Jules Laforgue, whose 1883 essay on Impressionism seminally widened understanding of French visual art.[2]

The composer personally closest to Impressionism is Chabrier, who built up one of the largest ever private collections of Impressionist paintings bought directly from his friends Renoir, Monet, Cézanne and Manet. Chabrier's neighbour and one of his closest friends, Manet painted two portraits of Chabrier and incorporated him in other paintings (as did Degas and Fantin-Latour), and their shared love of things Spanish is reflected in their bold outlines, rich mix of colour and intense emotional concentration.[3]

All this attracted the young Ravel, who considered his own heritage as much Spanish as French. A lifelong Manet admirer, Ravel once linked Manet's painting *Olympia* directly to Chabrier's piano piece 'Mélancolie' (more of this in Chapter 7). Ravel's paternal uncle Édouard was a painter of quiet distinction: opposite the piano in the music room of the Musée Ravel at Montfort l'Amaury hang his oil portraits of Ravel and his brother Édouard as children, facing his fine pastel of Ravel's mother and surrounding an equally fine 1896 oil portrait of Ravel's father by Manet's and Chabrier's old friend Marcellin Desboutin.[4]

A key technique of Impressionist (and post-Impressionist) painting was a new awareness of colour relationships, following discoveries about optics that showed how our perceptions are manipulated by juxtapositions of light and colour.[5] Equivalent sonorous explorations emerge from Debussy's *Prélude à l'après-midi d'un faune*, whose opening flute arabesque (at first unaccompanied) then returns twice at the same pitch, 'illuminated' by different harmonies each time. This matches Monet's varied portrayals of a subject in different lighting – Rouen Cathedral, a haystack, or trees reflected in the Seine. Similar shifts can be heard in some of Debussy's Preludes, with a moving bass under a fixed pattern ('La Cathédrale engloutie', bars 1–6, or 'Danseuses de Delphes', bars 3–4 and 18–20).

Ravel does the same in more exotic colours (rather like Cézanne relative to Monet) in the bars surrounding the cadenza of 'Oiseaux tristes' from *Miroirs*. A more spine-tingling example occurs across bars 20–4 of 'Le gibet' from *Gaspard de la nuit*, a slow two-bar progression then repeated with an even sharper modal flavour (as in Ex. 3.5a). Ravel's teacher Fauré had already made a habit of such juxtapositions, as in his *Ballade* op. 19 (the third bar of the *andante* linking passage between the *allegretto* and *allegro* sections), Sixth Barcarolle (bars 26–7) or Ninth Nocturne (bars 8–9). The coda of his *Pavane* of 1887 shows a particularly witty example, with doodling melodic repetitions of *f'♯* and *g'♯* kaleidoscopically varied by changing harmonies underneath (F♯ minor, G♯[7], F♯ minor[7] then B[7]). A dramatic version of the same technique can be heard at the climax of his Thirteenth Nocturne of more than thirty years later (bars 115–27, under the recurring melodic F♯–D).

Fauré's entrancing 'Air de danse' for piano duet (from *Caligula* op. 52, of which more in Chapter 14) reciprocates that technique by bringing back, in the middle of the piece, its opening G major theme, now a tone lower in F but with the accompaniment still in G. Some of his piano pieces have modal shifts that result in every note of a bar contradicting the key signature, the music then slipping back to the home key as effortlessly as a cat landing on all fours. The Third and Eighth Barcarolles typify this (look for the concentrations of accidentals), along with the last of the *Pièces brèves* op. 84 (alias the Eighth

Nocturne) and the main climaxes of the Sixth Barcarolle and the Fifth Nocturne (see Ex. 15.3c). Similar wit can be inferred from contrasted harmonizations by the mature Debussy and Fauré of a popular French lullaby, 'Dodo, l'enfant do' ('Sleep, child, sleep') (Ex. 1.1). This points up, in passing, the innate contrast between Fauré's virtuosity in modulation and the student Debussy who reportedly exasperated his improvisation teacher Franck by refusing to modulate until he felt like it.[6]

Example 1.1. Harmonizations of the song 'Dodo, l'enfant do' (words added editorially)

a: Debussy, 'Jardins sous la pluie' (*Estampes*, 1903), bars 27–31

b: Fauré, 'Messieu Aoul' (*Dolly* suite op. 56, 1893–6), bars 117–24

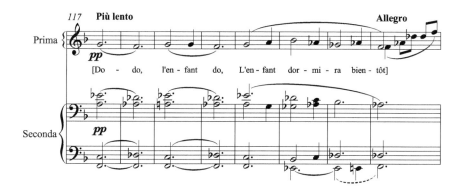

Even more interesting is when modal refraction operates on nested levels. Example 1.2a shows this first on a small scale over two bars, bridging a larger juxtaposition across the surrounding six bars (Ex. 1.2b–c). On a larger scale the latter two passages essentially stretch the same music, almost like a canvas, over two different modes, first a lydian-mixolydian mixture with raised fourth and flattened seventh (Ex. 1.2b),[7] then the whole-tone scale (Ex. 1.2c). If the first mode raises the modal temperature somewhat, the second one turns up the heat still further by removing the semitones, undercutting all sense of key in the approach to the main climax.

Example 1.2. Debussy, 'Hommage à Rameau' (*Images*, 1ʳᵉ série, 1905)

a: bars 46–7, with modal refraction

b: bars 43–5

c: bars 48–50

Similar modal relationships channel the energy of Debussy's *L'isle joyeuse*, a piece that stubbornly holds its key of A major even to start its main episodes from bars 28 and 67. This focuses attention on its modal contrasts, involving the piece's main theme (Ex. 1.3a) which alternates curiously yet logically between the 'overtone' scale already seen (bar 9) and pure lydian (bar 10). Over bars 20–1 the 'overtone' scale gives way to the whole-tone scale, involving a chromatic convergence (Ex. 1.3b) that replaces the first mode's E and F♯ by F♮, the note Debussy repeatedly emphasizes from bar 21. Later in the piece, as things intensify, the equivalent transition returns in more condensed form, jumping straight from lydian to whole-tone mode with a double chromatic convergence (Ex. 1.3c), the music again emphasizing the two new notes F♮ and G♮.[8]

Example 1.3. Debussy, *L'isle joyeuse* (1904)

a: bars 9–10 right hand (as in the *Œuvres complètes de Claude Debussy*)

b: modal transition across bars 20–1   c: across bars 165–6

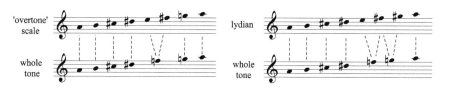

Even the arrival at the piece's triumphant coda, at last in normal A major (Ex. 7.17), is oddly anticipated by twelve bars that already harp on the tonic A. Behind this lies hidden tonal momentum, for the piece's two main key departures from A major – to B and E major at bars 36 and 99 – form a large-scale II–V sequence of descending fifths to the recapitulation's A major return at bar 160. Not only that, but the coda's decisive cadences to the tonic A, from F[7] and B♭[7] (bars 208–19 then 236–43), are anticipated by the long G pedal point from bar 115 then the C major climax at bar 141, planting a long background sequence of G–C–F[7]–B♭[7] behind the final A major resolution at bar 244.

Debussy's early works already tend to stay shy of modulation for its own sake – unlike those of Franck or Fauré – usually reserving key changes for new sections or episodes. (This may reflect the popular music most likely to have been heard around him as a small child.) Far from fighting the tendency in later years, mature pieces like *L'isle joyeuse* exploit it in dialogue with a modal variety that sometimes lets the music operate on two distinct levels of tonality: direct key relationships on the one hand against contrasts between tonal stability and instability (diatonality and chromaticism) on the other. An immediate quality of this polarity is its elemental audibility: even an untrained ear can hear the chiaroscuro contrast, with no more need to understand the techniques than an art gallery visitor needs to know colour theory or brush technique.

This was perhaps in Debussy's mind when he whimsically wrote to his publisher in 1905 that 'Reflets dans l'eau' would incorporate his 'most recent discoveries in harmonic chemistry'.[9] In fact 'Reflets dans l'eau' shows this dual tonal structure in concentrated form. Its identifiable keys are clearly defined and focused from bars 1, 35, 56, 69 and 77, forming a surprisingly classical sequence of Db–Db–Eb–Ab^7–Db (I–I–II–V–I), plus a strong whiff of V^7 from the dominant pedal across bars 24–34.[10] In between come dramatically contrasted chromatic passages (notably from bars 17 and 43) that defy any definable key. Part of Debussy's strategy is that his chromaticism allows a variety of tonal exit routes, letting him hold us in suspense until he decides which one to take. As early as 1889–90 he had talked about this, saying that with judicious use of intervallic structure 'one can travel where one wishes and leave by any door'.[11]

Playing with cadences

All we have just seen shows a masking of diatonic cadences and progression, transferring them to the music's less immediately perceptible background. The music's surface distracts us instead with a more varied range of modal cadences, something we might compare to the advances in colour mixing and composition in later nineteenth-century French painting. As often, Chabrier's *Pièces pittoresques* of 1880 lead the way: the penultimate bar of 'Mélancolie' features a cadence from VII^7 in third inversion to I in second inversion, and 'Idylle' provides a kaleidoscope of supertonic, mediant and other cadences. Poulenc insisted that Chabrier's 'Idylle' opened up 'a new harmonic universe' for him, and Manuel Rosenthal quotes Ravel as saying his own use of modes was prompted not by Gregorian chant (which he didn't know, having had a non-religious upbringing) but by Chabrier.[12] This may explain some of the distinction between him and Debussy: Julia d'Almendra has suggested that Debussy's childhood spell in Cannes, which possibly included training in the cathedral liturgy, sparked his lifelong liking for Palestrina, Gregorian modes and organum parallels (though Ravel too liked the last of these).[13]

Another case of tonic continuity over modal cadences ends the first of Fauré's early *Romances sans paroles* (Ex. 1.4). The two modal seventh chords involved – B♭⁷ and F♭⁷ against the tonic A♭ – manage to avoid sounding the home key's dominant, subdominant or leading note, and neatly relate to each other by chromatic contrary motion (𝄢). Although the piece was published only in 1881, it possibly dates from the early 1860s (Chapter 9 returns to this). Fauré's progression may have been still in Ravel's ears some decades later when he ended the Forlane of *Le tombeau de Couperin* with a sort of twentieth-century update (bars 157–8 in Ex. 12.5): Ravel's equivalent chromatic motion there is 𝄢 .

Example 1.4. Fauré, *Romances sans paroles* op. 17, no. 1, bars 61–4

With all this modal loosening, the conventional cadence can become apt fodder for 'old fogey' caricatures, as in Chabrier's piano duet *Souvenirs de Munich* of 1880, which turn the themes of *Tristan und Isolde* into quadrilles, each *Leitmotiv* in turn chopped off by a slap-happy cadence. (Fauré and Messager then did the same to Wagner's *Ring*, in the duet *Souvenirs de Bayreuth*.) Debussy's ragtime preludes 'Minstrels' and 'General Lavine' play similar pranks, with something of the air of a Toulouse-Lautrec poster.

OTHER MODAL MIXING

Modal juxtaposition can similarly serve pictorial ends. At bars 15–18 of 'Pagodes' (from *Estampes* of 1903) Debussy creates an apt sense of west views east by blending oriental-sounding pentatony in the outer voices with western chromaticism in between (Ex. 1.5). Ravel did the same a few years later in the middle of 'Laideronnette, Impératrice des Pagodes' from *Ma mère l'Oye*. 'Jumbo's Lullaby', from Debussy's *Children's Corner* of 1908, shows a deceptively innocent-looking example in a similarly exotic context (Ex. 1.6). Here each hand has almost the same pentatonic mode (Jumbo evidently being an Asian elephant), except that only the right hand has the leading note A, and only the left hand has the tonic B♭. The one can thus reach the other only via an elephantine three-octave lurch, a point humorously prodded home by Debussy's hairpin crescendo and staccato at the crucial moment.[14]

Example 1.5. Debussy, 'Pagodes', bars 15–16

Example 1.6. Debussy, 'Jumbo's Lullaby', bars 24–8

The whole-tone mode, a sort of musical colour sponge, has for many years been practically equated with Debussy, with dubious accuracy. It had long featured in Russian music: Dargomïzhsky's *The Stone Guest*, composed in the 1860s, uses it for an entire scene, as Ravel observed.[15] Apart from the prelude 'Voiles' (composed twelve years after Dukas's use of whole-tone mode in *L'apprenti sorcier*), Debussy tends to use the mode more as a tonal eraser, letting him move in and out of clear tonality as he wishes, or for building crescendos – equivalent really to Liszt's use of diminished sevenths.

Ravel, by his own account, largely abandoned whole-tone colour after his early *Shéhérazade* overture, opting instead for the more piquant octatonic mode of alternating semitones and tones. Like the whole-tone scale, octatony can act as a tonal solvent, but unlike the whole-tone scale it can accommodate diatonic triads, major-minor mixtures or triads a minor third or tritone apart, even the minor ninth chord. This versatility lets it run without monotony for longer spells than the whole-tone scale can, with the added bonus (for Ravel at least) of frequent semitone dissonances. The chromatic reduction shown immediately above Example 1.4 is basically a whole-tone dissonance followed by an octatonic one (corresponding to bars 157–8 in Example 12.5), showing the spicier, more sensual flavour of the octatonic semitone clashes. Indeed one of the main colouristic distinctions between Debussy and Ravel is their contrasting preference for respectively whole-tone and semitone dissonances. (Debussy's most 'Ravelian' moments of octatonic dissonance tend to coincide with his most overtly sensual music, for example the ballet *Jeux* and some Preludes from Book 2, as well as his earlier *Chansons de Bilitis.*)

The octatonic scale can also be formed from two diminished seventh chords a semitone apart, one sometimes acting as ornament to the other; older music used it this way, even up to some post-1900 Debussy.[16] Ravel's methodical exploration from the early 1900s of its harmonic piquancy includes the C–F♯ triadic mix that makes up the cadenza of *Jeux d'eau*, well before Stravinsky made a showcase of it in *Firebird* and *Petrushka.*[17] Arguably the scale relates to *pointillisme* in the sense of filling gaps in the octave with contrasted colours that blend into a larger whole. This rather nicely matches the way any piano music, by the nature of the instrument, has inevitably to be a *pointilliste* genre.

Modes can also work in several dimensions at once: as melody, as modal harmony or, in a more hidden way, stretched out over a slower bass line with varying harmonies above. In 'Scarbo' Ravel pulls us relentlessly into the piece's final climax via an octatonically descending bass line (leading into Ex. 3.6d). The opening section of his 'Alborada del gracioso' takes the bass line through an entire descending whole-tone octave, with just the occasional cadential diversion en route, notably where the halfway-stage A♭ turns into G♯. The long opening section of his ballet *Daphnis et Chloé* follows a similar whole-tone octave bass descent, marked more overtly with a key change at each step. Debussy's 'Reflets dans l'eau' – completed in 1905, like Ravel's 'Alborada' – has a bass line rising by minor thirds from bar 20, over which the right hand's arpeggios effectively mark out a combination of half-diminished 'Tristan' chords and major triads linked by octatonic scales. Shown in textural reduction here as Example 1.7, this echoes Ravel's String Quartet of two years earlier (first movement, from five bars before rehearsal figure 3). The next tonal departure in 'Reflets dans l'eau', from bar 43, has the bass rising instead by whole tones, over which half-diminished chords alternate with whole tones – again illustrating Debussy's remark about 'the latest discoveries in harmonic chemistry'.[18]

Example 1.7. Debussy, 'Reflets dans l'eau', bar 20 in polyphonic reduction

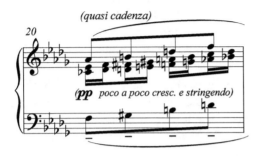

This active science of modal colour (Debussy did call it chemistry) can be traced back not only to Rameau's theoretical bent but also to Chabrier, who pioneered chains of ninth chords moving up or down by tones and semitones (notably in Act 2 of *Le Roi malgré lui*, an opera Debussy and Ravel adored). Such chains of ninths ellipticize diatonic logic by taking each resolution as read and replacing it with the next questioning ninth. Example 1.8 shows two instances, the unsounded resolutions shown in brackets in Example 1.8c. A variant emerges from Chabrier's two-piano *Valses romantiques*, where consonant grace notes 'resolve' to a ninth plus seventh (Ex. 7.26a), effectively retraining our ears about what constitutes consonance, and anticipating some similar redefinitions by Debussy and Ravel that we'll see in Chapters 2–3.

Example 1.8. Chains of ninths and their logic

a: Chabrier, *Le Roi malgré lui* (1887), 'Fête polonaise' (Chabrier's piano reduction)

b: Ravel, *Pavane pour une Infante défunte* (1899), bars 26–7

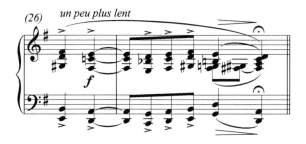

c: harmonic logic

In these respects the tonal thinking in this repertoire – despite what is often assumed – can be regarded as absolutely functional, in the basic sense that each step sets up implications that are answered, though not always exactly where or how we might expect. Debussy's piano *Image* 'Et la lune descend sur le temple qui fut' illustrates this by modally masking its E tonality with added fourths that chime throughout the organum-like opening phrase. Remove the fourths and the tonality becomes clear (worth noting when we voice the passage).

In Chapter 2 we'll see some pieces that end on a tonal question mark – like Debussy's preludes 'Voiles' or 'Brouillards' – but whose modality guides us to or through their centres of tonal focus. Other pieces, like Debussy's 'La terrasse des audiences' and 'Pour les sonorités opposées', use dominant harmonies and pedal points to imply a key that remains unsounded until the very end of the piece. In that regard 'Pour les sonorités opposés' shadows not only Ravel's 'La vallée des cloches' (*Miroirs* of 1905) but some of Debussy's own *Ariettes oubliées* of the late 1880s. One of them, 'L'ombre des arbres', unexpectedly ends in a different key from the one defined at the climax, like Debussy's later piano preludes 'Feuilles mortes' and 'Canope'.

GESTURAL EVOCATION

Like painters, composers usually work from sketches. With Debussy in particular, a miniature sketch of a finished work can surprisingly often be sensed in
its opening bar or bars, revealing thoroughly visual thinking. The asymmetrical
rise and fall across bars 1–2 of 'Reflets dans l'eau' sums up the piece's overall
shape (just how precisely will be seen in Chapter 5), while bar 1 of *L'isle joyeuse*
spirals outward, just as the whole piece does from its opening trill to a final
flourish across the whole keyboard. The opening two chords of Debussy's First
Book of Preludes (Ex. 1.9) even mark out the essential distinction between the
first two preludes themselves, the diatonic 'Danseuses de Delphes' followed by
the whole-tone 'Voiles'.

Example 1.9. Debussy, 'Danseuses de Delphes', bars 1–3

On a more immediate level Debussy and Ravel often carry their known
talent for mimicry into musical brush strokes. The rising arabesque in bars 4
and similar of 'Pagodes' from Debussy's *Estampes* gently yet evocatively traces
out the layered shape of a pagoda roof;[19] in 'Voiles' it's not hard to imagine
long silk veils trailing through the air (see Appendix 2 regarding this title);
the opening rhythm of 'Des pas sur la neige' deftly evokes a sense of snow
crunching gently underfoot; bars 1–5 of 'La Cathédrale engloutie' match
Debussy's indication *dans une brume doucement sonore* with a sense of gently
rising mist; bars 1–4 of 'Feuilles mortes' encapsulate a breath of wind followed
by leaves fluttering to earth; and 'Feux d'artifice' almost visibly conjures up the
motion of sparklers, rockets and Catherine wheels.

Likewise in Ravel's *Gaspard de la nuit* we can almost taste the sulking tear
at bar 87 of 'Ondine' (as in the poem that prefaces the piece), before the
witch's cackle erupts, followed by the bells and almost silent but relentless
spider in 'Le gibet', and the hidden nails scratching the curtain in 'Scarbo'.
Equally visual choreography emerges from Ravel's *Ma mère l'Oye*, reminding

us of the balletic element never absent from his or Debussy's music. Besides the Mallarméan way in which these passages evoke the feeling rather than just the object, the example of 'Feuilles mortes' just mentioned reflects Debussy's reported remark in an interview in February 1911, shortly before 'Feuilles mortes' was composed: 'Who can know the secret of musical composition? The sound of the sea, the outline of a horizon, the wind in the leaves, the cry of a bird – these set off complex impressions in us. And suddenly, without the consent of anyone on this earth, one of those memories bursts forth, expressing itself in the language of music.'[20]

In Fauré, less a man of the theatre and one who cared little for picturesque titles, the visual element is reflected more in an abstract sense, almost of doodling in colours and shapes (he was a chronic doodler, as many of his manuscripts show). He was also skilled at drawing caricatures of friends and colleagues, sometimes from memory – a talent shared with his teacher Saint-Saëns who just occasionally carried it sonically into his music, as in the *Danse macabre* and *Le carnaval des animaux*.[21] (*Danse macabre* can count here as piano music in the composer's scintillating two-piano version.)

For Fauré, as much as for Debussy and Ravel, evocations of bells are a recurring colour, standing out rather in the manner of Van Gogh's character-istic crimson splashes. Fauré's one explicit avowal of bell sonorities refers to the slow movement of his Second Piano Quartet (church bells he regularly heard in early childhood),[22] but they can equally be heard, as Jean-Michel Nectoux observes, in the central parts of his Fourth and Seventh Nocturnes and First Prelude (op. 103), as well as (obviously) around the word 'cloche' in the song *Prison* of 1894 (where the ⌐ articulation is a clear pointer for the sonority).[23] His First Nocturne, in the same E♭ minor key and metre as *Prison*, starts and ends with similar suggestions of B♭ tolling bells, anticipating Ravel's 'Oiseaux tristes' and 'Le gibet'. The tolling B minor chords that close his Thirteenth Nocturne (completed shortly after the death of his lifelong friend Saint-Saëns) make this sonority frame his entire Nocturne output. A *fortissimo* peal of bells seems to erupt from the final system of his *Thème et variations*, with more distant ones in the Seventh Barcarolle (the F major episode and coda) and bars 11–14 of the last of the *Pièces brèves*. That last piece ante-dates by a few years similar textures in Debussy's 'Cloches à travers les feuilles'. The chiming high C♯s in the middle of the Seventh Nocturne (answered by deeper bells from the left hand at bars 64–7) return in Debussy's prelude 'La terrasse des audiences du clair de lune' along with some markedly similar harmonies. In Fauré's Fourth Nocturne of 1884, the *Parsifal*-like opening theme, then the almost constant bell effects from bar 23 onwards, might be linked to Liszt's paraphrase on the *Parsifal* bell motive (*Feierlicher Marsch zum Heiligen Gral aus Parsifal*), published a year earlier in 1883. The Nocturne's ending also features two bars not so far removed from the swinging bell-like texture that opens Borodin's *Petite suite* with 'Au couvent'. As it happens, both that suite and Fauré's Fourth Nocturne were dedicated, within a year of each other, to the musical Comtesse Louise de Mercy-Argenteau, a friend of Liszt and Borodin.

Sometimes a title visibly or audibly matches larger symphonic aspects of the music's form. Debussy's careful wording 'Reflets *dans* l'eau' (as opposed to '*sur* l'eau') is neatly reciprocated, as Nicholas Routley remarks, by 'Des pas *sur* la neige' (rather than '*dans* la neige'), in ways that the music follows precisely, as we'll see in Chapters 2 and 5.[24] This relates to Vladimir Jankélévitch's observations about 'geotropism' – a tendency for lines and melodies to curl or tail downward – in many of Debussy's melodic shapes.[25]

An almost palpable example of rising and falling lines on a larger scale can aptly round off this chapter. 'Danseuses de Delphes' launches Debussy's Preludes with a thoroughly classical key structure – matching its classical title – of essentially I–V^7–II–V^7–I (plus a repeat of the initial I–V^7, balanced towards the end by alternations of V^7 and I). The piece's first half is characterized by rising melodic shapes right up to the central C major climax, reflecting the rising diatonic energy before its second half subsides again to the quiet closing B♭. While the piece's detailed textures are fluid rather than angular (the dancers' swirling robes), a schematic diagram of its overall energy can be drawn that neatly matches the frontage of a Greek temple like the one at Delphi (Figure 1.1).

Although not literal, this schematic representation is still very graphic in that it shows how the piece's climax straddles its exact centre, around which the main cadences mark out symmetrically spaced points of structural support rather in the manner of pillars. If the piece is viewed as primarily tripartite, this even more closely matches some smaller temple-like frontages in Delphi (with two central pillars), adjacent to its six-pillared main temple and the site of the caryatid dancers that inspired this prelude. In Chapter 2 we'll see that the buoyant yet robust musical structure of 'Danseuses de Delphes' is just an opening gesture in some larger symphonic sequences.

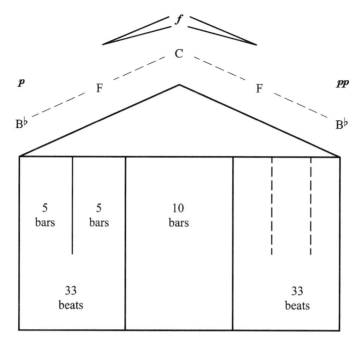

Figure 1.1. Debussy's 'Danseuses de Delphes' likened to a Greek temple frontage

CHAPTER 2

Painting in Musical Structure (1): Debussy's Preludes

Rien de plus cher que la chanson grise
Où l'indécis au précis se joint – Paul Verlaine

I_T's interesting to reflect that not until he was turning fifty was Debussy
heard premièring his solo piano music in public, in the form of some of his
Preludes between 1911 and 1913. Even these were extracts: he never said
whether he envisaged integral performance of either book.[1] Yet a brief study
of the Preludes shows structural threads wending their way through, in ways
that suggest an artist using a tonal or modal palette to produce very finely
coordinated combinations.

THE *1er LIVRE*

In Chapter 1 we saw Debussy toying with chromatic convergence in *L'isle
joyeuse* to turn tonally defined seven-note modes into the tonally unstable
whole-tone scale, as well as playing games in 'Jumbo's Lullaby' between the
notes A and B♭. A year after 'Jumbo's Lullaby' Debussy's attention was on the
first book of Preludes, whose very opening – in the same key as 'Jumbo's
Lullaby' – plays with the same material. For performers this merits investi-
gating, because Debussy's first three preludes, if played in sequence, put us in
the quandary of having to hold the audience's attention through three
opening pieces all fixated on B♭, with the first two marked at the same slowish
tempo ($\quarternote$ = 44 then $\eighthnote$ = 88). Coming from a skilled performer and freelance

musician like Debussy – whose professional survival depended, just like Mozart's, on not boring his audience – this apparent disregard of dramatic norms might seem lax if not downright stubborn. It certainly ought to raise our eyebrows. Naturally we can dodge the issue by not playing the pieces in sequence. Closer study, though, shows that it's even more interesting to stay with the sequence Debussy gave us and ascertain exactly what he was up to.

The shared tempo of 'Danseuses de Delphes' and 'Voiles' (allowing for some inherent flexibility) is mainly offset by their tonal makeup. After the very classical key sequence of 'Danseuses' (seen in Chapter 1), 'Voiles' has the most sustained use of whole-tone scale in Debussy's entire output, dominating all but the six pentatonic bars at the piece's climax.[2] Since the whole-tone scale *per se* can define no key, the only definable key in 'Voiles' has to be its pentatonic climax which ends with four clear cadences to E♭ minor, albeit modal ones from the flattened leading note D♭ – as though the 'veils' of the title lift for just a few instants. Debussy's five-flat key signature here typifies his precise thinking: he omits the normal sixth flat for E♭ minor because the passage uses only five notes of the scale.

Under its whole-tone spans the piece's opening section subtly marks out some distinct tonal implications. Debussy loses no time in emphasizing the note A♭ (or G♯), helpfully spelling it out for us by notating the piece's opening run (Ex. 2.1) from G♯ down to A♭. Then, from bar 10 and especially from bar 21, he increasingly emphasizes the note D, almost literally harping on it by bar 38.[3] Add the constant B♭ bass pedal from bar 5, and we have the dominant seventh of E♭ minor, turning bar 42 into a long-prepared perfect cadence. (This incidentally explains the high concentration of Ds across bars 38–41.)

Example 2.1. Debussy, 'Voiles', bars 1–2

Despite all those leading-note Ds, bars 42–6 carefully veil any sense of cadence, holding the pentatonic resolution in second inversion and constantly colouring the new tonic E♭ with D♭s. In effect this chromatically splits the Ds of bars 38–41 (rather than just letting them slip well-behavedly up to E♭). If we map the piece's two modes together, as in Example 2.2, we can see this forming part of a larger chromatic convergence, from the notes C–D–E to D♭–E♭, framed by the unchanging pitches around them. The resulting symmetry then relates to the piece's final C–E dyad, echoing the goal of the piece's opening phrase at bar 5.

Example 2.2. Modes in Debussy's 'Voiles'

'Voiles' emerges from this with five distinct tonal characteristics: (1) a fixation on B♭; (2) a modal polarity of whole-tone instability versus relative pentatonic stability, involving (3) mirrored chromatic motion; (4) an underlying dominant-tonic polarity; and therefore (5) a dual system of tonal tension: classical tonality in dialogue with modal polarity. All of these answer the opening bar of 'Danseuses de Delphes' (Ex. 1.9), whose key and diatonic progression match characteristics (1) and (4): the piece's first harmonic move splits the tonic B♭ chromatically to B♮ and A♮ (characteristic 3), resulting in a contrast of tonic stability with whole-tone instability across beats 1–2 (characteristic 2), before beat 3 resolves to a mixture of dominant and whole-tone colour (characteristic 5).

The two preludes are thus surprisingly reciprocal. 'Danseuses de Delphes' makes a great show of diatonic classicism but clouds it with whole-tones (those obstinate C♯s in the opening and closing bars). 'Voiles' conversely makes a show of whole tones but quietly underpins it with a large perfect cadence. It's tempting to view Debussy as manipulating our perception, Edgar Allan Poe-like, by sneaking in either an innovative idea under a conventional surface or vice versa. The two pieces' shared pulse can even make them seem like reciprocal parts of a single structure. This is underlined from the outset by the way the first two chords of 'Danseuses de Delphes' sum up the larger relationship across the two pieces (diatonic to whole-tone). Even the central cadences of 'Voiles' can be seen as having been prepared from the first chord of 'Danseuses de Delphes' onwards.

The next four preludes show variants of the same characteristics. 'Le vent dans la plaine' (Prelude no. III) is again permeated by a B♭ dominant pedal, which is chromatically split (to C♭ and B♭♭) at the piece's first harmonic departure at bar 15 – enharmonically the same process as across the first two chords of 'Danseuses de Delphes'. (The spelling is enharmonic because of the key. The note $c'♭$ is also present here from bar 1, but only as a passing appoggiatura with no harmonic function until bar 15.) The first two melodic notes of 'Le vent dans la plaine' (E♭ and D♭ in bar 3) also echo the climax of 'Voiles' and relate by contrary chromatic motion to the latter's closing C–E dyad, repeating the modal progression of Example 2.2. (A variant reading of bars 6 and 7 in 'Le vent dans la plaine', shown in the *Œuvres complètes de Claude Debussy*, pushes this a step further by then converging on the note *d'♮*.) We can thus discern the structural thread from 'Danseuses de Delphes' and 'Voiles' extending into 'Le vent dans la plaine', whose final chromatic rise from B♭ to D (bars 54–7) over the pedal B♭ echoes bars 1–3 of 'Danseuses de Delphes'.

After the isolated B♭s that end 'Le vent dans la plaine', the keys of the next two preludes, A and B, extend the opening chromatic split of 'Danseuses de Delphes' and 'Le vent dans la plaine' to a larger scale. The note B♭ or A♯ continues to permeate them, in *"Les sons et les parfums"* as an unresolved phrygian 'blue' note prominent from bar 1 onwards, and in 'Les collines d'Anacapri' as a non-functional seventh (avoiding cadences) from bar 4 through to the piece's last bar. These A♯s or B♭s continue to split chromatically at strategic points: for example, the whole last part of *"Les sons et les parfums"* from bar 38 is pervaded by added B♭s and A♯s that finally resolve in the last four bars to a tonic A, garnished each time with a B appoggiatura. The last page of 'Les collines d'Anacapri' mirrors this by constantly decorating the tonic B with a non-functional A, before the penultimate bar modally resolves it to B penta-tonic surmounted by a final high A♯. Debussy's constant unresolved sevenths towards the end of this piece so recondition our harmonic hearing that his final A♯ – technically an unresolved major seventh – acts on our ears like a resolution of the preceding repeated As.

The sixth prelude, 'Des pas sur la neige', returns to all those issues with a vengeance, leading them full circle in a number of ways. This process needs to be followed from a score of the whole piece (preferably the *Œuvres complètes*, which reproduces Debussy's voicing and articulation most accurately).

Bars 1–4 fill out a complete æolian mode on D, with B♭ emphasized as the one black key (the one that starts the melody, *tenuto*). It's tempting to see this as the first footprint in the snow of white keys – a synaesthetic element that becomes more explicit in Book 2, as well as a note that neatly picks up that final A♯ from 'Les collines d'Anacapri'. Bar 5, starting the answering phrase, withdraws B♭ in favour of B♮ strongly set off against A – a chromatic split by now familiar – and allows two more bars for that strong qualitative change to sink in.[4] Bars 8–15 follow through to complete the musical paragraph: after the B♮ of bar 5 Debussy adds F♯, then C♯ and G♯ together, then an emphasized E♭ in bar 12. These enharmonic rising fifths complete the twelve-note collec-tion – in the piece's first twelve bars, as it happens – with a strong sense of how the music's chromaticism intensifies step by step. If we continue rising by fifths, the next note is B♭, completing the circle; as if to say this, the paragraph closes in bar 15 on B♭, preceded by a B♮ that neatly mirrors how the process started.

Effectively Debussy has led us through the whole tonal or chromatic cycle without modulating, and there's characteristic irony in his having done this in the most static, ostinato-ridden of all his preludes. We might wonder how closely Schoenberg looked at this piece of proto-dodecaphony, albeit a completely tonal one. Seen from the other direction, it also puts in a kind of nutshell the rising fifths key cycle of Chopin's op. 28 Preludes – perhaps one reason why Debussy's Preludes avoid imitating Chopin's key sequence more overtly.

The remaining two main paragraphs of 'Des pas sur la neige' – bars 16–25 then bars 26–31 – play variants on this, by adding the same notes in different orders that follow the fan-shaped progressions of Figures 2.1 and 2.2. (The strictness of these is slightly more debatable: bar 20 reintroduces B♮ in a way that can justifiably be separated from the fan sequence of Figure 2.1 in that it recapitulates bar 5, whereas the note's reappearance in bar 27 is included in the fan sequence of Figure 2.2 because that context makes no back-reference to bar 5.) Were we to continue Figure 2.1 another step (as shown in parentheses), it would bring us back to B♭ and B♮; continuing it on from there would eventually make both branches converge on the piece's key of D. Figure 2.2 presents the added notes in an order from D♭ to E♭, the latter note emphasized by the melodic entry in bar 28 before bar 31 re-emphasizes D♭ (followed by the repeated C♯s of bars 32–3); a simple chromatic convergence of the two pitches then brings us back to the piece's closing tonic D. We might wonder in passing if Bartók – a Debussy devotee – observed these modal fan sequences before composing his fugal fan progressions by fifths in the *Music for Strings, Percussion and Celesta*.

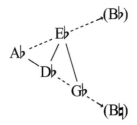

Figure 2.1. 'Des pas sur la neige', chromatic additions (other than B♮) in bars 16–25

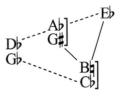

Figure 2.2. 'Des pas sur la neige', equivalent chromatic additions in bars 26–31

With these modal preoccupations worked through exhaustively in 'Des pas sur la neige', the remaining preludes of Book 1 explore other relationships.[5] Debussy's preoccupation through the first six preludes with B♭ and its chromatic neighbours thus divides the twelve preludes into two groups of six.

Similarly the first six preludes are divided into two groups of three, in that the first three are audibly dominated by B♭ before the note goes musically more underground. Debussy's manuscript reflects this by showing that the first six preludes were completed in two groups of three, before the remainder were added in a less certain order.[6] Debussy even embeds a witty touch of symmetry across the whole volume, since bars 1–2 of the twelfth prelude, 'Minstrels', are virtually a ragtime version of bars 1–2 of 'Danseuses de Delphes'.

THE 2e LIVRE

In Book 2 a new element comes from the many allusions to Stravinsky's *Petrushka*, whose première took place some months before Debussy started assembling this collection (an early draft of 'Brouillards' is dated December 1911). The impact of *Petrushka*, obvious from Debussy's letters of the time, can be read on two levels at the opening of 'Brouillards' (Ex. 2.3).[7] On its own the left-hand chord sequence echoes the closing mouth-organ motive from *Petrushka*, while the first eighth-note beat (both hands taken together) covers the 'Petrushka' chord of combined C and F♯ triads.

Example 2.3. Debussy, 'Brouillards', bars 1–2

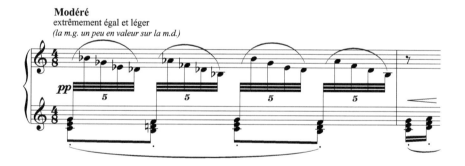

Any doubt over the link to *Petrushka* tends to be dispelled by the more texturally explicit C–G♭–C major fanfares in the middle of the piece (bars 29 and 30) or by the way the piece ends – plus the *Petrushka*-like bitonal arpeggios in bar 67 of 'Feux d'artifice', or the opening trumpet call of 'General Lavine – excentric', echoing the Appearance of the Ballerina in the Third Tableau of *Petrushka*. For all its brevity, this last example is telling because Lavine, an American clown who appeared in Paris theatres in 1910–12, was famous for a wooden puppet-like walk that prompts analogy with Petrushka. The opening figurations of *"Les fées sont d'exquises danseuses"* even suggest a direct answer to a prominent piano interjection in the Second Tableau of *Petrushka* (Ex. 2.4) – though any indebtedness here redounds to Debussy's favour, given the cadenza of 'Poissons d'or' from 1907, never mind that of Ravel's earlier *Jeux d'eau*.

Example 2.4

a: Debussy, *"Les fées sont d'exquises danseuses"* (1912–13), bars 1–2

b: Stravinsky, *Petrushka* (1911), second Tableau, bar 21, solo piano part

With this goes a newly piquant exploration, at least for Debussy's piano music, of octatonic colours. This is visible in Example 2.3, with the first two eighth-notes of 'Brouillards' exploring two octatonic collections (C–D♭–E♭ upwards then B–D♭–D♮ etc., before the episode from bar 32 explores the third collection (D–D♯/E♭–F upwards). Debussy's usage is not rigorous: many examples use incomplete collections of a mode, and he sometimes exploits similar semitone or major–minor clashes without being purely octatonic.[8] Although Ravel had consistently explored octatony since the early 1900s, it seems to have taken *Firebird* and *Petrushka* to spur Debussy to a similarly thorough investigation, from his ballet *Khamma* onwards.[9]

A third formative element of Book 2 involves a visual-tactile mix that has the left hands on white keys and the right hand (mostly) on black keys: this immediately links the opening of 'Brouillards', "*Les fées sont d'exquises danseuses*" and 'Feux d'artifice' (nos. I, IV and XII). Despite the tactile similarity, the three passages are tonally quite different. In 'Brouillards' the left hand holds the tonal fort against the right hand's incursions (Ex. 2.3); in "*Les fées*", by contrast, the tonality is defined by the right hand (Ex. 2.4a); and the start of 'Feux d'artifice' sits curiously on the fence, with no clear sense of key despite the one-flat key signature. 'La Puerta del Vino' explores a reciprocal permutation by opening with what, on its own, would be a right-hand C major melody interspersed with Moorish vocal ornaments – but over a left hand D♭–A♭ ostinato which is consonant only against the Moorish ornaments, each of which then 'resolves' to a dissonance.

To see the larger-scale consequences of all this, we must take a closer look at keys across the first four preludes of Book 2. On the last page of 'Brouillards' an attempt to install C♯ as the home key is thwarted when the bass slips back to the piece's opening key of C (bars 38–43). The following three preludes answer this by all being – or at least ending – in C♯ or D♭, an obstinacy of key surpassing even what we saw across the first three preludes in Book 1, and featuring a key curiously absent from Book 1. In fact each of those three preludes presents its C♯/D♭ key differently. 'Feuilles mortes' settles on it only at the very end. 'La Puerta del Vino', by contrast, imposes its D♭ ostinato from bar 1 (despite the right hand's contrary implications). "*Les fées sont d'exquises danseuses*" takes a page or more to settle into its D♭ major key, thus aerating the perceived sense of key after 'La Puerta del Vino'.

This is curiously reciprocated across the last three preludes of Book 2, as shown in Table 2.1. 'Canope' is mostly in a clear D minor (continuing the key signature of 'Hommage à S. Pickwick' before it) but suddenly slips into C mixolydian for its final cadence, just as unexpectedly as 'Feuilles mortes' had ended in C♯. 'Les tierces alternées' then holds to C major as firmly as 'La Puerta del Vino' had held to D♭, except for a reciprocally modulating episode shown in Table 2.1. The tonally ambiguous-sounding opening of 'Feux d'artifice' thus answers to a tonal dialogue that spans the whole of Book 2 and reaches its dénouement on the last page, where the two-hand glissandi down black and white keys sweep the board clean. A few fragments of the piece's opening then sputter out like damp squibs, before the tables turn in an exact reversal of what happened on the last page of 'Brouillards': the D♭ bass now takes over the key (as in 'La Puerta del Vino'), unshaken by the C major echoes of *La Marseillaise* over it.

Table 2.1. Tonal reciprocity across Book 2 of the Preludes

I. 'Brouillards'	II. 'Feuilles mortes'	III, IV. 'La Puerta', *Les fées*
opens with LH in C major, overlaid with RH chromaticism; last page 'foils' an attempt to install key of C♯	octatonic start over C♯, ends in C♯ major (modal)	D♭ major; central episode of III modulates down a minor third
X. 'Canope'	XI. 'Les tierces alternées'	XII. 'Feux d'artifice'
D minor with progressive modal overlay;[10] ends in C mixolydian	C major, central episode modulates up a minor third	tonally ambiguous start, ends with LH in D♭ overlaid with RH in C; last page 'foils' a RH attempt to restore key of C

SOME POSSIBLE SYMBOLISM

The picturesque nature of this structure and of the music, plus the allusions to *La Marseillaise*, *Petrushka* and much else, inevitably make us wonder if symbols might lurk inside (given Debussy's symbolist penchants). While it can be risky to over-read here (his music can stand up well enough on its own, and doesn't benefit from over-introspection in performance), related observations have been raised by numerous commentators. Carolyn Abbate and Peter Platt have suggested metaphors lurking in *Pelléas et Mélisande* that compare Golaud's shadow over Pelléas and Mélisande to the Wagnerian shadow looming over composers like Debussy, while the opera's ending suggests a dying old order giving way (or giving birth) to a new one.[11] Susan Youens similarly reads Debussy's song of 1904, 'Colloque sentimentale', as a metaphor for music shaking off the shades of dead habits and moving into the twentieth century (at a time when Debussy was in the throes of a similar domestic upheaval).[12] The tonal processes just seen in Book 2 of the Preludes suggest a similar metaphor, of the old order (C major in the book's opening triad and, *par excellence*, *La Marseillaise* on the last page) being literally outmoded by a newer, more supple approach to tonality.

Apart from anything else, the process is one into which Debussy may have been propelled willy-nilly by Stravinsky's rising star. It's very reasonable to speculate along these lines because, apart from *Tristan*, no single work by anybody – not even *Boris Godunov* – resonates so strongly in Debussy's music as *Petrushka* does in Book 2 of the Preludes. The density of this might be read as both a homage and something of an exorcism, not unlike Debussy's lifelong love-hate relationship with *Tristan*. Indeed, alert listeners may spot a 'Tristan' chord flitting, like a passing shadow, through the first bar of each book of Preludes. A telling pairing with Wagner emerges from Debussy's letter to Stravinsky of 13 April 1912, describing his admiration in *Petrushka* for 'orchestral *certainties* such as I have encountered only in *Parsifal*'.[13] If this was a rather backhanded compliment to pay the anti-Wagnerian Stravinsky, it suggests an edge to Debussy's reaction that later came to the fore.[14]

Not only *Petrushka* is involved. Book 2 of the Preludes was completed in January 1913, some seven months after the lunch party that Debussy and Stravinsky attended *chez* Louis Laloy where *The Rite of Spring* received an early private airing at the piano.[15] On 5 November 1912 Debussy reminded Stravinsky of this, writing: 'the performance haunts me like a beautiful nightmare and I try in vain to recall the terrifying impression it made.'[16] Well, perhaps not completely in vain, for we can hear him trying in 'Les tierces alternées', a piece he completed two months after writing that letter and which quotes – twice – a prominent motive from Part II of *The Rite* (Ex. 2.5: Debussy's tenuto dashes mark the allusion, which immediately repeats itself a semitone up). Whether Stravinsky ever noticed this is not on record; ironically, Debussy's prelude was published a month before the tumultuous première of *The Rite*.[17]

Example 2.5

a: 'Les tierces alternées', bars 75–8

b: Stravinsky, *The Rite of Spring*, 'Ritual action of the ancestors', Stravinsky's two-piano version, bars 19–20

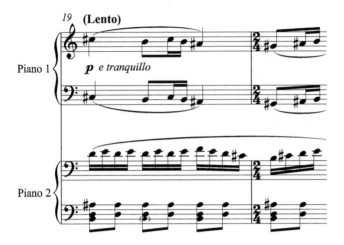

Debussy's mood of the time may be reflected in this. Stravinsky's ascendant star was doubtless one of various factors that sparked a crisis of confidence in Debussy, resulting in a mostly fallow period from late 1913 (after his ballet *Jeux* was virtually swamped in the wash from *The Rite of Spring*) until summer 1915. Cyril Scott reported finding his friend's confidence at a low ebb in 1913: 'That evening, although Debussy was charming and affable to me as usual, he spoke despondently of his own work and was, I gathered, in the midst of an unproductive period. "My style", he said, "is a limited one, and I seem to have reached the end of it".'[18] However literally we take this, we might see it paralleled by the mixed pathos and humour of his repeated *Petrushka* allusions, not least the melancholy mouth-organ echoes that close 'Brouillards'.

By contrast, the music of Debussy's creative resurgence in 1915 takes his language in new directions, avoiding Stravinskian or Tristanesque allusions or octatony except for the rapidly written third movement of *En blanc et noir*, a piece whose dedication to Stravinsky might in the context be read as a cheerful goodbye wave. If we wonder why it took *Petrushka* to propel Debussy into octatonic explorations that Ravel had already been enjoying for years, an obvious answer is that Debussy probably didn't want to be seen as aping the younger Ravel, given the minor *guerre des bouffons* already created between them by rival journalistic camps – but that *Petrushka* finally blared a summons too strident to ignore. Debussy's Preludes, however, show other links to Ravel, and these are explored in Chapter 3.

CHAPTER 3

Painting in
musical structure (2):
Ravel's *Gaspard de la nuit*

Composed in 1908, *Gaspard de la nuit* was newly in print and premièred by Debussy's friend Ricardo Viñes just as Debussy was assembling his first book of Preludes. Our interest in this chapter therefore relates specifically to Chapter 2, in terms of Ravel's virtuoso use of modes, keys and intervals.

A characteristic fingerprint (literally) of *Gaspard de la nuit* is the three-note motive or chord ♭♭♭♭♭, at various pitches with or without triadic filling (for example 'Le gibet' bar 6, 'Scarbo' bar 32 and much of 'Ondine', notably bars 55 and 89). A year after *Gaspard de la nuit* was first heard, the same motive forms an ostinato through the third of Debussy's Preludes, 'Le vent dans la plaine' which then teases out the motive in the piece's closing bars. The preceding prelude, 'Voiles', in turn features a B♭ bass ostinato rhythm that directly echoes (from bar 6) the B♭ bell ostinato of 'Le gibet'.

Unlike 'Voiles', Ravel's 'Le gibet' appears to divulge its key from the outset through its key signature, its opening B♭s and the first chord in bar 3. We could thus easily be gulled – as many have been – into considering it less sophisticated. This would invite the question of exactly how Ravel manages to hold us almost literally in suspense (given the title) through the slowest-paced piece of French music before Messiaen. In fact 'Le gibet' plays hide-and-seek with E♭ minor as much as 'Voiles' does, just in different ways. For example, while 'Voiles' is centred on a series of clear cadences to E♭ minor, 'Le gibet' has no climactic centre even to accommodate cadential resolutions. Indeed where is any tonic chord, or even any identifiable concord?

Tonally, Ravel's strategy follows two strands, the first of which is his constant use of appoggiatura. At bar 3 the first chord of stacked fifths implies E♭ minor (Ex. 3.1): we just need that F at the top to resolve up to G♭... At beat 3 G♭ duly arrives – and the rest of the texture shifts in parallel, thwarting the resolution. When the bass returns to E♭ in bars 4 and 5, the parallel motion immediately brings back that unyielding appoggiatura F above. Bar 15 offers another chance of resolution, now with an upper A♭ appoggiatura (Ex. 3.2); again the subsequent parallel chord motion thwarts the resolution. This continuing quiet drama eventually closes the piece in mirrored mode: bar 46 brings back the A♭ of Example 3.2; bar 47 resolves the melody to G♭ but renders the resolution futile by removing the tonic harmony underneath; and by the time tonic harmony returns in bar 48, the crucial voice with the G♭ has meanwhile continued down another degree to F. We are back where we started, and the piece fades out as it faded in.

Example 3.1. Ravel, 'Le gibet', bars 3–5

Example 3.2. 'Le gibet', bars 15–16

Ravel's second strand of tonal strategy is more chromatic, centred on F♭, a semitone from the (implied) tonic and a tritone from the B♭ ostinato. Bars 6–7 emphasize both relationships, letting the F♭ bite into what would otherwise be one of the piece's few consonances. (This nicely illustrates one of Ravel's rare reported remarks about how he composed: 'A note at random, then a second one and, sometimes, a third. I see what results I get by contrasting, combining and separating them.')[1] F♭ goes on to haunt much of the piece, sometimes spelt as E, sometimes acting as a sort of second-degree appoggiatura to F (as across bars 6–7 and 11–12, then in reverse at bars 28–9). From this comes one of Ravel's subtlest moments at bars 10–11, which repeat bars 6–7 but with an added voicing in parallel a third above, starting on F♭. This produces three fleeting E♭ minor chords (plus one of E♭ major), but in contexts that rob the chord of its tonic value, forcing it into the role of appoggiatura to the following diminished chord.

This ingenious reversal of tonal roles prefigures Debussy's technique in 'Les collines d'Anacapri' and 'La Puerta del Vino' (as seen in Chapter 2). Indeed, for the purposes of 'Le gibet' Ravel has effectively turned the stacked fifths of bar 3 into the piece's tonic, albeit a tantalizingly incomplete one. So effectively does he accomplish the illusion that by bar 28 he can give us an appoggiatura that leaves us the impression of resolving from an open fifth to a tritone (the F–E 'sigh' above the ostinato B♭). To top the irony, in bar 10 he lets the music rest for just a fleeting moment on a pure E♭ major chord – suggesting with programmatic aptness a ray of hope dashed by the following minor and diminished chords.

Around this, like a ghost scene, unfold the motions of classical sequence. The piece's first tonal excursion prepares a tonic cadence (via the dominant ninth at the end of bars 12, 13 and 14), only to be balked by the persistent A♭ (and F) at bar 15. Bars 17–19 repeat the sequence a fourth higher, as if to move to the subdominant A♭ minor, only for bar 20 to take off with other ideas above the A♭ bass resolution. Bars 35–9, as a condensed recapitulation of bars 12–19, balance this by implicitly preparing a cadence to B♭ minor (suggestions here of Chopin's 'Marche funèbre'), only to be balked at bar 40 by our F♭, which stubbornly refuses to resolve to what would now be a consonant F. On the way there we hear the only other E♭ minor triads of the piece, robbed again of their tonal function by the persistent bass C underneath.

The whole structure is as uncompromising as the gallows, and if the analytic language here keeps veering towards the picturesque, it's because of how strongly the music's structure acts out its story. It also gives an apt context to the way Ravel highlights the Wagnerian 'Tristan' chord from bar 12, as programmatically apt as is the tolling B♭ bell in relation to Chopin's 'Marche funèbre'. An equal link can be made to Fauré's song *Prison* of 1894, whose tolling B♭ bells and E♭ minor key explode into a series of chromatically rising Tristan chords from bar 15 (at the words '*Mon dieu, mon dieu!*').

Some of Ravel's techniques can be linked back to Chabrier's *Impromptu* of the 1860s, whose central section and coda feature what might be called dissonant 'daisy chains' across voices, a new dissonance sounding just as another one resolves. This technique became endemic to Ravel, who set it out clearly in partial analyses of a few works including the *Valses nobles et sentimentales*.[2] The technique can also be linked to the coda of Fauré's *Ballade* of 1879, where the tonic F♯ major has an E♯ above that works in a teasing seesaw action (Ex. 3.3): each time the leading note E♯ resolves up, the harmony underneath slips away from the tonic. This case retrains our ears at least momentarily to hear the seventh chord on beat 1 as consonant; a historic consequence of this can be heard in the unresolved major seventh that opens and closes Ravel's later *Jeux d'eau*, dedicated to '*mon cher maître Gabriel Fauré*'.

Example 3.3. Fauré, *Ballade* op. 19, coda

This prompts a second brief digression to note how many of Ravel's solo piano pieces – in something of a salute to Satie's *Gymnopédies* – either open or close (sometimes both) with a major seventh or minor second clash: *Sérénade grotesque, Menuet antique, Jeux d'eau, Sonatine*, the first four *Miroirs*, 'Ondine', 'Scarbo', every one of the *Valses nobles et sentimentales, Menuet sur le nom d'Haydn*, and five of the six movements of *Le tombeau de Couperin* – in sum, almost three-quarters of all his solo piano pieces, plus the two-piano 'Habanera' from *Sites auriculaires* and the outer movements of the Concerto in G. Before his second book of Preludes, Debussy's rare equivalences usually echo Ravel – the start of 'Poissons d'or' in 1907 relative to the end of the *Sonatine*, and the preludes 'Le vent dans la plaine' and 'La sérénade interrompue' relative to *Gaspard* and 'Alborada del gracioso'.

The sudden rush of semitone clashes in Debussy's second book of Preludes suggests that *Petrushka* may have tipped a long-accumulating balance rather than being the single active agent. The important role of semitone relationships (as seen in Chapter 2) in Debussy's first book of Preludes is distinct in that – for the main part – the semitones there act in horizontal rather than vertical juxtaposition, contrasting different modal areas. We might see that as the mature Debussy's way of veiling the continued operation of classical tonality at a fundamental level of his music. For Ravel, the equivalent veiling is achieved by his constant appoggiatura technique. In sum, Debussy (as in 'Voiles' or 'Reflets dans l'eau') lets non-cadential modal areas intervene between the essential motions of cadential tonality. With Ravel the latter is operating the whole time, its surface masked instead by his more piquant use of modal dissonance and overlapping appoggiaturas. It's tempting to compare the resulting difference in flavour to that between Monet and Manet, especially given Ravel's oft-expressed enthusiasm for the latter.

A lovely example of Ravel's blend of traditional and groundbreaking can be seen in the mock-chorale theme from bar 121 of 'Scarbo'. At first it sounds virtually atonal (Ex. 3.4a), each chord following different octatonic collections (as shown underneath). However, its underlying diatonic logic scuttles out if we let the two top voices resolve up a semitone, along with the inverted pedal point, as in Example 3.4b. (The result could amusingly pass for César Franck.) Ravel's ruse lies in running the top voices of Example 3.4a in constant appoggiatura mode until it eventually melts into consonance after a few lines, like Debussy's moorish chant five years later in 'La Puerta del Vino'.

Example 3.4. 'Scarbo', bars 121–3

a: Ravel's version

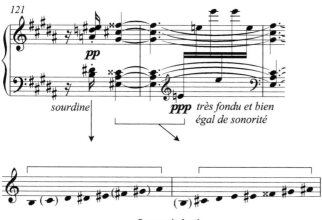

Octatonic basis

b: harmonically sanitized

The most spine-tingling octatonic sequence in *Gaspard* comes from bars 23–4 of 'Le gibet' (Ex. 3.5a): essentially a G[7] chord overlaid by triads of E, C♯ and B♭, it suggests Ravel's response – perhaps not unconnected with his love of fashionable cravats – to the poem's line about a spider spinning a macabre cravat around the hanged man's neck. From this emerges a slowly falling sequence to the major-minor chord of bars 26–7 (Ex. 3.5b), a haunting harmony that Debussy had already used in his *Proses lyriques* songs (see bars 17–18 of 'De fleurs') and which returns in his preludes 'Des pas sur la neige', 'Feuilles mortes' and 'La Puerta del Vino'. Example 3.5b in turn can be heard echoing in 'Pour la danseuse aux crotales' from Debussy's *Six épigraphes antiques* of 1914, and – more remarkably – in Alban Berg's macabre 'Warm die Lüfte' from his op. 2 *Lieder* of 1910.[3]

Example 3.5

a: Ravel, 'Le gibet', bars 23–4

b: 'Le gibet', bars 25–6 (bar 27 repeats the two lower staves of bar 26)

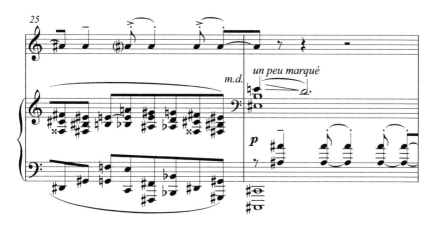

'Scarbo' resonates in Stravinsky's *Petrushka* in two sonorous ways, one of them being its opening D♯ tremolando, which Ravel reportedly wanted to sound 'like a drum'.[4] The other is the vigorous exploitation of the F♯–C major relationship, which becomes audibly Petrushka-like (before the event) by the last page of 'Scarbo' – though Ravel had already tested this tonal combination in *Jeux d'eau*.

The precisely calculated structure of 'Scarbo' is as programmatic as that of 'Le gibet', acting out the poem's recurring insomniac fantasy, combined with a progressive tightening of thumbscrews that gradually accelerates the piece (as we'll see) to no less than 27 times its opening speed. Each of the piece's three broad sections (exposition, development and coda) culminates in explosive fashion, the first two a tritone apart on F♯ and C (bars 204 and 366). Only at the final B major culmination (bar 563) is the tonal function of the previous two defined retrospectively, as dominant and neapolitan.[5]

Ravel links these keys through a subtle play of chromatic convergence and divergence. The three culminating keys are ingeniously prepared by the piece's second theme (Ex. 3.6a), a flamenco-like flourish that would unambiguously flag B major (the piece's closing key) from bar 52 were it not for the irritant of the mirrored semitonal appoggiaturas G♮ and F♮: if only they would resolve to F♯... Some pages later the exposition's culmination finally cadences thus to F♯ major (Ex. 3.6b) – only for the C♯ above to split immediately to C♮ and D♮, restarting the process (Ex. 3.6c). This in turn is finally resolved at the last climax (Ex. 3.6d): the descending bass line picks up the same C♮ and D♮ as its last two notes, resolving them this time downwards to B – just as the F♯ above it splits to F♮ and G♮, landing us back where we were at bar 52...[6]

The circular sequence perfectly encapsulates the piece's nightmare progression: just as the torment seems to resolve, the resolution turns back into the nightmare. The bass line leading to the final climax sums it up: with its complete octatonic octave descent of A–G♯–F♯–F♮–E♭–D–C–B (bars 556–63), it first retraces the approach to the piece's first climax (A–G♯–F♯), continues down to the C of the second climax, then finally sinks that extra dungeon step to B.

Locked in with this circular tonal structure is a large-scale rhythmic spiralling, accelerating the sounding tempo three times over the course of the piece, in each case by a factor of three. (Hence the 27-fold total increase referred to above: 3×3×3). The first such acceleration, across bars 17–22, locks itself cyclically into the structure with the indicated tempo equivalence at bar 395; the third accelerando, across bars 452–63, is similarly locked in across bars 615–17 (the opening motive returning at bar 617 at its opening speed). The second accelerando, harder to spot on the page, can be detected at bar 430 where once again a single beat of the bar continues the value of the preceding bar, betraying a tacit increase of speed written into the notation between bars 396 and 429.[7] Again the effect is of finding ourselves, each time we think we may have spiralled out of the Poe-like vortex, rhythmically and metrically back where we started. The effect is the more telling in the wake of 'Le gibet' with its remorselessly unchanging tempo.

An elemental distinction between Ravel's and Debussy's tonal thinking here lies in Ravel's characteristic use of cadence (often modal) as a dramatic focus for the main culminations, as opposed to Debussy's more characteristic placing of climaxes at points of tonal crisis, letting the resolution slip in more quietly later, often under modal disguise. (If 'Voiles' is something of a exception there, its climax coinciding with the piece's main cadence, it's still a more relaxed and (literally) veiled affair.)[8]

Given the links seen here across Chapters 2 and 3, Ravel's description of Debussy's first book of Preludes as 'marvellous masterpieces' (*'d'admirables chefs d'oeuvre'*) may have been penned with a touch of quiet satisfaction.[9] If Ravel, that ever-astute observer, observed the subsequent links across Book 2 of Debussy's Preludes, it may have pleased him to complete the circle modally two years later with another chromatic divergence, in the Forlane of *Le tombeau de Couperin* (see Ex. 12.5, along with the schematic reduction shown immediately above Ex. 1.4).

Example 3.6. Ravel, 'Scarbo'

a: bars 52–4   b: bars 203–6   c: bars 215–16   d: bars 561–3

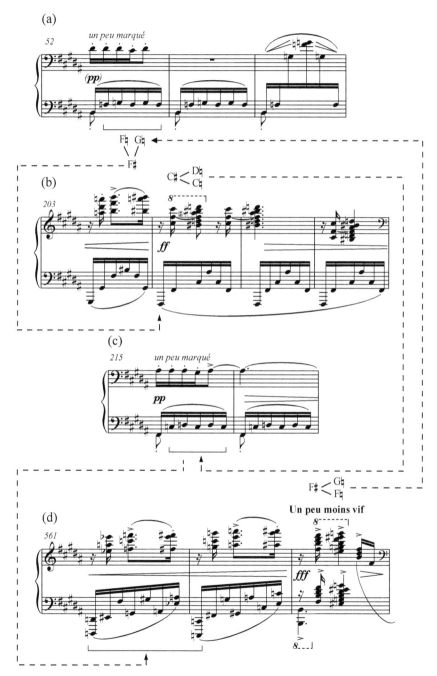

CHAPTER 4

SHAPES AND FORMS

A great painter who draws the naked human body sees with his X-ray eyes the skeleton, covered in living flesh, and not only the skeleton, but everything concealed by the skin.   – Heinrich Neuhaus

MUCH French music of this epoch has resisted classification in standard forms. We may well respond by saying bravo. For long enough a constant critical line – perhaps with a hint of sour grapes – was that it showed the composers to have been uninterested in form. We certainly have Debussy's repeated word that he was uninterested in parroting standard forms, but that's hardly the same thing. Ravel's structures, for their part, were judged, even by that veteran observer Charles Rosen in 1959, to be 'generally impeccable, if uninteresting' and those of Le tombeau de Couperin as 'traditional late-classical or romantic ones'.[1]

Chapter 12 offers a specific reply to this last case.[2] More generally – and even if we forget that Ravel was the son of a precision engineer and inventor – Rosen's verdict raises several questions, not least that of how 'impeccable if uninteresting' forms can grip and hold our attention as Ravel's do, with music that's constantly unpredictable yet architecturally cogent (a point repeatedly stressed by Ravel's colleague Vlado Perlemuter).[3] Perhaps Ravel is purring happily in his grave, having pulled the wool exactly where he intended. For him – he said as much – structure was a direct component or vehicle of the music's dramatic expression, one that shouldn't draw attention to itself and that doesn't need the listener decrypting more than that.

Indeed the strongest criticism Ravel made of Debussy was that the forms of La mer were over-intellectualized and thus drew unwelcome attention, by contrast with Chopin or even Debussy's own L'après-midi d'un faune, which

Ravel considered 'absolutely perfect' because 'it was impossible to say how it had been built up'.[4] Ravel's criticism remains one of the most illuminating ever levelled at Debussy, far from long-prevailing refrains of dreamy vagueness. Even before the artistic innovations of the early 1900s, the 1880s were a fertile decade for structural rethinking, following Liszt's and Chopin's inventiveness and the influence of literary and visual arts. Examples can be seen in the original yet disciplined combination of fantasy and strictness in Franck's two solo piano triptychs.

What Ravel said, of course, challenges the whole point of writing a chapter like this. Several instant answers arise. The 'formless' view of French music has assailed us long enough to have ingrained a rhythmically sloppy school of performance, in the teeth of everything the composers are known to have said. It's therefore pertinent to have an idea of exactly what we're shredding if, as performers, we let vagueness or sentiment on the rampage. More generally, no score can ever tell the complete musical story: it's inevitable that we still encounter problems of comprehension that the composers probably hoped would eventually take care of themselves. Chapters 15–19 deal with smaller notational aspects of this. On a larger scale, musical form is essentially a chart of the music's dramatic course; for us, sensing its logic is like reading the music's map.

DEBUSSY

In one respect it's odd that Debussy has long been touted as a formal iconoclast, for in practice few composers show us so exactly what they're doing – so long as we don't decide in advance what we're expecting to find. One of Debussy's most frequent templates, moreover, is Chopinesque modified ternary form. Incorporate in this a smaller first episode and a coda, and we have a somewhat flexible outline AbaCAc (upper case for main sections, lower for smaller episodes or returns, though final recapitulations are also sometimes condensed, as with Chopin). The initial 'Aba' segment often suggests a smaller ternary scheme within the larger one, creating the sense of a smaller structural wave followed by a larger one, while the 'c' coda then completes a reciprocal smaller ternary echo round the recapitulation. Particularly clear examples are *Masques* and *L'isle joyeuse* (whose close relationship is discussed in Chapter 14) and the *Images* 'Hommage à Rameau' and 'Mouvement'.

A quick survey of Debussy's mature piano music reveals this underlying template for one movement of *Pour le piano*, two out of three *Estampes*, four out of six *Images* plus one of the early *Images* of 1894, four out of six movements in *Children's Corner*, seven from each book of Preludes, and (at a stretch) six or seven out of twelve *Études*. (The exact tally can be debated but is based here on the presence of one main recapitulation which structurally dominates any other ritornellos.) The most frequent ambiguity lies in deciding exactly where an episode starts; this applies especially to the *Études*, where some 'b' sections grow almost imperceptibly out of the opening material and/or then grow into a 'C' section with little or no intervening ritornello. On the other side, the tally excludes pieces where an intermediate ritornello is substantial enough to suggest a rondo outline for the piece. Among the more recognizable (if sometimes irregular) rondos are the Toccata (and arguably the Sarabande) of *Pour le piano*, 'Reflets dans l'eau', the preludes 'La sérénade interrompue' and 'Brouillards', and the *Étude* 'Pour les notes répétées'.

In themselves these outlines are usually less revealing than what goes on inside them. Chapters 1–3 have already explored this in terms of the music's focal or nodal points of energy inside the larger outlines. Chapter 5 investigates it in 'Reflets dans l'eau', accounting for its peculiarly bi-thematic rondo sequence. Whatever we decide to call these forms, the labels are probably less important than a sense of how they curve or arch structurally, forming dynamic waves. With Debussy, the straighter his music is played off the page the clearer this large architecture usually becomes. As in any music, the balance between this and the placing in relief of small details is the performer's business; but awareness of the larger level – the one least visible in musical notation – brings a sense of how much its flow and balance constitute a vital part of the music's expression. A sense almost of precision engineering can be seen in an architecturally dramatic use of tempo shared by *L'isle joyeuse* and 'Hommage à Rameau' (both from the early 1900s). In a large-scale structural rubato, each piece starts its central section (bar 31 in 'Hommage', bar 67 in *L'isle joyeuse*) by pulling the basic tempo back, rather like the stretch of a large elastic, then gradually but inexorably releases the tension through a progressive increase of speed until the piece's main climax catches the built-up energy by instantaneously locking back into the basic tempo (bar 51 of 'Hommage', bar 220 of *L'isle joyeuse*).[5] These pieces incidentally date from shortly after Debussy had written this about the finale of his friend Paul Dukas's Piano Sonata: 'a powerful force . . . controls, almost imperceptibly, the rhythmic tension as if by a steel spring [*un mécanisme d'acier*] . . . the piece evokes a beauty comparable to the most perfect lines found in architecture.'[6]

We virtually know in advance not to bother looking for conventional sonata form in Debussy's piano music.[7] His nearest approach, one that allows bi-thematic recapitulation without the diatonic steps of sonata form, can be seen in the arch form of 'La terrasse des audiences du clair de lune' from Book 2 of the Preludes. (With geometric aptness the piece lies right at the centre of a larger arch sequence that spans the whole second book of Preludes, as we saw in Chapter 2.) In various of Debussy's ternary outlines listed above, a very late or short-seeming recapitulation can be attributed to elements of arch form, the rest of the 'recapitulation' having already been effectively dealt with. I say 'elements' because ternary and arch elements are often intermingled in ways that defy definition, and their logic becomes clear only if we follow the modal or other processes inside them.

One of Debussy's ingenious solutions at difficult transitions is simply to play with some of them rather like a cat with a mouse. Bars 17–20 of 'Reflets dans l'eau', like bars 27–34 of 'Poissons d'or', show him dovetailing contrasted material across a transition so that the new material first arrives like an interruption, then returns more solidly to take over a few bars later. A famous example of this links the last two movements of his orchestral *Image* 'Ibéria'.[8] Similar dovetailing, more discreetly hidden, performs a binding structural role in the Adagio of Ravel's Concerto in G, in the form of a cadential phrase across bars 31–4 (3 bars before figure 1) which reappears in varied forms across bars 34–7, 54–7, 62–5 and finally 93–6, performing a different binding function each time (with a magical interrupted cadence after its final appearance).

LITERARY INPUT

In Chapter 3 we saw Ravel translating literature into compelling musical structures; Chapter 12 returns to the topic. Literature plays a structurally vital role throughout Debussy's music. It was in song settings from the mid-1880s that he first found full musical confidence, at a time when his instrumental music was less structurally adventurous or fluid; his first fully mature instrumental work – the *Prélude à l'après-midi d'un faune* – achieves the equivalent by stretching its canvas (albeit somewhat freely) over Mallarmé's poem: as Arthur Wenk observed, its total of 110 bars matches the 110-line total of Mallarmé's poem.[9] Debussy's initial plan was for a *Prélude, Interludes et Paraphrase final* to accompany readings of Mallarmé's poem. David Grayson suggests that this tripartite sequence can still be read into the piece (a view I've long held), and even proposes the experiment of undoing the joins, inserting the text and venturing a theatrical performance, in the manner of the short interludes Debussy composed in 1900–1 for readings of Pierre Louÿs's *Chansons de Bilitis*, or his *Syrinx* for flute (originally composed as two fragments interspersed by spoken text: they were joined together when the music was posthumously published). In the case of the *Chansons de Bilitis*, Grayson observes that Debussy's interludes form such continuity across the text breaks that 'they are revealed to be, not isolated fragments, but a continuous music that has been interrupted by verse'.[10] This is proved by Debussy's reworking of the music thirteen years later as the *Six épigraphes antiques* for piano duet, in which he joined up several of the fragments in question. 'Not isolated fragments, but a continuous music' is an equally accurate description of what we saw in Chapter 2 linking various of Debussy's Preludes. Similar links across the piano *Images* as well as across the three movements of *La mer* are traced in Chapter 10 of my earlier book *Debussy in Proportion*; we'll see another case in Chapter 14 here.

DYNAMIC SHAPE

For Debussy and Fauré in particular, dynamics play a strongly defining role in structural arcs. (Chapter 3 has already touched on Debussy's and Ravel's differing structural treatment of dynamic culminations.) Dynamics can be viewed both as a formal element *per se* and as a barometer of the musical intensity defined by harmony, rhythm and texture: they set in relief those moments that the composer wants to stand out most prominently. Hence the structural distortion that results if we treat them carelessly. This will become clearer again in Chapter 5.

For all that, some leeway of dynamics is inevitably inherent, given different instruments, acoustics and performers. As we'll see in Chapter 16, Fauré constantly tinkered with dynamics when recopying or revising his music, mostly in ways that clarify rather than revise the music's architecture. In Debussy's case, it takes some acquaintance with the *Image* 'Et la lune descend sur le temple qui fut' to find the piece's main climax, one that becomes more obvious if we try the experiment of playing bars 32–3 as if the preceding build-up had continued through bar 31 (instead of being cut back again as Debussy marks). We can only guess if Debussy's decision to drop back to *p* for bar 32 was original to his plan or a daring afterthought. (He anticipates the sequence in miniature at bar 3 by suddenly dropping to *pp* for the opening phrase's culmination on the piece's first sounding main beat.) However we regard it, bar 32 needs a *p* or *pp* as intense as that of Pelléas's and Mélisande's whispered declaration of love in the opera's climactic Act 4 Scene 4. Debussy just counts on our understanding, along with the music's inbuilt rhythmic and harmonic intensification.

In fact Debussy's risk here initially backfired, for 'Et la lune descend' fell flat at its première on 21 February 1908: even the cultured Marguerite de Saint-Marceaux decided the piece was a hoax akin to 'a cat walking on the piano'.[11] This doubtless underlay Debussy's remark some weeks later to Georges Jean-Aubry: 'Viñes will have to be gently persuaded that he needs to put in some hard work on the new *Images*. He still doesn't sense their architecture clearly and, despite his incontestable virtuosity, distorts their expression'.[12] The remark revealingly shows architecture and expression inseparably linked in Debussy's mind.

The same problem of projecting intensity at low dynamics emerges from a dynamic variant at the final climax of Fauré's Fourth Barcarolle which, in the first edition of 1887, recedes *diminuendo* from bar 90 to a hushed *pp* for the harmonic sideslips in bars 92–4. Around 1923 Fauré revised this, making reprints maintain *f* for a few more bars until the sudden shift to F major in bar 92. This makes less difference to musical architecture than we might imagine, since the passage's harmonic twists make it intense at any dynamic. If Fauré's initial idea was to deliver them in a hushed whisper, his later emendation suggests he had heard too many performances that let the intensity collapse.

A complementary example is the climactic crescendo in Variation X of Fauré's *Thème et variations*, which is indicated to start from bar 69 in the original London edition of 1897 (probably following the now-lost manuscript) but only from bar 77 in the simultaneously issued Paris edition. We can doubtless read the latter placing as a revision designed to concentrate the crescendo and deter pianists from anticipating it. This ruse can misfire, though, if pianists misread it as letting the intensity drop before bar 77, since the build-up is structurally implicit from bar 69. (A critical edition can usefully flag such variants: each reading here provides vital context for the other.)

All those examples add colour to Charles Hallé's famed account of an ill and fatigued Chopin in 1848 successfully bringing off the latter part of his *Barcarolle* at a hushed *pianissimo* instead of the indicated *f* or more. 'Nobody but Chopin could have accomplished such a feat', Hallé hastened to add,[13] a remark that invites us to imagine Fauré or Debussy similarly sustaining a quiet intensity in the relevant passages of the Fourth Barcarolle and 'Et la lune descend'.

If 'Poissons d'or' saved the day at the première of Debussy's second series of *Images*, we can partly thank its virtuoso writing and clear dynamic outline, one that relates to several of Debussy's larger orchestral pieces, as well as to 'Jardins sous la pluie', *L'isle joyeuse* and 'Feux d'artifice' (all of which can be regarded as finales, as we'll see by Chapter 14). In all these pieces the opening events and episodes appear to play almost inconsequentially, only gradually coalescing into a much longer build-up (or sometimes two progressive ones) to the piece's main climax. This dynamic 'envelope', underlying the orchestral 'Jeux de vagues' from *La mer*, *Jeux* and the outer two of the orchestral *Images*, relates above all to *Pelléas et Mélisande*, and likewise to various dramatic archetypes.[14] It can also be linked more freely to some of Ravel's crescendo-driven forms like 'Scarbo' and *La valse*.

CHABRIER

As with Debussy, Chopin and Fauré, ternary outlines are a norm for Chabrier, most obviously in 'Danse villageoise' and 'Menuet pompeux' from the *Pièces pittoresques*, sometimes more compressed and integrated as in 'Idylle' or rhythmically transformed as in the compact *Ballabile*. In Chapter 13 we'll see some sophisticated ternary-within-ternary goings-on in 'Paysage', the first of the *Pièces pittoresques*, despite its deceptively simple-looking outline. His earlier *Impromptu* again seems at first unsophisticated in its ternary outline, until we look at not only what goes on inside but also its unconventional coda (more of this in Chapter 7). This anticipates the very compressed ternary-plus-coda envelope of *Bourrée fantasque*, including a complete rondo sequence inside its opening section. This piece somehow packs what feels like more than ten minutes of music into six, in a similar manner to *España* and *Joyeuse marche* (which equally count as piano repertoire because of Chabrier's sizzling two-piano version of *España* and solo and duet versions of *Joyeuse marche*).[15] It's an interesting reflection that while Chabrier's complete mature piano music (solos, duets and duos) fills a mere ninety or so minutes, few composers could serve up such a varied kaleidoscope of colour, rhythm and expression in twice that time or more. This quality especially endeared Chabrier to Ravel, that lifelong arch-enemy of musical padding.

A more sophisticated bending of ternary form (again with coda) can be found in Chabrier's 'Sous bois', whose middle section mostly consists of imitative development of the opening theme. Its bi-thematic outer sections can even tempt us to think of sonata sequence, but with the tonal variant that the second theme itself takes the music from tonic to dominant and then, in the recapitulation, flirts nostalgically with the flattened submediant.

'Mélancolie' explores a different direction again with a binary outline (plus brief culminating coda) that sets two contrasted sequences in juxtaposition, the metrically asymmetrical first part against the close imitation of the second part. 'Mauresque', another of the jewels of the *Pièces pittoresques*, compresses ternary form into almost a binary envelope, again anticipating Ravel. Ironically the strictest sonata form in Chabrier's whole output is the Schumannesque 'Improvisation'. Even more ironically, it manages to sound like an improvisation – though this is perfectly apt since strict forms, from fugue to sonata, were then a standard way of keeping improvisations on track. Chabrier had frequent experience of hearing mastery in that field from his friend César Franck.

FAURÉ

A peculiarly revealing aspect of Fauré's forms is his endings. Several of his manuscripts (including the Seventh and Eleventh Nocturnes, Fifth, Eighth and Tenth Barcarolles, C minor Piano Quartet and both violin sonatas) betray several attempts at ending a movement, including a few near misses judiciously rescued at the eleventh hour.[16] One implication is that his interest often lay – as with Debussy – in shaping wave forms that die away from a culminating 'peroration' (the word Fauré used), the ending being a less exciting task for the composer, however crucial for the listener. These often passive endings might be likened to water lapping after the boat has passed: since harmonic broadening is usually built into the endings – and since lapping water doesn't slow down – in performance it means avoiding any unmarked slowing or sagging except sometimes a marginal placing of the last cadence and final chord. (No student who ever slowed these endings in Vlado Perlemuter's hearing was likely to forget his admonition 'Ne faites pas comme une locomotive qui rentre en Gare Saint-Lazare!') Fauré is equally on record about this (as we'll see in Chapter 17), and his retouched endings usually show him tweaking the harmonic rhythm to ensure, as it were, that the boat draws up without either bumping the pier or needing any graceless last-second heave-ho.

Aside from Fauré's masterly treatment of symphonic forms in his chamber works, his piano music is mostly associated (again) with Chopinesque ternary or modified-ternary forms. This is an incomplete picture, though, not least because some of the ternary schemes disguise sophisticated goings-on inside: one of these, in the Fifth Nocturne, is explored in Chapter 15. Shorter pieces like the *Pièces brèves* show Fauré's skill at developing an idea seamlessly through a single architectural arch. The first *Pièce brève* caps the whole collection by developing its binary arc shape from an earlier single-arc version of the piece that ended just after the present halfway point (more of this on page 202).

The more rhapsodic structures of Fauré's Ninth to Twelfth Nocturnes have perhaps hampered their fame, leaving them less easy to bring off in concert than his straightforwardly ternary nocturnes (Chapter 18 returns to this topic). The Ninth to Eleventh Nocturnes share slightly asymmetrical binary sequences, each part of which develops almost monothematically in ways that convey a sense of almost botanical growth and variation, as hard to define as in Debussy's *Études* of just a few years later. The Twelfth Nocturne, not unlike

Debussy's 'Reflets dans l'eau', starts with a clear ABAB' sequence, the A reprise (bars 43–60) virtually identical with the first time round from bar 2. The B' reprise, by contrast, launches itself in the relative major of its earlier appearance (shades of Franck), and its progressive concentration culminates in a faster compressed A'B'' sequence across bars 76–90 before a stormy peroration dies away to echoes of the opening. (Fauré pushed this template farther again in the first movement of his Second Violin Sonata, composed just after the Twelfth Nocturne and in the same key.)

If such prose sounds inevitably banal beside the music, it signals Fauré's liking for two-threaded structures that can be related back to his *Ballade* op. 19. From a letter he wrote in September 1879 it emerges that the integrated *Ballade* we know was initially a group of separate pieces:

> My piano pieces nos. 2 and 3 have assumed considerably greater importance thanks to a no. 5, which is a link passage between 2 and 3. That is to say, by using *new* but at the same time *old* methods I have found a way of developing the phrases of no. 2 in a sort of interlude and at the same time stating the premises of no. 3 in such a way that the three pieces become one. It has thus turned into a Fantasy rather out of the usual run.[17]

In his editorial commentary to Fauré's letters, Jean-Michel Nectoux notes how Fauré's numbers can be matched to the sections of the complete *Ballade*: no. 1 as the opening *andante*, no. 2 the following *allegretto* and no. 3 the final woodland-like §8 *allegro moderato* (*allegro molto moderato* in the orchestral version) with the trills and bird calls.[18] Fauré's no. 5 (perhaps a slip of the pen for '4') would then be the intervening 4/4 *allegro* section, whose thematic processes exactly match Fauré's description. (He can't be referring to the §8 linking passages on each side of the 4/4 section, as they don't develop anything from no. 2.) A closer look reveals more again. After the inventively monothematic opening *andante*, the *allegretto* alternates two themes, the second of which is the opening *andante* theme. The 4/4 *allegro* then similarly adopts as its second theme the *allegretto*'s first theme, which it inventively develops in imitation and inversions. Finally the §8 *allegro moderato* continues to develop in tandem the two *allegretto* themes.

This instantly recalls the tandem-like sequential structure of *pantun* poetry, a form of Malayan origin popular among the Parnassian poets of Fauré's early years, in which the second and fourth lines of each stanza return as the first and third of the next stanza, each consequent line thus returning as an antecedent. In this context Fauré's mention of 'old' and 'new' takes on an intriguingly literal, almost crossword-like slant. (Chapter 12 returns to Ravel's and Debussy's involvement with *pantun*.) Besides its ingenious construction, Fauré's *Ballade*

rewards us doubly through its alternative, pianistically more manageable garb
with orchestral accompaniment, apparently devised following Liszt's advice.[19]
This version was doubtless a major prompt for Franck's sparkling *Variations
symphoniques* (in the same key) of five years later.

RAVEL

Binary sequences play several strong roles with Ravel. One can be seen in his
use of compact binary forms like the finale of the Concerto in G, whose second
part compresses an element of development together with irregular recapitulation of the first part. The themes thus return in unpredictable order, and
sometimes in changed harmonic contexts, making the whole second part a
long structural crescendo, rather along the lines of Chabrier's *España*. This mix
of quasi-sonata and binary also recalls Scarlatti (of whom Ravel was fond) or
the compact Mozart overture form. 'Ondine' and 'Le gibet' from *Gaspard de la
nuit* match this by the meticulous way even small passing motives make a
logical later return, again in changed order and transformed contexts. This can
be compared to some late Chopin works like the *Barcarolle* (which Ravel
adored), whose apparently loose-limbed rondo effortlessly allows a host of
passing motives or gestures to be recapitulated in unpredictable but musically
coherent order.

In an autobiographical sketch Ravel observed that *Jeux d'eau* 'is based on
two themes, like the first movement of a sonata, without however submitting
to the classical tonal scheme'.[20] This recalls what we just saw in Chabrier's
'Sous bois' (despite the two pieces' differences in character), and provides a
link to Ravel's largest piano pieces (besides the more overt sonata schemes of
the *Sonatine* and the Toccata in *Le tombeau de Couperin*). Ravel's ways of
disguising formal outlines include not only combining development with
condensed and reordered recapitulation (as already seen) but also blending
sonata elements with simpler shapes. 'Noctuelles' and 'La vallée des cloches'
from the *Miroirs* illustrate this by combining sonata-type recapitulations with
respectively ternary and arch forms; this points towards his more veiled
handling of structure in *Gaspard de la nuit*, where he evidently wants the
dramatic shape to be more perceptible than the technical forms that drive it.

If Ravel would hardly have wanted sonata form to be on our mind when
listening to *Gaspard*, closer study reveals its discreet ubiquity, holding each
piece taut without drawing attention to itself. 'Ondine', really a sonata form by
stealth, conceals its outlines by closely interlinking its themes in a long
blended line that motivically keeps wrapping around itself.[21] As Table 4.1
shows, the constituent thematic groups (insofar as one can isolate them)
return in reverse order. Only in retrospect can it be seen that by bar 47 a

characteristic Ravel development section (alternating two contrasted themes) is already under way, and that in bars 57–65 development turns imperceptibly into recapitulation. The development section (a much more Mozartian than Beethovenian affair) is thus inseparably dovetailed into the surrounding exposition and recapitulation; one of the movement's main motives (*c* in Table 4.1) is entirely contained inside it.

Table 4.1. Thematic sequence of 'Ondine'

Motive:		*x*	*a*	*a'*	*a"*	*t*	*b*	*c*
Exposition:	bar	0	2, 14	10	16	22	32	45
Development:	bar	—	42, 47	—	—	—	52	(45), 50, (57)
Recapitulation:	bar	89	80	84	88	72	66	57

Motives *a* and *b* are effectively the first and second themes, with *x* as accompanying texture (but an important element in itself, as the final bars show) and *t* as transitional theme (counted from bar 22 because of how closely bars 74–9 recapitulate bars 22–6 as an entity). The motives are closely interlinked: *a'* is derived from *a* at bars 5–6, *a"* from *a* at bar 4; *t* comprises two motives permanently linked together, the first of which (bar 22) is an intervallic augmentation of *a"*; the second phrase of *b* repeats the second phrase of *a'*; and *c* can be related to the rising part of *a* (across bars 2–3). Bar 88 also refers texturally back to bar 55. The opening incomplete bar is counted '0', as in the Peters edition.

Unlike in *Jeux d'eau*, Ravel sails close here to the classical tonal structure of sonata form: the way that motives *t* and *b* take the key via the supertonic to the dominant is entirely Mozartian. The veiled recapitulation from bar 57 is then quietly underlined by the enharmonic tonic, the only sounding tonic between the piece's first four and last three bars. (Bar 14 has a weaker tonal sense than bar 2 because of Ravel's careful removal of the tonic from the accompaniment.) Any sense of tonic return at bar 57 is masked by the added seventh, but this links naturally to the sevenths at bar 2. In the closing bars (from bar 89) Ravel emphasizes the arch shape by neatly embedding the G♯–A–G♯–G♯–A–G♯–G♯–A sequence of the opening *x* motive in the arpeggios of the last three bars. Vlado Perlemuter later recalled (in conversation) how Ravel pointed this out to him, adding '*comme si rien ne s'était passé*' ('as if nothing had happened').[22]

As we saw in Chapter 3, 'Le gibet' avoids such an overt tonal sequence, and again masks its quietly climactic development section (bars 28–34, mainly exploiting the 'sigh' from bar 7). This starts within a quarter-note of the piece's halfway point, giving the piece more the feeling of an overall binary sequence, before leading straight into an abbreviated recapitulation of bars 12–24. The piece then ends with a recapitulation of bars 1–11 in reverse thematic order, leaving an equal sense of arch form blended with the veiled sonata form.

The dramatic interest of what happens inside 'Scarbo' has already been explored in Chapter 3; its expansive sonata form – the most explicit in *Gaspard de la nuit* – is shown here as Table 4.2. Again the recapitulation is mostly in reverse order, the resultant sense of arch form running in ironic counterpoint with the piece's open-ended crescendo sequences and the repeated cyclic accelerandi that we saw in Chapter 3. Theme *F* has the character of a second theme proper, presenting a contrast to *a–e* whose close relationship forms a very extended first group rounded off by the return of *a'* at bar 110. This return conveys a whiff of sonata-rondo form, though the returning theme here performs a closing rather than opening role.[23]

Table 4.2. Thematic sequence of 'Scarbo'

Motive:		*a*	*a'*	*b*	*c*	*d*	*e*	*F*
Exposition:	bar	1	32, 110	52	65	80	94	121–213
Development:	bar	314	—	215	—	—	256, 318, 345	289, 303, 366
Recapitulation:	bar	395	386	431	437	448	—	477
Coda:	bar	617	580	593	—	—	—	586, 602

All motives are related by a rising semitone or tone, creating audible motivic continuity across transitions like bars 210–15 and 377–87. Motive *c*, a sort of skeletal derivative of *b*, is differentiated here because of its contrasted rhythmic character. As in 'Ondine', development and recapitulation are so mixed that the labels serve more for reference than for exact definition.

MEASURABLE SHAPES

In Ravel's Concerto in G, the finale's binary outline hides a small secret. Ravel's careful beaming of the first piano entry marks out the same melody as the bassoon solo that launches the recapitulation 153 bars later. Each of these entries is preceded by four bars of introduction. The second of these four-bar groups, marking the movement's main binary division at rehearsal figure 14, also divides its total of 306 bars in the exact ratio 153+153. This would be less remarkable were the two halves of the movement not structured in completely different ways, despite their shared material. Moreover, it forms part of a larger geometry. The tempo of this movement can be linked directly to that of the preceding Adagio. (Ravel indicated the Adagio ♪ = 76, and Vlado Perlemuter suggested ♩ = 72–76 for the finale, allowing for orchestral

articulation like the bassoon and contrabasses at the recap.) By that equivalence a bar of the Adagio (six eighth-notes) matches six bars of the finale – a
suggestive figure since the finale's total of 306 bars is conveniently a multiple
of six. If the entire length of the finale is thus mirrored backwards from the
end of the Adagio, by counting back 306 eighth-notes or 51 bars, it drops us
precisely – to the nearest note – at the Adagio's main turning point at rehearsal
figure 4 (bar 58). Similar geometry can be found in the Fugue of Franck's
Prélude, Choral et Fugue, whose subject inversion (upbeat to bar 218) marks
the exact halfway point to its *fff* climax, again with quite different internal
structures for each half. Further examples in Fauré will be seen in Chapters 15
and 18. Whether or not such balance is there through the composer's
conscious design, it can do performers no harm to be aware of the resulting
large-scale rhythm.

Unusual phrase balance can again be sensed in the almost mannered phrase
repetitions that pervade much of Debussy's *L'isle joyeuse*, notably the sections
in $\frac{4}{4}$ metre. These repetitions are so pervasive that they craftily distract us from
the discreetly appended odd bars which ensure that the piece's $\frac{4}{4}$ episodes
always amount to totals of three-bar or six-bar groups. (Try counting them:
you'll be surprised.) This is curious enough in itself, but becomes more intriguing again if we note that the many three-bar groups of $\frac{4}{4}$ match the eight-bar
groups that dominate the piece's $\frac{3}{8}$ sections (24 eighth-notes in each case,
following Debussy's indicated $\flat = \flat$ across the transitions). The implication suggests itself that Debussy somehow wanted this hidden hypermetric
equivalence running through the piece's structure; in Chapter 5 we'll see why.

'Reflets dans l'eau', Hokusai, Edgar Allan Poe and Leonardo of Pisa

A PHOTOGRAPH exists of Debussy in his study with Stravinsky;[1] on the wall behind them are two Japanese *estampes* including Katsushika Hokusai's *Great Wave off Kanagawa* (of which more below). Debussy had a stylized imitation of this *estampe* reproduced on the front cover of *La mer* in 1905, its looming wave aptly reflecting the momentum of Debussy's crashing waves at the end of the first movement and in the finale. Some deeper-lying links to Hokusai's print emerge from the musical structures Debussy was exploring around the same time as he was composing *La mer*, in 1903–5.

Chapter 1 observed the surprisingly classical way Debussy launches his piano *Images* and Preludes: in each collection the opening piece – 'Reflets dans l'eau' and 'Danseuses de Delphes' – follows a diatonic key sequence of essentially I–I–II–V^7–I (plus a passing V^7 in the first part). The symmetrical arch defined by that sequence in 'Danseuses de Delphes' (see p. 17) suggests that we check the shape produced by the equivalent sequence in 'Reflets dans l'eau'. The corresponding tonal touchdowns in 'Reflets' occur at bars 35, 56, 69 and 77 (the last one a cunningly delayed resolution of the near-cadence at bar 73), making up a sequence of 34+21+13+8 bars.[2] Any botanist's or mathematician's eyebrows are likely to rise on seeing this, for the numbers belong to a sequence that manifests itself in plant growth and has fascinated mathematicians since being written about in the thirteenth century by Leonardo of Pisa, the mathematician who brought Arabic numerals to the western world.

Leonardo's nickname Fibonacci (= Figlio Bonaccio) lives on in the number series that intrigued him, one that starts either 0+1 or 1+1, each succeeding term then being the sum of the two before: 1, 2, 3, 5, 8, 13, 21, 34, 55, 89 . . . What, we may ask, are Fibonacci's numbers doing forming the tonal skeleton of 'Reflets dans l'eau'? The fullest answer is in my book *Debussy in Proportion*, but a summary is relevant here. Two immediate questions suggest themselves. Do the numbers appear in other Debussy pieces? And can their apparent presence in 'Reflets' be related to the piece's other events, bearing in mind that its total length of 94 bars doesn't fit the series?

An answer to the first question emerges from the very defined 55-bar introduction to the finale of *La mer* (internally divided 21+21+13 bars), the 34 bars that build to the *ff* coda of *L'isle joyeuse* and similarly to the main recapitulation of *Masques,* the 34 bars constituting the song 'Spleen' from *Ariettes oubliées* (divided 13+8+13), and numerous other examples. Note that these all have to be counted in *completed* bars: an opening 34-bar group, for example, is thus completed at the start of bar 35, just as eight-bar groups are marked by the start of bars 9 and 17 (not 8 and 16); the start of (say) bar 34 is thus irrelevant in Fibonacci terms, alluring though the number may look.

Regarding the second question, a musical element of 'Reflets dans l'eau' that immediately invites comparative measurement is the piece's complementary tonal sequence of tonal stability versus chromaticism, already discussed in Chapter 1. The two long-term departures from diatonic stability occur at bars 17 and 43 – literally '*où l'indécis au précis se joint*' – diatonic order being finally restored from bar 69: this articulates a sequence right across the whole piece of 16+26+26+26 bars. Divide those numbers by two (or, equivalently, count the music in two-bar units), and the sequence becomes 8+13+13+13. The piece's intermediate point of tonal return at bar 35 forms a symmetrical division inside this, of 34+34 bars.

Something is clearly afoot, but to make any more of it we need to look at the unusual but simple properties of Fibonacci's numbers. Their most geometrically potent quality is that, as the Fibonacci sequence progresses, the ratio between successive terms comes ever nearer to an exact proportion widely known as golden section. This ratio, documented in Euclid's *Elements* as 'extreme and mean ratio', is obtained by dividing any fixed length in such a way that the shorter portion bears the same ratio to the longer portion as the longer portion bears to the whole length.

In Figure 5.1, the line from A to B is divided by golden section at C; D marks the complementary golden section if we measure from B back to A; the ratio itself approximates to 0.618 of the distance measured.[3] The special property of golden section is that D also divides the length from A to C in golden section. The system can be further extended or filled in to form an endless network of identical ratios, something no other ratio will do. This geometrically organic property (or 'dynamic symmetry' as Jay Hambidge's books term it) is accepted as the fundamental reason for the ratio's botanical prominence and its role through various epochs in art.[4] Besides its practical value in spatial or visual design, claims have long been made for the ratio's aesthetic qualities, mostly on

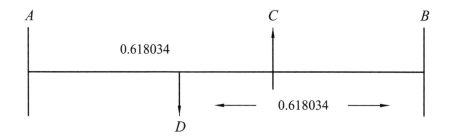

Figure 5.1. Golden section

the basis that the eye, for example, intuitively picks up the harmonious rhythm of a proportion that can constantly reproduce itself by internal division or external extension.[5]

However we regard the aesthetics, the Fibonacci bar groups in 'Reflets dans l'eau' mean that each point of diatonic definition in its I–I–II–V⁷–I key sequence marks a golden section (usually to the nearest eighth-note) en route to the next one: 34:21 bars, then 21:13 and finally 13:8. Likewise the piece's first large-scale departure from the tonic, after 16 bars, forms a golden section en route to the next one after bar 42 (16:26 bars = 8:13); the latter in turn marks the point of golden section between the start of the piece and the final return to diatonic stability at bar 68 (42:26 bars = 21:13).

It was as recently as the 1880s – and in Paris – that Fibonacci's name was first appended to his number series, by the French mathematician Édouard Lucas. Lucas noted that any such summation series with a memory of two progressively converges on the exact value of golden section. His own name graces the next such series, starting 1+3: from 3, 4 upward the 'Lucas series' expresses golden section to nearest whole numbers, continuing 7, 11, 18, 29, 47... In bijugate form – 14, 22, 36, 58, 94 etc. – this sequence coincides with the 94-bar length of 'Reflets dans l'eau'. Golden section division of this 94-bar span comes after 58 bars, that is, the start of bar 59, placing us right at the focus of the piece's main climax (after the indicated crescendo from *ff*) where Debussy's texture punches out a strident motive shared with *La mer*.

To observe how these elements and sequences interact, we need to chart the entire piece, as in Figure 5.2. At the top (**a**) is the diatonic key order, following a pure Fibonacci sequence. Next down, and linking into it (**b**), is the more elemental sequence of tonal stability versus chromaticism. This involves the focus of the piece's main climax (after 58 bars), which reinforces the logic of sequence (**a**) by completing golden section balances as well as forming them around itself. A logical tendency can be seen here for points of maximum musical tension to subtend golden sections (16:26, 42:26, 26:16, 16:10), while centres of tonal return or stability subtend symmetrical divisions, as shown here in parentheses (34:34, 26:26, 18:18).

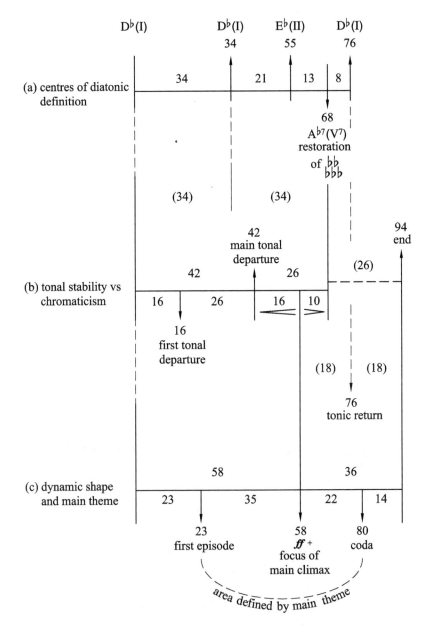

Figure 5.2. Proportions in 'Reflets dans l'eau'

Sequence (**c**) adds the broadest architectural touch of all. The main climax is dominated by a short theme or motive borrowed from *La mer*: this enters for the first time after bar 23 (starting the piece's first episode) and fades out for the last time after bar 80 (starting the coda). These points mark a pair of intermediate golden sections reflected around the piece's climactic centre, based on the bijugate form of the Lucas numbers.[6] The way all the sequences repeatedly interlink mathematically explains why the piece's total length is 94 bars rather than 89; the interrelationships of the sequences are based on the elementary way the Lucas numbers derive from the Fibonacci numbers (4, 7, 11, 18 etc. comes from $3+1, 5+2, 8+3, 13+5$ etc.).

Since sequence (**c**) in Figure 5.2 is visibly reflected around the piece's climax, the compression of its latter part can equally be viewed as a kind of refraction, just as an object appears compressed when viewed through a water surface. The main part of sequence (**b**) equally imitates, in diminution or refraction, the exact shape and proportions of sequence (**c**). All this neatly matches Debussy's titles *Images* and 'Reflets dans l'eau'; even the refractive element draws our attention to Debussy's careful wording 'Reflections *in* the water'.

In bald prose this may seem abstruse, but the expressive potential of these shapes can quickly be sensed on hearing or playing the music. 'Reflets dans l'eau' opens by evoking it all in miniature (Ex. 5.1): the three-note motive in the middle of the texture marks out a refracted sequence of $3+2$ semitones, surrounded by quietly flowing chords. Debussy reportedly likened this motive to a pebble dropping into water – after which our view of it would be refracted.[7] The surrounding ripples reach their peak after 5 out of a total of 8 eighth-notes; we can thus see and hear how the two opening bars sketch out the piece's large-scale refracted wave form, using the simple Fibonacci numbers 2, 3, 5, 8.

Example 5.1. 'Reflets dans l'eau', bars 1–2

Plate 1. Katsushika Hokusai: *The Great Wave off Kanagawa* from Thirty-six Views of Mount Fuji, c. 1820–9, with corner lines and arrows showing divisions by golden section

The relationship to Hokusai emerges from Plate 1 above, which shows his famous print *The Great Wave off Kanagawa* with added arrows round the edges that point to the print's main vertical and horizontal divisions – on left between wave and sky, and (top and right) by the peak of the wave and Mount Fuji. All the arrows divide the picture by golden section, showing one reason why its composition seems so harmonious.

Debussy was also a lifelong devotee of Edgar Allan Poe, and the structure of 'Reflets dans l'eau' can be related compellingly to Poe's essay 'The philosophy of composition'. Poe's essay purports to demonstrate how he wrote his poem 'The Raven' by calculating in advance every aspect of its effect, size, sonority and shape, focusing the tension towards the climax, so that the poem 'proceeded step by step, to its completion, with the precision and rigid consequence of a mathematical problem'. Even Poe's initial decision – on an optimum length for his poem 'of about one hundred lines' – sits nicely near Debussy's 94-bar total. While Poe's essay doesn't involve golden section, one could use his basic logic to design, step by step, a piano piece structured exactly like 'Reflets dans l'eau'. Ravel insisted that he composed exactly as Poe described, though he was undoubtedly aware of the beauty of Poe's position:

whether or not that was really how Poe wrote 'The Raven' (a point contested by Mallarmé), his essay strings the reader along in exactly that manner.[8]

One added circumstance supports viewing Debussy's piece this way. Although he had played an early version of 'Reflets dans l'eau' to Ricardo Viñes in December 1901, by August 1905 Debussy was still tinkering with it and finally, dissatisfied, wrote to his publisher Durand that he'd decided to scrap it in favour of a new version 'based on new ideas and following the most recent discoveries of harmonic chemistry'. He appears to have completed the replacement version in a matter of days; yet nowhere in his music is a logical structure more clearly integrated across all the musical elements 'with the precision and rigid consequence of a mathematical problem'. This suggests that the piece's final version was a recasting into optimum shape of extant material, carried out with the mental clarity of Edgar Allan Poe's methods.[9]

A wider account of this sort of structuring can be read in *Debussy in Proportion*, but a few small examples can aptly be summarized here. Of the remaining five piano *Images* of 1905–7, four show intricate use of golden section, two of them based on Fibonacci and Lucas numbers ('Hommage à Rameau' and 'Poissons d'or') and two of them featuring very sharply focused climaxes placed exactly at their overall point of golden section ('Mouvement' and 'Cloches à travers les feuilles').[10] *L'isle joyeuse*, with its wild ending, presents a very different structural and expressive challenge from 'Reflets dans l'eau': the stable phrasing and constant repetitions of its opening and central sections give way to increasing excitement later in the piece, via the build-up to the *fortissimo* coda. Making the most of the piano's dynamic range, Debussy constructs this as an expanding sequence of crescendos, interspersed with short passing climaxes that focus the accumulating tension. Starting from an eight-bar crescendo into the C major climax at bars 133–44, the progressive crescendos follow a now-familiar sequence of 8 bars, 13 bars, 22 bars, and finally 34 bars up to the *ff* of the coda. (The one slight departure, 22 instead of a theoretical 21, is dictated by needs of smaller-scale bar grouping within the passage.)

At the end of Chapter 4 we noted how the $\frac{4}{4}$ sections of *L'isle joyeuse* are curiously grouped in three-bar hypermetre, making it conveniently easy to measure them proportionally against whole-number groups of the piece's predominating $\frac{3}{8}$ metre. That equivalence lets us ascertain that the Fibonacci crescendo sequence just noted lies inside a larger network of proportions following the same sort of logic as 'Reflets dans l'eau' (Chapter 4 of *Debussy in Proportion* gives a fuller analysis). Most notably the piece's two transitions from $\frac{4}{4}$ to $\frac{3}{8}$ metre (bars 28 and 67) relate to each other and to the piece's entire length exactly by golden section, and the Fibonacci crescendo sequence starts to reveal its character exactly as the piece crosses its main point of golden section. Much of this can again be argued in terms of Edgar Allan Poe's 'Philosophy of composition', not least because one of the techniques Poe chooses there for discussion is the unusual hypermetre and verse structure he devised specially for 'The Raven'.

Debussy's music has no monopoly on this kind of musical structuring, though he appears to have used it more than any other major composer, even Bartók.[11] Two of Ravel's *Miroirs* – both composed shortly before Debussy's first series of *Images* appeared in print – reveal similar structuring; one of them, 'Alborada del gracioso', is examined here in Chapter 12. 'Oiseaux tristes' reveals a Fibonacci golden section arch (89 quarter-notes long) up to the start of its cadenza, after which its articulation changes in character.[12]

Fauré's concern with proportions is suggested by the bar counts visible in many of his manuscripts, though golden section schemes are rare. One appears tellingly in the song 'Reflets dans l'eau' from his late *Mirages*, composed just after Debussy's death.[13] From the other side chronologically, the song 'Tournoiement' of 1870 by Fauré's teacher Saint-Saëns not only has its brief *ff* climax exactly at its golden section (64:40 bars) but whirls off at the end with textures remarkably like the last page of Debussy's 'Mouvement', receding *sempre più pianissimo* to *ppp* without any slowing. If this song was in Debussy's mind, it might explain the curious echoes in 'Mouvement' of the *Dies irae*, a famous Saint-Saëns *idée fixe*. (Despite their mutual antipathy, Debussy openly admired several of Saint-Saëns's works.)

It's futile to try to define or forecast what repertoire is likely to show such proportions, and common sense warns against making this a yardstick of quality, since it's just one of infinite structural tools available to composers. However, some contexts are obviously apt for such devices, other less so: for example, the epigrammatic nature of Debussy's Preludes calls less for such symphonic structuring than the *Images* or *L'isle joyeuse*, though it can be found in some of the more extended Preludes, including 'La Cathédrale engloutie'.

As it is, we have no outright proof that such structures were designed consciously. In the absence of explicit comment from the composers,[14] our main question – as with any analysis – concerns the musical relevance of the structures. This can hardly be denied in 'Reflets dans l'eau' and *L'isle joyeuse*, where the proportional plans draw different aspects of the structure into an integrated dramatic entity, matching the music's pictorial and evocative intensity without drawing attention to how it was done. The most suggestive comment from Debussy is a letter to his publisher Durand, explaining that a bar he had added to the proofs of 'Jardins sous la pluie' was 'necessary from the point of view of number; the divine number.'[15] The bar in question (bar 123) adds no new music (it merely extends a trill): locally it turns a three-bar group into a four-bar one, but in a piece that maintains several other three-bar phrases in comparable contexts. On a larger scale it brings the overall proportions into a slightly more exact network of symmetry and golden section, though a less rigorous one than 'Reflets dans l'eau'.[16] Whatever we conclude, it certainly shows Debussy consciously alert to shape and proportion.

In any case, we search in vain for discussion from major composers before the Second Viennese school of almost any exact technique: not once, for example, do Debussy's writings mention the whole-tone scale. Such technical discretion is understandable in a Paris where divulgence would have handed gratuitous ammunition to hostile critics. As Debussy said about Rameau, 'He was perhaps wrong to write down all [his] theories before composing his operas, for it gave his contemporaries the chance to conclude that there was a complete absence of anything emotional in the music.'[17]

Among other evidence discussed in *Debussy in Proportion* (pp. 163–79), the first visible Fibonacci constructions in Debussy's music come in the wake of articles dealing with structural principles including golden section, which appeared from the mid-1880s in Symbolist journals which we know Debussy read avidly.[18] These were by the mathematician-cum-aesthetician Charles Henry, co-founder of the journal *La vogue* and artistic mentor to Symbolist groups including the 'Club des Hydropathes' that frequented the Chat Noir.[19] Although there's no trace of Debussy having been of their official number, he certainly knew many of them, including Verlaine's brother-in-law and Chabrier's friend Charles de Sivry (of whom more in Chapter 6).[20] Charles Henry and Debussy shared friends in the musical brothers Eugène and Théo Ysaÿe, whom Henry had befriended through Debussy's literary idol Jules Laforgue. Coincidences extend even to Édouard Lucas's mathematical writings having been printed by a publisher whose son and nephew Debussy knew well: the music critic Henri Gauthier-Villars ('Willy') and the painter Jacques-Émile Blanche, dedicatee of Debussy's *Estampes*.

Added to all that is the Symbolist preoccupation with numbers and para-science, involving many of Debussy's associates, not least Ricardo Viñes, a known numeromaniac.[21] Whatever we make of that (Debussy is on record as sending some of it up), one of the central symbols to all esoterica is the pentagram or five-pointed star, whose most basic geometric property is that its lines all intersect at their two points of golden section.[22]

In a reassuringly sceptical survey of golden section in art, science and experimental aesthetics, Denes Nagy uncovers Liszt's interest – documented in letters of 1859 – in the pioneering golden section researches of Adolf Zeising.[23] This adds intrigue to a question we'll return to in Chapter 11, of exactly what the elderly Liszt and the young Debussy might have discussed during their three meetings in Rome early in 1886 – just as Charles Henry's theories were appearing in Symbolist journals.

The topic is obviously a slippery one, in which plenty of nonsense has been written over the decades, indeed centuries. It may seem ridiculous to say how vital a sense of proportion is here. But the warning applies doubly in terms of ensuring that any associated musical structures relate sensibly in their own terms. We can't hear golden sections *per se* (this is their charm), but their role in linking and balancing events across long spans is an obvious attraction for artists known to have used them over the centuries. In medieval education mathematics, science and astronomy were regarded as essential parts of musical study, yielding relationships to be implanted as a matter of course. Several centuries later J. S. Bach still had apparent interest in number symbolism as well as (possibly) proportion, and numerical structures have been traced in Mozart, Haydn, Beethoven and even Schubert.[24] It may be that the tradition never really rested.

PART 2

MUSICAL ROOTS
AND ANTECEDENTS

CHAPTER 6

CHOPIN'S LEGACY

Half French by parentage, Chopin formed his unique piano style in his native Poland from a blend of Italian *bel canto* and the pianism of an Irishman based in Russia (John Field), before making his home in Paris. This rich mix underlies the way his music and teaching realigned much French pianism from its older, more finger-based habits.[1] In the later nineteenth century Chopin's most direct pianistic heir at the Paris Conservatoire was his student Georges Mathias, whose pupils included Dukas. Two other influential standard-bearers there were Antoine-François Marmontel and Émile Descombes: not Chopin pupils but on the periphery of his social circle, they knew and revered Chopin's playing and strove to convey its essence in their own teaching. Through these and other close musical contacts Bizet, Chabrier, Saint-Saëns, Fauré, Debussy, Ravel and Satie were all fairly direct recipients of 'Chopin tradition'.[2]

The year 1910 marked Chopin's centenary with the founding of Édouard Ganche's Société Chopin (with Ravel as vice-president), along with several other homages overt or implicit, such as Debussy's first book of Preludes.[3] In an article ten years earlier, celebrating the erection of the Chopin monument in Paris's Jardin de Luxembourg, Paul Dukas remarked that Chopin's main legacy to musical posterity was an unprecedented harmonic freedom and mobility.[4] This goes with an equal rhythmic mobility, letting a piece slip instantly across genres, like the sudden mazurka sections inside nocturnes or polonaises, or from slow to fast music and vice versa without changing the underlying pulse (as in the C minor and E major Nocturnes op. 48 no. 1 and op. 62 no. 2).

As Dukas observed, Chopin's influence reached far beyond the piano, notably into Liszt's orchestral poems and thence to Wagner. It's thus hard to tell if the climax of the Dawn scene in Ravel's *Daphnis et Chloé* (the *ff* 'Tristan' chord at rehearsal figure 163) more immediately echoes the climax of Wagner's *Tristan* Prelude (of the late 1850s) or the *fff* bars 124–5 of Chopin's First Ballade (of the early 1830s), both are so similar. In that regard Chopin's Ballades, F minor *Fantaisie* and *Polonaise-Fantaisie* effectively invented the symphonic poem at the keyboard, devising forms that cohere while defying conventional analysis, in ways that interested both Debussy and Ravel (as we'll see).

Fauré and Debussy, and to some extent Ravel, have long been seen as Chopin's natural heirs, velvet revolutionaries at the piano, and parallels have been drawn between Debussy's and Chopin's *Études* and Preludes or between Fauré's and Chopin's Nocturnes, Impromptus and Barcarolles, as well as Fauré's and Debussy's single early *Mazurka* and *Ballade* relative to Chopin's. On closer inspection, though, these connections betray several frayed edges. Fauré's use of the genres in question is often quite different and his titles bestowed more arbitrarily, while Debussy's titles often conceal different sources: Whistler's paintings for his orchestral *Nocturnes*, and Russian music for his piano *Nocturne* and *Ballade*, the latter originally titled *Ballade slave*.[5] Debussy's use of pictorial titles also follows a tradition ranging from Couperin to Chabrier via Schumann and Liszt, but emphatically not Chopin who was famously averse to overt pictoriality. As for Ravel, his only shared title with Chopin is a single short *Prélude*. Were that the whole story, this chapter might end here. A closer look, though, suggests otherwise, revealing affinities lying deeper under the surface, often in the most mature and individually characteristic works of the later composers.

FAURÉ AND CHOPIN

Fauré's most direct contact with Chopin's entourage came about in his twenties, when he was introduced by Saint-Saëns to Chopin's former pupil and protégée Pauline Viardot-García, one of the renowned Spanish dynasty of singers.[6] Fauré soon became part of her family circle (she nearly became his mother-in-law), and we can only imagine what Chopin reminiscences he heard there.[7] This doubtless fed Fauré's distaste for grandiose effect, in which respect his nature was always nearer Chopin than to his own teacher Saint-Saëns.

Fauré's independence from Chopin lies most clearly in his prolific song output and the urbane flightiness of even his earliest work, echoing Gounod, Saint-Saëns, Mendelssohn and Schumann – the latter two particularly in his bold sweep and breath, Gounod in many textures and modal shifts (Fauré's famous *Sicilienne* starts almost identically to Gounod's piano barcarolle *La veneziana*). This streak runs through to his full maturity in the *Valses-*

caprices, even if the breadth of Chopin's larger waltzes can often be heard in them, sometimes through intermediaries like Saint-Saëns or Chabrier's *Valses romantiques*. The chromatically rising sevenths in the middle of Fauré's first *Valse-caprice* certainly suggest an echo of those near the end of Chopin's *Nouvelle étude* in D♭, while his Second Impromptu mixes a native fluency with a distinct whiff of Chopin's *Tarentelle* op. 43. One of the main distinctions between the two composers lies in the Italian vocal origin of much of Chopin's melody and the more Slavic essence of his Mazurkas, beside the more Gallic flavour of Fauré's.

The Fauré scholar Jean-Michel Nectoux observes Chopinesque moments in Fauré's *Ballade*, First Impromptu, Second Nocturne and Fourth Barcarolle, mostly involving texture, rhythmic suppleness and sophisticated arpeggio figurations, plus the 'accompanied singing' that opens the Third and Fourth Nocturnes.[8] A little more covertly, Fauré's Second Nocturne exploits – from bar 24, but with the hands the other way round – the same combination of $3+3$ sextuplets against slower triplets as in Chopin's F minor *Étude* op. 25 no. 2. Some affinities are strong enough that they can amusingly trick our subconscious: I once heard a student intend to demonstrate the opening of Fauré's Third Impromptu, only to find herself suddenly playing Chopin's G major Prelude a semitone up. It's equally through our fingers that the last page of Fauré's second *Valse-caprice* suggests the contrary-motion arpeggios from the second page of Chopin's Third Ballade. That said, the Chopinesque surface of Fauré's Third Nocturne (complete with the recapitulation's cross-rhythms, like those of Chopin's C minor Nocturne op. 48 no. 1) is exceptional, for Fauré's piano writing is usually stamped more individually, not least by his fondness for sounding the bass off the beat (a device Chopin uses only rarely, as in the Prelude op. 45). This habit mainly serves to lighten solo piano textures: that it became a Fauré hallmark rather than a Chopin one may reflect the dramatic changes in piano construction and sonority across their lifetimes.

The most telling links lie under the surface of Fauré's fully mature idiom. By the Eighth Barcarolle of 1908, his modal adventurousness adds new flavour to a typical Chopin flourish (Ex. 6.1). Like Chopin, Fauré learnt early how to take the listener by stealth, something he exploits dramatically in his Fifth (and largest) Barcarolle of 1894. Taken in isolation, the accented unison *forte* F♯–C that recurs from the second page onwards (Ex. 6.2a) would suggest Musorgsky in Baba-Yaga mode. Fauré's harmony not only cushions it but relates it directly to the coda of Chopin's *Barcarolle* op. 60 (Ex. 6.2b). The full impact of the gesture emerges at the final reprise, where Fauré expands the falling tritone to a fifth (landing instead on B), setting off a series of subsidiary reprises and waves of intensity, just as the coda of Chopin's *Barcarolle* does.

Example 6.1

a: Chopin, Third Ballade, bars 126–8

b: Fauré, Eighth Barcarolle, bars 30–2

Example 6.2

a: Fauré, Fifth Barcarolle, op. 66, bar 12

b: Chopin, *Barcarolle*, bar 96 beats 3–4

On the way there the piece reveals another strong parallel with Chopin's *Barcarolle*, for each piece launches its lyrical central section over a rocking static bass with an abrupt minor-third modulation away from the tonic F♯: Chopin's swings to A major (bar 39), Fauré's conversely to E♭ major (bar 61).

Fifteen years earlier Fauré had vividly evoked Chopin's *Barcarolle* in the closing pages of his piano *Ballade* op. 19, ingeniously combining two of the *Barcarolle*'s most characteristic textures or gestures (Ex. 6.3). Example 6.3b is particularly telling, with its superimposed G⁷ chord on a bass F♯, resulting in a triple semitone clash (E♯/F♯/G♮). Prominent in several of Chopin's works from the B♭ minor Nocturne op. 9 no. 1 onwards, this harmonic and cadential device perhaps attests to Paganini's appearances in Warsaw in 1829, for it ends the first of Paganini's *24 Caprices* similarly over a static tonic bass. (Otherwise the harmony can be traced back via Beethoven to Bach.)[9]

Example 6.3

a: Chopin, *Barcarolle*, bar 24–5

b: Chopin, *Barcarolle*, bar 110

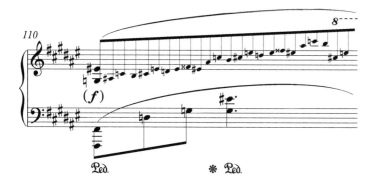

c: Fauré, *Ballade* op. 19, coda

DEBUSSY AND CHOPIN

Like Chopin, the young Debussy received his first music lessons from a violinist (in Cannes).[10] The Paris Commune of 1871 and its aftermath then brought Debussy's father into contact with the composer-pianist Charles de Sivry (already glimpsed in Chapter 5), who arranged for the nine-year-old to be taught by his (Sivry's) mother, Antoinette Mauté, a *soi-disant* Chopin pupil. No proof survives for this claim (which has often been summarily dismissed), but there's more to say about it below, and Debussy for the rest of his life remained in no doubt.[11] Mme Mauté taught him for a year, preparing him for his Conservatoire entrance exam. Their contact appears to have continued thereafter; more than forty years later Debussy's letters to his publisher Durand reveal vivid memories:[12]

> It's a pity Madame Mauté de Fleurville, to whom I owe the little I know about the piano, is not alive. She knew many things about Chopin.

> What Saint-Saëns says about pedal in Chopin [see p. 282] isn't – despite my respect for his great age – completely accurate, for I remember very precisely what Mme Mauté de Fleurville told me. [Chopin] advised practising without pedal, and, with only rare exceptions, never to hold it on.[13]

It speaks especially well for Mme Mauté that Debussy's memories of her were not swamped by those of the renowned Antoine-François Marmontel, his piano teacher for the next eight years at the Paris Conservatoire. Marmontel had lived near Chopin, probably met him, and often heard him play, an experience that indelibly marked his outlook. Marmontel's pupils included Bizet and Albéniz; on the wall in his house, where he often taught (apparently in a dressing gown), hung the famous Delacroix portrait of

Chopin now in the Louvre. We can imagine the effect on the young Debussy in the late 1870s – the heyday of the Impressionist painters – of being taught in such an atmosphere by the man who published this in 1878:

> If we draw a parallel between Chopin's sound effects and certain techniques of painting, we could say that this great virtuoso modulated sound much as skilled painters treat light and atmosphere. To envelop melodic phrases and ingenious arabesques in a half-tint which has something of both dream and reality: this is the pinnacle of art; and this was Chopin's art.[14]

The lasting effect of it can be read in Marguerite Long's memoirs of Debussy in 1914 and 1917:

> Chopin, above all, was a subject he never tired of. He was impregnated, almost *inhabited*, by [Chopin's] pianism. His own playing was an exploration of all he felt were the procedures of that master to us all.

> [Debussy] played nearly always in half-tints, but with a full, intense sonority without any hardness of attack, like Chopin, and was preoccupied by the latter's phrasing.[15]

It has often seemed puzzling that Debussy took much longer to find an assured compositional voice at the piano, his own instrument, than in song or orchestral music. One factor that helps explain this is the predominance of Chopin and romantic repertoire in his Conservatoire training, tempting young fingers into all-too-well-worn grooves. Chopin had the creative advantage here – one that could have worked only with him – of two music teachers in his childhood who were not primarily pianists.

Debussy's answer at the piano was at first to follow a more directly French idiom of Chabrier (a lifelong favourite), Fauré, Delibes, Massenet or Gounod (he always had sympathy for those last two, who were supportive to him in his early years). Since Chopin had never dominated song and orchestra in the same way, Debussy would have felt much less of a Chopinesque shadow in these genres. This perhaps underlies the close resemblance, observed by William Austin, between the long D♭ major melody in the middle of Debussy's *Prélude à l'après-midi d'un faune* and Chopin's Nocturne op. 27 no. 2 in the same key.[16] Debussy's increasingly confident muse here gives the recycled melody quite a different sense with its whole-tone harmonies and tritone progressions. (Massenet's 'Méditation' from *Thaïs*, contemporary with Debussy's *Faune*, is another close relative of this theme.)

The implication emerges that Debussy, away from Chopin's shadow, could approach him more fearlessly. One catalyst was certainly his experience of Javanese gamelan in 1889 and 1900. This is especially telling because of gamelan's distinctive sonority: the exotic surface of Debussy's 'Pagodes', for example, with its gamelan allusions (of which more in Chapter 8), suffices immediately to disguise the affinity between its opening arabesques and the opening of Chopin's *Polonaise-fantaisie* – in each case a leisurely exploration of the upper resonances of B major. One curious result of this mix is that the music of the French Debussy often has a more eastern-sounding melodic surface than that of his Polish precursor.

Indeed, the main climax of 'Hommage à Rameau' (contemporary with 'Pagodes') suggests how ingrained the *Polonaise-fantaisie* was in Debussy's fingers (Ex. 6.4). Many other passing details of Debussy's mature writing – once inoculated from dangers of pastiche – again suggest that such passing resemblances were often prompted as much by the fingers as by the ear. Sometimes a key suffices to set off a similar idea, especially when a different context ensures the integrity of Debussy's version: for example, under the hands the leisurely central episode of Debussy's 'Les collines d'Anacapri' (from bar 50) is surprisingly redolent of Chopin's *Polonaise-Fantaisie* in the B major episode from bar 153.[17]

Example 6.4

a: Chopin, *Polonaise-Fantaisie*, bars 214–15

b: Debussy, 'Hommage à Rameau', bars 54–5

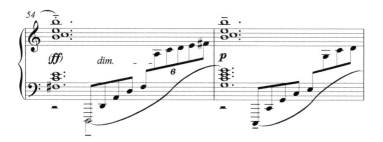

A striking echo of the Scherzo from Chopin's B minor Sonata op. 58 spans Debussy's two consecutive *Images* 'Hommage à Rameau' and 'Mouvement' (Ex. 6.5). (The motive returns again in Debussy's 'Les collines d'Anacapri'.) Matching this is the gestural (but not harmonic) affinity between Debussy's 'Et la lune descend sur le temple qui fut' (bars 25–6) and the end of Chopin's F♯ major Prelude from op. 28, both with a descant melody that sounds after the chords underneath, as indicated by similar vertical slurs in each piece.

Example 6.5

a: Chopin, B minor Sonata, op. 58, Scherzo (Trio), bars 81–4

b: Debussy, 'Hommage à Rameau', bar 14

c: Debussy, 'Mouvement', bars 30–1

Such Chopinesque elements in Debussy's 'body language' at the piano might support Mme Mauté's claim to have been a Chopin pupil – especially in view of how strong a part suppleness, free movement, hand weight and close key contact played in Chopin's teaching. One such trait appears in the wide bass arpeggios at bars 7 and 67 of *L'isle joyeuse* (Ex. 16.8), which Debussy reportedly wanted fingered *5–3–2–1 à la* Chopin with lateral wrist suppleness,[18] like the similar left-hand stretches in Chopin's *Étude* op. 25 no. 1, Second Scherzo, first movement of the B♭ minor Sonata – and perhaps particularly the central part of the B♭ minor Nocturne op. 9 no. 1. Another trait was observed with some surprise by the violinist Egon Kenton at a concert performance by Debussy around 1912: 'His hands never left the keys.'[19] Had Mme Mauté trained the young Achille-Claude with echoes of 'Vous brûlez-vous? [Did it burn you?]' (This was Chopin's facetious barb to pupils who threw their hands up from the keys.) Yvonne Lefébure similarly recalled Debussy saying 'Hands are not made to be in the air above the piano, but to go into it.'[20] While such habits could have been inculcated by Marmontel, it was revealingly to Mme Mauté that Debussy chose to refer in later years. To that we can add his love of tactile hand overlaps, like the opening of the Prelude 'Feuilles mortes' or the Sarabande of *Pour le piano* at bars 13–14 (compare with Chopin's E major Prelude from op. 28, the Trio section of the Scherzo in the B♭ minor Sonata or the overlapping arpeggios in the *Étude* op. 25 no. 1). Fauré enjoyed these overlaps too.

Subtler again is the sort of tactile voicing of inner parts characteristic of late Chopin works, often strategically placed to lead through a delicate transition. The transitional bar 61 of the *Barcarolle* shows an appealing *g′♯–f′♯–e′* under the top line's *b′–c″♯–d″*; in bars 76–8 the four-part writing disguises a strong line crossing the apparent voices (Ex. 6.6). These are reflected in similar implicit figures like the left thumb's *b♮–b♯–c′♯* in mid-texture leading into bar 38 of Debussy's 'Hommage à Rameau', a similar *d′♮–d′♯–e′* leading into bar 32 of his earlier Sarabande in *Pour le piano* and, in the second of Ravel's *Valses nobles et sentimentales*, the semi-hidden line rising through the off-beats of bars 37–41. (This kind of inner chromatic motion pervades the *Valses nobles et sentimentales*). One of the longest counterparts of Example 6.6 can be heard at the climax of Fauré's Fourth Nocturne, carrying a descending scale through the voices from a top *a‴♭* to a bass E♭, nearly four and a half octaves. Chopin's own intensely chromatic sequences of contrary motion, particularly in the *Polonaise-Fantaisie*, echo strongly in the third of Chabrier's *Valses romantiques* and Debussy's prelude 'La terrasse des audiences du clair de lune'.

Example 6.6. Chopin, *Barcarolle*, chromatic counter-voice in bars 76–8 (variant note sizes editorial)

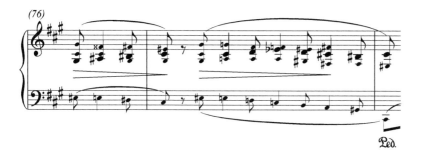

Debussy's pupil Mme de Romilly recalled Debussy's particular fondness for Chopin's *Barcarolle*: 'The way he explained and analysed this piece was something special.'[21] The texture of the *Barcarolle*'s culminating neapolitan cadence (Ex. 6.3b) echoes tellingly in the finale of Debussy's Violin Sonata of 1916–17 (at rehearsal figure 3), the last work he completed. Other appearances of the cadence, as often as not in Chopin's key, include the exact halfway point of Debussy's *Image* 'Mouvement' (bar 89), where it creatively mirrors Chopin's *Barcarolle*: whereas Chopin used the chord as the culmination of a long chromatic sequence over an F♯ pedal, Debussy reverses the process, using the chord to launch an equally chromatic sequence over an F♯ pedal leading to the piece's *fff* culmination. Chopin's *Barcarolle* is arguably pervasive in Debussy's whole manner of writing in *L'isle joyeuse*, notably the latter's opening trill and barcarolle-like central section – which intriguingly exchange positions with the same elements in Chopin's *Barcarolle* – and through the wave-like left-hand irregular metric groupings in each piece (from bar 67 of *L'isle joyeuse* and bar 78 of Chopin's *Barcarolle*). Under the hand the opening of *L'isle joyeuse* also strongly recalls the recapitulation of Chopin's D♭ Waltz op. 64 no. 1 (a trill gradually spiralling outwards).

A larger-scale link to Chopin is so skilfully embedded in *L'isle joyeuse* that only one gesture betrays it audibly. From the start of its culminating crescendo to its final bars, *L'isle joyeuse* shadows the structure of Chopin's Third Ballade as shown in Table 6.1. The detail that gives the game away is Debussy's similar bass ostinato of an octave with semitone appoggiatura (Ex. 6.7) – fortified by the texture of the right-hand chords. This large-scale relationship adds focus to Debussy's remark in the preface to his 1915 edition of Chopin's Waltzes: 'If [Chopin's] formal freedom has fooled his critics, we nonetheless must recognize the degree to which everything is in its place and carefully organised.'

Table 6.1. *L'isle joyeuse* in the footsteps of Chopin's Third Ballade

Chopin: bar 183	bar 213	bar 222	bar 231	end
ostinato build-up, rising textures	tonic arrival *f* or *ff*, thematic reprise	tonal interruption	tonic again, *più mosso*, other thematic reprise	final downward rocket across the keyboard with added sixth
Debussy: bar 186	bar 220	bar 236	bar 244	end

Example 6.7

a: Chopin, Third Ballade, bars 183–5

b: Debussy, *L'isle joyeuse*, bars 186–8

By the time of his Preludes a confidently mature Debussy could skirt even closer to Chopin in terms of sheer sound. Debussy's twenty-four Preludes avoid the sort of logical key sequence found in Chopin's twenty-four (or Bach's forty-eight), and appear to discourage classical analogy by the whole-tone chords that emerge from the opening bars of the first prelude, 'Danseuses de Delphes'. Yet closer study quickly reveals that the very first chord of this piece, with its unusual voicing of melody in mid-texture (Ex. 1.9), comes verbatim from the end of Chopin's B♭ Prelude op. 28 no. 21. (The full flavour of this can be sensed by playing from the one piece directly into the other.)

This aptly symbolic musical handshake is matched by pervasive links between 'Danseuses de Delphes' and the first of Chopin's Preludes, starting with a shared melodic *g'–a'* ostinato (despite their different keys: from bar 3 in Debussy, bar 1 in Chopin) and chromatically rising bass line (bars 3–4 in Debussy, bars 4–7 in Chopin). They even end with the same chord, just a tone higher and arpeggiated in Chopin's case. In Chapter 2 we saw the music and structure of 'Danseuses de Delphes' continuing into the preludes that follow it; we now see it equally emerging from two of Chopin's Preludes.

Nor is the key sequence of Chopin's Preludes completely ignored in Debussy's Preludes, if we consider the modal progressions by fifths that are embedded in 'Des pas sur la neige' (as we saw in Chapter 2). This also involves Debussy's second book of Preludes, in terms of how the opening C major of 'Brouillards' is progressively overlaid by chromaticism. Whether or not the analogies were deliberate, they are neatly summed up by the main motive of Debussy's last prelude, 'Feux d'artifice': sounding as a repeated fanfare at the piece's climax, it follows the exact shape of the motive ( ) that Jean-Jacques Eigeldinger postulates as running constantly under the surface of Chopin's Preludes.[22]

Debussy's *Études* suggest a culminating homage, not just through their dedication to Chopin's memory but also in tandem with the edition of Chopin's complete piano works in which Debussy was simultaneously involved for his publisher Durand. (Debussy's dedication on its own can't be read too definitively, because he long hesitated between Chopin and Couperin.)[23] The scarcity of identifiable Chopin allusions in Debussy's *Études* should hardly surprise us, coming from a composer ever determined to avoid the obvious. Again the links lie mostly under the surface, as in the physical patterns of 'Pour les accords' relative to the Scherzo of Chopin's B♭ minor Sonata, including the hemiola element (Ex. 6.8). Debussy's figurations in 'Pour les degrés chromatiques' (especially from bar 11) also echo the later parts of Chopin's B♭ minor Prelude from op. 28. Marguerite Long points at probably the closest link of all when she quotes Debussy as declaring he had 'worn down his fingers' playing Chopin's *Nouvelle étude* in A♭:[24] this can be vividly sensed by juxtaposing bars 13–14 of Debussy's 'Pour les sixtes' with Chopin's bars 75–6, or Debussy's bar 43 with Chopin's bars 38–9.

Example 6.8

a: Debussy, 'Pour les accords', bars 1–4

b: Chopin, B♭ minor Sonata op. 35, Scherzo, bars 50–3 (articulation as in Debussy's 1915 edition)

c: Chopin, B♭ minor Sonata, Scherzo, bars 75–6 (articulation as in Debussy's edition)

All this suggests a studied approach to both Chopin and pianism generally, something that emerges from Debussy's letters to Jacques Durand in 1915 discussing the editorial project in terms of accuracy, clarity, and comprehension of Chopin's notation.[25] By mid-1915 his comments to Durand about the Chopin editing are increasingly mixed with progress reports on his own *Études*, suggesting that, deliberately or not, the editorial project was prompting Debussy to write into his own *Études* all he wanted to cultivate in piano playing and in listening at the keyboard. Along with another stimulus we'll see in Chapter 8, his work on Chopin may have helped awaken his creativity after a depressed fallow period from the middle of 1913.

One of Chopin's most talented students, Friederike Müller-Streicher, quoted him as saying at one of her last lessons: 'Simplicity is everything. After having exhausted all the difficulties . . . then simplicity emerges with all its charm, like art's final seal. Whoever wants to obtain this immediately will never achieve it; you can't begin with the end.'[26] Half a century later, in 1899, Debussy wrote to his de facto publisher Hartmann, explaining the delays caused by his painstaking revision of two scores in progress: 'all that, to achieve "simplicity"'.[27] Chapter 21 below quotes a corresponding report of the 'great simplicity, at first disconcerting' of Debussy's piano playing in his late years.

RAVEL AND CHOPIN

Manuel Rosenthal has recounted Ravel's admiration for Chopin's *Barcarolle* as 'one of the most magnificent pieces in all music'. Besides its immense melodic, pianistic and harmonic originality, what Ravel especially loved was its '*souffle*', a word meaning both breath and sheer inspiration.[28] For the start of the 1910 centenary Ravel penned some reflections on Chopin, culminating again in the *Barcarolle*, which for him 'sums up the sumptuously expressive art of this great Slav of Italian education. . . . [In this piece] Chopin made real all that his predecessors managed to express only imperfectly.'[29] This doubtless echoes in the final cadence of 'Entretiens de la Belle et de la Bête' from *Ma mère l'Oye* – another work published in the Chopin centenary year – which exquisitely teases out (a semitone lower and over six bars) the culminating cadence of Chopin's *Barcarolle* (Ex. 6.3b).

Like Chopin, Ravel reached early musical maturity, and his most daring innovations are often similarly hidden under a concern for clarity of expression and perfection in taste and form, leaving no seams visible. Arbie Orenstein observes a close textural approach to Chopin's *Berceuse* in the similarly ethereal recapitulation of the Adagio of Ravel's Concerto in G (among the last works by each composer).[30] Several pianists have noted two strikingly Chopinesque textures in Ravel's *Valses nobles et sentimentales* – the repeated grace-note dominant *d"*s in the second *valse* (relative to the dominant grace-note *a"*♭s on the second page of Chopin's Waltz in D♭, op. 64 no. 1), and the two-in-a-bar melody across the $\frac{3}{4}$ metre in the central part of Ravel's seventh *valse* just as in Chopin's op. 42 Waltz in A♭. In his Chopin article of 1910 Ravel makes special mention of Chopin's lone Prelude op. 45, whose repeated appoggiatura ninths and offset left-hand figurations reverberate in Ravel's lone piano *Prélude*, written as a Paris Conservatoire sight-reading test in 1913. Unfortunately little documentation survives of Ravel's orchestrations of Chopin in 1913–14 for the ballet *Les Sylphides* (in a new Nijinsky version), now lost along with even a complete list of the works involved. Only a few tantalizing indications remain in surviving sketches for orchestrations of the *Étude* op. 10 no. 11, a Mazurka – and the *Barcarolle*.[31]

Gaspard de la nuit reflects Chopin's stormier side, most audibly in the funereal B♭ that tolls through both 'Le gibet' and the 'Marche funèbre' of Chopin's B♭ minor Sonata. The chromatic left-hand runs upward from bar 523 of 'Scarbo' also compare vividly with bars 187–9 of Chopin's Fourth Ballade. One of the most spine-tingling octatonic passages in 'Le gibet' (Ex. 3.5a) is just a slight, but strategic, reordering of the pitches from two octatonic bars in the first movement of Chopin's Sonata (Ex. 6.9). The motive that pervades *Gaspard* can equally be traced to Chopin's *Tarentelle* op. 43 (bars 20 and similar); the same clash repeatedly resounds in the first movement of Chopin's B♭ minor Sonata (for example at bars 151–2, G♭ clashing on F major).

Example 6.9. Chopin, B♭ minor Sonata, first movement, bars 91–2

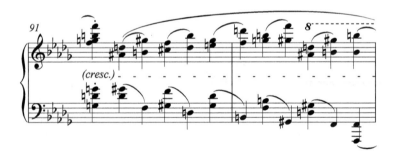

'Scarbo' doubly echoes Chopin, first through its ostinato rhythm ♩♪♪♪♪ (relative to the ♪♪♪♪♩ of the Scherzo in Chopin's B♭ minor Sonata), and secondly through its affinity of tempo to Chopin's four independent Scherzi. It also dramatically exploits sudden silences like those that punctuate Chopin's Second Scherzo (B♭ minor again, a piece that opens with almost the same rising motive as 'Scarbo'). The opening harmonic crunch of 'Scarbo' is exactly that of Example 6.3b, the three adjacent semitones again sounding together. While 'Scarbo' equally gleefully embraces elements of Mephisto Waltz, *Danse macabre*, *Islamey* and *España*, the whole of *Gaspard de la nuit* is inhabited by something akin to Chopin's darker moods.[32]

This macabre side is tempered – slightly – by an intriguing relationship between Ravel's 'Ondine' and Chopin's A♭ *Étude* op. 25 no. 1, whose many affinities include a shared ecstatic mood – until the sudden cackle of laughter on the last page of 'Ondine' gives at least Ondine's game away. The laughter might also be partly Ravel's, for his 'Ondine' suggests a classical parody of Chopin's A♭ *Étude* in the same sense that several paintings by his idol Manet are classical parodies of Raphael, Titian or Goya. (Perhaps Ravel knew that some of Chopin's *Études* play similar games, for example his chromatic op. 10 no. 2 relative to Moscheles's *Étude* op. 70 no. 3 of 1828.)[33] Besides the textural affinity between Ravel's 'Ondine' and Chopin's op. 25 no. 1 – a long entrancing melody spun out over rippling harmonies – the parallel becomes literal at the *appassionato* climax of each piece, where 'Ondine' (bar 66) briefly quotes Chopin's *Étude* (bar 30), a semitone higher and with hands an octave farther out. (Ravel's colleague Alfred Cortot perhaps spotted this, for his legendary recordings of this *Étude* add a bass octave there, as if for an ecstatic moment we had slipped into Ondine's watery arms.) The musical parallel continues, for Chopin's *Étude* then gradually subsides with a texture of quietly echoing octaves across the right hand (bars 41–3), just as 'Ondine' does at bars 75–8, before ending in a sudden flurry of arpeggios that equally suggest a ripple of laughter and a shower of spray. If Ravel's witch cackles a different laugh there from Chopin's more angelic muse, it's an essential part of the homage-parody.

A sophisticated aspect of Chopin's *Barcarolle* casts some more light on Ravel's 'Ondine'. Just as 'Ondine' suggests a hidden sonata form – its ideas all recapitulated but in juggled order, so that some shorter gestures are dislocated from their original contexts – Chopin's *Barcarolle* suggests a similar hidden orderliness by answering all its main ideas and gestures later in the piece. This extends even to gestures like the opening C♯ bass octave (cf. bar 92, which thus answers both bars 1 and 32) and the trill at bar 71 with its upbeat (cf. bar 102 with its upbeat). It's entirely characteristic of Chopin that such links may look thin on paper (for example because of the trill's different harmonic settings) but take on maximum force gesturally, through the ear or under the hand.

Chopin's boldness with the octatonic scale may surprise those used to considering it mostly a twentieth-century idiom (Ex. 6.10). If some of his earlier occurrences are essentially decorated diminished sevenths (Ex. 6.10a), as are some of Debussy's, Chopin's later usage increasingly resembles Ravel's by blurring major and minor and by mixing triads a tritone or minor third apart (Ex. 6.9 and 6.10c). Example 6.10b is one of the most quietly dazzling: common to octatonic and whole-tone scales, as well as to Debussy's 'overtone' scale, it would be equally at home in Ravel's 'Le gibet' (cf. Ex. 3.5b) or Debussy's 'La Puerta del Vino' and *L'isle joyeuse* (cf. Ex. 1.3).

Example 6.10. More octatony in Chopin

a: Nocturne op. 15 no. 3, bars 77–8   **b: Prelude op. 45, bar 79**
(cf. bars 37–42 of Debussy's 'Jardins sous la pluie')

c: Fourth Ballade op. 52, bars 223–4

Ravel might be seen here as heir to Chopin's demonic side, in the no-holds-barred *Gaspard de la nuit* or the savage end of *La valse* (a D major not so far from the D minor abyss that ends Chopin's op. 28 Preludes). By comparison, the more veiled nature of Debussy's or Fauré's (or even Schumann's) wildest moments can be sensed by comparing the end of Chopin's Preludes with Debussy's 'Ce qu'a vu le Vent d'Ouest' and Fauré's song *Prison* or the climactic Variation X of his *Thème et variations*. (All the more vital, therefore, not to weaken Debussy or Fauré by understating them in performance.) Not that this would have escaped Debussy for a moment: his many echoes of Chopin's Preludes and B♭ minor Sonata stand in relief against the way those works baffled (or even spooked) Schumann, just as Debussy's numerous echoes of Chopin's *Polonaise-Fantaisie* defy the way that last piece baffled even Liszt.

CHABRIER AND CHOPIN

Chabrier is somewhat complementary to Chopin, having brought to French music a concentrated orchestral brilliance, wit and emotional directness matching Chopin's pianistic revolution – not that Chopin is short of orchestral colours, as in the trumpet and horn calls in the G minor Nocturne from op. 15 and the *Polonaise-Fantaisie*, or the timpani rattles seen above in the Third Ballade. Chopin's circle touched the adolescent Chabrier peripherally, through his piano lessons from Chopin's friend Édouard Wolff – to whom the young Chabrier was sent on the advice of his fellow-Auvergnat Marmontel (Bizet's and Debussy's teacher).[34]

Dukas's 1900 article on Chopin twice singles out Chopin's impact on Chabrier.[35] To that we can add some exact detail like the chromatic sideslips over a dominant bass pedal in the last line of 'Mélancolie' (*Pièces pittoresques*), echoing the opening texture of Chopin's *Barcarolle* and the climax of the op. 28 no. 21. A few of Chabrier's textures audibly take over where Chopin leaves off. The finale of Chopin's B minor Sonata lets loose a brief but even rattlier version (Ex. 6.11) of the timpani-like ostinato already seen in Example 6.7a; Chabrier turned this figuration into a hair-raising ostinato in two of his fieriest works (see pp. 86–7 and Ex. 7.6a). These were not lost on Ravel, who was doubtless aware of the link back to Chopin.

Example 6.11. Chopin, B minor Sonata, finale, bars 189–90

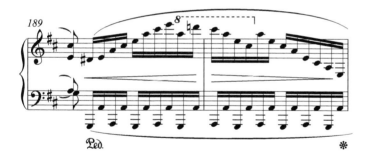

Another Chopin piece that must have dazzled Chabrier is Chopin's quietly astonishing D♭ *Nouvelle étude*, whose unusual texture – legato melody over staccato countermelody – echoes through the 'Idylle' of Chabrier's *Pièces pittoresques*. The same *Étude* prefigures several moments in Chabrier's 'Fête polonaise' from *Le Roi malgré lui*, notably its final chain of chromatically rising sevenths, not so far removed from Example 1.8a.[36] In another telling parallel, the vigorous fourfold chord sequence that rounds off Chabrier's

Joyeuse marche is essentially the final C⁷–F–A♭⁷–D♭ sequence of Chopin's Second Scherzo, down a semitone.

One outstanding Chabrier hallmark can similarly be traced back to Chopin (Ex. 6.12). Chabrier's quietly revolutionary contribution was to detach the leading-note melodic descent from Chopin's cadential context (the final small-note group bracketed in Example 6.12a); this turns the gesture, complete with its unresolved leading note, from a cadentially closing gesture into an opening one. In Chapter 7 we'll see more of where that led.

Example 6.12

a: Chopin, *Fantaisie* op. 49, bars 321–2

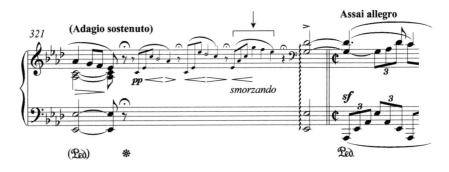

b: Chabrier, *Impromptu*, bars 84–8

CHAPTER 7

'MUSIQUE ADORABLE':
À LA DÉCOUVERTE
D'EMMANUEL CHABRIER

Example 7.1

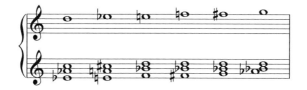

WHICH composer or generation does the progression above suggest? Listeners, given a blind test, usually reply along the lines of 'Messiaen' and '1930s or later'. In fact it comes (more or less) from Chabrier's *Ballabile* of 1889. Example 7.2 shows the start of the sixteen-bar sequence from which it is abstracted: even if we read the harmonies in resolved form (the top line of Ex. 7.1 up a semitone), the progression remains fresh.

I learnt Chabrier's piano music with Debussy and Ravel already thoroughly in my ears and fingers. Time after time it surprised me with sonorities, harmonies and characteristic gestures that I'd long regarded as hallmarks of his successors. From that it was a short step to trying the corresponding Debussy or Ravel passages as if they were Chabrier: as often as not the music seemed to reply, 'Ah, now you've found me!' Tellingly, the major part of Chabrier's output corresponds with Debussy's most formative years, the decade 1880–90 when he was aged between eighteen and twenty-eight. The two composers certainly met on occasion – they both travelled to Bayreuth in summer 1889 – and shared friends and acquaintances including Charles de Sivry and Jules de Brayer (of whom more in Chapter 9).

Example 7.2. Chabrier, *Ballabile*, bars 33–7

Debussy's *Ariettes oubliées* of 1885–8 are especially revealing in this regard: showing him for the first time in fully confident maturity, they were composed around the time when Debussy and Paul Vidal played Chabrier's two-piano *Valses romantiques* to Liszt (of which more in Chapter 11), and swarm with echoes of Examples 7.5a and 7.27a. Debussy's next set of songs, the *Cinq poèmes de Baudelaire* of 1889, take a more overt lead from Wagner in much the way that Chabrier's *Gwendoline* did in the mid-1880s, a matter that Georges Servières observed in 1912.[1] (The first of them, 'Le balcon', also echoes Chabrier's song *L'île heureuse* more than once.) Our focus sharpens again if we consider that these song groups surround Debussy's *La Damoiselle élue*, whose debt to Chabrier's *La Sulamite* Debussy openly admitted, plus Debussy's plans for an opera based on the play *Axël* by Villiers de l'Isle-Adam – who, as Debussy would have known, took music lessons from Chabrier.

Perhaps the most telling tributes below are those from Ravel and Poulenc. Poulenc not only ranked Chabrier's *Pièces pittoresques* alongside the Preludes of his lifelong hero Debussy but took time off from a busy composing schedule to write a book about Chabrier, one that crucially records Chabrier's impact on two generations of composers.[2] Poulenc's adoration for Chabrier's 'Idylle' shines a light on Chabrier's almost alchemical skill in blending ostensibly unpromising elements: taken separately, those of Example 7.3 would seem unviable to the point almost of stubborn silliness – until their combination produces the haunting Example 7.4a. Example 7.4b shows exactly the same three elements resonating in Ravel's *Miroirs*.[3]

Example 7.3   a: melody   b: accompaniment

c: bass

Example 7.4

a: Chabrier, 'Idylle' (1880), bars 18–23 and 26–31

b: Ravel, *Miroirs* (1905), 'Noctuelles', bars 47–8

A related quiet revolution slips out of the second page of Chabrier's *Pièces pittoresques*, combining a bluesy mix of major and minor thirds with an equally bluesy chromatic line to and from the minor seventh (Ex. 7.5a).[4] The combination echoes in a range of pieces including the Ritual Fire Dance from Falla's *El amor brujo*; fifty years later it had lost none of its edge in Ravel's Concerto for Left Hand (Ex. 7.5b), nor in his Concerto in G (notably just after rehearsal figure 5 in the first movement). Even taken singly, those two elements colour subsequent works from Debussy's *Ariettes oubliées* to the F♯ major-minor blur that ends Ravel's *Sonatine* of 1905, a colour that then reverberates in Debussy's 'Poissons d'or' (Ex. 15.5) and 'Golliwogg's cake walk' (middle section).

Example 7.5

a: Chabrier, *Pièces pittoresques* (1880), 'Paysage', bars 55–7

b: Ravel, Concerto for Left Hand (1930), orchestra (piano reduction), rehearsal figure 29

Combine Example 7.5a with the chromatic pendulum of Example 7.3c and we virtually have the first solo entry in Gershwin's *Rhapsody in Blue* (and the essence of his second piano Prelude). Add the strings of ninths from Chabrier's 'Fête polonaise' (Ex. 1.8a), and we have the backbone of most light music (and some not so light) of the twentieth century – even if many of the composers who benefited may not have known its origins.

Example 1.8a also forms part of a larger original context, for it leads into two passages with equally dramatic later reverberations (Ex. 7.6a–b). If Example 1.8a can be heard echoing in Act 4 Scene 4 of *Pelléas et Mélisande* or the finale of Debussy's Violin Sonata of 1917 (from bar 51), the ostinato from Example 7.6a returns verbatim at exactly the equivalent point in Ravel's 'Scarbo', the start of the final dramatic accumulation. (It also features, a tritone lower, at the equivalent point in Chabrier's two-piano version of *España*.) That passage's resolution (Ex. 7.6b) reverberates just as vividly in

Ravel's *La valse* (Ex. 7.7), along with two further ricochets: Chabrier's hemiolas resonate elsewhere in *La valse* and in the fourth of Ravel's *Valses nobles et sentimentales*, while Ravel's chromatically rising tenor line in Example 7.7 mimics another Chabrier footprint, prominent in *Ronde champêtre*, 'Improvisation', *Aubade* and *Bourrée fantasque*, as well as in Examples 7.16a and 7.25. (Ravel's *Menuet sur le nom d'Haydn* features the same gesture.)

Example 7.6. Chabrier, *Le Roi malgré lui* (1884–7), 'Fête polonaise', Chabrier's piano reduction

a: climactic ostinato

b: resolution of the passage above

Example 7.7. Ravel, *La valse* (1906–20), Ravel's solo piano version, leading into the coda

These and the following musical extracts are best savoured at the piano. Particularly striking is the concentration of 'Chabriesque' moments in late Debussy (Preludes Book 2, *Études*, the Sonatas), including his only known use of the word *ballabile* (in 'Pour les quartes'). This was also the time of Debussy's two-piano suite *En blanc et noir* (1915), whose manic opening waltz suggests a crowning homage to Chabrier's *Valses romantiques*. This is supported by a curious notational quirk at the climax of the second movement in *En blanc et noir*, in the form of grace notes apparently tied to following main notes which, in practice, obviously have to be re-sounded (that is, the apparent ties read as slurs). The one other piece in the repertoire that shows this odd notation is Chabrier's *Impromptu*.

The occasional composer-cluster occurs. Example 7.21, partly noted by earlier observers, shows Fauré holding Chabrier's metre while Debussy holds Chabrier's pitch.[5] The most amusing such cluster is Ravel's concoction in *À la manière d'Emmanuel Chabrier* of 1912, deftly retouching Siebel's Flower aria from Gounod's *Faust* just enough to turn it into pure Chabrier (helped by the Chabriesque *do-re-mi* in Gounod's theme). To appreciate the full wit of Ravel's pastiche we have to remember what a warhorse Gounod's original was (and still can be), gleefully sent up backstage or at parties – it's easy to imagine Chabrier doing this – sometimes with spoof words. (I once memorably heard it sung to 'C'est aux pieds que j'ai froid; réchauff'-les-moi!' ['It's my feet that are cold; do warm them up!'])

Ravel's double-take adds exactly the sort of retouches we might imagine Chabrier perpetrating at a party, turning Gounod's innocuous melodic and bass descents from c'' and c into sensuously Chabriesque 7–6–5 sequences (bracketed in Ex. 7.8b: cf. Ex. 6.12b and 7.16). Bar 12 of Ravel's affectionate spoof adds another unmistakable Chabrier thumbprint (*un peu en dehors* in Ex. 7.8b: cf. Ex. 7.15); bars 15–18 turn Gounod's rising seventh chords into Chabriesque sliding ninths; and bars 22–9 indulge Chabrier's beloved two-octave unisons (as in 'Paysage', 'Mélancolie' and many of his songs). The bass line in bar 8 having aped Chabrier's *Impromptu* (from just before the coda), bars 19–20 and 31–4 pursue brief diversions into *Bourrée fantasque*, *Chanson pour Jeanne* and *Caprice* before the closing bars deliver the *coup de grâce*, a triple-take combining Gounod's opening *do-re-mi* with the final cadence of Chabrier's 'Sous bois' at exactly the point where the latter skirts, by a tingling hair's-breadth, the end of Wagner's *Tristan* (Ex. 7.9).

Example 7.8

a: Gounod, *Faust*, 'Flower song' (vocal score), bars 11–15

b: Ravel, *À la manière de Chabrier*, bars 9–13

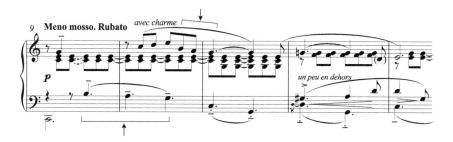

Example 7.9

a: Chabrier, *Pièces pittoresques*, 'Sous bois', bars 101–3

b: Ravel, *À la manière de Chabrier*, bars 44–6

c: Wagner, *Tristan und Isolde*, 'Liebestod' (Wagner's vocal score)

A whole culture of sophisticated wit can be adduced from these bars, which could be likened to paintings depicted in another painting, like Turner's evocation of Watteau's studio (of which more in Chapter 10), or Renoir's portrait of the two Lerolle sisters sitting in front of a Degas canvas. In that sense Ravel's *À la manière de Chabrier* simultaneously depicts two other pictures, at least one of which depicts a further one ...

To Poulenc's bold declaration about the *Pièces pittoresques* (see below) I'd unhesitatingly add that Chabrier's *Impromptu*, for all its ostensibly simple form, marks the start of modern French piano music. Composed apparently in the mid- to late 1860s, it antedates even Bizet's marvellous *Jeux d'enfants*, which it harmonically and rhythmically outdoes with modal surprises, dissonances and textures that already suggest mature Debussy and the Ravel of the *Valses nobles* (see Ex. 7.18 and 7.24). Not least of its delights is the different way the closing E♭ augmented triad of its central section resolves by semitones each time (first time to A♭ major, second time to C major)[6] – a good reason for observing the repeat, as well as a healthy challenge to the pianist's right foot in the descending arpeggio (to avoid either smudging or losing the continued resonance). The coda's ingenious layers of overlapping dissonances form something of a bridge between the likes of Schumann's 'Vogel als Prophet' and Ravel's 'Le gibet'.[7] Although *Impromptu* was out of print between the early 1890s and the early 1920s, Debussy may have acquired it at an early stage, for his song *Jane* of around 1881 and the Menuet of his *Suite bergamasque* make something of a refrain of Chabrier's central theme shown in Example 6.12b.[8]

To Dukas's list of Debussy's Chabrier favourites (quoted below) we can add the opera *Gwendoline*, which Debussy's stepdaughter Mme de Tinan remembered often seeing on his piano, and after which he named a magnificent ornamental Chinese toad (whom we'll meet again in Chapter 8).[9] Indeed, the only orchestral work Debussy ever conducted by a non-living composer was the overture to *Gwendoline* (in Turin in 1911) – a piece one would hardly choose as an easy option. The last of Debussy's *Ariettes oubliées*, 'Spleen', opens with a deadly-apt quotation from the 'Epithalame' (bridal song) of *Gwendoline*, published just a few years earlier.[10] This beautiful Chabrier chorus features daringly chromatic strings of parallel sevenths that prefigure the Menuet of Ravel's *Sonatine* and *Jeux d'eau*. The musical extracts that complete the present chapter take added force from the following remarks by numerous composers; see also the start of Chapter 10 for a far-reaching remark by César Franck.

Francis Poulenc:[11]

I have no hesitation in declaring that [Chabrier's] *Pièces pittoresques* are as important for French music as Debussy's Preludes.

How often Ravel talked ecstatically to me about 'Sous bois'. For him it was one of the summits of Chabrier's output.

When I first heard 'Idylle' in February 1914,[12] I lost my head to it. On my piano then were *Petrushka*, *Le sacre*, Schoenberg's *Six pieces* [op. 19]: but, ignoramus that I was (as many still are today), I thought Chabrier, much though I already loved his music, was a minor musician. Having gone into the Pathé record listening booths one day ... out of admiration for [the pianist Édouard] Risler, I put a coin in the slot and pressed the number to hear 'Idylle'. Even today [1961] I tremble with emotion at the memory of the ensuing miracle: a harmonic universe suddenly opened up before me and my music has never forgotten that first *baiser d'amour*.

I've often played two bars of the 'Menuet pompeux' [Ex. 7.21a] to music enthusiasts who disdained Chabrier, and asked them what it was. 'Well of course! it's Debussy', they'd exclaim.

Maurice Ravel:[13]

I would rather have composed [Chabrier's] *Le Roi malgré lui* than the whole [of Wagner's] Tetralogy.

The première of *Le Roi malgré lui* changed the whole orientation of French musical harmony. (Ravel in conversation with Poulenc, said on several occasions according to the latter)

The other day [I attended] the performance of *Le Roi malgré lui*, a work which I can play by heart from beginning to end, and which I was seeing for the first time ... You know of my great sympathy for the one musician who has influenced me above all others. (Letter of 1929 to Chabrier's daughter-in-law)

Of course, I was influenced above all by a musician: Chabrier, who more-over still does not have the recognition he deserves, for all of contemporary French music stems from his work. His role was as important as that of Manet in painting ... If the Debussyan revelation did not touch me deeply, it's because I was already conquered by Chabrier ... To return to the connection which, in my view, exists between Chabrier and Manet, it is not restricted to the influence which they exercised on their respective arts. This connection strikes me as more profound: I discovered the same impression created by Chabrier's music in Manet's *Olympia* ... In *Olympia*, I always had the feeling of rediscovering the essence of Chabrier's 'Mélancolie', simply transferred to another medium.[14]

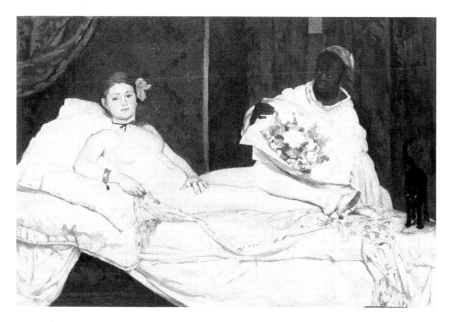

Plate 2. Édouard Manet: *Olympia* (1863), Musée d'Orsay, Paris

[Ravel] used to come to my apartment to rehearse and as soon as he arrived he often would sit down at the piano and start playing Chabrier's *Chanson pour Jeanne* which he loved; and he would say, 'Why don't you sing it, it's so lovely?' (Recounted by Madeleine Grey)

Claude Debussy:[15]

Chabrier, Moussorgsky, Palestrina, voilà ce que j'aime (To Alfred Mortier, c. 1892–3)

[Debussy], who knew Chabrier [personally] only a little, loved his whole output, but above all *La Sulamite* and *Le Roi malgré lui*. (Paul Dukas to Robert Brussel)

One of [Debussy's] joys was to sing, accompanying himself, from one end to the other of Chabrier's [operetta] *L'Étoile*, for whose brilliant invention and verve he had unbridled enthusiasm. (Recounted by René Peter)

Apparently Debussy was in tears of laughter when he heard the 'Duo de la chartreuse verte' [an aria in *L'Étoile* that parodies Donizetti: see Ex. 7.13a].

For the inaugural concert of the Théâtre des Champs-Élysées on 2 April 1913, Inghelbrecht started the programme with [Chabrier's] *Ode à la musique*. Debussy came to hear the final rehearsal. After the *Ode*, he made some comments to the young Inghelbrecht, who ran the piece again. When Inghelbrecht asked Debussy if he was now satisfied, he replied, 'It was fine the first time, but I so love the piece that I wanted to hear it twice.'[16]

Manuel de Falla:

I do not think any Spanish composer has ever succeeded as Chabrier has [with *España*], in achieving so genuine a version of the *jota*, as it is shouted out by the people of Aragón dancing in rings at night.[17]

Gustav Mahler:

In this work [*España*] I see the beginning of all modern music.[18]

Constant Lambert:

It is impossible to praise too highly the wit, charm and skill of this composer ... Above all, Chabrier holds one's affection as the most genuinely French of all composers, the only writer to give us in music the genial rich humanity, the inspired commonplace, the sunlit solidity of the French genius that finds its greatest expression in the paintings of Manet and Renoir ... He was the first important composer since Mozart to show that seriousness is not the same as solemnity, that profundity is not dependent upon length, that wit is not always the same as buffoonery, and that frivolity and beauty are not necessarily enemies.[19]

Jean Françaix:

So, as Roland-Manuel used to say, let's stop rediscovering Chabrier every twenty years. Let's put him once and for all in his true place, right at the top. Ravel insisted that this stocky little man from the Auvergne had changed the course of French music; Stravinsky that, without him, his *Petites suites* could not have been written.[20]

CADENCE CORNER

Example 7.10

a: Chabrier, *Gwendoline* (1885), Overture, bars 45–6 (following Chabrier's piano duet reduction)

b: Ravel, *Menuet antique* (1895), bars 7–8 and similar

Example 7.11b also has a place here, along with the Adagio of Ravel's Concerto in G (bars 44–5) as well as Debussy's Cello Sonata (bars 2–3) and 'Hommage à Rameau' (bars 27–8).

Example 7.11. The soft timpani touch

a: Chabrier, 'Menuet pompeux' (1880),   b: Ravel, *Sonatine* (1905),
bar 75   'Menuet', bars 11–12

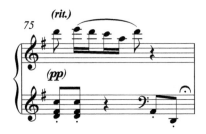

c: Debussy, *Images [oubliées]* (1894, published 1977), I, bar 11

The gesture also characterizes the second of Chabrier's *Valses romantiques* and his *Lied* of 1890 (the latter at the same pitch as Ex. 7.11b). This whole section of Chabrier's 'Menuet pompeux' (second part of the trio, from bar 73) echoes through the equivalent part of Ravel's *Menuet antique* of 1895 (from bar 54).

Example 7.12. Syncopated hemiolas

a: Chabrier, *Valses romantiques* (1880–3), I, bars 46–9

b: Ravel, *Valses nobles et sentimentales* (1911), I, bars 17–20

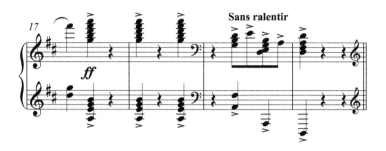

Example 7.13. The mock-courtly bow

a: Chabrier, *L'Étoile* (1877), 'Duo de la Chartreuse verte', bar 24

b: Debussy, *Suite bergamasque* (c. 1890), Prélude, bar 19

(If this cadence can often be found in older music (Ex. 11.1, for example), the extracts here share a particular mock-antique mood partly characterized by the texture and thirds.)

Example 7.14

a: Chabrier, *Le Roi malgré lui* (1887), Overture, bars 15–16 (Chabrier's piano reduction)

b: Debussy, *La mer* (1903–5), first movement, figure 14 (Debussy's piano duet version)

Poulenc (*Emmanuel Chabrier*, p. 96) links Chabrier's progression here to Satie's *2ᵉ Sarabande*: in fact Satie's *1ʳᵉ Sarabande* echoes it more closely, from its first two chords. Ravel perhaps had Satie's *Sarabandes* in mind when he remarked (as quoted above) on the harmonic impact of *Le Roi malgré lui*: Satie's *Sarabandes* date from September 1887, a few months after the première of *Le Roi malgré lui*.

Example 7.15. The falling melodic fifth to the dominant

a: Chabrier, *Pièces pittoresques* (1880), 'Mélancolie', bar 8

b: Chabrier, *Pièces pittoresques*, 'Scherzo-valse', bars 138–9

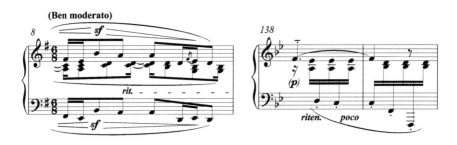

c: Franck, *Variations symphoniques* (1885), solo part, 8–9 bars after rehearsal figure R (also 4–5 bars after figure W)

The same gesture permeates Chabrier's *Ballabile*, *Ode à la musique*, parts of the *Bourrée fantasque*, and many of his songs and operatic numbers. The unusual *Ben moderato* heading of 'Mélancolie', incidentally, returns to open Franck's Violin Sonata of 1886.

Example 7.16. The 7–6–5 fall-away from the leading note (see also Example 6.12b)

a: Chabrier, *España* (1883), bars 312–15 (Chabrier's two-piano version, Piano 2)

b: Debussy, 'Hommage à S. Pickwick Esq.' (1913), bars 52–3

c: Ravel, *Pavane pour une Infante défunte* (1899), bar 39

This gesture (which also permeates the central section and coda of *Bourrée fantasque*) became virtually a Debussy signature, as at the end of 'Jardins sous la pluie' (Ex. 20.8) and 'Les collines d'Anacapri' (and 'Poissons d'or'), bars 4 and similar of both 'Bruyères' and *Page d'album*, the coda of *L'isle joyeuse* (the bracketed tenor line in Example 7.17) along with virtually the same ostinato in 'La soirée dans Grenade' (bars 50–1, 57–9 and 72–3), *Ballade* (bars 11, 14, 26–7 and 74), 'La Cathédrale engloutie' (bars 19–20), 'Pour les octaves' (bars 12 and similar and bar 94), and even his Piano Trio of 1880. It also appears in Fauré's Fourth Nocturne of 1884 (the climactic bar 56) and Sixth Barcarolle of 1896 (bars 82–3).

Example 7.17. Debussy, *L'isle joyeuse* (1904), bars 220–3

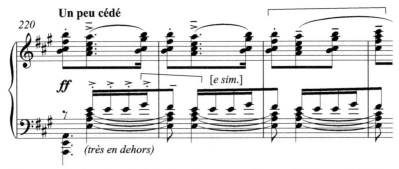

Compare the bracketed right-hand sequence here with Example 7.9a and the *do-re-mi* melodic endings of Debussy's preludes "*Les fées sont d'exquises danseuses*" and 'Feux d'artifice' (Ex. 15.4a) and Chabrier's *Joyeuse marche*.

Example 7.18. Decorated hanging second inversions

a: Chabrier, *Impromptu* (1860s), bars 252–4

b: Debussy, 'La terrasse des audiences du clair de lune' (1912–13), bars 44–5

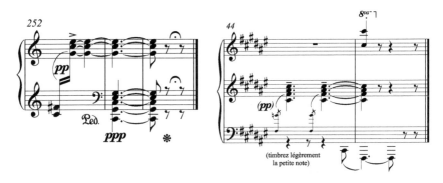

Example 7.19. The bold E major waltz opening that slips down a semitone

a: Chabrier, *Valses romantiques* (1880–3), II, bars 1–4

b: the same, bars 29–32

c: Debussy, *Études* (1915), 'Pour les octaves', bars 1–3

d: the same, bars 21–4

This E–E♭ sideslip is a Chabrier favourite: see also Example 7.14a (relative to the key signature) and no. 4 of *Une éducation manquée* (the Gontran-Pausanias Duetto bouffe, central $\frac{3}{8}$ episode).

Example 7.20. Chromatic chains of second-inversion triads

a: Chabrier, *Valses romantiques* (1880–3), III, coda

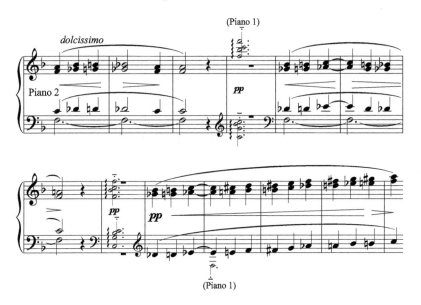

b: Debussy, 'La terrasse des audiences du clair de lune' (1912–13), bars 39–42

Compare also the end of Debussy's *Prélude à l'après-midi d'un faune*.

BEYOND THE CADENCE

Example 7.21

a: Chabrier, *Pièces pittoresques* (1880), 'Menuet pompeux', bars 82–3

b: Fauré, *Clair de lune* (1887), bars 51–2

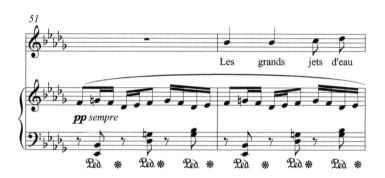

c: Debussy, *Suite bergamasque* (1890), Prélude, bars 33–4

(See note 5 to this chapter.)

Example 7.22

a: Chabrier, *Habanera* (1884–5), bars 80–3

b: Debussy, 'La soirée dans Grenade' (1903), bars 130–3

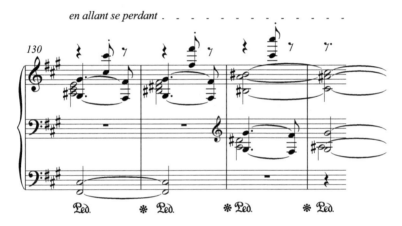

('La soirée dans Grenade' is Debussy's first piano piece to use three staves.)

Example 7.23

a: Chabrier, 'Sous bois' (1880), bars 10–13

b: Debussy, *Études*, 'Pour les agréments' (1915), bars 31–2

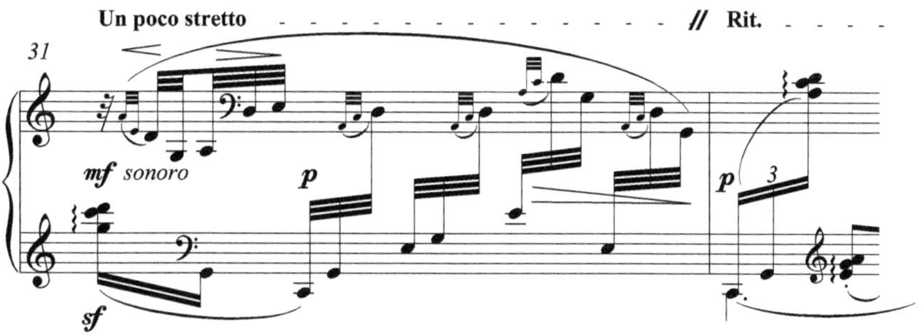

Example 7.24

a: Chabrier, *Impromptu* (1860s), bars 202–3

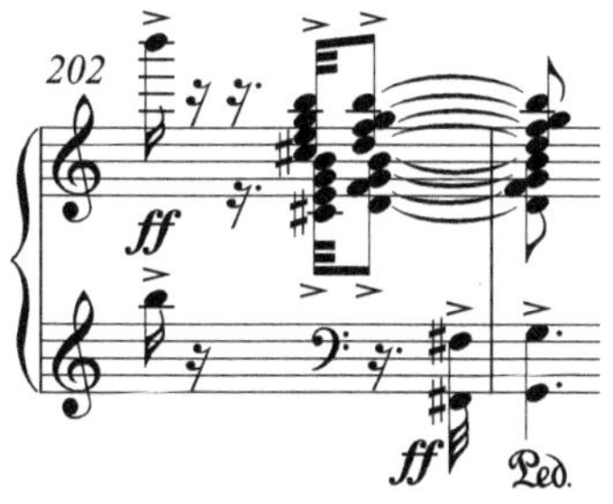

b: Debussy, 'Hommage à Rameau' (1905), bars 51–2

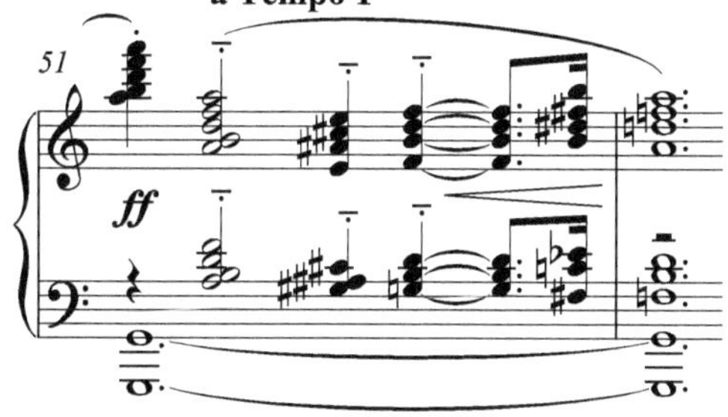

c: Chabrier, *Impromptu*, bars 205–6

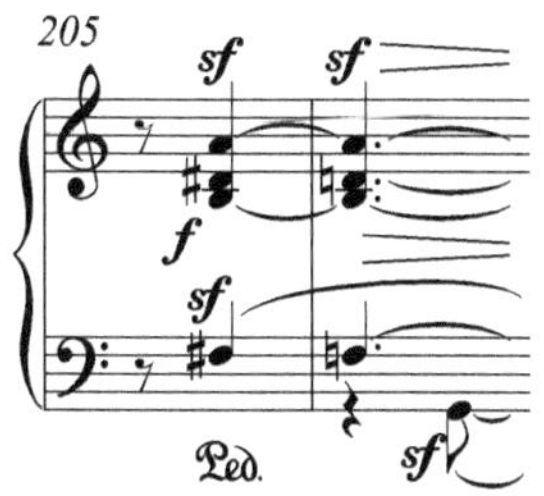

Example 7.25. The decorated chromatic rise (see also Example 7.16a)

a: Chabrier, *Aubade* (1883), bar 82   b: Debussy, 'Reflets dans l'eau'
(1905), bar 10

c: Debussy, *Études* (1915), 'Pour les arpèges composés', bar 41

Example 7.26. The appoggiatura tenth 'resolving' to the ninth

a: Chabrier, *Valses romantiques*   b: Debussy, *Petite suite* (1888),
(1880–3), III, bar 71   'Cortège', bar 30

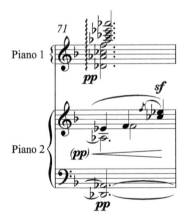

c: Debussy (1901), *Pour le piano*, Toccata, bar 149

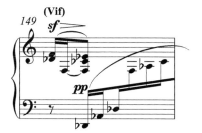

See also Act 2 Scene 2 of Debussy's *Pelléas et Mélisande* and variants of this gesture in 'Poissons d'or' (Ex. 15.5), 'Voiles', the coda of *Masques*, etc.

Example 7.27. Ninth chord trails

a: Chabrier, *Valses romantiques* (1880–33), III, bars 66–7

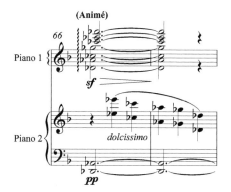

b: Fauré, Eighth Barcarolle (1906), bar 69

Compare also the opening of Debussy's *Ariettes oubliées* (1885–7) and the second page of Fauré's Fourth *Valse-caprice*.

Example 7.28. The extended chromatic pendulum

a: Chabrier, *España*, bars 145–8, Chabrier's two-piano version

b: Ravel, *La valse*, E♭ episode, Ravel's two-piano version

More examples along those lines are shown in my article 'Chabrier "par" Debussy'. Nor should the Chabriophilia of some eminent conductors be overlooked. Sir Thomas Beecham's various recordings of *España, Joyeuse marche* and the *Gwendoline* overture are widely regarded as unsurpassed. Ernest Ansermet named his rural retreat 'La Chabrière' and left some historic Chabrier recordings (radio tapes and discs). D.-E. Inghelbrecht's conducting career showed a lifelong preference among French repertoire for the four composers central to this book, and his Chabrier and Musorgsky enthusiasm played a major part in his friendship with Debussy – one reason perhaps for the sudden increase of Chabriesque allusions in Debussy's music from around 1912, as their friendship grew. Ravel's student Manuel Rosenthal, a lifelong Chabrier devotee on the rostrum, titled his musical reflections *Musique*

adorable (the opening words of Chabrier's *Ode à la musique*), including a chapter on Chabrier ('adorable musicien') plus several puns on Chabrier titles ('Monsieur, Madame Orchestre et leurs enfants'). Paul Paray's Chabrier recordings for Mercury from 1957–61 exude similar concentrated energy to Beecham's, echoed again in recent recordings by Sir John Eliot Gardiner.

CHAPTER 8

DEBUSSY AND THE ORIENT

Debussy regarded the piano as Balinese musicians regard their gamelan orchestras. He was interested not so much in the single tone . . . as in the patterns of resonance which that tone set up around itself — E. Robert Schmitz

W E might aptly say that Debussy re-oriented western music, given his fascination with oriental cultures and art. Without attempting (or needing) risky proofs of influence, this survey lets us sort some wheat from chaff and delve deeper into Debussy's normal techniques relative to the oriental traditions that most fascinated him.[1] That particularly marks him out here: attracted though many composers of the time were by the orient, Debussy is the one who made much of it his own language, even identity.[2]

His exposure to oriental art and philosophy is well known. In the Symbolist milieux he frequented, oriental-cum-esoteric ideas from Buddhism to Sufism to Hermeticism had been endemic since Baudelaire's time. Among his close associates were at least three ethnomusicologists with oriental interests. In the years around 1890 there was Edmond Bailly, esoteric and oriental scholar, who published some of Debussy's music from his bookshop L'Art Indépendant, a rallying point for Symbolist artists. From 1902 there was Louis Laloy, orientalist, ethnomusicologist, music critic and one of Debussy's most trusted friends.[3] From 1906 there was Victor Segalen who mixed his career as ship's doctor with passions for archaeology, writing and music.[4] Debussy avidly attended the various Asian music and theatrical performances at the Parisian Expositions universelles of 1889 and 1900, and was a lifelong devotee and collector of oriental art and artefacts, apparently from adolescence onwards.[5]

From that we can extract three strong links to his music. One is gamelan music, most immediately that of Java, but broadly encompassing a tradition of percussion-based ensembles and rhythmic layering common to much of South-East Asia.[6] A second source is Indian music, a compendium of cultures, Hindu and Muslim, North and South, all characterized by the technique of *rāga*, a spiritual philosophy of the different colours, moods and 'affects' of different scales or modes.[7] Thirdly we have Asian art and artefacts generally. Blended with all that is the way oriental philosophies can be seen reflected in Debussy's outlook and aesthetic.

GAMELAN

Debussy was entranced by the performances of a north Javanese gamelan that he first heard at the 1889 exhibition: the impression haunted him for years.[8] To pursue any analogies with Debussy's music, we need a brief outline of how a gamelan sounds – hard though this is to convey without hearing the characteristic 'carpet of sound' produced by its pointillistic textures and rhythms. Example 8.1 shows approximate pitches of the two basic Indonesian modes, *slendro* and *pelog*: their exact temperament defies western notation and varies from district to district and from gamelan to gamelan. Most gamelans have two sets of instruments, in pelog and slendro tunings: players can change from one to the other to play many pieces of standard Javanese *balungan* repertoire in either of two modal forms.

Example 8.1. Slendro and pelog scales (approximate pitches)

As for the instruments and their interplay, metre and period are marked by the largest gong, which completes a measure or cycle usually every fourth, eighth or sixteenth beat, depending on tempo and context. (In western notation this would mark the first beat of the bar; the sounding effect is the same.) The remaining percussion interlocks with this in intricate set patterns, filling the intermediate and off-beats, the highest instruments struck most frequently in keeping with their faster tonal decay. In rising order pitch-wise from *gong, kempul* is slightly smaller, pitched about a fifth higher; *kenong* and *kethuk* (the names are all onomatopoeic) are two smaller gongs laid horizontally on cords; *bonang* is a two-octave range of smaller gongs laid horizontally on cords, prominent in introductory passages and off-beat interlocking, along with *gambang* (xylophone) and *panderus* (metallophone). *Gender* and *saron*

metallophones sound the most prominent lines, in addition to any vocal participation or sustaining instruments (fiddles, flutes and oboes), something that varies from piece to piece (some can be played purely by percussion).

We have to be wary of equating Debussy's use of pentatony *per se* with slendro, since pentatony occurs worldwide, usually closer to western pitch. Asian (most specifically Chinese) flavour can of course be evoked from it by concentrating melodically on its fourths and minor thirds (rather than fifths and major thirds), as Ravel does in 'Asie' from *Shéhérazade*, 'Laideronnette' from *Ma mère l'Oye* and the surreal Chinese teacup foxtrot in *L'Enfant et les sortilèges*. The surest way of evoking gamelan at the piano, though, is by emulating pelog, as Poulenc does in his Concerto for Two Pianos and Orchestra, composed just after the 1931 Paris Exposition universelle.[9] Debussy's avoidance of that suggests his interests lay deeper. Nor can whole-tone scales be likened (as has sometimes been attempted) to pelog, whose varying intervals make for quite different colours. More fruitful insights emerge from Debussy's use of rhythm, timbre and structure – the aspects of gamelan he himself singled out – even if his pentatony sometimes is obviously gamelan-like when the accompanying rhythms and textures support the analogy.

The piece that most obviously invites comparison with gamelan is 'Pagodes', the first of Debussy's *Estampes* composed in 1903. (*Estampes* is the standard French term for Japanese prints.) Debussy's title 'Pagodes' is matched by the music's mix of pentatonic arabesques and its relative lack of diatonic cadences or modulations: the piece's only sounding keys, B major and G$\sharp$ minor, share the same pentatonic scale. Louis Laloy, who had known Debussy for a year when the *Estampes* were composed, regarded the piece's main stimulus as the Exposition universelle of 1900, which the painter Jacques-Émile Blanche recalled attending with Debussy specifically to hear the gamelan.[10] However, gamelan is just one of several possible images blended in 'Pagodes', embracing a westerner's perception of 'pagodas' and all they imply.[11]

My own position with 'Pagodes' is a personal but vivid one. For years the piece had puzzled me, and I was less than convinced it was one of Debussy's better pieces. In 1985 I had the chance of joining a gamelan (at the University of Western Australia); some months later I returned, almost idly, to 'Pagodes' and was astonished to hear its allusions and nuances fall easily into place. For example, if bars 1–2 already suggest rhythmically layered gongs and bells, bars 3–4 more exactly follow the normal rhythmic sequence of *gong* and *kempul*. At bar 11 the first shift in the bass (not in itself a standard gamelan gesture) is accompanied by a new right-hand motive whose semi-muffled sonority and varied syncopations (duplets, triplets and off-beats) immediately evoke the timbre and patterns of bonang (Ex. 8.2). Probably the most specific allusion of all is the oddly-placed *Rit.* across bar 30, imitating the sudden slowing of a gamelan piece into a new cycle. In 'Pagodes' this introduces an ostinato (from bar 37) particularly suggestive of a group of *gender*. Finally, the piece's coda is dominated by the nearest that two hands at a piano can produce to the inter-locking of high metallophones, with fast motion in high voices layered against progressively slower motion in the lower ones. The piece ends with an entirely gamelan-like slowing into what one can only describe as the final gong.

Example 8.2. Debussy, 'Pagodes', bars 11–12

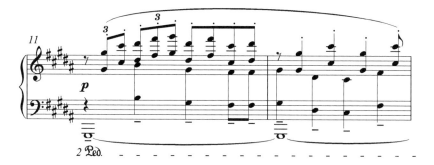

The crux here lies in how often Debussy's instructions and unusual textural balances in 'Pagodes' make little sense by western norms but fall into place when treated as gamelan gestures. This particularly affects voicing and rhythm. If we treat the top line of bars 3–4 like a western melody, the texture immediately clogs; the tune (marked *presque sans nuances*) neither asks nor merits such attention. Left to itself it becomes a quieter, impassively decora-tive arabesque, sharing attention with the texture below and beyond. The bass and tenor fifths sound particularly gong-like on upright Bechsteins of the sort Debussy had at that time, and his tenuto accent at bar 1 beat 3 encourages the left thumb to let the top notes ring like *kethuk* (as in bars 3–4, strict timing is vital). In Example 8.2, voicing the right thumb slightly stronger than the octave above it brings out the bonang-like colour, as does some fractional rhythmic freedom (anticipating the off-beats and marginally stretching the triplets): hard to define on paper, the effects are easier at the keyboard and quickly grasped by anyone familiar with gamelan.

After the *Rit.* at bar 30 (often ignored by pianists because it makes little sense in western terms), at bar 38 we can let the top line ring out in a context that western norms would normally forbid (the repeated ringing *c‴♯*s), while the figure underneath can rattle percussively as Debussy's notation invites. A basic opening tempo of ♩ = c. 80–84 (keeping exact time as in gamelan) lets all that voicing register easily; the tempo accumulation from bar 23 can then reach as much as ♩ = c. 100, letting bar 30 then pull back dramatically to ♩ = c. 60

before restoring basic tempo again from bar 31. Maximum sense then emerges from all Debussy's indications, letting the piece cohere naturally.

Bearing in mind that a piano can't reproduce exact gamelan pitch, we have to be alert for where 'Pagodes' points elsewhere. Taken more broadly, the piece is a picture, a westerner's perception of another continent, culture, climate and way of life. This is where other aspects emerge, in Debussy's best nature-painting vein, like the pagoda roof outline noted in Chapter 1 (which Debussy then elaborates in bars 23–6), various suggestions of temple bells, drums and chants, or just a breath of tropical air through the palms (see Ex. 1.5).

A few structural aspects of 'Pagodes', like the occasionally roving bass line, are also at variance with gamelan.[12] Perceptions of its relation to gamelan can thus vary widely with the observer's degree of specialization. My experience has repeatedly been that musical amateurs familiar with Indonesia, on hearing 'Pagodes', tend to exclaim 'gamelan!' (especially if the piece is played with rhythmic clarity), while ethnomusicological specialists are much more sceptical. In short the newcomer, viewing the canvas from afar, is struck by the affinities while the specialist, close up with a glass, is all too aware of the differences. This was probably Debussy's aim, and confirms how well he succeeded in covering his tracks.

Some other works continue this filtering of gamelan-related techniques into Debussy's normal technique. The gong and bell evocations on the last page of 'Reflets dans l'eau' (composed first in 1901 then rewritten in 1905) stand out against the piece's more occidental structures already seen. The matching *Image* from the second series, 'Cloches à travers les feuilles', mirrors this by starting with a layered texture (Ex. 8.3) which, despite its whole-tone mode, imitates gamelan textures and rhythms: in particular the encircled As in bars 3–4 emulate a standard rhythmic sequence of kethuk and kenong, relative to a kempul that corresponds with the Gs of bars 1–2. Debussy's non-gamelan mode and different tessitura show his own voice, though, and the gamelan analogy fades from bar 5 (though some aspects return later in the piece). Most remarkably, Example 8.3 often sounds just one note at a time, never more than four, yet marks out seven differently voiced lines, five of them interlocking in bars 3–4. Besides what that tells the performer, it reflects Debussy's declaration that 'Javanese music obeys laws of counterpoint that make Palestrina seem like child's play'.[13]

Example 8.3. Debussy, 'Cloches à travers les feuilles', bars 1–4

Debussy's orchestral *Images* 'Gigues' and 'Rondes de printemps' carry gamelan-like layering to something of an apogee, mixing their arabesques and themes in rhythmic augmentation and diminution: 'Rondes de printemps' superimposes voices respectively in $\frac{9}{8}$ and $\frac{3}{4}$ over other voices in hemiola hypermetre of $\frac{18}{8}$ or $\frac{3}{2}$ (most clearly from rehearsal figure 20, the fastest-moving lines at the top just as in gamelan). 'Rondes de printemps' also revisits the stylized gamelan-ritardando, slowing to exactly half speed as it moves into rehearsal figure 11. In 'Pagodes' the equivalent slowing acted as a gesture; in 'Rondes de printemps' it goes deeper, slowing the whole tempo and structure for the next section (or cycle) exactly in gamelan manner. The gamelan-like colours inherent in these pieces emerge more explicitly from their two-piano or four-hand transcriptions, prepared with Debussy's blessing by André Caplet.

One more matter brings us back to 'Pagodes'. Chapter 6 mentioned the curious way Debussy reached full maturity last of all in his solo piano music. The piano's percussive nature would have been a factor in this, far from the qualities of the singing voice that always inspired the best from him in his young years. 'Pagodes' suggests that it was gamelan that showed Debussy how to embrace and exploit the piano's intrinsic percussiveness in creating a gamelan-like 'carpet of sound' (an expression used by many westerners after hearing gamelan), its varied reverberation and tonal decay working in the music's favour.

Since 1903 was well after Debussy first heard gamelan in 1889, the crucial catalyst may have been his re-hearing of it in 1900, just as he was most ripe for it.[14] The Toccata of *Pour le piano* (early 1901) may be a preliminary spring: Debussy's pupil Mme de Romilly considered it an evocation of 'the gongs and Javanese music to which [Debussy] spent entire days listening at the Paris

Exposition universelle'.[15] If that reflects gamelan at its most exuberant, the more pointillistic textures of 'Pagodes' and the last page of 'Reflets dans l'eau' suggest the key to Debussy's later remark that 'if we listen without European prejudice to the magical beauty of Javanese "percussion", we are obliged to admit that our own is a barbarous noise fit only for a travelling circus'.[16]

INDIAN MUSIC

The role this plays is more elusive, for we don't know what Indian music Debussy may have heard before 1913, except for his expressed interest already seen in 1907 and the probability that he learnt something of its theory around 1890 during his daily discussions with Edmond Bailly at the Librairie de l'Art Indépendant. Bailly was something of a specialist on the topic, and his short book *Le son dans la nature* of 1900 devotes a section to Indian spiritual philosophy relative to music.[17]

In a study not primarily concerned with Debussy, Elisabeth de Jong-Keesing singles out his piano *Image* 'Et la lune descend sur le temple qui fut' as 'using melody in authentic Indian style'.[18] This is probably the present Example 8.4a (the only material in the piece that bears the analogy). The passage closely resembles a fragment headed 'Bouddha' in a sketchbook Debussy used around 1907–8 (Ex. 8.4b), probably intended for Victor Segalen's 'Buddhist drama' *Siddhartha*.[19] This fragment is doubly interesting for being Debussy's most explicit emulation of oriental sonority, albeit qualified by its western ending and by having remained unpublished.

However, if Example 8.4a might be heard as Indian, the mode of Example 8.4b sounds Japanese. To muddy things further, the shared theme resembles a quasi-Chinese motive (Ex. 8.4c) that had recently appeared in Ravel's song 'Le paon' (from the *Histoires naturelles* of 1906), complete with the same distinctive ornamentation. (Nectoux plausibly likens the octave ornamentation in Example 8.4a to effects from Asian string instruments;[20] Ravel's version also neatly evokes the peacock's strut.) To diffuse matters even more, Louis Laloy defines the title 'Et la lune descend sur le temple qui fut' – which he possibly dreamt up with Debussy – as 'in Chinese style'.[21]

Example 8.4

a: Debussy, 'Et la lune descend sur le temple qui fut' (1907), bars 12–14

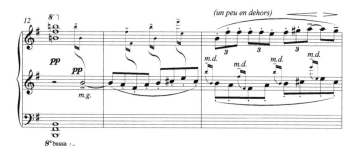

b: Debussy, 'Bouddha' sketch fragment (c. 1907)

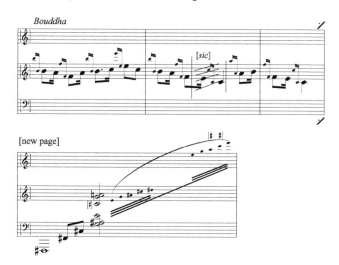

c: Ravel, *Histoires naturelles* (1906), 'Le paon', bars 7–9

Such ambiguities make us look more under the music's surface, where analogies start to emerge with the theory and structure of Indian music. Debussy's love of drones becomes especially interesting when combined with tonal procedures that relate less to western norms of the time than to those of Indian *rāga*.[22] Common to North and South Indian music, *rāga* is not just a mode or scale but the order in which notes are first introduced – the way the musician progressively colours in the tonal canvas. Sometimes specific notes have to be preceded or followed by others, defining melodic shapes or turns. Its character is reflected by the origin of the word *rāga* in the Sanskrit word for colour.[23]

Debussy's affinity with this emerges from his habit of building up a tonal palette in an ordered way that defines a strong modal colour or character while avoiding western-type modulation. This informs exactly those aspects of 'Pagodes' that are unrelated to gamelan. Opening with pentatony (B–C♯–D♯–F♯–G♯), the piece gradually adds five more pitches in the order A♮ (bar 3), E♮ and A♯ (bar 7) and G♮ and E♯ (bars 15–17). At the piano we can sense how each of these progressively modifies and builds the piece's modal 'affect'.

Two pitches, C♮ and D♮, remain unsounded throughout the piece, which is immediately followed by the second *Estampe*, 'La soirée dans Grenade'. This opens on a C♯–G♯ drone (somewhat redolent of Indian tanpura, despite the outwardly Spanish context), but its real 'rāga' begins in bar 7, with a melodic turn that circles chromatically around *c″*♯: sounding as Indian as it is Spanish, its colours are quickly characterized by the notes *d″*♮ and *c″*♮ (= *b′*♯) – the very two pitches Debussy withheld from 'Pagodes'. 'La soirée' thus continues and develops the *rāga* from 'Pagodes', in the same way that Chapter 2 showed larger structures linking various Preludes. Once again, the ostensible evocations in 'Pagodes' and 'La soirée', respectively South-East Asian and Spanish, show how thoroughly Debussy assimilated his *rāga*-like techniques, far beyond surface evocation.

Chapter 2 has shown Debussy's *rāga*-like procedures reaching a peak in the prelude 'Des pas sur la neige', with its repeated and methodical progressive saturation of the chromatic octave (beyond the pitch norms of Indian modes, even if the latter compensate with micro-intervals foreign to western usage). Debussy achieves his 12-note cycles in that piece without leaving the home key, which is held through most of the piece by a simple, almost Indian-sounding ostinato drone. The underlying techniques thus relate to Indian practice exactly where they depart from western norms. A further whiff of *rāga* comes from Debussy's penchant for combining non-western modes with a drone bass: for example the 'overtone' scale already seen in *L'isle joyeuse* and 'Hommage à Rameau' (Ex. 1.2b and 1.3) is a standard South Indian mode classified as *Vachaspati*.[24]

Debussy's best-documented link with Indian music is his meeting in May 1913 with the Indian Sufi Inayat Khan who, for some years, had been performing in Europe and America with an ensemble including his two younger brothers and cousin.[25] Virtually the first person to befriend them in Paris was Debussy's old friend Edmond Bailly, though it was the pianist Walter Rummel who introduced them to Debussy. In a letter to Rummel, Debussy, apparently sensitive to the matter of time of day in Indian music, asks Rummel to let Inayat Khan 'come with his brother on a day of his choice, at about 5 o'clock, which appears to be his usual time'.[26]

Years later, Musharaff Khan, the youngest brother, recalled this occasion (which he says Debussy referred to as 'the evening of emotions'): Debussy listened to their music and then 'sat down at the piano and played, calling out titles that resembled the rāgas' descriptive names'.[27] Musharaff Khan remembered titles including 'rainy season', 'spring' and 'autumn'. Was Debussy improvising? Or, bearing in mind the translations involved, might he have been playing 'Jardins sous la pluie', a spontaneous piano reduction of *Printemps* (a youthful work in two-part form akin to the Indian *alap–tala* sequence, and which had received its première just the previous month) and the newly published prelude 'Feuilles mortes'? Another candidate might be the newly published, Indian-inspired prelude 'La terrasse des audiences du clair de lune'.

The Dutch musician Hakiem van Lohuizen, who worked with Musharaff Khan, considers that musical echoes of Inayat Khan's music might be discernible in Debussy's *Berceuse héroïque* of 1914, or even in parts of *La boîte à joujoux*, composed later in 1913.[28] According to Musharaff Khan, his older brother gave Debussy instruction on his melodic instrument, the vīna; when the brothers had to leave Paris hurriedly on the outbreak of war in 1914, the instrument was left with Debussy. Musharaff Khan reports delivering it there himself, with some difficulty in the face of a concierge who suspected he was delivering a weapon.[29]

Inayat Khan's affinity of musical outlook with Debussy emerges from his posthumously published musical writings, part of whose first page could almost come from Debussy's mouthpiece 'Monsieur Croche':

> What do we see as the principal expression of life in the beauty visible before us? It is movement. In line, in colour, in the changes of the seasons, in the rising and falling of the waves, in the wind, in the storm, in all the beauty of nature there is constant movement. It is movement which has caused day and night, and the changing of the seasons; and this movement has given us the comprehension of what we call time.[30]

We could hardly ask for a better definition of most of Debussy's evocative titles; it also matches the tenor of Debussy's already extant writings, a constant exhortation to listen to nature's rhythm and avoid recipes. It could as easily have been Inayat Khan who wrote, 'Only musicians have the privilege of capturing all the poetry of night and day, of earth and sky, of reconstituting its atmosphere and immense rhythm.' In fact the sentence came from Debussy's pen in November 1913, in the early months of their friendship.[31]

The friendship evidently yielded more than just pleasing sympathy. Musharaff Khan later recalled that Debussy 'encouraged us by his real understanding and interest in our art, and by the new and sincere emotion that my brother's music inspired in him'.[32] They in turn may well have helped Debussy emerge from his creative crisis of mid-1913 to mid-1915: in 1916 Debussy thanked Walter Rummel, who had introduced them, 'for having reawakened in me the appetite for music at a time when I fully believed I would never again be able to compose'.[33] The very first bars of his creative resurgence in summer 1915 – launching the two-piano suite *En blanc et noir* – are anchored by the nearest approach in all of Debussy's music to an Indian tanpura (bottom staff of Ex. 8.5: the bass continues thus to bar 12). Add Debussy's harmony over it (upper staves) and any risk of blatancy melts in his characteristic blend of East and West.

Example 8.5. Debussy, *En blanc et noir*, first movement, bars 1–4 (reduced from two-piano original to show polyphony)

ORIENTAL ART

Debussy's beloved *objets d'art* came from many countries. While Egypt was the source of his two cherished Canopic jar lids, from China came his ornamental toads – the wooden Arkel who lived on his work table, travelled everywhere with him and refused to be shut in cases, and the hollow green Gwendoline already encountered in Chapter 7.[34] Japan took on special importance in the wake of the 1868 Meiji restoration when its paintings and artefacts found their way to the west after more than two centuries of isolation.

Like French painters of the time, Debussy was fascinated by *estampes*, the brilliantly and subtly coloured Japanese woodcut prints: with the sculptress Camille Claudel he used to peruse albums of Hokusai as they became available. Besides the *estampes* by Hokusai and Utagawa Hiroshige that hung on his wall, in 1896 he gave his friend René Peter a print of Hiroshige's *Minakuchi* (one of the series Fifty-three Stations of the Tōkaidō).[35] Other oriental objects seen by visitors to Debussy's home in 1911 included a *kito* and some rare Japanese instruments, a Buddha, jade animals and pieces of Chinese pottery.[36] Preserved in the Musée Debussy at Saint Germain-en-Laye are his nineteenth-century Chinese screen and a lacquered Japanese cigarette case depicting carp, ornaments from his desk including two small Japanese pencil (or pen?) holders and a nineteenth-century Chinese porcelain *écritoire* featuring a reclining Buddha plus inkwell, and the famed lacquered ebony plaque with inlaid brass depicting two carp in a sweeping current under a willow branch, the inspiration of his piano *Image* 'Poissons d'or'.[37] Manuel de Falla intriguingly remembered an additional small study in Debussy's house 'full of Japanese and Chinese masks'.[38]

From the 1890s onwards Debussy plagued his publishers with a mania for reflecting the character of Japanese prints on the cover pages of his music. Besides the cover of *La mer*, which copied part of Hokusai's *Great Wave off Kanagawa*, one of Debussy's own printed exemplars of *Pelléas et Mélisande* has a flyleaf adorned with a beautiful hand-painted colour and ink drawing of the two lovers in Japanese style (by an unidentified artist).[39] He also viewed the graphics of his manuscripts in terms of the meticulousness of Japanese prints.[40]

One oriental technique almost visible on the paper of Debussy's music is the pen-and-brush technique of Chinese ink drawing, where the pen first etches a line that is then gently washed over by the damp brush. This can be sensed across the hands in the opening gestures of (notably) 'Reflets dans l'eau' and 'Brouillards', or, on a larger scale, in the way the clear underlying tonal skeleton in pieces like 'Reflets dans l'eau', 'Danseuses de Delphes' and 'Voiles' (as seen in Chapters 1–2 and 5) is gently washed over and disguised, or softened, by the music's surface chromatic episodes or whole tones.

On a larger scale Claude Monet emerges as a major catalyst, according to the researches of the art historian David Bromfield. In a fascinating chapter entitled 'Japanese art, Monet and the formation of Impressionism' Bromfield makes numerous references to Monet that can equally be applied, almost word for word, to Debussy. Bromfield explores Monet's avowals that Japanese prints and etching were the mainspring of his mature art (as suggested by the Japanese prints that festoon his house in Giverny), and centres on the changes in Monet's brush techniques from the late 1860s after encountering Japanese art, plus Monet's evolving approach to composition and depiction of subject.

Bromfield regards Monet's three views of 1867 from the colonnade of the Louvre as being his first canvases based on principles absorbed from Japanese painting, the model being Hiroshige's *Asakusa Kinruzan*, depicting an important Buddhist temple and the life surrounding it. Bromfield describes Monet as translating into western terms what John LaFarge called the Japanese way of depicting 'the illuminated air of the scene of the action'.[41] For 'Monet' read 'Debussy' along with *Estampes* and 'Pagodes', and the parallel starts to speak for itself.

Bromfield also sees Monet's late preoccupation with water reflections as the final embodiment of what he had learnt from the 'treatment of subject' in Japanese art. As illustration, Bromfield contrasts Monet's direct view of the water with the earlier European approach, as in the treatment of Narcissus by Poussin or Claude Lorrain, with Narcissus the focus rather than the water.

This prompts comparison with Debussy's 'Reflets dans l'eau'. Chapter 5 has already traced how the piece's two main arches open with the same basic motive (the dropping pebble and spreading ripples), taken up again from bar 35. Thereafter the piece's two arches diverge. In the first one, bar 16 suggests the skyline coming to meet its reflection in the water (Ex. 8.6), in a shape uncannily like Monet's 'Seine at Giverny' paintings of the late 1890s. As they meet in bar 17, it is as if Narcissus sees his reflection: bars 18–19 sound the *Tristan* love-spell chord before a web of arpeggios ensnares the music, carrying the circling melody to a harmonic impasse at bars 30–1. Whatever else it may embody, this passage translates to perfection the essence of Claude Lorrain's *Narcissus*. The piece's reprise from bar 35, after a similar start, bypasses the 'Narcissus' material and, via a series of more turbulent figurations, plunges us straight into the water for the piece's climax, before the last page settles into a reflective calmness akin to Monet's later water paintings. The piano's closing evocations of gongs and bells might even be read as saying that from the east came the symbol and the story. In its structure and its sequence the piece effectively recreates where western depiction of water had gone from Claude Lorrain to Claude Monet.

Example 8.6. Debussy, 'Reflets dans l'eau', bars 16–18

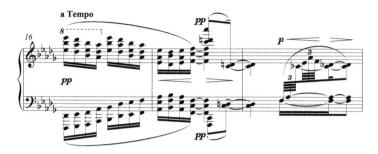

   Such a reading is inevitably subjective, supported though it may be by the music's allusions. A rounder view of Debussy's musico-visual interests takes us back to the *Estampes*, a creatively ingenious formula that allowed him to portray both exotic and home scenes as interchangeably familiar and exotic perceptions. 'Jardins sous la pluie', with its woven-in nursery songs, thus suggests France viewed in the manner of Hiroshige or Hokusai viewing their own country, with a finesse equivalent to their eye and engraving knife: even the look of the music's opening figurations on the page recalls the diagonal lines of rain on Japanese prints. Similar observations can be made for Debussy's later 'The snow is dancing' (*Children's Corner*), which exploits a delicate gamelan-like texture to suggest the snow of a Japanese print, just like the printed front cover of the suite's first edition, drawn by Debussy himself. Both gamelan and Japanese prints bear on playing this piece, suggesting a gamelan-like veil of discreet half-pedal under a delicate touch, letting the listener's ear be caressed as by snowflakes. (Too much pedal risks turning it into rain, too little into hail.)

   In the course of this chapter, oriental allusions have been seen in all three pieces constituting the second series of piano *Images*. Take this together with Debussy's cover design for the latter's edition – which expressly matches not the first series of *Images* but the *Estampes* – and an implication emerges that they equally make up an unspoken second series of *Estampes*. The different title may simply reflect that Debussy, by the time he completed *Estampes* in 1903, had already signed over the two planned series of *Images* – part of a larger project – to the publisher Durand: any re-titling at that stage would have caused complex disruption.[42] This elasticity is inherent in many of Debussy's titles: not only could 'The snow is dancing' have been equally an *estampe* or prelude, or the prelude 'Les tierces alternées' equally an *étude* (or *estampe*), but as late as 1915 Debussy's letters show him viewing his *Études* in terms of *estampes* (see note 40 to this chapter). Even his title *Études*, in the manner of his Whistler-like use of the title *Nocturnes*, suggests the painter as much as the musician.

EASTERN PHILOSOPHIES

Besides the visual and literary Buddhist interests already seen, a distinct tint of Buddhist philosophy emerges from the way Debussy introduces 'Monsieur Croche' to the world in 1901 – notably when he follows some daydreaming reflections with the sudden conclusion, 'The alchemy of that is far more complex, for it requires the sacrifice of one's whole precious little personality.'[43] In another article two years later we find Debussy lampooning dilettantish orientalism in a way that quietly betrays the adept:

> Nothing is more exciting than pretending one is some little Buddha, living on an egg and two glasses of water a day and giving the rest to the poor, mulling over ideas of 'nature naturing' and pantheistic thoughts about the cosmos, and indulging in those attractively confusing arguments about the self and the not-self. All bound together, of course, by the theory of the Universal Consciousness... All very nice as conversational topics, but unfortunately not worth a penny in practice, and possibly even dangerous.[44]

To link this to music can be risky, yet viable when discussing a composer as steeped as Debussy was in symbols and images, provided we do it in a way that avoids rigid interpretation. Two central pieces here are *Masques* and *L'isle joyeuse*, composed in 1903–4, the heyday of 'Monsieur Croche' and around the time of *Estampes*, the first series of *Images* and *La mer*. Under their contrasted surface *Masques* and *L'isle joyeuse* are closely twinned (of which more in Chapter 14), to the extent that they can seem like opposed dances of death and life, opposite sides of the same, the archetype of karma, the circle of our desires and fears. This matches Debussy's remark to Marguerite Long that *Masques* was 'not the Italian *commedia* but the tragic expression of existence'.[45] The contrast between these paired pieces can be related to the contrast already seen between the two musical arches that make up 'Reflets dans l'eau', completed less than a year after *Masques* and *L'isle joyeuse*. 'Reflets' in that regard compresses the archetypes of *Masques* and *L'isle joyeuse* into a single piece. As David Bromfield observed for Monet, the final fusion of subject and water in 'Reflets' (as in the western ritual of baptism) can be read as the surrender of self, or, in Debussy's words, 'the sacrifice of one's whole precious little personality'.

Some of this extends to matters surveyed in Chapter 5. In his discussion of Charles Henry, José Argüelles not only examines the Buddhist preoccupations of Henry's close friend Jules Laforgue but is even prompted by his findings to wonder if Henry was trained in Sufism.[46] Some of his arguments suggest asking the same of Debussy, or at least if he was conversant with its principles, even before he knew Inayat Khan. Surveys of Sufism by modern writers such as Idries Shah fuel the question, even if conclusions are risky, given the variant streams of Sufism with differing ideals and symbols.[47] Shah's insistence that the harlequin is of Sufic origin prompts reflection on a composer whose harlequinesque works range – as with no other composer – from his earliest songs to his last three sonatas.[48] Shah even claims related Sufic origin for face-corking, which could draw in 'Minstrels', and repeatedly emphasizes Granada as a major ancient centre of Sufism, a place that obsessed Debussy's imagination to the extent of yielding us *Lindaraja*, 'La soirée dans Grenade' and 'La Puerta del Vino'. The implications arising from all this can now only be open questions, and certainly shouldn't impose weight on music designed to speak for itself. If it prompts us to treat the music with heightened attentiveness, that can do no harm.

CHAPTER 9

THE EXOTIC VIA
RUSSIA AND SPAIN

The new era in our music really begins with Musorgsky – Manuel de Falla

THIS dual exoticism is the more intriguing for its many interactions. Not the least of these comes through Glinka, whose two-year sojourn in Spain and close study of its music left an indelible imprint on subsequent Russian music. Manuel de Falla had quite a bit to say about that, involving the two countries' modal links to church music[1] – to which we can add their traditional use of drones and their sheer emotional full-bloodedness. If Glinka's role helps explain why innumerable eastern European boleros, besides existing at all, can sound uncannily like polonaises or vice versa, Gypsy peregrinations can partly account for why phrygian turns and flamenco-like footstamps emerge as readily from Borodin's *Prince Igor* as from Falla's *La vida breve*, or even why a recognizable fragment of Rimsky-Korsakov's *Scheherazade* sounds happily in place in the first Spanish dance of Falla's *La vida breve* – just as Stravinsky gets away (barely) with ending the Infernal Dance of *Firebird* with pretty well the last fourteen bars of Ravel's *Rapsodie espagnole*.[2] As Falla well understood, purist attitudes can find no home here, the most markedly national styles being in constant interactive evolution. One major distinction between the two sources in this chapter is that the Spanish element worked through direct contact and friendships, whereas the Russian one comes mostly from a generation or so earlier.

RUSSIA

André Schaeffner's survey 'Debussy et ses rapports avec la musique russe' provides vital background to this whole field: ranging well beyond Debussy, he evokes a generation and more of musical russophilia in France from the 1870s involving Liszt, Saint-Saëns, their friend the Comtesse Louise de Mercy-Argenteau (composer, author of a book on César Cui and promoter and friend of Borodin), the conductor Charles Lamoureux (close colleague of Chabrier) and his enterprising concerts administrator Jules de Brayer, an École Niedermeyer graduate and friend of Saint-Saëns, Fauré, Chabrier and – from the late 1880s – Debussy. De Brayer's exploits included not only introducing Renoir to Wagner but also playing extracts from Musorgsky's *Boris Godunov* on the organ of the Trocadéro at the end of the 1878 Paris Exposition universelle. The same Exposition had just been the venue for the first French concert performances of Musorgsky, conducted by Nikolai Rubinstein, the dedicatee of Balakirev's *Islamey*.[3]

This followed the donation of twenty-seven new Russian works, including a vocal score of Musorgsky's *Boris Godunov* in its authentic non-Rimsky edition, to the Paris Conservatoire library in autumn 1874, during Debussy's third year of study there. Schaeffner notes that these scores were much borrowed and circulated, and that by 1877 Debussy was often seen in the library.[4] Musorgsky's *Sunless* songs, published in 1875, just missed the 1874 *envoi*, but de Brayer was soon promoting them among his colleagues.[5] This could explain a startling moment of near identity between the cycle's final song and the last page of Chabrier's *Caprice* for piano of 1889 (Ex. 9.1). Almost a decade earlier, a less literal but texturally vivid echo of the same song emerges from (again) Chabrier's 'Sous bois' of 1880 (Ex. 9.2) – in each case almost as if he had quietly set the stage for it.[6] His song *Sommation irrespectueuse*, again of 1880, contains an equally Musorgskian episode across bars 150–62, while one of his melodic thumbprints from around 1880 onwards, the II–V descent in Example 7.15 (spoofed by Ravel at the end of Ex. 7.8b), echoes a sequence in Musorgsky's song 'In the corner' from *The Nursery* (published in 1872). Arguably the earliest traces of Musorgsky assimilated into French music, these various passages suggest that Chabrier had digested Musorgsky song cycles well before they were first heard publicly in Paris in the mid-1890s.

Example 9.1

a: Chabrier, *Caprice* (1889), bars 31–2

b: Musorgsky, 'On the river' (*Sunless*, 1875), bars 34–5

Example 9.2

a: Chabrier, 'Sous bois' (*Pièces pittoresques*, 1880), bars 75–6

b: Musorgsky, 'On the river', bars 26–7

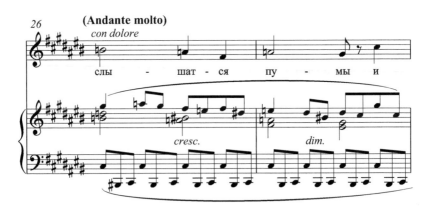

It's tempting to bracket Chabrier and Musorgsky together in a similar way to Manet and Goya – yielding another natural Russo-Spanish affinity, given that Musorgsky as the Goya of music is no new idea. Even by the 1900s

Chabrier was being touted as a French Musorgsky (albeit without the latter's darker colours), a topic cautiously summed up by Roger Delage, who observes that Chabrier could have had early access to *Boris Godunov* via Jules de Brayer, but above all that both composers were 'de la même famille spirituelle'.[7] Both composers left one towering piano cycle plus other piano pieces, operas, a smallish body of songs that transformed the genre, orchestral showpieces of dazzling brilliance and, alas, no chamber music.

The other Russian piece that suggests particular impact on Chabrier is Balakirev's *Islamey* of 1869 (published in 1870), whose vigorous repetitions and densely packed textures and structure anticipate partly *España* but even more *Bourrée fantasque* (especially the latter's opening). Balakirev's subtitle 'Oriental fantasy', along with what is known of how he collected and developed the piece's material from folk sources in the Caucasus and Crimea, suggests a venture in many ways analogous to *España*.

Fauré's music might initially seem to exude little Slavic flavour except, perhaps, through his penchant for bell sonorities (something that runs through Russian music from Glinka onwards, though it can also be linked to Liszt). However, Fauré's immersion during the mid-1870s in Pauline Viardot's family circle warrants a closer look, involving as it did the novelist Ivan Turgenev. It was through Turgenev that Fauré, in autumn 1876, befriended the young Sergei Taneyev, who had just arrived to spend a year in Paris. Fauré's single *Mazurka* op. 32 – almost certainly composed around then, when Russian music was still a novelty in Paris – may well bear witness to evenings they spent around the piano. As shown in Example 9.3, its first episode and coda harp on a gesture that Richard Taruskin dubs the '*nega*' progression, a chromatic sideslip to the relative minor that almost hand-stamps much Russian music of the era, notably by Balakirev and Borodin. Balakirev's *Islamey* is permeated almost to saturation point by the device: Examples 9.3b–d show it underpinning each of the piece's main themes.[8]

Example 9.3. Russian-style *nega* progressions

a: Fauré, *Mazurka* op. 32 (mid- to late 1870s), bars 47–54

b: Balakirev, *Islamey* (1869), bar 14   c: *Islamey*, bar 48

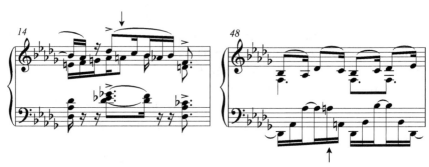

d: *Islamey*, bars 95–6

Fauré's pastiche suggests a sort of *À la manière de* . . . not so far removed from his caricature doodles, an affectionately witty nod to Russia just as his later 'Le pas espagnol' from the *Dolly* suite is to Spain. It also suggests some prescience, probably in the wake of *Islamey*, since most of Borodin's works featuring the device (the *Petite suite*, string quartets, *Prince Igor* and full scores of his symphonies) reached print only in the 1880s, and the *nega*-laden second movement trio in Tchaikovsky's Sixth Symphony (remarkably similar to Example 9.1a) dates from 1893.[9] (Tchaikovsky thought highly of Fauré – they met through Taneyev – and may well have known his *Mazurka*, a piece he might even have heard Fauré play at a Viardot soirée.)[10] A clear *nega* progression features early in Taneyev's song 'Summer night' of 1874, the first of a set of *Romances* that he completed in Paris; this and *Islamey* (dedicated to and premièred by Taneyev's piano teacher Nikolai Rubinstein) are obvious candidates for what he is most likely to have shown or played to Fauré and Turgenev.[11]

A darker Musorgskian gesture in Fauré's Fifth Barcarolle has already been seen in Chapter 6, differentiating the passage from its otherwise Chopinesque makeup. From Fauré's later years, when his companion was the Russian-speaking Marguerite Hasselmans, the sixth of his op. 103 Preludes from 1910 (in E♭ minor) is pervaded by an unusual blend of Russian-style chant and Bach-like chromatic counterpoint, while the end of his Tenth Barcarolle of 1913, with its growling A major-minor alternations, sails daringly close to that of Rachmaninov's famous 1892 setting of Pushkin's 'Ne poy, krasavitsa'. Two years later again, the final *fortissimo* outburst at bar 91 of Fauré's Twelfth Nocturne, with its starkly opposed E major and B♭ major triads low on the instrument, would not be out of place in Stravinsky's *Firebird*.

Ravel's boundless enthusiasm for the Russian 'Five' (known also as the 'Mighty Handful') can be linked to their modal variety and adventurousness; while Ravel gave primary credit in that regard to Chabrier, Chabrier too owed arguable debts eastward, as we've just seen. Ravel's exploration of octatony from the early 1900s has been particularly related to Rimsky-Korsakov (and thence back to Liszt),[12] though the greater harmonic or 'vertical' bite of Ravel's usage can also point to Chopin, as we saw in Chapter 6.

Russian flavour and techniques are so thoroughly assimilated in Ravel that it can take close observation to spot them. A strong tactile affinity links 'Noctuelles' from the *Miroirs* to Balakirev's *Islamey*: even if the two pieces' right-thumb scurries share Lisztian ancestry, their use here highlights several similar contexts, not least the flurry down to the long bass ostinato at bars 178–80 of *Islamey* relative to Ravel's reverse-motion version of it at bars 472–6 of 'Scarbo'. The structure of *Islamey* also resonates in 'Alborada del gracioso': each piece has its main break at the end of the opening section, stamped with virtually the same *fortissimo* chord (bar 70 in 'Alborada', bar 86 in *Islamey*), before the lyrical central section launches itself melodically from the trichord $d'–f'\sharp$ and promptly comes to rest on the note b in the relative minor. Such affinities doubtless reflect the many performances of *Islamey* by the Catalan pianist Ricardo Viñes (of which more below): Ravel later quipped that one of his aims in *Gaspard de la nuit* was to write something harder than *Islamey*.[13]

Gaspard shows a complementary Russian side to this through the way that 'Ondine', particularly from bar 32, recalls the 'Serenata' from Musorgsky's *Songs and Dances of Death* (from bar 11) – in each case a circling theme with rising fourths, aptly linking two songs of macabre entrapment. In 'Ondine' this leads to brusquely alternating sevenths ($C^7/F\sharp^7$, then $C\sharp^7/G^7$ and $B\flat^7/E^7$) in the manner of Example 9.5a. More general is Ravel's love of bell sonorities, as in 'Entre cloches' (from the two-piano *Sites auriculaires*), 'La vallée des cloches', 'Le gibet' and the finale of *Ma mère l'Oye*. While some of this can equally be linked to Liszt's (generally lighter) bell evocations, when it involves pentatony and low registers, as at the end of 'La vallée des cloches', the suggestions point more decisively eastward, notably to the sonorous impact of Musorgsky as in Example 9.5a.

Apart from his orchestration of *Pictures from an Exhibition*, Ravel's most overt Russian homage comes in *À la manière de Borodine* of 1912, a part-salute to his *Apaches* friends, whose mutual call-sign was the opening theme of Borodin's Second Symphony.[14] Ravel's initial quarry here is the 'Sérénade' of Borodin's *Petite suite* (try his bars 1–20 alongside Borodin's bars 7–24, with their shared *nega* sequence and final shift up the octave). His opening texture also neatly blends the waltz theme from the scherzo of Borodin's Second Quartet with Chabrier-like hemiolas (cf. Ex. 7.6b). It can be highly entertaining to perform this piece as a guess-the-composer encore.

Stravinsky recalled Debussy saying he first encountered Musorgsky's music during one of his summers working for Nadezhda von Meck (probably 1881, spent in Russia).[15] Over the previous summer Debussy had played piano duet reductions with Mme von Meck including Glinka's *Jota aragonese* and Tchaikovsky's newly published Fourth Symphony, and made duet transcriptions (which were promptly published) of the Russian, Spanish and Neapolitan dances from Tchaikovsky's *Swan Lake*. Tchaikovskian echoes are thus hardly surprising in Debussy's lively *Danse bohémienne* and 'Scherzo-Intermezzo' of his Piano Trio, both from that summer of 1880, as well as in his Second Arabesque (published in 1891 but possibly composed earlier) with its pizzicato-like bass passages. The pianist Bennett Lerner has remarked on this piece's close affinity of texture and key with Tchaikovsky's 'Chant de l'alouette' from *Album for the Young* op. 39.[16]

By the early 1890s Debussy's loyalty had audibly shifted towards the 'Five', a matter we can attribute in part to the large amount of Russian music played at the 1889 Paris Exposition universelle against the background of the strengthening Franco-Russian rapprochement of these years. Debussy's *Ballade slave* of 1891 (later retitled *Ballade*) and *Nocturne* of 1892 exude the sort of quasi-narrative air that underlies Balakirev's *Tamara*, one of his perennial favourites. *Nocturne* amplifies this in its unusual $\frac{7}{4}$-metre central section, mixing *nega* progressions with modal turns that suggest Debussy's own implicit *À la manière de Borodine* (or Balakirev). Like Example 9.3a it anticipates (by a year) the asymmetric metre and *nega* repetitions of the second movement trio in Tchaikovsky's Sixth Symphony.

The neglect of this single piano *Nocturne* by Debussy probably stems in part from the first edition's disastrous omission of many necessary accidentals in the modal central section. Only after Debussy's death was the problem addressed, in a 1920 reprint edited by Isidor Philipp, a pianist who had little sympathy for Debussy's music.[17] Several of Philipp's added accidentals tend towards the anodyne, and the edition has misled readers ever since by not showing that the offending accidentals are not Debussy's. Example 9.4a shows the bars most afflicted, with brackets added to identify Philipp's additions.

An alternative solution is proposed by the *Œuvres complètes de Claude Debussy* (Ex. 9.4b), matching a related passage in the central part of Debussy's piano duet *Marche écossaise* of 1891. (Example 1.9 shows much the same

Example 9.4

a: Debussy, *Nocturne*, bars 39–42, Isidor Philipp's additions (1920) shown in [ ]

b: the same bars as in *Œuvres complètes de Claude Debussy* 1/1

repeated progression opening Debussy's first book of Preludes two decades later again.) This analogy takes support from the way *Marche écossaise*, like the *Nocturne*, frames its lyrical central section by harmonizing its Scottish theme with repeated *nega* cadences – an amusing juxtaposition that might suggest Debussy's preference for caviar over porridge. If the modal nature of Example 9.4 inevitably leaves some modal options open, it's revealing that Philipp's accidentals more romantically emphasize downward chromatics and perfect cadences (E♮–E♭ resolving to D over each barline and D–C♯–C ending bars 40 and 41) as against the more exotic-sounding upward chromatics of Example 9.4b (B–C–C♯–D leading into bar 40, then a triadic C♯/E/A to D/F/B♭ across the next two barlines).

If Debussy's *Ballade* and *Nocturne* are less audibly groundbreaking than his songs of the late 1880s, they reveal what he was still digesting and illustrate his reported remark around 1893, 'Chabrier, Moussorgsky, Palestrina, voilà ce que j'aime' (see p. 93). They equally reflect accounts of Debussy playing and singing his way through *Boris Godunov* for Chausson's friends in 1893 and borrowing, with Chausson's blessing, the most recently acquired Musorgsky scores. A clear reminiscence of this emerges towards the end of the piano *Images* that Debussy dedicated early in 1894 to Chausson's niece Yvonne Lerolle, with bell-like alternations of D major and G♯[7] that echo the 'Kremlin Bells' from the coronation scene in *Boris Godunov* (Ex. 9.5). The allusion is underlined by Debussy's indication *une cloche qui ne garde aucune mesure* at the start of the G♯–F♯ ostinato a few bars before Example 9.5b.

A decade later we have to look harder to spot a similar allusion in 'Hommage à Rameau' (see Ex. 1.2a, one bar of Debussy matching each of Musorgsky's chords). The implied quotation marks are now gone and the gesture assimilated into Debussy's everyday modal fluency, one that conveys more sense of the ingenious polyphony ( ) underlying Musorgsky's progression.

In his penetrating essay already discussed, André Schaeffner challenges an old fable according to which Debussy, lent de Brayer's exemplar of *Boris Godunov* in 1889, seemed uninterested in it. As Schaeffner observes, Debussy could easily have had earlier access to the score in the Conservatoire library.[18] His *Ariettes oubliées* of 1885–7 are already so saturated with seventh and ninth chords juxtaposed by the tritone or minor third as to add fuel to Schaeffner's argument that he had probably encountered *Boris Godunov* before 1889, even if his acquaintance with it later deepened. The impact of all this on *Pelléas et Mélisande* (explored in detail by Schaeffner), plus some exaggerated Parisian gossip on the topic in the 1900s, perhaps underlies a cheekier moment in

Example 9.5

a: Musorgsky, *Boris Godunov*, Coronation scene, bars 7–8 (1874 vocal score)

b: Debussy, *Images* [*oubliées*], III, bars 145–52

Debussy's second book of Preludes of 1913: Example 9.6 appears literally to 'rag' Musorgsky's chord sequence in cakewalk rhythm. Even the rhythm can be linked to Musorgsky's scene, where it joins in across bars 11–14 of the ostinato. Viewed thus, Example 9.6 aptly answers Debussy's similar 'ragging' of *Tristan* in 'Golliwogg's cake walk', of which more in Chapter 11.[19]

Example 9.6. Debussy, 'General Lavine – excentric', bars 25–6 (repeated in bars 27–8 and 84–7)

Shades of Musorgsky remain around Debussy's later piano works. His *Children's Corner* of 1908 arguably owes much of its concept to Musorgsky's *Nursery* songs (*La chambre d'enfants* in French), to which Debussy devoted a critical panegyric in 1901.[20] The quiet pentatonic bass that opens 'Jumbo's Lullaby' has a distinct Musorgskian flavour, one that continues in the first book of Preludes – arguably in the pentatonic colours of 'La fille aux cheveux de lin', famously in the *fortissimo* of 'La Cathédrale engloutie' (relative to 'The great gate of Kiev'), and more quietly verbatim in 'Ce qu'a vu le Vent d'Ouest' whose opening arpeggios and recapitulation embody the same D^7–$G\sharp^7$ alternations as Example 9.5a. By Debussy's second book of Preludes this is overlaid by a new Russian element, his artistic interaction with Stravinsky, as already explored in Chapter 2.

A stronger sense again of Musorgsky returns to permeate Debussy's wartime *Berceuse héroïque* of 1914 and the central movement of *En blanc et noir* (1915), with their iron-treaded long crescendos.[21] Besides reflecting a bleak era, they amplify Debussy's friendship with the Musorgskophile D.-E. Inghelbrecht, whose scintillating run of performances at Astruc's new Théâtre des Champs-Élysées in 1913 culminated in the first performance of *Boris* in French, with considerable rehearsal participation from Debussy.[22] A few months earlier Diaghilev had staged *Khovanshchina* there, as partly reconstructed by Ravel and Stravinsky. This thoroughly Russian year for Paris ended by taking Debussy back to Russia on tour for the first time since 1882, where he enjoyed *inter alia* a performance of Musorgsky's *Sorochintsï Fair*.

In 1902 Balakirev's *Islamey* appeared in a new edition, one that for the first time printed the piece's indications of tempo and character in Italian rather than Russian. Over the next few years Ravel's and Debussy's friend Ricardo Viñes – who had just toured Russia and met Balakirev – repeatedly programmed the piece. Several of Debussy's visible interests from those years, like the modal techniques in Example 1.2, relate to elements of *Islamey* such as Balakirev's enjoyment of modally varied repetitions and harmonic switches in bars 172–6 and 206–13.

By summer 1903 Debussy was drafting *L'isle joyeuse*, whose dazzling ending recalls both the last bar of *Islamey* (the rapid whip down the keyboard) and the end of the Polovtsian Dances from Borodin's *Prince Igor* (in the same key of A and published in an 1889 Belaïeff duet reduction that Debussy certainly knew).[23] The piece's exceptional virtuosity suggests that *Islamey*, and Viñes's playing of it, had spurred Debussy to contribute something of comparable brilliance to the French repertoire. Some uncannily close links between *L'isle joyeuse* and *Islamey* bear on this. The second theme of *Islamey*, in its second guise (from bar 45, incorporating Example 9.3c), forms a remarkably similar dance to bar 9 onwards in *L'isle joyeuse* (as well as to generically similar themes in 'The little shepherd' and 'La danse de Puck' – the last of which interestingly has the same idiosyncratic phrasing as Example 9.3c). Balakirev's chromatic counter-voice *ab–g–gb* in this same passage of *Islamey* (bars 46–7) finds an echo in Debussy's repeated *f'♯–f'♮–e'* at bars 12–13 of *L'isle joyeuse*. Add to all that the long crescendo ostinato in *Islamey* (Ex. 9.7), comparable to that of *L'isle joyeuse* (Ex. 6.7b), and we may wonder if *Islamey* is one reason for that curious 's' in Debussy's *isle* (rather than *île*): the two similar ostinati even share the left hand's cross-bar beaming. (Balakirev's right hand then similarly beams across the barline from bar 184 onwards.) As Example 6.7 shows, the relationship also involves Chopin's Third Ballade – logically in view of Balakirev's veneration for Chopin. From that vantage point Balakirev's ostinato occupies a very apt pivotal position between Chopin's and Debussy's.

Example 9.7. Balakirev, *Islamey*, bars 181–3

Along with *L'isle joyeuse* and *Bourrée fantasque*, no French piece echoes *Islamey* more vividly yet originally than 'En tartane' from *Cerdaña* of 1910 by the Languedoc composer Déodat de Séverac (another close associate of Viñes) – a piece replete with repeated B♭s, *nega* progressions and many similar textures under the hand. Its evocative Catalan setting again serves to point up ingrained Iberian-Russian affinities.

SPAIN

Audible interaction between 'modern' Spanish and French music reaches back well before the mid-nineteenth century. Bizet's *Carmen* of 1875 reflects the impact of the French-Spanish singer Pauline Viardot-García whom – as Manuel de Falla observed – we can largely thank for the French love affair with the habanera.[24] If Chabrier's four-month stay in Spain in 1882, where he methodically transcribed the music and dances he heard, most immediately yielded *España*, it also brought to fruition dreams sparked off by his childhood music lessons from two expatriate Spaniards.[25]

Defining French or Spanish music in relation to each other becomes more elusive if we remember that both Albéniz and Falla conceived many of their most 'Spanish' masterpieces in France, under the acknowledged influence of pieces like Debussy's 'La soirée dans Grenade' and Ravel's 'Alborada del gracioso'. Falla repeatedly takes this up, emphasizing how these pieces reach far beyond earlier *espagnolade* by taking their Spanish content creatively to deeper structural levels.[26] In the process Falla confronts accusations by several Spanish critics of the time – this may seem hard to believe now – that his own *Nights in the Gardens of Spain* and even Albéniz's *Iberia* had sold out Spanish heritage to 'foreign influence'.[27] By acknowledging the degree of interaction, Falla balances the Spanish impact on Debussy and Ravel with how handsomely (in his view) they repaid the debt.

Our view becomes clearer again on learning that on 25 April 1889 (that amazing year for Paris) Debussy, Ravel, Fauré, Dukas and Ricardo Viñes were all present at Albéniz's Parisian début concert, featuring entirely his own works.[28] Albéniz's ensuing friendships with Debussy, Dukas, Chausson and Fauré have recently been explored by Michael Christoforidis and Elizabeth Kertesz; they may bear on Falla's view that the scherzo of Debussy's 1893 String Quartet could pass as 'one of the most beautiful Andalusian dances ever written'.[29] It emerges that Debussy entertained hopes of visiting Granada in the late 1890s, possibly prompted by the paintings of Santiago Rusiñol who was then working in Granada after spending several years in Paris. Albéniz in turn had just completed the epic piano piece 'La vega' that opens his *Alhambra* suite. Although Debussy never did visit Granada, its attraction may account for the sudden emergence of the two-piano *Lindaraja* from his pen in 1901 and 'La soirée dans Grenade' in 1903. Debussy's fluency in Andalusian musical idioms, which Manuel de Falla ascribed to the Parisian Expositions universelles of 1889 and 1900, may owe particular debts to the nocturnal gypsy performances 'L'Andalousie au temps des Maures' (Andalusia in Moorish times) at the 1900 Exposition.[30] Edward Lockspeiser amplifies this with a detail unmentioned by Falla, Maurice Emmanuel's discovery of Debussy one day 'carrying about *in his pocket* [Felipe] Pedrell's collection of Spanish folk-songs'.[31]

To all this can be added Debussy's friendship from 1901 with Ricardo Viñes, who premièred most of Debussy's and Ravel's new piano works in the decade 1903–13 (and several of Ravel's before that). Elaine Brody considers Viñes's whole way of playing to have played a significant part in Debussy's piano writing from the *Estampes* onwards (though we've already seen other possible factors).[32] Besides embedding flamenco-like episodes in pieces like *Masques* or 'Pour les arpèges composés', Debussy left three solo pieces in explicitly Spanish character, 'La soirée dans Grenade', 'La sérénade interrompue' and 'La Puerta del Vino', plus the two-piano *Lindaraja*. Each of them suggests something of a story as well as bearing witness to friendships.

If 'La soirée dans Grenade' points towards Debussy's friendship with Albéniz and Viñes, his later prelude 'La sérénade interrompue' (completed around New Year 1910) so strongly echoes Albéniz's *Iberia* – including moments of 'El polo' and 'Málaga' but most of all 'El Albaicín' – as to suggest a quiet tribute to Albéniz, who had died in May 1909. This lies naturally in the old tradition of *déploration*, where such allusions are often quietly buried in the music. Example 9.8 shows the clearest shared gesture across the two pieces, though several others can easily be found.[33] (The dynamic contrast between them tempts us to imagine what a conversation might have sounded like between the gruffly ebullient Albéniz and the soft-spoken Debussy.) The Catalan composer Carles Guinovart has suggested (in conversation) that we might read 'La sérénade interrompue' on one level as an allusion to Albéniz's all-too-short life. According to Falla, 'El Albaicín' fascinated – almost obsessed – Debussy to the point that he planned to orchestrate it, even 'to make a free transcription of it for orchestra'.[34] If this idea remained unrealized, 'La sérénade intérrompue' may be its distilled remnant.

Example 9.8

a: Albéniz, refrain of 'El Albaicín' (*Iberia* Book 3, 1907), bars 49–50

b: Debussy, refrain of 'La sérénade interrompue' (Preludes Book 1, 1910), bars 19–20

Debussy's cordial friendship from autumn 1907 with Manuel de Falla reached its most artistically intense phase around 1912, when he helped Falla recast *La vida breve* in its final two-act form.[35] I once related this to a class of Spanish pianists before playing the opening bars of 'La Puerta del Vino' – composed late in 1912 – whereupon the whole class spontaneously exclaimed

'Falla!' No words could better sum up the distinctive voices of Albéniz and Falla than 'La sérénade interrompue' relative to 'La Puerta del Vino'.

Earlier than all of these is a two-piano habanera dated April 1901 that Debussy left unpublished: it appeared posthumously in 1926 as *Lindaraja*, a title not visible on the piece's autograph. (The reference is to a small tower and courtyard in the Alhambra palace in Granada named 'Mirador de Lindaraja' after a Moorish princess.) No clear context is known for the piece's existence, except that in December 1901 Debussy talked to Ricardo Viñes about twelve pieces he was planning, six for solo piano and six for two pianos.[36] By 1903, on a contract between Debussy and the publisher Durand, the second of the two-piano pieces was titled 'Ibéria'. The planned two-piano pieces eventually became Debussy's orchestral *Images*, including the triptych *Ibéria* published in 1909, whose expansive symphonic dimensions suggest something quite different from the single two-piano piece he had first envisaged. Could the latter have been the piece now known as *Lindaraja*? It would give it a logical *raison d'être*, in exactly the right year.

We might also conjecture that Debussy withheld *Lindaraja* from print because of a rather emphatic harmonic resemblance, over bars 117–41, to Ravel's still-unpublished two-piano 'Habanera' of 1895, of which Debussy had reportedly borrowed a manuscript. In 1903 Debussy put almost the same harmonic combination (of C♯ and G[7]) into 'La soirée dans Grenade' (bars 23–8), prompting a minor *scandale* over who had invented what. In fact Debussy is clear of blame, because exactly the same harmonic combination appears in his *Prélude à l'après-midi d'un faune* of 1894, a piece Ravel unreservedly adored (at rehearsal figure 3, the piece's only anacrusis).[37] It can even be heard in Debussy's *Chanson espagnole* of 1883, a song probably unknown to Ravel as it remained unpublished until 1980. Whatever the exact story behind *Lindaraja*, we can doubtless thank Ravel's 'Habanera' for some of its flavour, as well as that of 'La soirée dans Grenade'.

As for Fauré, a diary entry by Ricardo Viñes in March 1902 records an evening spent in the company of several composers:

Later, Fauré asked me to play Spanish things: full of enthusiasm, he made me repeat the Sevillanas del Valle which he said he could listen to all night! He finds . . . in Spanish music something that goes beyond music . . . [and] of which one never never tires! It's what I also find in Russian music. He added, 'Why compose if one can never attain the emotional intensity of such music?'[38]

If Fauré has rarely been viewed in relation to Spain (apart from the one-off 'Le pas espagnol' from *Dolly*, an obvious riposte to Chabrier's *España*), clarification comes from Jean-Michel Nectoux's publication of Fauré's letters to Albéniz.[39] Their close friendship, especially from 1905, prompts a closer look at what linked Fauré, the child of the southern French Ariège, to the Catalan Albéniz, both from similar landscapes with a degree of shared folk culture and dialect quite distinct from touristy flamenco Spain. This background helps explain why Saint-Saëns, Charles Koechlin and Marguerite Long all thought fit to mention Fauré's swarthy, almost Arab appearance as relevant to his music.[40] We may hear it mirrored in the Moorish tinge of his Ninth, Tenth and Eleventh Barcarolles, notably the phrygian turns that open the Tenth and Eleventh. Hannah Wallace has observed that the sudden exuberant ending of Fauré's Eighth Barcarolle (of 1908), with its wide-spaced texture, is most unusual for Fauré but quite typical of Albéniz.[41] It's tempting to wonder if Albéniz had a hand (or literally two) in it, as could easily have happened around the piano if Fauré played him an early version of the piece (especially bearing in mind page 45 above).

Underlying all this are strong affinities of pianistic polyphony and metrical patterns between Fauré's Barcarolles and Albéniz's *Iberia*. The alternations of $\frac{6}{8}$ and $\frac{3}{4}$ across hands or successive bars in 'Rondeña' and 'Almería' from *Iberia* are equally endemic to Fauré's Barcarolles from the early 1880s, well before Albéniz's arrival in Paris. The central E♭ episode of Fauré's Fifth Barcarolle (1894) even mixes and juxtaposes $\frac{3}{4}$, $\frac{6}{8}$ and $\frac{2}{4}$ patterns within the same bar length, just as 'Rondeña' and 'Almería' do. Add to that the whole-tone lead-in to the coda of 'Almería' – which smacks more of Fauré's usage than Debussy's – and 'Almería' and Fauré can almost seem to start melting into each other. The main sounding difference between them lies in Albéniz's overt rhythmic and modal exploitation of flamenco.

The ailing Albéniz was certainly much on Fauré's mind at the time of the Ninth Barcarolle, written just after the completion of Albéniz's *Iberia* and on the heels of the rustic *Sérénade*, which Fauré composed in 1908 for the Catalan cellist Pau Casals. Fauré's Eleventh Barcarolle of 1913, dedicated to Albéniz's daughter Laura, might equally be read as a tribute to her father (at whose funeral Fauré's Requiem was performed). Carlo Caballero has suggested (in conversation) that Fauré's first three Preludes from op. 103, published before the other six early in 1910, can be read similarly as a tribute to Albéniz. The second one – which echoes in the middle of Debussy's *Étude* 'Pour les cinq doigts' – feels particularly redolent of guitar and flamenco.

The futility of apportioning specific influence there is clear, especially given the long history of $\frac{3}{4}$ and $\frac{6}{8}$ alternations in traditional Mediterranean music. Fauré's and Albéniz's modal flavours similarly reflect their Mediterranean heritages (as a child at the École Niedermeyer, Fauré was regularly called on to sing *ariégeois* folksongs for official visitors). More plausible is the high degree to which they prompted and inspired each other, rather as Debussy and Ravel did (eventually at one remove) through the 1900s. Whatever the exact case, such comparisons do no harm if they remind us that Fauré's Barcarolles have modal and rhythmic teeth.

Our most unusual case is probably Ravel, born near the Spanish border to a Basque mother who had lived and worked in Madrid. His parents reportedly first met in Aranjuez in 1873; when the family moved to Paris a few months after Maurice's birth in 1875, Marie Delouart Ravel would sing her infant son to sleep in Spanish.[42] This doubtless helps explain a musical output framed by Spanish pieces, from his 1893 piano *Sérénade grotesque* (of which more in Chapter 14) to the *Don Quichotte à Dulcinée* songs of 1932–3. On a postcard sent from Spain to Joaquín Turina in Paris in 1911, Ravel signs himself off, 'Very best wishes from your (or my) fatherland', and his letters from the Basque region, or to friends and relatives there, are peppered with Basque phrases as well as Basque forms of place names.[43] Manuel de Falla later recalled their first meeting in 1907, when Ricardo Viñes and Ravel played him Ravel's newly completed *Rapsodie espagnole* in two-piano form:

> How was I to account for the subtly genuine Spanishness of Ravel, knowing, because he had told me so, that the only link he had with my country was to have been born near the border? The mystery was soon explained: Ravel's was a Spain he had felt in an idealised way through his mother . . . a lady of exquisite conversation . . . I understood with what fascination her son must have listened to these memories that were undoubtedly intensified by the additional force all reminiscence gets from the song or dance theme insep-arably connected with it.[44]

Immediate shades rise of the expatriate Chopin and his idealized Poland: Ravel similarly could paint his idealized Spain in sound while breathing its idioms like a native. Most explicit in 'Alborada del gracioso', *Rapsodie espag-nole* and *L'Heure espagnole* (from 1905–7), this is balanced by the asymmetrical Basque *zortzico* rhythms that open Ravel's Piano Trio and his early Violin Sonata of 1897 – besides the fanciful associations of antique Spanish infantas in the *Pavane pour une Infante défunte*. Ravel's friend, student and biographer Roland-Manuel enlarged on this from Ravel's own memories: describing Ravel as 'a Basque for whom Spain is another homeland, and for whom the Pyrenees do not exist', he quotes the Basque Eduardo López Chavarri's asser-tion (echoing Falla) that Ravel, Debussy and even Stravinsky, stimulated by Gypsy music, didn't 'make music in the Spanish style, like Bizet, but in the Spanish tongue, or more correctly, in the tongue of Andalusia'. Roland-Manuel also quotes Ravel's admission of having made varied Iberian idioms his own in an entirely French way, including what Ravel amusedly called 'the Louis-Philippe habaneras'.[45]

Ravel's adolescence was enormously marked by his friendship with the young prodigy Ricardo Viñes, who arrived from Barcelona with his mother to study in the Conservatoire piano class of Charles de Bériot (the nephew of Pauline Viardot and Manuel García). Ravel joined Bériot's class in 1891 and later dedicated *Rapsodie espagnole* to him. The two boys' friendship started in 1888, initially through their mothers each of whom was delighted to discover a fellow Spanish-speaker. (Viñes's first written mention of Ravel calls him 'Mauricio'.)[46] Together they explored the piano duet repertoire (in particular by the Russian 'Five') along with Paris's museums and exhibitions, including the 1889 Exposition universelle (with its imposing new tower by Ravel *père*'s erstwhile employer Gustave Eiffel). By 1893 Viñes had lent Ravel a rare book of prose poems by Aloysius Bertrand titled *Gaspard de la nuit*; in 1907 he introduced Ravel to Manuel de Falla. Again we may ask how many of the now-famous French piano masterworks of those years would exist without the enthusiastic input of Viñes who, with his supple technique and near-photographic memory, quickly assimilated whatever was put before him. (He reportedly learnt Ravel's *Miroirs* from manuscript in under two weeks.)[47] It was Viñes too who maintained the current of musical stimulus between Debussy and Ravel after 1905 when the two composers were no longer in personal contact, playing the latest pieces by each composer to the other.

That background, together with Falla's observations about the vital interaction between new Spanish and French music, helps explain Ravel's present stature as a national icon throughout the Basque region (French and Spanish), even throughout Spain where most conservatoires boast a Sala Mauricio Ravel. Ravel may have partly earned this through his unrealized plan for a piano concerto on Basque themes with the provocative Basque title *Zazpiak bat* ('The seven [provinces] are one'), a slogan that can still attract unwelcome police attention on either side of the border. Among many Spanish musicians with whom I've conversed, all identify easily – much more unanimously than anglophone or even French musicians – with what they consider Ravel's concentrated emotional intensity. The tenderly ironic humour that dreamt up a title like *Pavane pour une Infante défunte*; the quixotic, melting sensuality of the *Miroirs*, redolent of Antoní Gaudí's architecture; the wilder sensuality that ends *Rapsodie espagnole*, 'Alborada del gracioso', *La valse* and *Boléro* and that permeates the Concerto for Left Hand:[48] all suggest a temperament nearer Spanish art, humour and literature of the time – as did the luxuriant Spanish-style moustache that Ravel sported up to the age of about thirty.

Spanish musicians similarly (in my experience) tend to consider all Ravel's music Spanish-tinged, even more than Debussy's overtly Spanish works. If this involves complex interaction and some retrospective colouring (as Falla knew), it draws our attention to the flamenco elements pervading 'Scarbo', or to a repeated rhythm like ♪ ₇ ₇ ♫ | ♪ ₇ ₇ ♫ | ♫ ♫ | ♪, which I quote here not from Ravel's *Boléro* but from the finale of his Concerto in G (eight bars after rehearsal figure 7). Ravel's surreal *Boléro* – it goes at almost half normal bolero speed, like the rhythmic figure just quoted – came about because his plan to orchestrate some of Albéniz's *Iberia* was thwarted by copyright restrictions. (Shades here of Debussy's preoccupation with 'El Albaicín' are bolstered by a strong resemblance between Example 9.8a and the piano accompaniment to the 'Chanson espagnole' of Ravel's *Chants populaires* of 1910.)

Most revealing of all is to view Ravel beside his friend Falla, two self-consciously small musical giants who infused their music with explosive emotional energy, from the fiery hispanicism of the mid-1900s to the concentrated classicism of their late works. Under the contrast between Falla's piety and Ravel's determined agnosticism – a matter lightly written off (in conversation) by Carles Guinovart as merely 'the difference between an Andaluz and a Basque' – lie two similarly intense temperaments. In the course of balancing Ravel's 'subtly genuine Spanishness' with his 'strong French character', Manuel de Falla shows an understanding of his friend that I think no commentator has surpassed:

> Ravel's style, so firm and delicate in its boldness, so clear, orderly and precise, offers us another outstanding quality: the absence of vanity. This virtue is the more noteworthy if we recall that Ravel composed most of his work at a time when, under foreign influences, music was required at least to affect a certain haughty aspiration to what was thought to be transcendental. I think that the composer's refusal to yield to such requirements reveals a rare discernment.[49]

CHAPTER 10

THE CLAVECINISTES

Nothing can make us forget that slyly voluptuous perfume, the unavowed fine perversity that innocently hovers around 'Les barricades mystérieuses'.

– Claude Debussy

I'M long used to hearing harpsichordists and viol players say that Debussy, Ravel and Chabrier sound to them remarkably like Rameau or Couperin.[1] In fact their music was composed in an atmosphere of quite intense interest in older French music. A 'Festival Rameau' in April 1880 for example, with Franck on the organizing committee, brought Saint-Saëns onstage with the cellist Jules Delsart and the flautist Paul Taffanel – all of whom were also champions of young composers such as Fauré. This provides context for Franck's reaction a year later on hearing the première of some of Chabrier's *Pièces pittoresques*: 'We have just heard something extraordinary. This music links our era to that of Couperin and Rameau.'[2]

The *Pièces pittoresques* amply justify Franck's remark, not least in the luxuriant ornamentation of 'Sous bois': far from pastiche, the piece reinvents the art of *agrément* in ways that undoubtedly marked Debussy (Ex. 7.23). Even if the piece's title was an afterthought, it reflects a whole range of past pieces in the genre of Dandrieu's 'Le ramage des oiseaux'. The rustic textures and bass drones of Chabrier's 'Scherzo-valse' in turn suggest Rameau in *tambourin* mode, as does the central section of Chabrier's 'Danse villageoise'. The most startlingly close moment of resemblance undoubtedly springs from the opening rhythm of 'Danse villageoise' (♩♩♩♩♩♩♩♩♩♩) relative to that of the 'Rigaudon' in Couperin's Fourth *Concert royal* (♩♩♩♩♩♩♩♩♩) or even to that of Rameau's opera *Les Boréades* (♩♩♩♩♩♩♩♩♩).[3]

Regardless of what specific pieces Chabrier knew, a major point there is a shared generic character that was certainly in musicians' ears at the time.[4] Anthologies of French harpsichord music had been increasingly available since the 1840s; among numerous pianists who featured it in concerts, the most prominent was Louis Diémer who, according to Katharine Ellis, 'turned Couperin and Daquin into household names'.[5] In the course of constantly performing this repertoire from the 1860s well into the twentieth century, Diémer published several anthologies, the best known being his volumes of *Les clavecinistes français* issued by Durand in 1887 (François Couperin, Daquin and Rameau) and 1896 (Dagincourt, Dandrieu, Daquin and Lully), a project that eventually extended to the complete keyboard *ordres* of François Couperin (Durand, 1903–5). *Les vieux maîtres*, his collection of keyboard transcriptions of Boismortier, Chambonnières, Couperin, Frescobaldi, Gervaise and Rameau, was published in 1896 by Heugel.[6] From 1888 Diémer took equally to the harpsichord, prompted by a 1769 Taskin two-manual instrument which the maker's grandson exhibited at the Salons Erard in 1888 and then at the 1889 Paris Exposition universelle.[7]

In a series of high-profile concerts mixing old with new at the 1889 Exposition universelle, Diémer played both piano and the Taskin harpsichord, with colleagues including Taffanel on flute and Louis van Waefelghem and Delsart on viols as well as viola and cello respectively.[8] 'None of the [older] pieces was unknown to Parisian audiences', notes Annegret Fauser, 'and some of the works by Couperin and Rameau were even favourites from . . . over the past decades.'[9]

The continuing momentum from the Exposition concerts led Diémer, van Waefelghem and Delsart to found the hugely popular Société des instruments anciens which, from 1895, played period-instrument concerts to packed houses at the Salle Pleyel. In 1895 and 1896 Diémer's performances of Rameau's *Gavotte et six doubles* [*Gavotte et variations*] reportedly brought the house down at concerts by the Société.[10] Fauré just then was composing his *Thème et variations*, whose very first variation opens remarkably like Rameau's, the theme transferred to the left hand under a similar descant (Ex. 10.1).[11] Fauré's Variation VIII is particularly harpsichord-like under the hand, its contrapuntal texture highly redolent of Rameau's 'Les triolets' or 'La Timide' (which Diémer featured in a Société concert in May 1896). From 1896 also dates one of Ravel's first published songs, 'D'Anne jouant de l'espinette' with accompaniment for 'clavecin ou piano (en sourdine)'.

Example 10.1

a: Rameau, *Gavotte et six doubles*,
1er Double, bar 1
(as in Diémer's 1887 edition)

b: Fauré, *Thème et variations*,
Variation I, bar 1

In his piano recitals Diémer's former pupil Édouard Risler maintained the huge popularity that Diémer had generated for pieces like Rameau's 'Le rappel des oiseaux' and Daquin's 'Le coucou', with programmes that simultaneously promoted Chabrier and Fauré. (In 1897 Risler gave the première of Fauré's Sixth Barcarolle, which is dedicated to him; in 1898 he and Cortot premièred Fauré's *Dolly* suite, and in 1903 he premièred Dukas's *Variations sur un thème de Rameau*.) 'Le coucou' resonates in three twentieth-century toccatas, two of them also in E minor: Debussy's 'Jardins sous la pluie' and the Toccata of Ravel's *Tombeau de Couperin* (with a similar opening texture and tempo) – plus the Toccata of Debussy's *Pour le piano*, to which we'll return later.

In our urtext-informed age it's salutary to view Debussy's or Ravel's scores alongside Diémer's anthologies, replete with his added phrasing and dynamics and the ornament signs renotated as grace notes, as in Ravel's *Tombeau de Couperin*. The whole appearance of *Le tombeau de Couperin* is not dissimilar to Diémer's editions, and parts of Ravel's Toccata, with its overlapping hands and fast note repetitions, look and sound not so far from Rameau's *Gavotte et six doubles* with the dynamics and articulation of Diémer's 1887 edition, or indeed from Couperin's 'Le tic-toc choc' as it sounds on Risler's brilliantly poised 1917 piano recording. Risler's recordings include not only 'Le coucou' but also 'Le rappel des oiseaux' and 'Tambourin' from Rameau's *Pièces de clavecin* of 1724.[12] If, as is quite feasible, Risler ever programmed the last of these alongside Chabrier's *Bourrée fantasque* or *Ballabile*, alert listeners might have noticed that Chabrier's two pieces launch themselves with something very near Rameau's opening rhythm and melodic outline respectively.

We might also hear Rameau's 'La poule' answered in the rooster-like call that launches Chabrier's *Aubade* (Dawn song).[13] The tradition of bird calls runs through to pieces like Ravel's 'Oiseaux tristes' and *Ma mère l'Oye*, en route to the more specialized world of Messiaen. (Rameau's operas teem with bird scenes prefiguring those in Ravel's *Daphnis et Chloé* and *L'Enfant et les sortilèges*.) Even Schumann's 'Vogel als Prophet', with its quiet French overture rhythms, suggests influence from west of the Rhine. (Beethoven's Pastoral Symphony, for example, goes about the matter in a very different way.) Chapter 11 returns to this extraordinary piece by Schumann and his links to older French tradition.

In letters to two of his friends in summer 1916, Ravel, on army service as a truck driver, wryly notes his unsuitability for a military career, having spent spare moments notating bird calls. (Two of them are quoted in *A Ravel Reader*, p. 176, one of them whimsically notated in waltz time.) Ravel was then working on *Le tombeau de Couperin*, and a curious episode blends all this with popular old titles including Couperin's 'Le rossignol en amour' and 'Les fauvètes plaintives' as well as Rameau's 'L'indifférente'. Arriving at a scene of devastation after the battle of Verdun, Ravel found the area abandoned and in ruins, every tree defoliated – and a bird singing obliviously on a bare branch. According to Hélène Jourdan-Morhange and Manuel Rosenthal, he determined to incorporate this haunting scene in *Le tombeau de Couperin* as 'Le rossignol indifférent' (according to Rosenthal) or 'La fauvette indifférente' (according to Jourdan-Morhange).[14] Both of them regretted that no such piece eventuated, but it's possible the experience is quietly encapsulated in the Menuet of *Le tombeau*, just as the central *musette* gives way to the reprise at bar 73, the returning Menuet theme piping as a quiet descant over the last echoes of the desolate *musette* (see Ex. 12.2a). However we view that, it highlights the quiet intensity of a passage whose descant demands an expressionlessly calm *pianissimo indifférent*.

Ravel's publisher Jacques Durand may be partly to thank for the title *Le tombeau de Couperin*: he had doubtless told Ravel of Debussy's quandary in deciding between Chopin and Couperin as dedicatee of his *Études*. Ravel's title neatly reciprocates both that and Debussy's earlier 'Hommage à Rameau', even if he later said his own homage was addressed 'less . . . to Couperin himself than to French music of the eighteenth century'.[15] As preparatory exercise for his own Forlane, Ravel transcribed the Forlane from Couperin's fourth *Concert royal*. A comparative survey of the two can be read in Barbara Kelly's essay 'History and homage', to which Chapter 12 here adds some rhythmic analysis. Reluctantly eschewing a tango movement (in facetious reaction to a church edict that had outlawed the tango), Ravel did tell Roland-Manuel to expect a 'gigue';[16] this we can probably hear in the suite's Prélude, albeit unlabelled (like the unlabelled gigue in the opening movement of Rameau's first book of *Pièces de clavecin*).[17]

Even the frequent glint of near-jazz in *Le tombeau de Couperin* matches the popular and humorous touches that permeate the suites of the clavecinistes (or the guitar-like strums in Scarlatti). The daringly calculated dissonances on the last page of Ravel's Forlane – which defeated the ears of several of his contemporaries – lie absolutely in the tradition of Rameau's 'L'enharmonique'. Ravel's decision to dedicate these dance-like pieces to comrades fallen in the war shocked several people at the time but tallies with the old French tradition that a posthumous tribute had no need to be sombre.

Both Ravel's and Debussy's preoccupation with the imagined world of Louis XIV involves (particularly for Debussy) the Italian *commedia dell'arte* and the world of *fête galante* as encapsulated in the paintings of Antoine Watteau, who used the latter – just as the Italian actors used the *commedia* – as a cover for portraying human nature and public and private *mores*.[18] Watteau's brief career (he died aged only 37) coincided with both Couperin's and Rameau's, and Debussy once described Rameau as Watteau's exact counterpart.[19] I use the phrase 'imagined world' above, because for post-revolutionary France it could only be a freely nostalgic reconstruction, first through the Parnassian poetry of the 1860s and 70s with its re-celebration of the *fête galante*, then through Verlaine with his more incisive *fête galante*-based exploration of the human psyche.[20]

The thread of Pierrot and the *commedia* runs right through Debussy's output. Anyone in doubt need only wonder what his *Étude* 'Pour les arpèges composés' of 1915 is up to between bars 29 and 45, where it abandons any pretence at *arpèges* in favour of an outright harlequinade. A sketch page for one of his *Études* shows annotations on the verso for a ballet titled *Fêtes galantes* that Debussy was planning with Louis Laloy.[21] Pieces like Couperin's 'L'Arlequine' are a natural antecedent to these and to Debussy's 'Minstrels' or 'General Lavine', in a line that also dog-legs via Manet's *Polichinelle* and Chabrier's 'Mauresque'. Couperin's heading for 'L'Arlequine' – *grotesquement* – resounds amusingly in the heading *bêtement* to Chabrier's song 'Les gros dindons' and in Debussy's facetious instruction *sagement* at the start of his *Études* (for which, in the context, one could almost equally read *grotesquement* or *bêtement*). Another claveciniste tradition, that of portraits of (or tributes to) friends, personages or creatures real and mythical, resurfaces in Fauré's *Dolly* as well as in several Debussy Preludes (which feature not only the clown Edward Lavine but also Albéniz, Falla, Mr Pickwick, Loïe Fuller and the Delphic bacchantes: see Appendix 2). To that we can add the title and whimsy of *La plus que lente*, a piece we'll revisit in Chapter 17.

In one vital respect all this follows a very real element of Louis XIV France, one that David Tunley addresses in his study of François Couperin:

As we learn through the courtesy books and dance manuals of the time, the five basic positions of social dance (which were to form the basis of

nineteenth-century classical ballet) were also the basic 'positions' of deport-
ment cultivated during the reign of Louis XIV. (He can be seen in many of
his portraits holding one of the dance positions – even when playing
billiards!) It is not the least surprising, therefore, that a society which developed physical movements to the level of an art, and which regarded the fine
arts as a means of pleasing and touching its audience, should have cultivated a style of music in which subtle and expressive 'gestures' were
preferred to thematic argument.[22]

That last sentence easily embraces Debussy, from the *Petite suite* of 1888 to
the *Études* of 1915, or Ravel from the *Menuet antique* to *Le tombeau de
Couperin* via the *Sonatine* or *Ma mère l'Oye*. Tunley qualifies matters by
quoting from a seventeenth-century 'courtesy manual' which criticizes any
affectation in this art of movement and gesture as 'something that "tarnishes
and soils the most beautiful things".[23] Debussy's advice to Maurice Dumesnil
matches that ('Pas d'affectation, surtout !' ['No affectation, above all!']),[24] as
do Ravel's *sans expression* indications in passages that provide their own
carefully poised, often gestural, expression. Tunley continues with a survey of
how dance forms pervade French keyboard music into the eighteenth
century;[25] Chapter 17 below suggests carrying this through to the twentieth
century.

Stylistically Debussy's *Petite suite* and *Suite bergamasque* stand out against a
background that had hitherto restricted 'classical' suites to the 'pastiche' box
(like Pierre-Alexandre Boëly's *Suites dans le style des maîtres anciens* of the
mid-1850s, even Saint-Saëns's op. 49 *Suite en ré* of 1883). Early in his career
Debussy thus launched a renewing impetus that led to Ravel's *Tombeau de
Couperin*, via *Pour le piano*. In line with much of the poetry he was setting at
the time, Debussy's *Suite bergamasque* blends harmonic and textural modernity with antique gestures: its opening harpsichord-like flourish could suggest
a curtain rising on a Molière play, décor *à la* Poussin. As it is, the first two
movements of *Petite suite*, like the third one of the *Suite bergamasque*, take
their titles from poems in Verlaine's *Fêtes galantes*. 'En bateau' also reflects
Watteau's epoch-making painting *L'embarquement pour Cythère*, and the
suite's Menuet is derived from Debussy's song *Fête galante* of 1882 (to a poem
by Banville) – one of whose manuscripts Debussy whimsically subheaded
'*Musique Louis XIV avec formules de 1882*'.[26] A complement to these suites
comes from Debussy's two *Arabesques* of the same years, reflecting the role of
arabesque decoration in the art of Watteau, pieces that already skilfully blend
delicacy with rhythmic and dynamic vigour.[27]

Wider perspective again comes from the recent first publication (in *Œuvres
complètes de Claude Debussy* 1/7) of Debussy's earlier duet suites from the

1880s, notably the robust yet poised *Divertissement* and *Le triomphe de Bacchus*. In the volume's preface, the editor Noël Lee observes Debussy's archaic use of rhythmic augmentation and diminution in the finale of *Divertissement*. Similar augmentations appear on the last page of *Suite bergamasque* (in the left hand) and close both the Prélude and the Toccata of *Pour le piano*; another can be found in *Danse* (from bar 251), and the closing pages of *En blanc et noir* show him still indulging the habit in 1915. Other dance-like plays on metre emerge from the Menuet of the *Suite bergamasque*: a hemiola-like $\frac{4}{4}$ pattern embedded across bars 5–8 means that the piece opens with a pattern of four bars of $\frac{3}{4}$, then three sounding groups of $\frac{4}{4}$, then three of $\frac{3}{4}$ (the first of which really belongs with the preceding $\frac{4}{4}$ sequence). This explains why the piece's first paragraph can round off after eleven bars without feeling short-changed. Other antique-style hemiolas can be sensed over bars 22–5 and 63–4.

Fifteen years later, in 1905, the 'sarabande' sub-heading of Debussy's 'Hommage à Rameau' invites analogy with Rameau's Sarabandes – notably the rich A major one from the *Nouvelles suites de pièces de clavecin* of the late 1720s – but even more interestingly draws attention to the piece's wider setting within Debussy's first series of *Images*. Debussy starts the suite with 'Reflets dans l'eau', which has the eye-catching instruction *Mesuré* after an opening page in rubato rhythm – an echo, perhaps, of the way the initial Prélude in Rameau's first book of *Pièces de clavecin* goes into regular $\frac{12}{8}$ metre after an opening page of unmeasured prelude. (It's equally tempting to see this gigue revisited ten years later, in the first of Debussy's *Études*.) Debussy had easy access at the time to Rameau's collected *Pièces de clavecin* in the edition by Saint-Saëns – a much cleaner urtext than Diémer's anthologies – published in 1895 as part of Durand's complete Rameau edition, which involved Debussy from 1905 onwards. We might even read Rameau's theory of invertible dominants into the unusual key relationship between 'Reflets dans l'eau' and 'Hommage à Rameau' (D♭ major and G♯ minor). As it happens, the first harmonic move in Rameau's first book of *Pièces de clavecin* follows exactly the same progression to the dominant minor.

All this colours Debussy's *L'isle joyeuse* of 1903–4, originally intended as the finale of a three-movement *Suite bergamasque* entirely different from the *Suite bergamasque* we now know (Chapter 14 returns to this). In the course of discussing *L'isle joyeuse* in a letter of July 1914, Debussy muses affectionately on Couperin's 'Les barricades mystérieuses', then adds that *L'isle joyeuse* is 'also slightly *L'embarquement pour Cythère*, with less melancholy than in Watteau'.[28] A different connection, however, emerges from the diaries of Ricardo Viñes: when Debussy played him an early version of the piece in July 1903, Viñes was immediately reminded 'of paintings by Turner [. . .; Debussy] replied that, indeed, before composing [it] he had spent a good while in the Turner gallery in London.'[29] It's possible that Debussy saw a painting there that unites both strands, Turner's *Watteau Study by Fresnoy's Rules* of 1831 (see Plate 2), depicting Watteau at the easel alongside two of his major canvases, *Les plaisirs du bal* and *La lorgneuse*. The latter translates as 'The flirt', a title as redolent of Couperin or Rameau as *Les plaisirs du bal* is of *L'isle joyeuse*. This just touches on Debussy's view of Turner as 'the finest creator of mystery in the whole of art', part of a line that rebounds to classical France through Turner's veneration for Claude Lorrain.[30]

If Rameau's earthy virtuosity is echoed most immediately in Chabrier, Debussy's fastidious textures often suggest Couperin, not least in a shared fondness for tenor register (as in 'Les barricades mystérieuses'). Other

Plate 3. Detail from J. M. W. Turner: *Watteau Study by Fresnoy's* Rules (1831), Clore Gallery, London

Couperin pieces in sensuously low tessitura include 'Le Dodo ou L'amour au berceau', a rondo on a nursery song that Fauré and Debussy later revisited (as shown in Ex. 1.1).[31] Debussy's fondness for lower registers includes a few passages in later pieces that he had to rewrite in higher tessitura before publication, having evidently found them too growly at the piano – perhaps with the likes of 'Les barricades mystérieuses' in his ears? If this seems far-fetched, try the start of 'Pour les agréments' on harpsichord, an instrument Debussy had in mind at exactly that time for the (never-written) fourth of his chamber sonatas.[32] Indeed 'Pour les agréments' is one of the pieces that most shows these revisions of tessitura (visible in the Minkoff facsimile of the *Études*), along with 'La terrasse des audiences' (whose original ending is printed in the Appendix to *Œuvres complètes* 1/5 and also at the end of an older Kalmus edition of the Preludes).

This returns us to Debussy's quandary about whether to dedicate his *Études* to the memory of Couperin or Chopin. His manuscripts of the *Études* show that he changed the pieces' order more than once, most radically just before they went to engraving. His original order – it's tempting to call it '*ordre*' – ended with 'Pour les agréments', the most Couperin-like of the collection, as Claude Helffer observes in his *Œuvres complètes* preface. Although the published order ends instead with the more vigorously Chopinesque 'Pour les accords' (see p. 75–6), that piece equally bows to Couperin in its central section, for Debussy's fair copy shows two groups of grace-note ornaments in bar 86, both carefully aligned to start on, not before, the beat. Overlooked in the first edition, this telling alignment was spotted by Claude Helffer who restored it in the *Œuvres complètes*.

While such grace-note treatment is certainly exceptional for Debussy, it points up his wider penchant for starting measured ornamental flourishes on the beat, for example the repeated bass turn in the closing bars of 'Bruyères'; a close antecedent of this in Schumann (which we'll see in Chapter 11) conversely sounds before the beat.

From his Preludes onwards Debussy adopts Couperin's use of poised breathing commas,[33] and the manuscripts of his Preludes show rhythmic groups like ♩ ♪ or ♪ ♪ which, like similar Couperin notations with single dots, don't always add up exactly. Although Debussy's first editions arithmetically correct a few of these occurrences (to ♩ ♪ or ♪ ♪ etc.), his notation might be read as aiming, consciously or not, for the best of both worlds in *clavecin* style, poising the long notes without scrambling the short ones. (The same can be found in his song 'En sourdine' of 1892, another of his Verlaine *Fêtes galantes* settings.) Chapters 15 and 17 return to the elasticity of various dotted or dance-like rhythms in Debussy and Ravel.

Debussy's fervent advocacy of Rameau (particularly the operas, given that Rameau's keyboard music was already well known) started in 1903, in the direct wake of *Pelléas*, and in the same year as Dukas's *Variations sur un thème de Rameau* ('Le Lardon')[34] and the part-performance of *Castor et Pollux*, directed by Vincent d'Indy, that prompted Debussy's first Rameau panegyric in February 1903.[35] Within a few months followed Debussy's inclusion of the title 'Hommage à Rameau' on the contract for the piano *Images* (July 1903) and his growing friendship with Louis Laloy, who published a monograph on Rameau in 1908. To that we might add Debussy's adoption of evocatively picturesque titles in the wake of the Société des instruments anciens craze. (Obviously shared by Schumann and Liszt, this titling tradition was primarily launched in François Couperin's *Pièces de clavecin*.) Although a definite degree of polemic can be read into Debussy's pro-Rameau stance[36] – understandable in the Paris of the time – his unflagging enthusiasm for this repertoire over the rest of his life suggests primarily musical inspiration. (He doubtless equally sympathized with Rameau as a school dropout who later more than compensated in self-education.)

Rameau's music has its own say. Apart from semi-stunt pieces like 'L'enharmonique', his norms emerge from the outset in *Les fêtes de Polymnie* (which Debussy edited in 1905–8 for the Durand complete Rameau edition, with the help of Francisco de Lacerda). In keeping with Polymnie's reputation as the inventor of harmony, Rameau starts his opera with an initial unison tonic to which he then adds an open ninth (or second), followed by a rising ladder of (mostly) dissonances that makes interesting textural comparison with the opening of Ravel's *Daphnis et Chloé*.[37] Far from being exceptional for the era, this sort of daring matches some of the usages observed in Lucy Robinson's study of the Forqueray *Pièces de viole*, published in 1747, which show dominant ninths, tonal and modal ambiguity such as leaps between major and minor, even the odd whole-tone flurry, and frequent harmonic elisions – that is, missing resolutions between dissonances, exactly the sort of compression seen in Chapters 1–4 from Chabrier, Debussy and Ravel.[38]

Couperin's *Pièces de clavecin* answer this with not only 'La superbe ou la Forqueray' but also Couperin's own startling harmonies and ellipses in pieces likes the dramatic Passacaille from the *8ᵉ Ordre*. These all reflect the adventurous, enquiring mind of a self-educated connoisseur of literature (as Couperin was), again just like Debussy.[39]

Louis Laloy links Debussy's Preludes not only to Chopin and Couperin but also to the preludes of the lutenists, with their traditional role of checking the instrument and its tuning.[40] Jean-Jacques Eigeldinger's observation of this last characteristic in the opening Prelude of Chopin's op. 28 extends effortlessly to the almost identical 'tuner's chords' that open and close Debussy's 'Danseuses

de Delphes'.[41] Debussy's older interests equally embraced renaissance literature, as manifest in his settings of Charles d'Orléans, Tristan Lhermite and
François Villon around the time of his *Images* and Preludes.

As for Fauré, his oft-observed influence on Debussy's *Suite bergamasque*
centres on the bergamasque of his own *Pavane* op. 50, first published for solo
piano in the late 1880s, then with an added SATB text by Robert de
Montesquiou in spoof *fête galante* style. Fauré's Watteau-esque dream of
having his *Pavane* danced outdoors in period costume, with an invisible choir
and orchestra, was realized in 1891 at a party in the Bois de Boulogne on the
outskirts of Paris. (Chapter 18 returns to this aspect of the piece.) In 1902,
when the society hostess Madeleine Lemaire – one of Proust's models for
'Madame Verdurin' – asked Fauré for music for a *Fête galante* evening, he was
able to comply with existing music including his *Pavane* and the op. 35
Madrigal; sixteen years later he added to these, including some unpublished
pieces from his early years, to make up the Watteau-inspired ballet *Masques et
bergamasques* op. 112.[42] Surviving proofs show that the final Passepied of
Debussy's *Suite bergamasque*, in the same key as Fauré's *Pavane*, was even originally titled 'Pavane', a heading Debussy doubtless changed at the eleventh
hour to avoid finger-pointing comparisons (Debussy's piece, anyway, is
somewhat frisky for a pavane).

All this colours our perception of intermediate pieces or passages like the
somewhat antique modal minuets in Fauré's Fifth and Sixth Nocturnes (the
latter's *allegretto* section), plus arguably the whole ethos of his Barcarolles and
Valses-caprices. To my ears the Sixth to Eighth Barcarolles particularly epito-
mize Watteau, the restless melancholy of the Seventh answering a sensuous
insouciance in the Sixth that skilfully veils its enormous compositional wit
and virtuosity (of which more at the end of Chapter 18). A careful look at the
Sixth Barcarolle's robustly focused dynamics, accent articulations, bass
breathing rests and pedal releases should be enough to warn us not to be
fooled by its deceptively nonchalant surface.

If it's surprising not to see more of Domenico Scarlatti in *fin de siècle* special
events, it's mostly because he was never neglected enough to become a *cause
célèbre* (and wasn't French at a time when much of the polemic was about
Frenchness). Roland-Manuel recalled Scarlatti sonatas as virtually the only
score he ever saw on Ravel's piano (another taste shared with Chabrier);[43] the
D minor Sonata K.141 suggests itself as one possible favourite with its fast
repetitions *quasi alla* 'Alborada del gracioso'. A famous Scarlatti trait, the
dissonant notes integrally written into chords (literally *acciaccature* or
'crushed'), can be heard across the hands at the start of Ravel's Concerto in G,
the left hand providing colour without harmonic function relative to the right

hand. (Judicious balance across the hands is thus of the essence, as in the somewhat related opening of Debussy's prelude 'Brouillards'.)

BACH

As Joël-Marie Fauquet notes, Franck's *Prélude, Choral et Fugue* suggests a homage to the Bach bicentenary of 1885.[44] It's easy to overlook Franck's boldness there in combining new and old without self-conscious archaism: the 1881 première of his friend Chabrier's *Pièces pittoresques* was perhaps still fresh in his mind, and he doubtless knew that Chabrier considered himself 'steeped in *père* Bach'.[45] The halfway point of Franck's *Fugue* (the inversion of the subject going into bar 218) is especially redolent of the equivalent point in the A minor Prelude from Book 2 of Bach's '48', with a similar chromatic rising line in a texture dominated by fourths and sixths. In turn, Durand's editions of J. S. Bach from 1915 onwards entailed the editorial participation of Fauré (for the organ works and the '48') and Debussy (the six sonatas for solo string instrument and keyboard).

Debussy fondly recalled how his first piano teacher Mme Mauté played Bach 'as nobody does now, putting life into it'; in the mid-1890s he would spend Sunday afternoons playing Bach in duet transcription with his fellow-composer Ernest Le Grand.[46] Debussy's *Pour le piano* of a few years later appears to echo these sessions: the Prélude evokes various textures and lines from Bach's A minor organ Prelude BWV 543 (as shown in the Foreword to the *Œuvres complètes de Claude Debussy* 1/3), before the Toccata cheekily blends the opening of Bach's E major violin Partita with a repeated pivotal bar from Daquin's 'Le coucou' (Ex. 10.2).

Example 10.2

a: Claude Daquin, 'Le coucou', bars 23–4 (as in the 1887 Diémer edition)

b: Debussy, *Pour le piano*, Toccata, bars 1–6

c: J. S. Bach, Partita for solo violin, BWV 1006, Prelude, bars 1–6

Coming between Debussy's earlier suites and Ravel's *Tombeau de Couperin*, *Pour le piano* suggests a particularly original initiative: its overall title ('For the piano'), its classical movement titles, and the omission of Debussy's name from the first edition's front cover all lend it an air of classical anthology in the manner of (say) Diémer's collections. Debussy even had the dynamics set in mock-editorial small type, a practice absent from Diémer's editions but already applied in some German editions of old classics. (He might have laughed at the quandary this recently caused in the *Œuvres complètes*, which had to render his dynamics full size to prevent confusion.)

If Fauré is more often associated with barcarolles than Bach chorales, his lifelong enthusiasm for Bach is confirmed by his fellow-enthusiast the organ-playing Princesse de Polignac (née Winnaretta Singer).[47] A glance under the rippling surface of Fauré's Sixth Nocturne instantly reveals its underlying chorale texture (see Ex. 20.4–5). An affinity has long been noted between the opening of Fauré's First Nocturne (in E♭ minor) and Bach's corresponding Prelude from Book 1 of the '48'; even more telling is the top of the next page (as observed in conversation by the pianist Roderick Chadwick), where Fauré's ostinato from bar 21 shadows almost verbatim Bach's fugue subject from the same pair. The central section of Fauré's Second Nocturne then features the same hand acrobatics as the Gigue from Bach's B♭ Partita or the quasi-flamenco cadenza from the Fifth Brandenburg Concerto (one of Diémer's known *pièces de résistance*). That could be one reason why Fauré's Second Nocturne was a special favourite of Saint-Saëns, coming on the heels of the latter's Second Piano Concerto with its opening salute to Bach's G minor Organ Fantasia, BWV 542.

Behind all that lies Fauré's polyphony-based École Niedermeyer training in Palestrina, Vittoria and Lassus as well as Bach and Handel. It explains Fauré's easy blend of sensuously veiled modernity with fugue or strict canon in works like the *Dolly* suite or the *Pièces brèves*, sometimes incorporating music from his adolescent years.[48] It also points to his supple bass lines, structurally melodic as with virtually no other composer. Another Bachian element, inseparable from Fauré's polyphonic thinking, emerges from the all-purpose nature of pieces like his famous *Sicilienne*: eventually published as op. 78 the piece exists, like much baroque repertoire, in various transcriptions by the composer (piano solo, or cello and piano with violin or viola options, or for orchestra as in his *Pelléas et Mélisande* music, all in addition to its unpublished first version for a small ensemble of woodwind and strings).

If Chopin openly regarded J. S. Bach as fundamental to his musical thinking, we have clear reason to view Bach's era and its specialized French manifestations as equally influential over the end of the nineteenth century.

CHAPTER 11

ROMANTICISM

Elegant society lady to Fauré (affectedly): 'Ah, *cher Maître*, I can no longer bear to listen to Wagner.' Fauré (affably): 'Rest assured, Madame, that's not of the slightest importance'   – recounted by Hélène Jourdan-Morhange

W<small>HILE</small> this topic could fill a book, a few glimpses here usefully complement Chapters 6 and 9. They also let us consider the oft-posed question of whether music like Debussy's or Ravel's (even Chabrier's) counts as classical or romantic. If their picturesque titles can point in either direction (given the claveciniste tradition), the undoubted romantic expression in their music is countered by the way formal clarity and balance play a vital expressive role, as seen throughout Chapters 1–4 (not least Debussy's comment on page 42 above linking form and expression in the second series of *Images*). Mixed implications underlie Ravel's quip that he had intended *Gaspard de la nuit* as a caricature of romanticism, 'but perhaps I let myself be taken over by it'.[1] Ravel's pleas to performers just to 'play, not interpret my music' – even with all the caveats such a statement invokes – can be read as both a classicist's declaration and an assurance that any romanticism is inbuilt.

SCHUMANN

Schumann's immeasurable effect on French music is hardly surprising given his literary francophilia and his exploration of *Innigkeit* and tenderness, qualities close to the aesthetic of the French clavecinistes. Should this appear far-fetched, we need only consider the impact of his francophone *Carnaval*, arguably the first substantial musical tribute since the clavecinistes to the world of *comédie italienne* and *fête galante*. (Telemann provides one of the early German links to that world.) Schumann's fondness for French overture rhythm underlines this (*Etudes symphoniques*, *Kreisleriana*, *Waldszenen* in both 'Verrufene Stelle' and 'Vogel als Prophet'); his inclusion of Paganini and Chopin in *Carnaval* joins a musical portrait or *à la manière* tradition stretching from the clavecinistes to Ravel and beyond; and its ironically titled final 'Marche des "Davidsbündler" contre les Philistins' (in $\frac{3}{4}$ metre), with its 'seventeenth-century' bass theme, has distinct shades of the raspberry blown by Couperin, in his *11ᵉ Ordre de Pièces de clavecin*, at the perceivedly philistine society of Ménestrandeurs.[2]

Debussy's main success as a Conservatoire piano student was in the 1877 *concours* with the first movement of Schumann's G minor Sonata; twenty years later the first work he assigned his piano pupil Mme de Romilly was *Kreisleriana*.[3] In later years again he talked fondly of Schumann to Cyril Scott, and the pianist Marcel Ciampi recalled having never heard Schumann played more beautifully than by Debussy (he remembered in particular the *Arabeske*).[4] Debussy's transcriptions include a solo piano version ('À la fontaine', printed in 1903) of 'Am Springbrunnen' from Schumann's op. 85 piano duets, plus a two-piano version (1891) of Schumann's *Sechs Stücke in canonischer Form* (op. 56) for pedal piano or organ.[5] The gently ornamented close of the fourth of these *Stücke* seems to echo at the end of Debussy's prelude 'Bruyères'. Louis Laloy reports that Debussy's unbounded affection for Schumann was tempered only by a regret that Schumann had 'put the ideas best suited to the orchestra into his works for piano'.[6] Nor can Schumann's essential character as an exotic outsider – a *Vogel als Prophet* in his own land – have failed to catch Debussy's sympathy.

Chabrier's fascination with Schumann (plus Berlioz and Bizet) included an enthusiasm for playing Schumann's symphonies in piano duet. He may well have enjoyed the four-hand transcription by Bizet of Schumann's above-mentioned *Sechs Stücke*, for the chromatic sideslips that end the barcarolle-like second one (Ex. 11.1) suggest a spur for the end of his own *Valses romantiques* (Ex. 7.20a) and also for the final cadence of his piano 'Improvisation' from the *Pièces pittoresques*. (The end of Chabrier's song 'Les cigales' comes even closer to Schumann's repeated cadence.)

Example 11.1

Schumann, *Sechs Stücke in canonischer Form* for pedal piano op. 56: no. 2, bars 53–5

The constant on-beat dissonances of Schumann's 'Vogel als Prophet' in turn anticipate Chabrier's *Ballabile* (Ex. 7.2) or the contrapuntal daisy-chains of dissonance in the central part and coda of his *Impromptu*. (Bar 11, like Example 6.3b, sounds F, F♯ and G simultaneously.) The way Schumann's flighty ornaments momentarily resolve the on-beat dissonances points farther again, via 'Les bulles de savon' from Bizet's *Jeux d'enfants*, to Debussy's 'La Puerta del Vino' (see p. 25 above). Roger Delage suggests 'Vogel als Prophet' as the main textural antecedent of Chabrier's 'Sous bois', a point arguable in terms of either the arpeggiations or the left-hand semitone dissonances, as well as the pieces' very muted dynamics – though see also p. 145 above.[7]

If Chabrier's 'Improvisation' could almost pass for Schumann (on one of the latter's best days, too), its nearest literal approach emerges from bars 61–4 (leading into the recap) relative to bars 16–19 of 'Coquette' from *Carnaval*. 'Coquette' also echoes in Chabrier's 'Mauresque', another piece associated with clown figures (see note 14 to Chapter 7). The first movement of Schumann's C major *Fantasie* has an even more Chabrier-like extended sequence of chromatically rising lines (from bar 105, leading to the reprise): out of context it would be hard to tell which passage is by whom. The *Fantasie*'s finale again echoes in Chabrier's *Pièces pittoresques*: besides its rolling figurations (cf. again 'Improvisation'), the alternation of double-octave unisons and canonic imitation across bars 48–59 could be read as a miniature template for Chabrier's 'Mélancolie'. As for the vigorous bass cross-beats that close the 'Préambule' of *Carnaval*, we can hear them again under the main theme of *España* (from bar 52, especially in Chabrier's two-piano version). Indeed, the curious bar of $\frac{7}{4}$ that goes with them uncannily prefigures the 'drunken sailors' wild trombone irruption in *España*. We can also sense Florestan and Eusebius in Chabrier's extremes of gaiety and intro-spection: Manet's 1881 oil portrait of Chabrier captures the latter aspect, conveying – as vividly as his painting *Olympia* did for Ravel – the spirit of 'Mélancolie', 'Improvisation' and the intense *Caprice* of 1889.[8]

Ravel's occasional anti-Schumann *boutades* can't be taken over-literally:[9] they reflect his delight in debunking *idées reçues* and might be read in part as ersatz defence of Mendelssohn. Three of Ravel's piano-playing triumphs as a Conservatoire student again involved Schumann at his far from easiest, with movements from the G minor Sonata in 1890 and the C major *Fantasie* in 1894, plus – at a Salle Erard public concert in 1892 – the Andante and Variations for two pianos with his old teacher Henry Ghys, part of an all-Schumann programme. Indeed Ravel's first known composition, now lost, was a set of variations (at his own initiative) on a chorale by Schumann.[10] Strong shades of Schumann's *Carnaval* – including its own 'Valse noble' – pervade Ravel's *Valses nobles et sentimentales*, mixed with echoes or aspects of

Schubert, Chopin, Weber, Johann Strauss II, Chabrier and even Satie. Besides a general affinity between Ravel's opening *valse* and the start of Schumann's 'Préambule', the rubato bars 25–8 and 57–60 of Ravel's second *valse* suggest echoes of Schumann's double-dotted theme (from bar 86) that returns in the finale of *Carnaval*: the shared chromatically rising harmonies suggest reading Ravel's rubato as a gentle hurrying through the rising sequences. As it happens, it was just three years after the *Valses nobles* that Ravel orchestrated *Carnaval* for Nijinsky's ballet troupe.[11]

Schumann's tonal daring echoes again in the Prélude of Ravel's *Tombeau de Couperin* whose key, as in the opening song of *Dichterliebe*, seesaws between relative minor and major (as does Debussy in the Prélude of *Pour le piano*, *Masques* and the *Étude* 'Pour les accords'). Schumann might even be viewed as the boldest of them all there for letting his song end on a hanging dominant (to the relative minor). According to Manuel Rosenthal, Ravel reflected '*sans cesse*' on the 'humanity of Schumann's music', saying in private what reserve kept him from printing:

> Yes, I'm well aware there are awkward, even clumsy turns, but even so [Schumann] invented much of our pianistic writing . . . of our harmonic feeling . . . we must place very, very highly – perhaps higher even than all the others – a musician who, with the seven wretched notes of the scale, somehow expresses so fully what lives in the human heart.[12]

Along with Chabrier, Fauré is especially close to Schumann, a point Ravel observed in an article about Fauré's songs that singles out *Au cimetière* in relation to 'Ich grolle nicht'.[13] The opening of Schumann's G minor Sonata (plus that of the C major *Fantasie*) is particularly strongly suggested by the start of Fauré's Second Piano Quartet. Less immediately obvious is the blend of plagal harmony over a V–I bass that opens the *Fantasie* and ends 'Die Rose, die Lilie, die Taube' in *Dichterliebe*. Exactly the same blend pervades Fauré's violin *Berceuse* op. 16 as an ostinato, and features in Chabrier's 'Scherzo-valse' from *Pièces pittoresques* (the B♭ episode), as well as such contrasted later pieces as Debussy's 'La fille aux cheveux de lin' (bars 9–10) and the repeated cadence of the Rigaudon in Ravel's *Tombeau de Couperin*.

Equally remarkable is the IV[7]–I cadence that ends Schumann's *Humoreske* op. 20, or the startling modal cadences on the last page of 'Abschied' from *Waldszenen* (bars 46–7, starting with C[7]–B♭): only one note of Schumann's sequence needs to be changed (*c'* to *d'♭* at bar 47 beat 3) to make the sequence tally exactly with the end of Fauré's first *Romance sans paroles* (Ex. 1.4). Texturally the end of 'Abschied' resonates even more in the closing bars of Fauré's *Romance* op. 28 (in the same key) for violin and piano. Chapter 6 has already discussed a related cadence (from Schumann's 'In der Fremde') in connection with Chopin with enormous repercussions for later French music (see note 9 to Chapter 6).

Interval character plays its role – something Ravel perhaps had in mind when he remarked on Schumann's 'marked individuality'.[14] The strings of sixths for both hands in Schumann's *Humoreske* (the *einfach und zart* section) and in the fifth of the op. 21 *Noveletten* (bars 205–30) return in Debussy's *Étude* 'Pour les sixtes' and Variation V of Fauré's op. 73 *Thème et variations* (from bar 9, reportedly one of Fauré's favourite passages in the work).[15] Fauré's love of stepwise sequences of seventh chords (diatonically and chromatically) again echoes the finales of Schumann's Third and Fourth Symphonies (in the latter case from bar 59). The abrupt stepwise key shifts in the middle of Fauré's *Pavane* op. 50 (D to C then B♭) likewise hark back to the outer movements of Schumann's Fourth Symphony, including their stark way of landing on a vigorous unison.[16]

It was Saint-Saëns who introduced Fauré (and other École Niedermeyer students) to the music of Schumann, Liszt and Wagner, unofficially lengthening piano lessons to include them along with general musicianship and composition.[17] Fauré's appreciation of Schumann (who was still alive when Fauré enrolled at the École Niedermeyer) thus had a savour of daring modernity from the outset, and helps explain why, years later, he made a dawn-to-dusk trip just to visit Schumann's grave in Bonn.[18] It was against that background that Jacques Durand asked Fauré in 1915 to edit Schumann's piano music, and that Winnaretta de Polignac recalled that Fauré 'used to play most of [Schumann's] works better than any other pianist I've heard, including the great names of the keyboard'.[19]

It has often been observed that Fauré's *Thème et variations* suggest something of a homage – though Fauré said nothing about it – to Schumann's *Etudes symphoniques*. Besides their shared C♯ minor key and similarities of internal structure (notably a plagal penchant toward F♯ minor), the numerous correspondences of texture, voicing and harmonic colour include a neapolitan tint in Fauré's Variation XI that looks back to Schumann's Variation VII. Other Schumannesque colours include – besides the chains of sixths already noted in Fauré's Variation V – the way his epilogue-like Variation XI echoes both the opening of Schumann's op. 12 *Fantasiestücke* ('Des Abends') and the final *Dichterliebe* postlude. It speaks eloquently for Fauré that he could sail so close yet retain his own distinct voice.

MENDELSSOHN, WEBER

Besides Ravel's constant defence of Mendelssohn (and editing of his piano works for Durand in 1915), an outright tribute can be sensed in Fauré's early *Romances sans paroles* op. 17 (literally *Songs without Words*), published in 1881 but probably composed in his teens. Mendelssohn's frequent usage of busy piano figurations in otherwise light textures resurfaces in Saint-Saëns and Fauré, not least the second of Fauré's *Romances sans paroles*, which takes its texture almost literally from Mendelssohn's G minor *Lied ohne Worte* op. 102 no. 4 (at almost double tempo) while quoting 'Oh for the wings of a dove' in the minor! If this was unconscious it reveals, with a vengeance, Mendelssohn's impact on Fauré; if conscious it reflects the same gently pungent wit as Fauré's many skilfully drawn caricatures (answering Mendelssohn's talent at the easel). A sense of Mendelssohn under the fingers remains in some of Fauré's mature masterworks, not least the opening layout of the Sixth Nocturne relative to Mendelssohn's *Lied ohne Worte* op. 53 no. 1 in A♭.

In countries less opera-obsessed than nineteenth-century France it's easy to overlook Weber, whose impact is impossible to evaluate without his operas: according to Manuel Rosenthal, Ravel knew *Oberon* and *Freischütz* entirely from memory.[20] Besides the popularity of *Invitation to the Waltz* (both the piano original and Berlioz's magnificent orchestration), Weber's piano works were standard (if advanced) Conservatoire fare: Debussy's final piano *concours* of 1878 featured the demanding Second Piano Sonata, op. 39 in A♭. In a lengthy letter of 1887 Chabrier vigorously defends Weber's *Oberon*, particularly its first chorus and its overture, which Chabrier insisted he could happily hear twenty times over: most newer operas, he adds, sounded dated alongside Weber's lasting freshness.[21]

Debussy was probably unaware of Chabrier's letter when, in January 1903, he mounted his own vigorous defence of *Oberon*: in a *Gil Blas* article and again in a longer interview with Robert Godet, he affectionately introduces Weber almost in the manner of 'Monsieur Croche' – that is, as a mouthpiece for Debussy's artistic ideals.[22] Several pieces by Chabrier and Debussy end with apparent echoes of the *do-re-mi* horn call from *Oberon* (often observed in Debussy's *"Les fées sont d'exquises danseuses"*, this can also be seen in some examples in Chapter 7). Weber resurfaces later in Debussy's second book of Preludes: bars 54–61 of 'Ondine' echo the final part of Weber's *Concertstück* for piano and orchestra.

LISZT

The traditional bracketing 'Liszt–Ravel' and 'Chopin–Debussy' is not without reason even if, like any generalization, it tells only part of the story. Ravel was quite open about it, and his own musical library was replete with Liszt scores, many in first prints.[23] If his *Jeux d'eau* invites immediate comparison with Liszt's 'Les jeux d'eau à la Villa d'Este', the most audible moment of musical approach is Ravel's opening and closing exposed major seventh (relative to bar 4 of Liszt's piece) – though more harmonically disguised textural parallels have been observed by Dominique Merlet.[24] Other textures in Ravel point particularly to Liszt's 'Waldesrauschen' and 'Au bord d'une source': at the piano we quickly sense the tactile and sonorous affinity between the *leggiero* left-hand leaps that open 'Waldesrauschen' and bars 31–2 of *Jeux d'eau*. Intriguingly, bars 33–6 of Ravel's 'Noctuelles' – spiralling upward figurations to a tremolando that then flutters down again – suggests a neat compaction of elements from both 'Au bord d'une source' (bars 10–11) and 'Waldesrauschen' (bars 79–84).

This case is particularly striking, coming on the first page of a suite (*Miroirs*) in which Ravel's specific aim was to explore new paths. For all the ways he did that over the following years, Liszt is rarely far away: try playing from bar 5 of 'Waldesrauschen' straight into the opening theme of 'Ondine', or compare the teasing minor-major resolution at bar 30 of 'Ondine' with the one that frames 'Waldesrauschen' (four bars from its start and end), likewise the wilder virtuoso shades of (mostly the first) Mephisto Waltz with 'Scarbo', or the end of the Toccata in *Le tombeau de Couperin* with that of Liszt's 'Légende du Saint-François de Paule marchant sur les flots'.

A generation earlier, Liszt's long friendship with Franck linked two of the great virtuosos of their era. Alfred Cortot notes strong echoes of Liszt's Variations on Bach's *Weinen, Klagen, Sorgen, Zagen* in the fugue of Franck's *Prélude, Choral et Fugue*.[25] As for Chabrier, it speaks for his force of character that he remained one of the few who could write overt piano virtuosity without aping Liszt, and Vincent d'Indy rated Chabrier's expressive capabilities at the piano almost on a par with those of Liszt (see p. 320 below). Chapter 4 has already discussed a symphonic aspect of Liszt's impact on Fauré; anyone in doubt about their proximity both musical and pianistic need only compare the start of 'O Lieb' from Liszt's *Liebesträume* (with its famous A♭ major rising sixth) with the start of Fauré's Third Nocturne and *Romances sans paroles*, or its cross-hand melodies with Fauré's First and Fourth Barcarolles. The wood-rustling echoes in Fauré's *Ballade* op. 19, taken with the Chopinesque links seen in Chapter 6, suggest a piece that pays simultaneous tribute to Chopin, Liszt and the lighter-footed side of Wagner. If the overt showman in Liszt seems less to Fauré's taste, it didn't discourage him from taking over and developing the (originally Lisztian) *Valse-caprice* genre.

As for Debussy, important Lisztian elements include the tritonal cadences that end *Pour le piano* and *La mer* (G to C♯/D♭), answering the end of Liszt's B minor Sonata (F to B) of half a century before. (The final chord of Liszt's Sonata, hanging on second inversion, also echoes at the end of Chabrier's *Impromptu* – Ex. 7.18a.) One of Debussy's first piano pieces (now lost) was reportedly a *Rhapsody in the style of Liszt*: contact at just one remove came in his late teens when he spent three summers as resident pianist for Nadezhda von Meck, several of whose children studied with Liszt. Many pianists have noticed an early echo of Liszt in Debussy's First Arabesque (the descending pentatonic arabesques from bar 6, relative to the coda of 'Sposalizio'). A much later one can be heard across bars 49–52 of Debussy's *Étude* 'Pour les notes répétées' relative to 'La campanella' (particularly the 1851 version, bar 50 onwards). From the late end of Liszt's output, pieces like *Nuages gris* are sometimes likened to Debussy, though the analogy is arguably limited because any 'impressionism' in Debussy tends to be more precisely and audibly structured.

Debussy's one personal contact with Liszt came about in January 1886, while he was *Prix de Rome pensionnaire* at the Villa Medici in Rome and the elderly Liszt was spending the winter (his last) at the Hotel Alibert. On 8 January Debussy and Paul Vidal were guests at dinner with Liszt at the Villa Medici (they then played his Faust Symphony in duet reduction, during which the tired and well-fed Liszt understandably fell asleep). The next day appears to have been the one when Vidal and Debussy visited Liszt and played him Chabrier's *Valses romantiques*, before Liszt dined again at the Villa on 13 January and played a recital including 'Au bord d'une source', his transcription of Schubert's *Ave Maria*, and an unnamed third piece.[26] That evening would have been the basis for Debussy's vivid recollection, almost thirty years later in 1915, of how Liszt used the pedal 'as a kind of *respiration*' (of which more in Chapter 19). Meanwhile in 1904 Debussy had written *L'isle joyeuse*, whose accompaniment from bar 7 recalls – as many have observed – Liszt's 'Les jeux d'eau à la Villa d'Este' (Ex. 11.2; cf. Ex. 16.8). Debussy's carefully notated arpeggio figurations invite exactly the sort of pedal respiration that his recollections of Liszt imply.

Example 11.2. Liszt, 'Les jeux d'eau à la Villa d'Este', bars 44–7

Besides *L'isle joyeuse*, no piece brings out the Lisztian lion in Debussy more than his prelude 'Ce qu'a vu le Vent d'Ouest'. Under the mane lies an extraordinary link, a highly unusual ostinato shared with a *Trauermarsch* that Liszt composed in September 1885 (Ex. 11.3: Debussy marks the ostinato with the crescendo-driven bass note that completes each half-bar, as arrowed under Example 11.3b). Incorporated that same year in Liszt's *Hungarian Historical Portraits* as the Funeral music for László Teleki, his *Trauermarsch* was published separately in 1888.[27] It was thus one of Liszt's most recent compositions when he played at the Villa Medici in January 1886. Might it have been the unnamed third piece in his recital, perhaps unidentified through being new and unpublished (and already having two titles)? Or might Liszt have shown or played it to Debussy when they met? It was his habit to do exactly that sort of thing.[28] With Liszt in Rome was his pupil and factotum Arthur Friedheim, who used some of the time there to orchestrate four of the *Hungarian Historical Portraits*, before conducting them in Liszt's presence in June 1886. There's no doubt these pieces were very much in Liszt's mind around the time he met Debussy. Nor can we assume Debussy wouldn't have remembered the piece or at least its ostinato by 1909–10: besides the existence of the 1888 edition, his recollections of Liszt in 1915 suggest an indelible impression, and Debussy had perfect pitch.

Example 11.3

a: Liszt, *Trauermarsch* (1885; also no. 3 of *Hungarian Historical Portraits*)

b: Debussy, 'Ce qu'a vu le Vent d'Ouest', bars 15–16, bass ostinato (repeated with octave then whole-tone doubling over bars 17–20)

WAGNER

> Earlier detractors failed to understand Wagner's greatness. Nietzsche's hostility was different: he understood Wagner all too well.
>
> — Robin Holloway, *Debussy and Wagner*

While existing Wagner-related surveys (like Robin Holloway's) range far beyond what can be attempted here, the present context allows a glance where they rarely venture, into piano music. The problem is typified by how much Wagner's impact is assumed in Chabrier's operas *Gwendoline* and *Briséïs*, while Chabrier's piano music is virtually deemed a separate species. Not quite so, as we saw lurking under the ending of 'Sous bois' (Ex. 7.9a and c). More immediately startling is a sudden incursion of what seems like the 'curse' motive from Wagner's *Ring* in the middle of *Bourrée fantasque* (at bars 133–6, *a Tempo vivo*). However we read those – almost certainly not programmatically – the salient point is that Chabrier at the piano, like Debussy, could combine Wagnerian intensity with concision, intimacy and clarity. No piece displays this more than his *Caprice*, already glimpsed in Chapter 9; Example 11.4 shows something of how it translates – and compactly harnesses in three pages – the chromatic essence of the *Tristan* opening. (The passage returns near the end of the piece, over the Musorgskian bass of Example 9.2).

Example 11.4. Chabrier, *Caprice*, bars 7–12

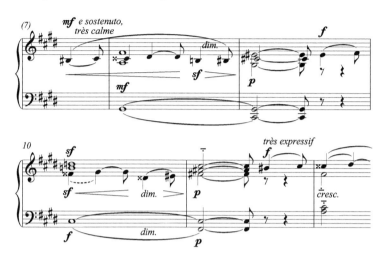

Part of Chabrier's quiet originality here lies in his harmonic independence from the *Tristan* gestures and polyphony that he still manages to evoke vividly. César Franck by contrast, in the *Choral* of his *Prélude, Choral et Fugue*, happily uses Wagner's opening two 'Tristan' chords at enharmonically sounding pitch (Ex. 11.5a–b), albeit with some polyphonic disguise.[29] The first 'Tristan' chord then returns at pitch as the harmonic highlight of Franck's theme at bar 63 and bar 67 beat 2, before launching the *poco allegro* transition to the *Fugue* from bar 116. A decade later Debussy embeds the same *Tristan* opening progression in his *Images* of 1894 (Ex. 11.5c; see also Ex. 1.7). Intriguingly, before he republished this Sarabande in 1901 as the middle movement of *Pour le piano*, Debussy covered his tracks by removing all the naturals from Example 11.5c.

Example 11.5

a: Franck, *Prélude, Choral et Fugue*, bars 60–1

b: Opening progression (texturally reduced) of Wagner, *Tristan und Isolde*

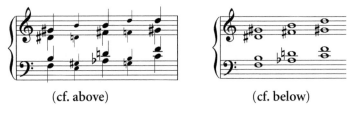

(cf. above)   (cf. below)

c: Debussy, 'Sarabande' from *Images* [*oubliées*], bar 1

Without vocal texts, Debussy's piano music offers fewer handles for symbolic interpretation – though Nicholas Routley's article 'Debussy and Baudelaire's *Harmonie du soir*' takes a bold grasp at the Wagnerian undertones in the prelude *"Les sons et les parfums"*. Odder Wagnerian echoes link two texturally related pieces of Debussy's last years, the *Étude* 'Pour les tierces' (notably bars 43–4, Tristan chords rising again by minor thirds) and the prelude 'Les tierces alternées' (*Siegfried* in the opening bars, then low-lying *Tristan* chords rising by minor thirds in bars 121 and 123).

We have to be wary of over-reading meanings into that familiar chord (the standard half-diminished), for which reason I'm ignoring countless occurrences in Debussy's piano music: our interest lies in when Debussy's usage maintains the Wagnerian gesture or mood-related setting, for example by rising through minor thirds even when the register is disguised, sometimes almost grotesquely so as in 'Les tierces alternées'. One of the most picturesquely cogent examples, from bar 18 of 'Reflets dans l'eau' – rising through minor thirds from bar 20 – has already featured in Chapters 1 and 8.

These serve as background to the burlesque of 'Golliwogg's cake walk', not only the famous mockery in its central section of the opening phrase of *Tristan*, but also the way Debussy's opening arpeggios of bars 2–4 and off-beats of bars 10–11 (etc.) literally and relentlessly 'rag' the Tristan chord. The undignified thump with which Debussy, in bar 4, ousts the Tristanesque C♭ with B♭ continues the burlesque tradition of slap-happy floor-thumping cadences that characterizes Chabrier's 1880 *Souvenirs de Munich*, a deliciously irreverent piano duet quadrille based on the leitmotifs of *Tristan*. Written a few months after Chabrier had been reduced to helpless sobs on hearing

Tristan live for the first time, *Souvenirs de Munich* prompted Fauré's and Messager's *Souvenirs de Bayreuth* in the same vein, with backward glances to Offenbach's Wagner satire 'Le musicien de l'avenir' in *Carnaval des revues*.[30] Another amusing echo comes in Chabrier's *Pas redoublé* for piano duet (published posthumously as *Cortège burlesque*): originally conceived as a march for military band, the piece at one point narrowly averts falling into the arms of *Lohengrin* (Ex. 11.6: the analogy is added underneath, in transposition).

Example 11.6. Chabrier, *Pas redoublé* (*Cortège burlesque*), bars 53–8 (two-hand reduction)

Fauré's piano music is often viewed as relatively Wagner-immune, his most Wagnerian moments concentrated in his opera *Pénélope* (and the earlier choral work *La naissance de Vénus*). Even the example of *Pénélope*, though, prompts attention to the climaxes of his Ninth and Tenth Nocturnes (contemporary with *Pénélope*), both dominated by half-diminished Tristan chords, at exact Tristan pitch in the Ninth Nocturne (bar 53). Before them comes the fourth of the *Pièces brèves* of 1902 with its *Tristan*-like chromatic sequences of rising thirds (bars 21–4 and 41–4), culminating in the unresolved Tristan chords of bars 52 and 54. Earlier again are the possible echoes of *Parsifal* in the Fourth Nocturne (see p. 15 above) whose central section features one of Fauré's favourite thematic shapes, a falling fifth followed by a rising scale like the start of his *Ballade* op. 19, the orchestral 'Nocturne' from his music to *Shylock* – and Wagner's *Siegfried Idyll*, a piece Fauré once conducted.[31] Balancing that, it has to be added, is the similarly shaped second theme in the first movement of Schumann's Piano Quintet. Fortuitous, maybe, but it reminds us in turn that the exact opening progression of *Tristan* is anticipated a decade earlier, in the same key, by the first half-close in Schumann's Cello Concerto.

The famous programmatic associations of these motives are, of course, largely Wagner's, and this underlies some strategically placed Tristan chords already seen in Fauré and Ravel (p. 31 above), in the latter case used as a focus for the concentrated *tristesse* of 'Le gibet'. The chord's emotional potential is harnessed again at the climax of the Adagio in Ravel's Concerto in G (bar 71). From the other side – and beyond this book's remit – comes Ravel's almost hyper-Wagnerian deployment of the Tristan chord for the love spell in *Daphnis et Chloé*, milking Wagner with virtuoso impunity.

Political vagaries of the era easily distract us from some telling cultural overlaps. Throughout the 1880s the conductors Felix Mottl and Hermann Levi were the two staunchest champions in Germany and Austria of both Anton Bruckner and Emmanuel Chabrier. (Mottl, a Bruckner pupil, orchestrated Chabrier's *Valses romantiques* and *Bourrée fantasque* and staged two of his operas. We can now only guess if Mottl or Levi acquainted either composer with the music of the other one.) In a commentary printed in the *Allgemeine Deutsche Musik Zeitung* in June 1889 Oskar Grohe, a friend of Bruckner's pupil Hugo Wolf, likens Chabrier's melodic and harmonic boldness to Bruckner but concludes that with Chabrier 'everything sounds more organic, more essential, while the Viennese master's music always has something more rhapsodic ... Despite the German elements [Chabrier] has assimilated, he has remained French.'[32] The underlining of these qualities at that time by a German commentator is striking.

While Debussy is unlikely to have known Bruckner's music, his Chabriophilia may offer a source for some shared traits – along with his youthful improvisation classes with César Franck, who never forgot hearing Bruckner improvise in Paris in 1869.[33] Debussy and Bruckner also share a love of fanfare-like alternating duplets and triplets, providing what initially would seem an odd link between Bruckner's Fourth Symphony and the first of Debussy's piano *Images* of 1894, the two-piano *Lindaraja* of 1901, the 1904 *Morceau de concours* for piano, and Examples 6.5 and 7.14b.[34] 'Hommage à Rameau', moreover, yields one brief but startling resemblance to the first movement of that same Fourth Symphony, for its central section glides off in a remarkably similar way to the structurally equivalent start of the symphony's development section. John Phillips draws attention to the core role in Bruckner's Ninth Symphony of the chromatically split tonic (D to C♯/D♯ in the first movement);[35] in Chapters 2–3 we saw the similar role of this as a binding thread through the first book of Debussy's Preludes and Ravel's 'Scarbo'. Such affinities remind us that there are always more links under the surface than we'll ever fully know.

PART 3

FRESH PERSPECTIVES

CHAPTER 12

RHYTHMIC GAMES IN RAVEL

Voici venir les temps où vibrant sur sa tige
Chaque fleur s'évapore ainsi qu'un encensoir;
Les sons et les parfums tournent dans l'air du soir;
Valse mélancolique et langoureux vertige!

Chaque fleur s'évapore ainsi qu'un encensoir;
Le violon frémit comme un cœur qu'on afflige;
Valse mélancolique et langoureux vertige!
Le ciel est triste et beau comme un grand reposoir.

Le violon frémit comme un cœur qu'on afflige,
Un cœur tendre, qui hait le néant vaste et noir!
Le ciel est triste et beau comme un grand reposoir;
Le soleil s'est noyé dans son sang qui se fige.

Un cœur tendre, qui hait le néant vaste et noir,
Du passé lumineux recueille tout vestige !
Le soleil s'est noyé dans son sang qui se fige. . .
Ton souvenir en moi luit comme un ostensoir!

'Harmonie du soir' (from Charles Baudelaire, *Les fleurs du mal*)

Even without a knowledge of French, visual examination of this sixteen-line poem soon shows that it is made up from just ten lines. Baudelaire is playing on the Malayan-derived *pantun* form – already seen in Chapter 4 – in which the contrasted couplets of each stanza play leapfrog over each other to the next stanza, at the same time as the second and fourth line of each stanza become the first and third of the next. Many *pantuns* also start and end with the same line (though not 'Harmonie du soir'). This invites passing comparison with many of Ravel's mirrored gestures, like the major seventh clash that starts and ends *Jeux d'eau* or the figurations that start and close 'Ondine' or 'Le gibet', even the identical start and close of the Rigaudon in *Le tombeau de Couperin* and the finale of the Concerto in G.

Pantun structure has many musical resonances, not least the antiphones of its alternating strands of couplets. It also performs a graceful dance, each recycled line taking a new partner in the next stanza. 'Harmonie du soir' has the added resonances of its title and the poem's euphony of words and rhythm, including the cadential effect of its two rhyming end syllables, -*ige* and -*oir*. Small wonder that the poem inspired a song setting from Debussy as well as a piano Prelude (named after the poem's third line), both of which observe aspects of its *pantun* form.[1] Ravel would have been well aware of all this in 1914 when he headed the second movement of his Piano Trio 'Pantoum'. For decades Ravel's title was accepted without query, until Brian Newbould in 1975 illustrated how the movement follows a compositionally virtuosic two-strand *pantun* form.[2]

Our main interest here is in the way each consequent line of a *pantun* changes role to become an antecedent in the next stanza. Ravel shows a love of using this musically, exploiting ambiguities between antecedent and consequent to build up large-scale forms, while catching and holding our attention by letting the ambiguities surprise us. The basis of it is nicely illustrated by one of Poulenc's (and probably Ravel's) favourite anecdotes, according to which the hapless Benjamin Godard was overheard telling Emmanuel Chabrier, 'What a pity, *mon cher* Emmanuel, that you took up music so late', only to wilt under the retort 'An ever greater pity, *mon cher* Benjamin, that you took it up so early.'[3] Banal though it may seem to analyse such a squib, the structural nub is the way the consequent line ousts the initiating role of the antecedent, retrospectively stealing its thunder.

Le tombeau de Couperin

Composed after Ravel completed his Piano Trio, *Le tombeau de Couperin* teases us with a constant play on such elements, the suite's ostensibly classical outlines forming a fairly thin veil over its compositional sophistication. This emerges from the very start of the opening Prélude. Is its key E minor or G major? Bars 1 and 3 suggest the former, bars 2 and 4 the latter. The first-time repeat bars on the second page opt clearly for G major, making that the closing (consequent) key for the first time round and the opening (antecedent) key for the second time round; but the Prélude ends in a modal E minor, closing the circle with bar 1. The rest of *Le tombeau* – notably the opening page of the Toccata – plays on this dichotomy, resolving it only with the Toccata's final triumphant E major.

The metre of the Prélude plays the same game. If bars 1–2 (and again bars 3–4) follow a strong–weak or antecedent–consequent sequence, their apparent answer across bars 10–13 is more ambiguous. This is partly because bars 10–13 invert the textural order of bars 1–4, but mainly because the sequential sense has just been upset by the single bar 9. A sort of tag added to the already consequent bar 8, bar 9 leaves ambiguity about whether bar 10 (an apparent reprise of the consequent bar 2) is a consequent to the texturally dissimilar bar 9 or a new antecedent. Such ambiguities can be found throughout the suite, like the feint treble entry at bar 43 of the Fugue that makes the real entry a bar later sound like a consequent.

The suite's Menuet exploits similar ambiguities at several levels. At first glance its opening eight bars look like a harmless antecedent–consequent 4+4 sequence (Ex. 12.1a). In fact they reverse the classical norm by placing the full close before the modal half-close (bars 4 and 8). Ravel neatly follows through at the end of the Menuet's opening section (Ex. 12.1b), where the melody from bars 1–4, initially an antecedent, now returns as a consequent, the full close now in its 'proper' place. As the Menuet's recapitulation moves into the coda, Ravel gives this an extra nudge by continuing the opening melody over the transition (Ex. 12.1c), so that the original antecedent–consequent melodic trope now becomes consequent–antecedent, carrying the music gracefully into the coda. The transition is further disguised by the left hand starting its new figuration a bar early, on the weak or consequent bar 104.

Example 12.1. *Le Tombeau de Couperin*, Menuet

a: bars 1–8 (all grace notes start on the beat)

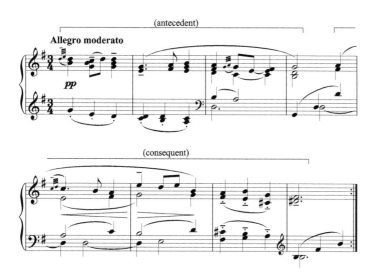

b: bars 29–32 (the repeat goes back to bar 9)

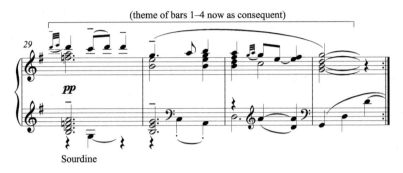

(theme of bars 1–4 now as consequent)

Sourdine

c: bars 101–6

consequent (ending the recap)   antecedent (starting the coda)

Sourdine

In between these, the piece's central Musette section starts from bar 33 with an eight-bar phrase repeated in ornamented form, another simple antecedent–consequent sequence. Ravel follows this through after the *ff* climax, as the Musette gives way to the return of the Menuet. Bars 65–72 recapitulate the Musette's opening eight bars as antecedent, followed by its repetition as a consequent from bar 73, the latter now changed to major mode while the Menuet's opening melody enters above it (Ex. 12.2a). The latter, normally an antecedent gesture, thus slips in under cover of a consequent. Bar 81, featuring the surprise transposition up a major third (Ex. 12.2b), thus manages to act simultaneously as a formal consequent (to the descant theme across bars 73–80) and an antecedent (following the same bars' tenor theme). Musically Ravel has obtained exactly the effect he wants, diverting our attention past the transition at bar 73 towards the surprise modulation at bar 81: we arrive there with a sense of impending recapitulation, only to discover we're already eight bars into it.[4]

Example 12.2. *Le tombeau de Couperin*, Menuet

a: bars 72–6

b: bars 79–82

The suite's Forlane applies this sort of play within the bar, opening with a first beat that can equally be heard as an upbeat to the second beat's accented dissonance (Ex. 12.3a). The phrasing and accentuation of the next seven bars maintain the ambiguity. As the movement nears its end, Ravel makes the point explicit by recapitulating the piece's opening beat as a notated anacrusis (Ex. 12.3b); in between he exploits the ambiguity in ways that constantly play with our expectations. His precedent is the Forlane from François Couperin's fourth *Concert royal*, which he used as something of a model. In Couperin's piece the strong beat sounds throughout on the half-bar, reversing the roles of antecedent and consequent beats within the bar (a quirk of notation from an era that paid less attention to barlines); Ravel's Forlane does this more selectively, making it explicit only through the first and second episodes (in E minor and B minor).

Example 12.3. *Le tombeau de Couperin,* Forlane

a: bars 1–5

b: bars 156–7 (numbering as in London Peters edition)[5]

Between the E minor and B minor episodes comes an abbreviated eight-bar ritornello, with one playful addition: halfway through it Ravel points up the metrical ambiguity by adding an imitative left-hand entry at the half-bar (just as Balakirev's *Islamey* does from the rhythmically similar bar 124). This means that whether we initially regarded the theme's opening beat as an upbeat or a main beat, we're now forced to hear it both ways. It also allows this short ritornello to be heard as continuing the offset sounding metre of the first episode (the strong beat on the half-bar), carrying it through to the second episode.

The second (B minor) episode develops the metrical play in two stages. Stage one is a hemiola by diminution (two sounding groups of $\frac{9}{8}$ in place of three of $\frac{6}{8}$), as shown in Example 12.4a, the effective metre indicated editorially above the system. Ravel's ploy lets the main sounding accent flirt momentarily with the barline then land gracefully back on the half-bar as before, just as we reach the first cadence. This decorative effect then becomes more structurally active as the episode yields to the final ritornello (Ex. 12.4b): the $\frac{9}{8}$ momentum now vaults the transition, reconciling with the barline one bar into the ritornello. The music can thereafter be heard either in $\frac{6}{8}$ (synchronous with the barline) or as continuing the $\frac{9}{8}$ momentum, at least up to and over the left hand's imitative entry three bars later.

Example 12.4. *Le tombeau de Couperin*, Forlane

a: bars 66–71 (the repeat goes back to bar 64)

b: bars 92–7

This ambiguity persists through the Forlane's final episode and coda, until the last seven bars effectively mark out four $\frac{9}{8}$ groups (Ex. 12.5), emphasized by the savoury modal contrast across bars 157–8 (whole-tone against octatonic). Ravel's calculated risk here emerges from an overall view of the piece. A rondo with two ternary episodes plus a binary third episode and coda, much of it repeated, the piece could easily appear – or sound – overlong. A closer look reveals how literally Ravel has offset his risks, relying on the performer's intelligence to catch the rhythmic play without exaggeration (doubtless why he left the metric notation simple).

Example 12.5. *Le tombeau de Couperin,* Forlane, bars 156–62

The Rigaudon leads us yet another dance, alternating phrases of varying lengths with its opening and closing two-bar cadential gesture. Everything sounds unpredictably irregular, and only a careful count reveals that the larger resulting bar groupings nonetheless manage to comprise multiples of sixteen or twelve. This effectively softens us up for the piece's central section (from bar 37), where the left and right hand take us off in two directions at once with different bar groupings. While the left hand marks out a relatively clear opening sequence of 4+4+8 bars, in the right hand the fourth bar doubles as antecedent to the fifth bar. (Any attempt to mark the fifth bar as a right-hand antecedent quickly makes this clear.) The section's fifth bar thus pits a right-hand consequent against a left-hand antecedent, the right hand meanwhile allowing no audible phrase break until eight bars later, when both hands metrically reunite to round off the sixteen-bar paragraph with a pair of hemiola-like $\frac{3}{4}$ groups (Ex. 12.6). The following sixteen bars again articulate the left hand 4+4+8, but differently again in the right hand, this time ending with two three-bar groups (bars 63–8, sounding as two $\frac{3}{4}$ groups then three $\frac{2}{4}$ ones). In each case it proves impossible to divide the first thirteen then ten bars (respectively) of right-hand phrasing into viable smaller groups, despite a few repeated rhythmic patterns inside the long phrases.

Example 12.6. *Le tombeau de Couperin*, Rigaudon, bars 48–53

From bar 69 (the larger consequent, or answering part of the piece's middle section), this phrase structuring is compressed, making up a 'sentence' of 3+2+3 bars (the last three bars articulated as one sounding group of $\frac{3}{4}$ plus two of $\frac{2}{8}$); this complex eight-bar sentence is then innocently reciprocated by a simple 4+4-bar group. A further eight bars (4+2+2) lead back into the reprise, virtually annexing the opening two bars of reprise in the process. Yet all this unpredictable variety makes up a central section of 16+16+16+16+8 bars – the most ostensibly innocent regularity imaginable, were it not for the rhythmic intrigue almost literally leaping around inside it.

'ALBORADA DEL GRACIOSO'

A related rhythmic play informs Ravel's 'Alborada del gracioso' of 1905, and helps explain an otherwise mysterious anecdote according to which Ravel once demonstrated to Maurice Delage how the piece's structure was 'as strict as that of a Bach fugue'.[6] The piece's first section opens out in three expanding paragraphs, bars 1–11, 12–29 and 30–70. As Example 12.7 shows, motive *a* begins the piece and almost immediately (in bar 5) forms an antecedent to the consequent motive *b*. Motive *b* then opens paragraph 2 as antecedent to the consequent *c*. Motive *c* accordingly opens paragraph 3 as antecedent to the consequent *d*. Motive *d* returns after the piece's central section, as an antecedent launching the recapitulation at bar 166. This enchanting surprise, after several bars that lead us to expect a regular reprise in D major, is therefore built absolutely logically into the sequence.

Example 12.7. 'Alborada del gracioso', motivic sequence

Paragraph 1:

motive *a* (antecedent), bars 1, 3 (5, 7)   motive *b* (consequent), bars 6, 8

Paragraph 2:

motive *b* (antecedent), bars 12, 13   motive *c* (consequent), bar 14

Paragraph 3:

motive *c* (antecedent), bars 31, 32   motive *d* (consequent), bars 33, 34

Recapitulation:

motive *d* (antecedent), bars 166, 167

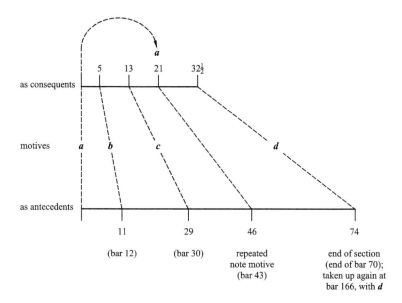

Figure 12.1. 'Alborada del gracioso', motivic appearances

Figure 12.1 shows the ingenious geometry of this sequence, closely related to what we saw in Chapter 5. Measured by constant completed units of $\frac{6}{8}$ (this varies slightly from bar totals because of some passages or bars in $\frac{6}{8}$ and $\frac{9}{8}$), the initial planting of motives as consequents (or as a structural close at bar 22) sets in motion a sequence of numbers (5, 8, 13 and 21) that follow the Fibonacci series already encountered in Chapter 5. The motives' return as antecedents then sets off the same proportional sequence on a larger scale, following the numbers of the related Lucas series (11, 18, 29, etc.). In this way the beginning of paragraph 3 at bar 30 divides the whole extract by golden section, as does the entry of the flamenco sub-episode at bar 43; the beginning of paragraph 2 at bar 12 marks a similar golden section (11:18 units) on the way to paragraph 3. As it progresses, the sequence is compressed from the theoretical Lucas numbers of 47 and 76 to an actual 46 and 74 (and from a theoretical 34 to 32½); far from invalidating the proportional logic, this makes dramatic sense to the piece's increasing urgency.[7] This proportional structure extends throughout the piece, and is even allowed for in Ravel's revised dimensions for the orchestral version; it also adds an interesting gloss to Ravel's reported childhood interest in mathematics.[8]

How characteristic this is of Ravel's thinking can also be seen by comparing it with 'Ondine'. Table 4.1 (p. 48) has already shown how motives *a'* and *a"* in 'Ondine' first appear as consequent offshoots of theme *a*, before returning as antecedents to launch new melodic waves. We begin to sense some of the ways in which Ravel, in 'Ondine', managed to spin out such a long, apparently seamless melody so resistant to cut-and-dried analysis. We can also better understand Ravel's reported remark to Maurice Delage, 'My *Trio* is finished. I only need the themes for it.'[9] What he meant becomes literally visible when we observe his small-scale melodic and rhythmic structuring, plus the large-scale architecture that then grows naturally out of it.

CHAPTER 13

RHYTHMIC GAMES IN CHABRIER

In Molière's *L'école des femmes*, the devious young Agnès utters the line 'Le petit chat est mort' to deflect her elderly husband's curiosity about what she had been up to all week while he was away. The line has become a standard practice range for French actors, inviting different inflections from varying stresses (Le petit chat est *mort*; Le petit chat *est* mort; Le pe*tit* chat est mort, even Le *pe*tit chat est mort). A musical equivalent of this is suggested by the opening of Chabrier's piano *Caprice*, the same trichord repeatedly subjected to different emphases and syncopations. A more humorous equivalent explodes from the opening orchestral wallops of his *Joyeuse marche* (Ex. 13.1). Originally composed to follow a peacefully lyrical *Prélude pastoral*, the piece's initial clog-stamp is startling enough (especially in the orchestral version), before the rhythmically offset repetitions buck us like a wilful horse. Chabrier's daring is clear if we imagine the second of the three cadences placed a banal eighth-note earlier; as it is, the effect of the metrical displacement can be read as shown above Example 13.1. (This matters in performance, for the impact is fatally weakened if the end of bar 2 is played like an upbeat.)

Example 13.1. *Joyeuse marche* **(solo piano version), bars 1–4 (effective metre shown above)**

THE *PIÈCES PITTORESQUES*

Chabrier's *Pièces pittoresques* are replete with such play, in ways that not only anticipate (and match) *Le tombeau de Couperin* but also bind the suite together, just as much as Debussy's Preludes are bound in tonal and modal terms.[1]

Rhythmic intrigue quickly emerges if we observe that the opening 'Paysage', a five-minute piece in clear ternary form, yields not a single unambiguous four-bar phrase. By contrast, the third piece of the set, 'Tourbillon', consists uniquely of four- and eight-bar groups (but with a few surprises inside). Between them comes 'Mélancolie', whose long bars initially form four-bar groups but can hardly be heard thus because of the constantly changing asymmetrical metres. (Only twice does the piece have consecutive bars in the same metre, and they occur within three-bar groups). 'Sous bois', after an opening four-bar feint, has outer sections mostly in six- and five-bar phrases, with just a few four-bar phrases tucked into the more compressed sequences at the middle of the piece. 'Mauresque', following it, disguises most of its eight-bar groups by subdividing them $3+3+2$. 'Idylle' opens with two distinctive five-bar phrases before letting four-bar phrasing take over. 'Danse villageoise' then launches itself with vigorous eleven-bar groups that appear to be indivisible; 'Improvisation' again starts with an eleven-bar paragraph. Finally, 'Menuet pompeux' and 'Scherzo-valse' relent by giving us predominantly four- or eight-bar phrasing in their outer sections, but these enclose episodes which either studiously avoid four-bar groups or play a sort of football with them.

Besides the inherent curiosity of all this, a closer look helps us in performance to deal with a few conundrums. In 'Paysage' the entire outer sections (structurally identical) can be counted in three-bar groups, the only doubt occurring at two apparent feints wittily embedded in the music's articulation. The first one comes with the curiously placed *rit.* and *a tempo* across bars 16–17 (Ex. 13.2), an effect one would generally expect a bar earlier. Like Example 13.1, the essence is humorous timing, momentarily leading us to expect an extension of the three-bar group from bar 13 to four bars – until bars 17–18 pull bar 16 into their fold, and the rug from under our feet. (The crucial point for pianists is to resist any – ANY – temptation to slow in bar 15.)

Example 13.2. 'Paysage', bars 13–18

A page or so later Chabrier follows through on a larger scale. This time the feint comes with an apparent two-bar phrase from bar 64, followed again by three-bar phrases as if nothing had happened (Ex. 13.3a), until a single extra bar acts as a link into the local recapitulation (Ex. 13.3b). This of course balances out the earlier ellipsis, allowing the overall sequence to maintain multiples of three. In fact, exactly how we read the bar grouping here depends – as in the central part of Ravel's Rigaudon from *Le tombeau de Couperin* – on which hand, or strand of the metrical counterpoint, we follow: if we read it through the left hand, the imitative bass line allows the whole passage to be felt in constant three-bar groups. (It might therefore be viewed as a large-scale version of the classical or Chopinesque rubato where the left hand keeps strict metre – in this case hypermetre – under an offset right hand.) Rather neatly, the 3+1-bar feint of Example 13.3b rhythmically echoes the 3+1-bar feint of Example 13.2 by ending with a bar of *ritenuto*.

Example 13.3. 'Paysage'

a: bars 64–8

b: bars 75–9

These levels of hypermetre bring perspective to Chabrier's tempo heading *Allegro non troppo, avec calme* (followed by ♩ = 132). Even if the musical sense might suggest easing the metronome mark back a notch, the resulting *allegro* is still vigorous enough to make '*non troppo, avec calme*' seem odd. Slowing below ♩ = 120 allows some immediate *calme*, but the musical line then sags.

Sense can emerge, however, if we read Chabrier's heading at a higher metric level and imagine the piece's outer sections notated in $\frac{3}{2}$, $\downarrow$ = c. 63: from that level a broader underlying minuet emerges, underpinning the lively surface and encouraging a gentle dance through the intermediate barlines. Chabrier's *calme* then comes into focus.

Once we imagine the music thus notated in $\frac{3}{2}$, the question naturally follows, how are these larger $\frac{3}{2}$ units grouped? If we might expect to see groups of four at this higher level, we are again thwarted by an initial clear structural grouping of the $\frac{3}{2}$ units as 5+5. Only after that does the music relax (or appear to) into fourfold groupings of $\frac{3}{2}$ units, across bars 31–78. This draws attention to the way the piece's outer sections each comprise their own smaller ternary form. Not only that, the central part of this ternary outer flank (bars 31–78 the first time round) even contains *its* own ternary sequence, giving the whole piece a sense almost like *matryoshka* dolls-within-dolls. (The piece's central section, as we'll see, is also in ternary form.) This is worth a closer look.

Bars 31 onwards make play of two alternated motives, a *scherzando* variant of the piece's opening theme plus the somewhat bluesy chromatic slide of Example 7.5a. For twenty-four bars the former motive acts as antecedent to the latter; for the next twelve bars they change positions (the reversal emphasized by *pressez* then *rall.* across bars 49–54), the former antecedent thus now acting as consequent and vice versa in a way already familiar from Chapter 12. The piece's opening theme then returns in the last of these twelve bars (bar 66 in Example 13.3a), starting the imitation across the hands already noted, with the added result that these last twelve (or thirteen) bars of imitation belong as much to the following reprise as to the section's central episode.

We may wonder why Chabrier didn't notate the piece in $\frac{3}{2}$. The most probable answer is that he decided on $\frac{2}{4}$ to show continuity into the piece's *Vivo* middle section, which takes up a different but equally methodical metric play, first of all with five- and six-bar phrases. These are alternated to make up two paragraphs each of twenty-two bars, the first one articulated 5+6+5+6, the second one 5+5+6+6. Each of these last 6+6 is further subdivided as 3+3, and at least the penultimate '3' group is further compressed into inverse hemiolas of sounding $\frac{3}{4}$. The final group is then wittily articulated as three bars of $\frac{2}{4}$ in the right hand but two units of $\frac{3}{4}$ in the left. (This makes fascinating comparison, both on paper and in sound, with bar 37 onwards of Ravel's Rigaudon.) 'Paysage' then completes its central section with fifteen bars divided 5+7+3, in a way that not only echoes the start of the section but also links neatly into the following three-bar phrases of the recapitulation.

With all that packed under an innocent-looking surface, it's easier to understand why Chabrier cast 'Paysage' in its apparently transparent ternary form:

the closing section, a more-or-less straight recapitulation of the opening section, lets us hear again, and digest a little more, all the sophistication inside.

'Mélancolie', following on the heels of 'Paysage', could hardly present a more contrasted surface, with its more fluid rubato, unhurried tempo, long bars and visibly complex metrical structure, plus the imitative voicing from bar 9 onwards. But is imitation across the hands not already familiar from 'Paysage'? It's not the only element. If we asked why Chabrier didn't notate 'Paysage' in $\frac{3}{2}$, the most immediate answer (continuity of metre through the whole piece) poses the reciprocal question of why 'Mélancolie' isn't notated in $\frac{3}{8}$. An immediate answer this time is that the longer bars better convey this piece's less dancing character and *legatissimo* phrases.

But let's imagine for a moment that Chabrier *had* notated the outer parts of 'Paysage' in $\frac{3}{2}$, and 'Mélancolie' in $\frac{3}{8}$; how do they compare? The answer is, astonishingly closely. The ♪ of 'Mélancolie' (at Chabrier's indicated ♪ = 80) moves only a little faster than the metrically corresponding ♩ of 'Paysage'. The first eight bars of 'Mélancolie' make up clear phrases that group the basic $\frac{3}{8}$ units in groups of five – just as happens with the opening hypermetric grouping of $\frac{3}{2}$ units in 'Paysage'. Bars 9–16 of 'Mélancolie' then modify that (with the interposed $\frac{9}{8}$ bars) so that the $\frac{3}{8}$ units now form groups of eight, again just as 'Paysage' does in its first episode . . .

Table 13.1 shows this graphically, and reveals how closely 'Mélancolie' echoes the metrical structure that directly preceded it, the closing (and opening) sections of 'Paysage'. Only the pieces' two different metrical indications disguise the resemblance, letting us wonder if it was an additional factor in Chabrier's decision to notate one piece in effective hypometre ($\frac{2}{4}$ instead of $\frac{3}{2}$) and the other in effective hypermetre ($\frac{9}{8}$ + $\frac{6}{8}$ instead of $\frac{3}{8}$). While the basic $\frac{3}{8}$ unit of 'Mélancolie' moves slightly faster than the equivalent $\frac{3}{2}$ unit of 'Paysage', this is neatly balanced by the way the proportions and dimensions of 'Mélancolie' form something of an augmentation to the outer parts of 'Paysage'. If Chabrier was aware of this relationship, his *avec calme* heading to 'Paysage' makes even more sense.

Table 13.1. Metrical comparison of 'Paysage' (outer sections) and 'Mélancolie'

'Paysage': outer sections (metrically identical), measured in hypermetric units of $\frac{3}{2}$		
5+5	4+4; 4+4	5+6
(each subdivided 2+3)	(the metric counterpoint across the hands affects the last 4)	
'Mélancolie', measured in hypometric units of $\frac{3}{8}$		
5+5+5+5 (each subdivided 3+2)	8+8 (each subdivided 3+3+2)	5+5

'Tourbillon' is a dramatic foil to all this, with its constant four- and eight-bar groups of $\frac{3}{4}$ metre. Within these, however, Chabrier creates some pleasing creative mayhem. The opening ritornello can equally be heard in $\frac{3}{2}$ hemiolas, contrasting with the first episode that emerges at bar 5, unambiguously in $\frac{3}{4}$. When the ritornello returns at bar 21 Chabrier adds a further squeeze, letting the second episode cut in a quarter-note early (bar 22 beat 3), setting off a new chain of hemiolas that completely defies the barlines (Ex. 13.4). The effect is similar to Example 13.1 except that here the offset momentum rampages for six bars until bar 28 closes the short paragraph by restoring the 'stolen' beat (like the single bar 78 of 'Paysage' in Example 13.3b). Bars 29–36 repeat the sequence, so that the sounding metrical sequence between bars 21 and 36 coincides with only three barlines en route. Yet all this rumbustious pandemonium fills two innocent-looking eight-bar groups – again like the internally unpredictable sixteen- or twelve-bar periods of Ravel's Rigaudon.

Example 13.4. 'Tourbillon', bars 21–8

The rhythmic makeup of the following transition (bars 37–48) makes it readable either in the printed $\frac{3}{4}$ metre or in hemiola $\frac{3}{2}$, preparing the way for the final ritornello from bar 73. This initially echoes the opening until an incursion of B♭s and a sudden swing into E♭ across bars 74–5 articulate a new layer of double hemiola in effective $\frac{3}{1}$ metre. Were 'Tourbillon' notated throughout in its sounding metre, the changes on the page would relate its appearance interestingly to 'Mélancolie'.

A telling Ravelian analogy comes at the start of the seventh *Pièce pittoresque*, 'Danse villageoise', a piece that Alfred Cortot specifically likened to the Rigaudon of *Le tombeau de Couperin*.[2] The piece launches itself with what initially feels like a four-bar start until bar 5, echoing bar 3, attaches itself to bar 4 in such a way as to make any real division impossible until the end of the eleven-bar period (like the first thirteen bars of the central part of Ravel's Rigaudon). Even in that tautly-knit sequence, the last four bars plus their upbeat neatly echo the opening, framing the undetachable three bars in the middle.

In the lyrical central episode of the ninth *Pièce pittoresque*, 'Menuet pompeux', a repeated figuration beamed across the barline (Ex. 13.5) betrays again that all is not exactly as the barlines would have it. This case involves an ingenious nesting of hemiolas readable in various ways: the interpretation shown above the system follows Chabrier's curious stemming, but an equally viable one shown underneath yields the entrancing effect across the extract (repeated in the following six bars) of four progressively compressed triple units, of $\frac{9}{4}$, $\frac{9}{8}$, $\frac{3}{4}$ and finally $\frac{3}{8}$. Chabrier's *rall. poco* across the last two bars delicately sets off the compression, whichever metric reading one opts for. His beaming later in this episode reveals more sequences of $\frac{3}{8}$ within – and sometimes offset from – the printed $\frac{3}{4}$ barring. Ravel's special affection for 'Menuet pompeux' is evident not only from Chapter 7 but also from his orchestration of the piece: his majestic treatment of the outer sections prompts our imagination at the piano, where Chabrier's writing is near the limits of what two hands can do.

Example 13.5. 'Menuet pompeux', bars 61–6

To round off the *Pièces pittoresques*, 'Scherzo-valse' revisits various of the metrical ruses just seen. A rondo with two episodes (in D and B♭), its outer sections maintain a rollicking continuity of four-bar phrases, setting off contrasted games in the two episodes. The first episode (an ingenious four-part structure that exploits binary form on several simultaneous levels) steps just slightly outside the circle with an initial sequence of 4+4+5 bars, repeats the process, then continues with four-bar phrases ('as if nothing had happened') until the lead back into the ritornello, a page later, answers with a compensatory sequence of 4+3.

The B♭ episode (in itself a ternary form) indulges something of a last metrical fling before the cycle ends. The matched outer parts of this episode each comprise twenty-four bars, divided into three six-bar phrases (hypermetric units of $\frac{18}{8}$); the central part does the same. Internal contrast comes from the way the episode's outer parts subdivide those hypermetric $\frac{18}{8}$ units into $\frac{6}{8}$ groups, whereas the central core subdivides them into $\frac{9}{8}$ groups. If we imagine this notated in (first-level) hypermetre of $\frac{6}{8}$ and $\frac{9}{8}$, its rhythmic relationship to 'Mélancolie' suddenly becomes visible.

Compare that with the ritornello's $\frac{9}{16}$ metre, and constant variety emerges. From the smallest units ($\flat$) upwards the ritornelli are articulated 3×3×4 (or 3×3×2×2 if we count the sub-articulation of the bars in pairs), while the B♭ episode is articulated (counting from the basic ♪ unit upwards) partly 3×2×3 and partly 3×3×2, the latter a direct augmentation of the ritornello's paired $\frac{9}{16}$ bars. In sum, nothing in this piece is quite as simple as appears on the surface. It's tempting to speculate that this sort of reciprocal yet ever-playful and ever-varied orderliness reflects something of Chabrier's years at the Ministère de l'Intérieur, where his tasks of organizing and classifying (for which he was highly regarded) perhaps mingled creatively with the music forming in his mind.

The picturesque titles of the *Pièces pittoresques* reflect publishing fashion of the time: not part of Chabrier's original conception, they were added at the behest of a publisher who at first could make so little sense of 'Idylle' that he had to be pressed hard to publish it. Forty years later, fashion might have let them be titled *Études de rythme* (they can equally be regarded as *études* in much else). Chabrier's ingenuity, though, is so unpredictable as to defy the sort of classification such a title might demand. All the same, viewing the *Pièces pittoresques* through such an alternative perspective is a useful antidote for anodyne postcard interpretation – the problem that has equally dogged Debussy's Preludes despite his placing of titles *after* the pieces.

More analogies offer themselves with Debussy – with the hidden $\frac{4}{4}$ patterns in the Menuet of the *Suite bergamasque* or, on a larger scale, with *L'isle joyeuse*, whose hidden continuity of hypermetre we glimpsed in Chapters 4 and 5. If Chabrier's larger-scale proportions reveal no sign of recondite proportions like golden section, the way he (and Ravel) visibly build overall forms from smaller-scale metre nonetheless follows similar logic.[3]

Chabrier was also an habitué of Parnassian literary circles (who took up structures like *pantun* with such gusto) and, like the younger Debussy, of Symbolist groups that frequented the Chat Noir. His writer friend Maurice Rollinat (the 'singing poet' of the Chat Noir) appears to have been one of the Hydropathe group influenced by Charles Henry's mathematical-cum-aesthetic theories, and Chabrier's social habits leave every chance (though no documentation remains) that he had contact with it. His song setting of Rollinat's poem *Tes yeux bleus*, with its undercurrent of $\frac{6}{8}$ across its slow $\frac{3}{4}$ metre, is the clearest precedent for the same combination in the *Adagio* of Ravel's Concerto in G.

A direct musical link can also be drawn to Fauré (Chabrier's friend and Ravel's teacher), some of whose early chamber music shows hypermetre deployed with extreme wit and sophistication: the curious $\frac{1}{4}$ barring in the scherzo of his First Violin Sonata op. 13 hides systematic alternations of $\frac{2}{4}$ and $\frac{3}{4}$ pitted against longer $\frac{3}{4}$ sequences, and the scherzo of his First Piano Quartet op. 15 methodically groups the $\frac{6}{8}$ bars in threes and fours to produce larger patterns of $\frac{18}{8}$ against $\frac{24}{8}$.

Table 13.2 sums up some of the creative metrical organization and contrasts packed into Chabrier's *Pièces pittoresques*, showing them in order of most visible comparison across pieces. (The table is intended more for leisurely exploration at the piano than for digestion at a single sitting. Again, if its listings might appear laborious on paper, the associated effects assure constant musical variety and freshness.) It's some measure of Chabrier's professionalism that – as with Debussy's golden sections or any other hidden structuring – he buried all this virtuoso intrigue under the clearest possible instructions for the player, letting the hidden sophistication work for itself.

Table 13.2. Selected metric, hypometric and hypermetric games in the *Pièces pittoresques*

'Paysage': outer sections (structurally identical), hypermetric units of $\frac{3}{2}$		
2+3; 2+3	4+4; 4+4 (the last 4-group contains the imitation across the hands)	2+3; 2+4

'Mélancolie', entire piece, hypometric units of $\frac{3}{8}$		
3+2; 3+2; 3+2; 3+2	8 + 8 (3+3+2; 3+3+2) (this section starts the imitation across the hands)	3+2; 3+2

'Paysage': central section, bars of $\frac{2}{4}$		
5 + 6 + 5 + 6	5 + 5 + 6 + 6 (the last 12 subdivided 2+2+2 + 1½+1½+1½+1½)	5 + 5 + 5 (or 5; 5+2; 3)

'Sous bois', modified ternary form (bar groups always include the previous upbeat)		
(4); 6+5; 6+6; 5+5; 5+4	4+4; 4+4	5+5; 7+5; 1+7+1+3; 4+4+4 (disguising a closing symmetry of 12+12+12)

This reads the transition into the central section through the bass; the imitation across the hands from bar 46 makes it also readable through the right hand as 4½+4½, or 4+5 (going by his *poco rit.* and double bar)

'Mauresque', modified ternary form (with repeat of last 2 sections); bars of $\frac{3}{4}$

(2); 3+3+2; 3+3+2 (the 3-bar groups internally asymmetric, primarily divided as 2+3+4 beats)	6+2; 2+2+2+2 (containing varied hemiolas by augmentation and diminution)	3+3+2, then a repeat from the central section onwards that extends the recap to 3+3+4+4

The recapitulation is masked by melodic continuity from a bar earlier (bar 34) with a degree of hemiola over the barline

---

bars 21–28 (and 29–36) of 'Tourbillon', ♩ units

2+2+1; 2+2+2; 2+2+2; 2+2+3
only the final group of 3 tallies with the barlines

Scherzo-valse:

ritornelli: 8-bar groups of $\frac{9}{16}$ (♪ × 3 × 3 × 2 × 4)

comparative metric organization of ternary second episode:

♪ × 3 × 2 × 3 × 4 (repeated)	♪ × 3 × 3 × 2 × 4 (augmentation of ritornellos)	♪ × 3 × 2 × 3 × 4

ternary first episode, $\frac{9}{16}$ bars: 4 + **4** + *4+1* (all repeated); 16+16+8;
4 + **4+4** + *4+3*
(Bold and italic type show passages that are extended in the recapitulation)

CHAPTER 14

REPERTOIRE DISCOVERIES
(AND A FEW MYSTERIES)

SOMETIMES a hitherto unknown piece emerges from a sale, attic or archive, or a long-inaccessible one finally becomes available. Most of these merit exploration as unusual and worthwhile repertoire. All the Debussy items figure in the *Œuvres complètes*: his *Nachlass*, much the largest of our four main composers, is most easily dealt with here in semi-tabular form.

DEBUSSY

In 2001 a manuscript copy of an *Intermède* was discovered, constituting a solo version of the 'Scherzo–Intermezzo' movement from Debussy's Piano Trio of 1880. In the hand of the pianist Maurice Dumesnil, it initially raised a query of whether it might be a copy of an original Debussy solo version now lost. Although it was later identified as a transcription by Dumesnil, it retains interest as a thoroughly viable solo piano version of some remarkable early Debussy, arranged by a skilful pianist who had worked with Debussy. In the same key (B minor) as *Danse bohémienne* of 1880, this version appears as an appendix in *Œuvres complètes* 1/4.[1]

Images of early 1894: long known to exist, these three pieces were published in 1977 by Theodore Presser as *Images (oubliées)*. They survive in a fair copy dedicated by Debussy to Yvonne Lerolle, adolescent daughter of the painter Henry Lerolle, niece of Chausson and piano pupil of Cortot (who later acquired the manuscript from her). The middle piece, an early version of the Sarabande in *Pour le piano*, was published by itself in a Parisian journal in 1896. The third piece is thematically related to Debussy's String Quartet (as well as to the start of Debussy's later uncompleted opera on Edgar Allan Poe's

Fall of the House of Usher) and shares its second theme (the children's song 'Nous n'irons plus au bois', 'We'll go no more to the woods') with several Debussy pieces including 'Jardins sous la pluie'. The haunting first piece has affinities with the Passepied from *Suite bergamasque*, *Prélude à l'après-midi d'un faune* (an opening flute-like melody punctuated by arpeggios), and ends very much like 'La soirée dans Grenade' and Act 1 of *Pelléas et Mélisande*. Already 'first vintage' instrumental Debussy along with his String Quartet and the *Faune*, this remarkable suite merits a full place in the repertoire.

Regarding *Lindaraja* for two pianos, see page 140.

Morceau de concours, forgotten until the 1970s (published by Durand in 1980), was Debussy's contribution to a spot-the-composer contest in the January 1905 issue of the magazine *Musica*. (The winner's prize was a piano.) Debussy's short, wittily ragtime-like piece uses material – probably part of the planned overture – from his unfinished sketches for an operetta on Poe's *The Devil in the Belfry*.

Étude retrouvée (1914–15; the title is editorial): discovered in 1976 and published in 1980 (Theodore Presser), in facsimile along with a performing realization. Headed 'Pour les arpèges composés', the manuscript presents a completely drafted but incompletely filled-in alternative version of that *Étude*, written on the same type of paper as the drafts of the other *Études* (reproduced in the Minkoff facsimile edition). The unusual fact that Debussy preserved it suggests he may have contemplated it for later use elsewhere, an idea thwarted by the collapse of his health. In the same key as the published 'Pour les arpèges composés' but otherwise entirely different, it can be of practical use in recitals featuring the complete *Études*: placed between Books 1 and 2 it provides contrast between 'Pour les huit doigts' and the similarly paced 'Pour les degrés chromatiques'.

Pour Le Vêtement du blessé (spring 1915): published in 1933 as *Page d'album* (Theodore Presser, reissued in urtext form in 1980). Debussy reportedly played this specially written short waltz at a fundraising concert for 'Le Vêtement du blessé' (Dressing the wounded), a war charity supported by his wife Emma. Like *La plus que lente* it plays repeatedly on its opening cadence and humorously takes a few deliberate wrong turns just before the end.

Élégie (December 1915): published in manuscript facsimile in a 1916 war-relief publication (*Pages inédites sur la femme et la guerre*), rediscovered in the 1970s (republished in 1978 by Éditions Jobert but slightly more accurately in

Œuvres complètes 1/4); until 2001 it was thought to be Debussy's last piano piece. Its D minor tenor melody suggests overflow from the Cello Sonata of summer 1915.

"*Les soirs illuminés par l'ardeur du charbon*" (early 1917): discovered in 2001, published in 2003 (Durand). This neat manuscript served as a gesture of thanks, possibly payment, to Debussy's coal merchant Monsieur Tronquin, who had diverted scarce fuel supplies to the Debussy household during a harsh wartime winter.[2] Debussy, seriously ill at the time, was just completing his Violin Sonata, whose outer movements share with this piece the curious metronome marking 55, the age Debussy turned in 1917 (and at which he died in March 1918). The title ('Evenings lit by glowing coal') is a repeated line in Baudelaire's poem 'Le balcon', set by Debussy in the late 1880s as the first of the *Cinq poèmes de Charles Baudelaire*. The piano piece opens with the same phrase as Debussy's other Baudelaire-titled piece, the prelude "*Les sons et les parfums tournent dans l'air du soir*". Along with brief echoes of a few other preludes, bars 5 and 17 sound a characteristic rhythm from the second interlude in Act 1 of *Pelléas et Mélisande*.

A dispersed *Suite bergamasque* of 1903 – quite distinct from the familiar *Suite bergamasque* of 1890 – is a different kind of discovery, putting a new complexion on pieces already known. According to adverts by the publisher Eugène Fromont, *Masques* and *L'isle joyeuse* (then spelt 'L'Ile joyeuse') were originally intended as the outer pieces of a three-movement *Suite bergamasque*, a suite already under way by summer 1903 when Debussy played parts of it through to Viñes, before playing him the whole suite on 2 January 1904.[3]

Fromont's announcement names the middle piece as '2e Sarabande', a title that might seem to point to the then-unpublished 'Hommage à Rameau'. By July 1903, however, Debussy had allocated 'Hommage à Rameau' to his piano *Images*,[4] so by January 1904 he must have had another piece in mind. As it happens, in that same month he completed *D'un cahier d'esquisses*, which appeared a month later in the magazine *Paris illustré*. The piece makes an astonishingly effective prologue to *L'isle joyeuse*: compare for example its cadenza and closing motive with the identical left-thumb ostinato in the coda of *L'isle joyeuse* (Ex. 7.17). One can even play directly from *D'un cahier d'esquisses* into *L'isle joyeuse* without any need to change the pedal. It feels almost like watching the glass shoe slip onto Cinderella's foot: the opening *quasi-cadenza* to *L'isle joyeuse* suddenly makes complete sense.

No solid evidence survives of why the pieces were not published together. Debussy had sent *D'un cahier d'esquisses* to Manzi (the publisher of *Paris illustré*) in response to a request for pieces that had the character of musical sketches.[5] Since Debussy at that time tended to write piano pieces only in suites, he probably took advantage of what was at hand, perhaps hoping that a magazine publication would help publicize the new suite. Indeed the title *D'un cahier d'esquisses* – literally 'from a sketchbook' – can equally be translated as 'work in progress' or even 'watch this space'; it might have been intended as provisional at that stage. Manzi, however, passed *D'un cahier d'esquisses* on to the Brussels publisher Schott, who published it just before the Paris publisher Durand persuaded Debussy to sell him *Masques* and *L'isle joyeuse* (which Debussy revised over summer 1904). By then his life was in some disarray following his elopement with Emma Bardac to Jersey (his own *isle joyeuse*, perhaps one more reason for that added 's' in *isle*). Meanwhile, for legal reasons beyond his control, Debussy was obliged to give Fromont publication rights for his old four-movement *Suite bergamasque* of 1890 – thus losing that title for his new suite. It may be that, amidst all the upheaval, a mundane conflict of publishers simply peeled one piece away from its companions.[6]

Masques and *L'isle joyeuse* remained something of a pair (Viñes premièred them together in February 1905), and show this structurally. Despite their contrasted moods, bars 1–4 of *Masques* mark out a similar rhythm to bar 7 of *L'isle joyeuse*, where rhythmic articulation takes over from the piece's opening *quasi-cadenza*. Table 14.1 juxtaposes the two pieces' dimensions accordingly: after a series of constantly twinned transitions, the darkly turbulent *Masques* closes at exactly the equivalent point where the extrovert *L'isle joyeuse* opens out into its triumphant coda (Ex. 7.17).

Two important tempo corrections are involved. The implausibly fast ♩. = 104 printed in early editions of *Masques* is undoubtedly an error (as discussed in the *Œuvres complètes*): in practice the piece demands a tempo roughly matching the quarter-note beat of *L'isle joyeuse*. Conversely, the *très lent* heading of *D'un cahier d'esquisses* is probably an erroneous transposition of an indication meant for the last page: the opening (Ex. 20.1) responds naturally to a more flowing barcarolle tempo which then makes it possible to follow the indicated ♩. = ♩ equivalence into the piece's final ⁶₄ section.

If no documentation survives to explain exactly what happened in 1904, adopting *D'un cahier d'esquisses* as a central piece solves three practical problems at once: the incomplete-seeming context of *L'isle joyeuse* on its own, the lack of key and tempo contrast between *Masques* and *L'isle joyeuse*, and the relative neglect of *Masques* and *D'un cahier d'esquisses*. It also answers most of the historical questions and yields a triptych of comparable strength to the first series of *Images*, perhaps even to *La mer*. Even playing *D'un cahier d'esquisses* and *L'isle joyeuse* in sequence produces an effortlessly integrated entity well beyond the sum of the parts.

Table 14.1. Structural comparison of Debussy's *Masques* and *L'isle joyeuse*

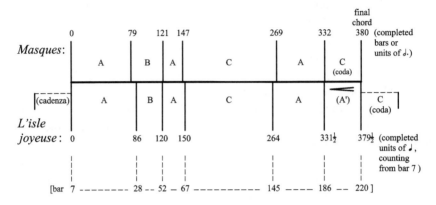

A triptych of 1891? This is less certain again, but worth consideration for programming. In 1891 the publisher Choudens issued Debussy's *Tarentelle styrienne, Ballade slave* and *Valse romantique* (a later edition of 1903 retitled the first two pieces *Danse* and *Ballade*) separately but all with the same title page, which lists them as *Pièces pour piano* nos. 1–3.[7] Though not explicitly a suite, they make an apt set (note the neatly matched original titles); *Valse romantique* again emerges more strongly as a finale. Scathing though Debussy later was about some of his early pieces – few composers are indulgent on that front – he took the trouble to revise these three pieces carefully before their 1903 republication. He could also sometimes be surprised: Paul Loyonnet reports playing him the Passepied from his *Suite bergamasque* in 1917, prompting Debussy's reaction, 'I had no idea it was so attractive!'[8]

FAURÉ

A long life, plus a carefully planned bonfire a few weeks before it ended, ensured that most of what Fauré wanted to survive went into print under his eyes. A shorter early form of the first of the *Pièces brèves* – written as a Conservatoire sight-reading test in 1899 and printed as an appendix in the Peters edition – prompts appreciation of what Fauré later grafted onto it, not least the gently spine-tingling modulations of bars 19–24. Some of his earliest pieces, from years when he had no publisher, were later revised and incorporated in the *Pièces brèves* (the two fugues) and the late Watteau-based ballet *Masques et bergamasques* (see p. 155). Durand published four movements of the latter in Fauré's piano duet version (Ouverture, Menuet, Gavotte and Pastorale). If this ordering makes for a rather weak concert ending (the

Pastorale was not intended to end the *spectacle*), a mundane reason is that some numbers in the ballet belonged to a different publisher. With ingenuity and the help of one or more singers, the original sequence can even be reconstructed, as Ouverture, Pastorale, the choral *Madrigal* (op. 35), the song *Le plus doux chemin* (op. 87 no. 1), Menuet, the song *Clair de lune* (op. 46 no. 2), Gavotte, and finally the op. 50 *Pavane*.[9]

A hidden gem of the repertoire is Fauré's original duet version of the 'Air de danse' from his 1888 incidental music (op. 52) to the play *Caligula* by Dumas *père*: at present (2009) it can still be found only in the original *Caligula* vocal score. The piece became a favourite of Fauré's son Philippe, for whom Fauré wrote a brief but lucid analysis of it, quoted in *Gabriel Fauré: His Life through his Letters*, pp. 260–2. Devotees can also seek out a brief *Prélude* for solo piano that Fauré contributed to a collection of *Études d'octaves* compiled by Isidor Philipp in 1897, plus Fauré's own piano duet transcription of the Andante from his String Quartet op. 121 (to which Cortot added a matching duet transcription of the Quartet's outer movements).

RAVEL

Arbie Orenstein's access in the early 1970s to the Ravel manuscript archives allowed several publications by Editions Salabert in 1975, notably of the *Sérénade grotesque* and two-piano *Sites auriculaires* (whose Habanera Ravel slightly revised for the later *Rapsodie espagnole*), plus Ravel's duet version of his early *Shéhérazade* overture. One idea from *Sérénade grotesque* (bars 35–40) returns in 'Alborada del gracioso' (from bar 6); the manuscript facsimile of the *Sérénade* published as Plate 19 in Orenstein's *Ravel, Man and Musician* also suggests that the top note in bar 11 is probably a badly written *b″* rather than the printed *g″*. Still unpublished for copyright reasons (but performed in recent decades by many who have hand-copied it) is a short but appealing menuet-like piece that Ravel wrote out for his student Maurice Delage. Perhaps once intended for his *Sonatine*, its main curiosity is its odd phrase structure of 8+8+7 bars, requiring some skill at the end to avoid either a sudden 'lights-out' effect or a stylistically gauche rallentando. (Some missing accidentals also have to be assumed, notably a few ♮s to D.)

Untraced since its sale at auction in 1977 is Ravel's last known piece of solo piano writing. Probably intended for orchestration, it comprises connecting passages between the existing *Pavane pour une Infante défunte*, 'Alborada del gracioso' and *Rapsodie espagnole* to make up a continuous ballet suite, *Le portrait de l'Infante* (or alternatively *L'Infante rose*), commissioned in 1923 by the dancer Sonia Pavlov, to a Madrid-based scenario by Henry Malherbe. Publication (which Ravel never intended) would have been problematic because of the pieces' different publishers; at present this *olla podrida* (*potpourri*), as Ravel called it, exists only as a tantalizing shadow.[10]

CHABRIER

Chabrier's main piano *Nachlass* was issued as *Cinq pièces* in 1897, three years after his death, by the same publisher (Enoch) who had refused at least two of them while Chabrier was alive. Far from being a set, they have varied origins. *Ronde champêtre*, whose main theme comes from his early *buffo* operetta *Fisch-Ton-Kan*, was initially meant for the *Pièces pittoresques*. *Aubade* of early 1883 (just after Chabrier's return from Spain) might be taken as a companion piece for *Habanera*. *Ballabile* and *Caprice* form a pair (sketches for both appear on the same sheet of paper), probably the two sight-reading test pieces (heaven help the candidates) that Chabrier wrote for the Bordeaux Conservatoire in 1889. Their ingenious derivation from the same simple scalic trichord (see Ex. 7.2) embraces the remaining posthumous piece, *Feuillet d'album*, suggesting that the three pieces may have been intended as a set or part of a larger collection.

A sad note is the passionate but incomplete *Capriccio* of 1883: its 1914 publication (completed by Maurice Le Boucher with a disappointingly verbatim recapitulation) gives no indication of where the now unlocated manuscript tails off: in 1960 Le Boucher recalled (in a letter to Roger Delage) that his contribution made up roughly the second half. The piece was omitted from the Dover edition for copyright reasons but has subsequently appeared from other reprint houses.

(A FEW) OTHER COMPOSERS

This could fill a book. Still little-known repertoire ranges from the best of Gounod (well suited to the less virtuoso, and sometimes with Fauré-like modal sophistication) via the light touch of Delibes and Massenet to the more rigorous yet still atmospheric Roussel, Dukas (arguably rigorous only at the piano) and Magnard. Debussy thought highly of Dukas's Piano Sonata, and the Passepied of his *Suite bergamasque* suggests that he enjoyed the Passepied in Delibes's incidental music for *Le Roi s'amuse* (long available in piano transcription). *Nachlass* is something of a Satie speciality thanks to his penchant for leaving manuscripts in disused jacket pockets or letting them drop behind pianos; most of it is known to Satie adepts and fairly easily found. Besides his famous duet *Jeux d'enfants*, Bizet's main piano offering is the *Variations chromatiques* of 1868, based on a rising and falling chromatic octave, an idea that arguably echoes in the rising and falling octaves that frame Fauré's *Thème et variations.*

Something of a sibling to both Debussy's *Children's Corner* and Fauré's *Dolly* can be found in André Caplet's piano duets *Pour les enfants bien sages: un tas de petites choses.* Although published only in 1925 (by Durand), the suite's opening Berceuse existed as early as 1909 as a gallant offering for Chouchou Debussy, aged 'three years and eight months', to play with her father.[11] (As we'll see in Chapter 21, she may well have been able to.) In a quietly dextrous *tour de force* Caplet restricts the primo part of each piece to the pentachord C–D–E–F–G, hands in unison, blending with sophisticated secondo parts *pour le professeur* in keys ranging from D♭ major to B major. The overall effect is sophisticated and brilliant.

An enjoyable education in French children's songs can be had from the six piano duet volumes of D.-E. Inghelbrecht's *La Nursery* (again reflecting his Musorgskophilia). Debussy also thought highly of Déodat de Séverac, whose suites *En Languedoc* and *Cerdaña* emulate Albéniz in technical challenge and sometimes in discursiveness: the scintillating 'En tartane' that opens *Cerdaña* can confidently stand alongside anything in the repertoire. Séverac's children's suite *En vacances*, with its endearing 'Boîte à musique' in the tradition of Gounod's *Les pifferari*, would probably enjoy more enduring fame had Séverac remembered that children have small hands. Long out of print but worth the search is the choral-sounding *Le petit chat est mort* by Séverac's friend René de Castéra, a wistfully tender exploration of a stock phrase (see the start of Chapter 13).

PART 4

AT THE KEYBOARD

CHAPTER 15

What do we interpret?

Jackets must be worn – sign in smart London restaurant

Dogs must be carried – sign on London Underground escalators

AT the start of his prelude 'Des pas sur la neige' Debussy pampers us with instructions: the evocative heading *Triste et lent* is amplified with a metronome marking plus a comment under the left-hand ostinato, '*(Ce rythme doit avoir la valeur sonore d'un fond de paysage triste et glacé)*'.[1] Even the parentheses are a nuance in themselves, conveying an added aura of intimacy. Six years earlier, for the central episode of *L'isle joyeuse*, Debussy stipulated (♪ = ♪) then qualified it with *un peu cédé* plus *molto rubato* and, above the bass arpeggios, *ondoyant et expressif*. Amid all that we can picture him thinking 'well, more or less' or 'but nevertheless' – if not 'how does one explain all this?' Meanwhile Ravel, at the most intense and hushed moment of 'Le gibet' (bar 28), laconically instructs *sans expression*.

What does all this tell us? Debussy's appeal to our imagination and feeling reflects that musical notation itself consists of *des pas sur la neige*, ink marks where the composer's inspiration passed. Like a recipe book, notation instructs us in two ways, either by telling us exactly what to do or by defining the desired result. The former method is prescriptive, like instrumental tablature (or fingering), the latter descriptive, like open staff notation. If Debussy's descriptive exhortations are aimed at our sensibility, Ravel's *sans expression* is a clever prescriptive ruse to deter us from botching the inbuilt expression by emoting. Both approaches can be seen as their ways of idiot-proofing their beloved creations – or, to put it more kindly, of communicating with us, the unknown performer. Most composers' scores show a mix of prescriptive and descriptive indications that reveal much about how they ticked – not least by suggesting how they expect *us* to tick.

Despite their contrasts of approach, Debussy and Ravel are both on record as imploring performers to pay close attention to all their markings: Ravel's colleagues repeatedly quoted his pleas to 'play my music, not interpret it'.[2] We can even argue that music *per se* can't be 'interpreted' without distorting it. What we can't help interpreting is musical notation, with all its symbols and their varied meanings in different countries and eras. In that context Ravel's *sans expression* is obviously calculated in relation to his assumption of the performer's training and musical sense.

Debussy's descriptive habits echo his literary and Symbolist tastes (he doubtless savoured the multiple echoes of titles like 'Des pas sur la neige'). The opening bars of his *Image* 'Cloches à travers les feuilles', luxuriantly spread over three staves, primarily show the music's polyphonic lines, leaving us to sort out which hand plays what (mostly a matter of common sense). This sybaritic three-stave notation runs through his second series of *Images* and second book of Preludes, even where the music doesn't need it (editions of the latter work omit some of the unused staves). Indeed, Debussy's manuscript of the first four preludes in Book 2 brackets *four* staves to a system, though the music never uses more than three at a time. While this delicious extravagance never reached print, it helps set the evocative scene, part of Debussy's mania for visual presentation. Once we're aware of this, it encourages us to play as if we're reading from a *particelle*, the sort of 'short score' in which Debussy always drafted his orchestral works.

Even pedalling tempts Debussy to luxuriant description. *Quittez, en laissant vibrer* ('let go and leave to resonate on the pedal'), he enjoins us at the tied-over notes in bar 2 of 'Les collines d'Anacapri' – doubtless aware that were the pedal not already down, now is a bit late to be telling us. The prescriptive equivalent – a simple *Ped.* ✳ across bars 1–2 – would theoretically do the job (we can read Debussy's comma at the end of bar 2 as his release sign), but might prompt us less to listen for what is obviously delighting his imagination, the lingering resonance of distant bells, maybe on the goats that give Capri its name. Apart from anything else, the way we listen to bar 2 bears vitally on how we practise and play bar 1.

By contrast, Fauré's prescriptive pedalling sometimes appears overly laconic, just confirming where the pedal absolutely needs to be down. This is most obvious from the sparse pedal markings in his song *Prison* (he can't possibly mean no similar pedal in the surrounding bars). In the first of his *Romances sans paroles* op. 17, in bars 39–46 his pedal markings are an equivalent minimum to ensure legato over the left-hand leaps from beat 2 to beat 3. (Experiment quickly suggests that the pedal sometimes needs to go down as much as a beat earlier to avoid disparity of resonance in the melody, and is often best not released too audibly where marked.) Like Debussy's evocative prose in 'Les collines d'Anacapri', Fauré's markings count on our intelligence for integrating specified cases into surrounding tacit norms.

TEMPO

A shared characteristic among our composers is that – like Chopin – they unanimously regarded sloppy rhythm or abuse of rubato as anathema. French music can be seen, sometimes amusingly, defending itself against the progressive incursion over the years of the Germanic expressive rallentando: when Debussy wants no slowing he mostly leaves it unmentioned; Ravel, thirteen years younger, forestalls it by writing *sans ralentir;* for Poulenc, a generation later, this regularly becomes *surtout* [above all] *sans ralentir.*

This bears on Debussy's and Ravel's contrasted notation for hemiola contexts: compare Example 15.1 (the time signatures above the system are Debussy's) with Examples 12.4 and 12.5. If Debussy's meticulously descriptive notation guards against misaccentuation, it leaves a risk of slowing and disrupting the descant ostinato across bars 14–15. Ravel's laconically continuous $\frac{2}{4}$ metre guards against slowing but at the price of risking misaccentuation, as can be heard on plenty of recordings. Neither notation can be foolproof, and we can see each composer appealing to our intelligence to complete the sense.

Example 15.1. Debussy, 'Feuilles mortes', bars 11–15

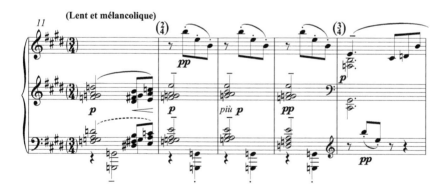

Not that our composers were exclusive about notational tools. Debussy neatly conveys hemiolas in *L'isle joyeuse* and the Prélude of *Pour le piano* by beaming across the barlines. Other prescriptive ruses in his armoury include the alternating accents and staccato dots in 'General Lavine – excentric' which automatically ensure a degree of ragtime swing at bars 51 and 63 (Ex. 17.3a), and again in parts of the *Étude* 'Pour les notes répétées'.

One curious notation by Fauré suggests a craftily prescriptive ruse. In the Tenth Nocturne his key change from E major to E minor, printed at the end of bar 66, would appear to make better sense after bar 67 (avoiding the need for most of the accidentals in bar 67). Were it placed there, though, its coincidence with the cadence point could easily tempt players into Fauré's *bête noire* of slowing. Fauré neatly averts the hazard by moving the double bar forward to mid-phrase, the musical equivalent of between the diving board and the water.

Several apparent oddities make sense once we become accustomed to Debussy's descriptive habits. A notorious one is the indication *Le double plus lent* in old editions eight bars from the end of the Toccata in *Pour le piano*, where all musical sense suggests maintaining the quarter-note pulse unchanged. The indication makes some sense if read as descriptive confirmation of an augmentation already written in ('yes, the motive here *is* meant to be twice as slow this time' – actually four times as slow). Debussy later became aware of the danger of its being read prescriptively, and told Marguerite Long to ignore it.[3] A similar case appears on the penultimate page of his song 'Chevaux de bois'.

This intriguingly mirrors 'La Cathédrale engloutie'. Debussy's piano roll recording of the piece (of which more in Chapter 21) plays the half-notes through bars 7–12 and 22–83 at the same sounding speed as the quarter-notes in the rest of the piece, a relationship not explicitly shown in the score but which results in a sounding continuity of triple time. This equivalence makes it much easier (indeed, possible) to establish and maintain a steady tempo through the piece, and is corroborated by several people who heard Debussy play the piece, on recordings by some of his associates, by an orchestration of the piece by Henri Busser that Debussy reportedly supervised, and even by analysis of the piece's proportions.[4] While we may chide Debussy for omitting to mark this explicitly, one can well understand why he didn't indicate anything like *Le double plus vite* (or *lent*), which would descriptively contradict the continuous sounding metre.[5]

Nor are such tacit equivalences so rare: two passages where pianists habitually make the same adjustment without noticing are in Franck's *Prélude, Choral et Fugue* (the *poco allegro* transition after the *Choral*, where one has to assume ♩ = ♪ *precedente*, as can be seen by analogy with bar 11 of the *Prélude*), and in the first movement of Ravel's Concerto in G (figure 29 in the first movement, completing the accelerando with an automatic ♩ = ♩ *precedente*). For almost thirty years after its publication Fauré's Sixth Nocturne lacked the necessary indication ♪ = ♩ *precedente* at the main climax (bar 111) until the pianist Robert Lortat alerted Fauré to the omission. Another case occurs in a song Debussy composed in 1898 but left unpublished;[6] a more complex one affecting the *Étude* 'Pour les quartes' is discussed in Chapter 17.

All this provides perspective for the many passages where Debussy uses descriptive indications to confirm effects already embedded in the rhythmic notation. The last page of 'Reflets dans l'eau' would grind to an ungainly halt were we to impose his indications *en retenant jusqu'à la fin* and *Lent* prescriptively: if we hold a steady pulse they happen anyway.[7] This usage can be traced back to Chabrier's *Impromptu* where the sounding contrasts of the central section (*Molto meno mosso* then sudden spurts of *Vivo*) are all written into the notation and assure themselves if played in a fairly constant ♪ pulse. Example 6.5 shows a similar identity of pulse and gesture across two otherwise contrasted Debussy *Images*.

Debussy's *Études* are specially prone to this. At bars 7 and 37 of 'Pour les quartes' the *stretto* (along with the following *rit.*) needs only a slight nudge from the performer relative to the basic tempo that Debussy defines at bar 1 or bar 49. At bar 33 of 'Pour les sixtes' we can (ironically) best assure the *molto rit.* by momentarily counteracting it, so that the eighth-note triplets flow naturally out of the preceding sixteenths (Ex. 15.2). A similar relationship is implied across bars 77 and 79 of 'Pour les quartes' and over the last three bars of 'Brouillards', as well as across bars 86–7 of Fauré's Second Nocturne. Such descriptively duplicate indications are rarer in Ravel, though 'Ondine' shows one example, the expanded metre in bar 29 that assures the indicated *un peu retenu* relative to bar 28.

Example 15.2. Debussy, 'Pour les sixtes', bars 32–3

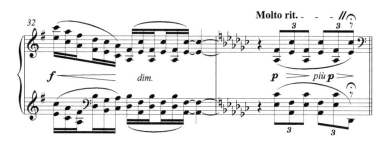

Debussy's comments to performers show him keeping this delicate balance between the music's fluid surface and its underlying firm structure. Marguerite Long, who could be needle-fingered, was told, 'Seule compte le plaisir de l'heure!' – a picturesque way of saying 'enjoy the moment' – whereas Ricardo Viñes was faulted (as we saw in Chapter 4) for incompletely grasping the architecture of the second series of *Images*.[8] Viñes's 1930 recording of 'Poissons d'or' suggests a possible reason why: for all its mastery, a flaw in architectural awareness emerges as he lets the dynamics and intensity peak around bar 80, inevitably fading before the *sff* focus of bars 84–5.[9] We can easily sympathize with Viñes in the heat of performance, because the thinned texture at bar 84 doesn't let the instrument's resonance work in our favour. Still, Debussy made his intentions as clear as possible (holding off *ff* as much as one dare in the context), and our challenge through that passage is to balance large-scale shape optimally with the kaleidoscope of colours he offers us on the way. Useful comparison comes from the similarly structured main climax and its approach in 'Jeux de vagues' from *La mer* (around rehearsal figure 38).

Standard staff notation, too, is just one type of musical notation. As we'll see in Chapter 17, titles also yield performing instructions. If analytic graphs are a specialized form of notation that marks key events, normal staff notation is reciprocally an all-embracing kind of analysis (literally a 'partition', as French usage has it), one that allows some leeway of prescriptive and descriptive options. Inevitably it can't show the structural significance of every moment. Any pianist familiar with Fauré's Fifth Barcarolle knows that defining moment at bar 111 where the ritornello-like triple unison drops not from F♯ to C♮, as on every previous occasion, but to B, swinging the piece into its final peroration. In the score Fauré just has to let this diversion speak for itself, hoping for enough performer awareness to let it register without under- or overemphasis. The same goes for any of the important turning points seen in the analytic chapters above.

FOREGROUND AND BACKGROUND NOTATION IN FAURÉ

Fauré's Fifth Nocturne subtly illustrates several of those matters. Example 15.3a shows how its opening section, *andante quasi allegretto* in ¾, gives way at bar 70 to a contrasted *allegro* in ⁶⁄₈. What the contrast neatly hides is the way Fauré's two (absolutely viable) metronome markings ensure a virtual eighth-note equivalence across the transition (♪ = 192 and 198 respectively). The bar duration thus stays the same, allowing Fauré a little *coup de théâtre* at the main climax from bar 121: the earlier *andante* second theme from bar 49 returns at its original sounding tempo, but now in hemiolas across the flying arpeggios of the ⁶⁄₈ *allegro* (Ex. 15.3b–c). Nor is that Fauré's only *coup de théâtre*, for he has the entire climactic page sounding in B major, despite the five-flat key signature and the lack of a B major chord anywhere in the piece.

Example 15.3. Fauré, Fifth Nocturne, op. 37

a: bars 64–70

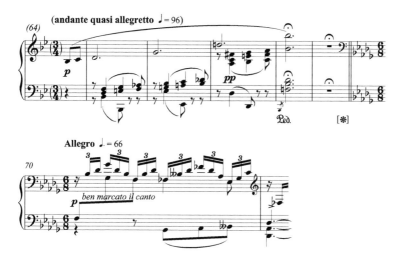

b: bars 49–52

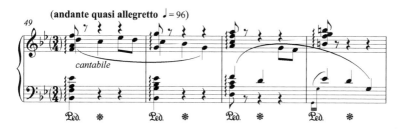

c: bars 121–2

It's easy to take Fauré's notation in all these passages for granted, until we consider the options. For example, let's imagine Example 15.3c respelt in five sharps (anywhere from bar 117 onwards), and bar 121 respelt in $\frac{3}{4}$ metre. It would leave the passage pleasingly free of ties and accidentals; but the large-scale symphonic sweep of the whole middle section would be visually fractured on the page. More radically, let's imagine Example 15.3a with the tempo modifications (𝄴, *allegro*, ♩. = 66) moved five bars back to bar 65 or its upbeat. Played straight off the page, the music would sound not a whit different. The changed notation would merely draw our attention to different relationships. As it is, bars 65–9 relate to both the piece's opening and to bar 70, neatly dovetailing the two sections together.[10] Fauré leaves us a hint of this with the left-hand rests in bars 65–7 (𝄾𝄾 instead of 𝄽), as if the time signature were already 𝄴.

His score thus neatly analyses the piece in the ways that most help us, while his stealthy dovetail into the *allegro* section takes care of itself in performance. Under it all lies a larger coherence: not only are the piece's opening and central sections exactly the same length (69 bars each, but different internally), but the first appearance of the 'climax' theme occurs exactly halfway to where the central section takes it up again (48 + 48 bars, a figure whose roundness defies the irregular phrase lengths through the first 48 bars). Not surprisingly, Fauré appears to have had a soft spot for this piece, for its rhythms echo ten years later at the main climax of his Fifth Barcarolle and in the *allegretto* section of his Sixth Nocturne. One can even play straight from bar 39 of the Fifth Nocturne into bar 45 of the Sixth Nocturne without any audible join – an amusing party trick with which to tease connoisseurs, though best avoided too near concerts in case it confuses the memory . . .

DEBUSSY'S ORCHESTRA AT THE PIANO

Debussy's descriptive habits match the evocative range of his titles: taken together, his *Estampes*, *Images*, *Children's Corner* and Preludes evoke sonorities ranging from orchestra to voice (including Spanish *cante jondo*), whistling,[11] gamelan, guitar, shepherd's pipe, harp, café violin ("*Les sons et les parfums*" as well as *La plus que lente*), horns, trumpets, bugle, cathedral organ, bells large and small, finger cymbals, timpani, tamtam, brass band and banjo – or just the patter of rain and roar of the wind.[12] 'Make me forget the piano has hammers', his publisher Durand quoted Debussy as saying;[13] far from suggesting anything anaemic, it can be read as a call for imaginative boldness, effectively meaning 'Make me forget it's a piano.' As further indications of Debussy's orchestral thinking, up- and down-bow signs appear on the first page of 'Les collines d'Anacapri', plus the brass indication *cuivrez* (recte *cuivré*) and another down-bow sign for piano in the closing pages of his Violin Sonata. Equally graphic are Debussy's *portamento* lines in bars 35 and 36 of 'La Puerta del Vino', literally unrealizable at the piano but an illusion he clearly wanted us to sense and evoke as best we can through agogics or voicing.

Anyone still in doubt about reading Debussy's piano notation in this manner need only look at bar 1 of 'Des pas sur la neige' which, in purely pianistic terms, appears to be marked nonsensically. Does the tenuto dash on the opening double-stemmed *d'* mean it should be stronger than the following *e'*? If so, what can the crescendo hairpin to the *e'* mean? It makes sense only if read as quasi-orchestral short score, exhorting us to imagine (say) a cor anglais on the rising figure over a sustained horn or viola. The melodic entry in bar 2 might then be imagined as an oboe or even a vocal line.[14] Other cases of outright orchestral writing in Debussy's Preludes include bars 29 and 31 of 'Bruyères', where the rising sixth inside the rhythm ♪♫ is impossible to voice at the piano without obscuring an equally important line above it: only an orchestration could make the polyphony audible. Another case flagged in the *Œuvres complètes* is bar 8 of 'La Cathédrale engloutie', where Debussy's piano roll avoids re-sounding the printed octave Es, obviously to prevent them intruding on the melodic line, a purely pianistic problem.[15]

This relates equally to a sometimes awkward-looking element of Debussy's piano notation, the fully measured-out tremolos in inner parts which can often be awkward to articulate. Several passages suggest they're not meant to be too articulated or even played too literally. The most obvious one is in the closing lines of 'Feux d'artifice', where bar 96 isn't literally playable by two hands (Ex. 15.4a). Common sense tells us to 'fake' the bass continuity with pedal, to assume unmeasured bass tremolo rather than pedantically measured 32nd-notes from bar 90 onwards (Ex. 15.4b), and to interrupt the tremolo briefly for the grace notes at the end of bar 90. This follows a standard old usage of orchestral reductions, which habitually notate tremolo as 32nd-notes regardless of the tempo in force.

Example 15.4. Debussy, 'Feux d'artifice'

a: bars 95–6   b: bars 90–1

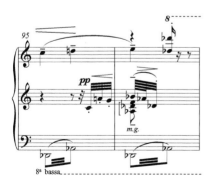

aussi léger et **pp** *que possible*

This has a considerable impact on how we read the opening of 'Poissons d'or'. Example 15.5a shows the passage's notational and interpretative quandary: we can either aim somewhere near Debussy's indicated ♩ = 112 or try to play all the notes, but hardly both. Even if ♩ = 112 seems more apt for the central part of the piece (around bar 58) than for the opening, starting it too much slower puts evident strain on the piece's architecture. Implicit comment comes from bars 18–21 where the tremolo is replaced by simple trills, a notation Debussy couldn't use at bar 1 merely because the intervals concerned are too wide. At the reprise from bar 86 Debussy simplifies his notation further by stemming the theme separately from the accompaniment and replacing its double dots and 32nd-notes with grace notes. Why then didn't he do the same from bar 1, in the manner of Example 15.5b? An immediate answer is that it would look too blatantly like unrealized orchestral reduction, and anyway the rhythmic notation needs more exact definition from bar 6. As it is, Debussy talked of the passage orchestrally: Maurice Dumesnil reports him as wanting the tremolo 'almost immaterial, so one could hear "two clarinets" up above'.[16] In a close parallel, 'Jeux de vagues' from *La mer* features a clarinet solo similarly in $\frac{3}{4}$ metre indicated ♩ = 112 (two bars before rehearsal figure 30); Debussy's piano duet transcription of *La mer* spells the figuration out fully in 32nd-notes, whereas his orchestral score partly renotates it as trills. The passage is particularly similar to bars 16–17 of 'Poissons d'or'.

Example 15.5. Debussy, 'Poissons d'or'

a: bars 1–4 as notated by Debussy

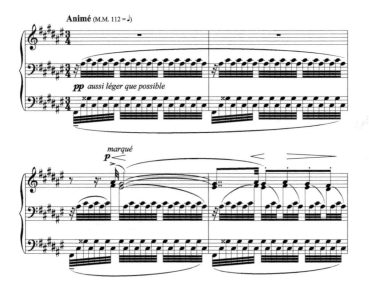

b: a renotation of bars 1–5 in the manner of orchestral reduction

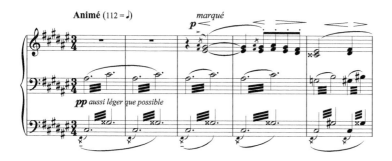

More insight on this comes from a letter to André Caplet in June 1913, written by Debussy a few days after he and Ricardo Viñes premièred Caplet's two-piano transcription of Debussy's *Ibéria*. Debussy's letter laments that Viñes's overly brilliant tremolos sounded 'like the rumble of so many dead pebbles'.[17] Comparison with Viñes's 1930 recording of 'Poissons d'or' is revealing. One of the nimblest performances on record, it starts at c. ♩ = 84 before moving on progressively from bar 5 onwards, with quiet but brilliant articulation of the opening figurations. Breathtaking though it is, it may well have been too defined for the ever-demanding Debussy, whose indication *pp aussi léger que possible* suggests something more orchestrally shimmering ('make me forget the piano has hammers').

At the other dynamic extreme, timpani-like explosions like the bass octave tremolo at the climactic bar 52 of 'Ce qu'a vu le Vent d'Ouest' suggest starting with a simultaneous octave attack on both notes, rather than a too-literal start with the weakest finger. As for the fussy-looking dynamics in bars 54–6, reading them orchestrally makes simpler sense in terms of clarifying the voicing across the effective F♯–G♮ and F♯–G♯ bass tremolos, and even suggests that we somehow make each upper note appear to sound on rather than after the beat.

Other tremolo notations by Debussy can be explained in terms of specific contexts. From bar 126 onwards of 'Jardins sous la pluie' his use of tremolo (rather than trills) was probably intended to show the accented upper-note start to each trill. In bars 22–7 of 'Le vent dans la plaine' his sextuplets (instead of trills) suggest a sort of continuous shimmer, avoiding accents at each change of pitch. In *"Les fées sont d'exquises danseuses"* (Ex. 15.6) the suddenly measured notation from bar 13 shows the optimal hand layout, but common sense suggests that the texture otherwise imitate the trills in bars 11–12.

Example 15.6. Debussy, "*Les fées sont d'exquises danseuses*", bars 11–14

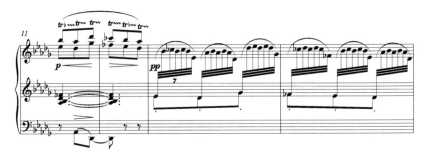

In bars 63–6 of 'La danse de Puck' musical sense suggests treating the minor third of the left hand tremolo (first bar of Ex. 15.7a) like the trills in the texturally similar bars 87–90. In bars 67–8 the upper voice of the tremolo shorthand echoes that of the trills of bars 55–60 (as shown under Ex. 15.7a–b): the context again suggests making each upper note there sound (or appear to sound) on the beat. It then aptly prepares the return of the same trope, notated explicitly, in bar 71.

Example 15.7. 'La danse de Puck'

a: bars 66–8

b: bars 55–7 (likewise bars 59–61)

Other cases of Debussy wavering between alternative notations can be seen in 'Voiles', where an *acciaccatura* gesture like that in bar 3 of 'Poissons d'or' is rhythmically measured out at bars 2, 16 and 59 but simplified to grace notes at bars 62–3. Chabrier's 'Mauresque' shows similarly mixed notation for the same basic gesture (bar 2 versus bars 18–19 and similar). This is one of several ways in which Debussy's sometimes fussy notation echoes Chabrier, who often marked articulation densely to underline a constant wish for liveliness of colour.[18]

All composers ultimately depend on the performer's sense, and it's therefore sometimes a matter of discretion where we take the composer's word exactly and where a quiet degree of licence is needed. While it's traditionally regarded as improper to omit notes in this repertoire, but acceptable to treat dynamics and rhythm with 'artistic discretion', the composers' own remarks often suggest they viewed things the other way round. Along with all his insistence on strict rhythmic observance, Ravel is reported as saying that in the opening of his 'Ondine' he was more interested in a sense of rippling water than in hearing every note, in a way that matches the contexts discussed above.[19]

Would using a variety of note sizes have helped in some of these cases? Debussy did just that in 'Feux d'artifice', whose first edition has four different note sizes. While his model may have been Chopin's A♭ *Étude* op. 25 no. 1, he may also have been prompted by notational problems already encountered in 'Poissons d'or' and 'La danse de Puck'. This raises an intriguing question: given a second chance, might Debussy have opted for more varied note sizes in 'Poissons' and 'Puck'? Indeed, when the second book of Preludes first came to reprint, he had some arpeggios in 'La Puerta del Vino' changed to smaller type (Ex. 20.7a–b). His manuscripts provide mixed evidence: his writing is generally small, and noteheads in quick figurations often look slightly smaller, though usually without any instructions for the printer.

In a few pieces – 'Bruyères' immediately comes to mind – smaller note sizes for light arabesques could arguably help keep the music moving by directing attention to the main melodic lines in the middle of the texture. Given the lack of explicit source evidence, such renotation normally lies beyond the remit of critical editing. But there's nothing to stop us imagining, and the thought of variable note sizes – in the manner of Chopin's A♭ *Étude* – for 'Poissons d'or', 'Bruyères', 'Les tierces alternées' or even Ravel's 'Ondine' is no bad exercise.

Debussy's differing ways of notating related textures matches a notational subtlety in 'Reflets dans l'eau'. At first sight the arpeggios from bars 18 onwards look unrelated to the steady four-voice texture of bars 9–14. Example 1.7, however, shows how they quietly continue it – with, as so often, the main melodic and modal interest in the middle of the texture. A thorough professional (*anti-dilettante*), he was evidently happy there to let this hidden textural continuity work by itself.

Sometimes a conflict of two notations suggests something in between them. At bar 58 of 'Hommage à Rameau' there seems no reason to treat Debussy's ♩. ♪ differently from his ♩.. ♪ in the corresponding phrase at bars 2, 11 and 27. Experiment suggests in practice something between the two, and that the double dot aims to avoid flaccid rhythm. It can doubtless be related to Debussy's careful alignment of the rhythm ♪ ♪. in bars 34 and 37 of 'Brouillards' against the arpeggios above, forcing it into sextuplet value. Bars 15–20 of 'Ce qu'a vu le Vent d'Ouest' are a more special case (Ex. 15.8). In bars 19–20 the rhythmic values fail to add up unless we read Debussy's ♩.. ♪ as an intended ♩... ♪. This matches his ♩ ♩.. ♪ in bars 15–18 (cf. also Ex. 11.3b), a notation he was unable to continue in bars 19–20 for obvious reasons of space.[20] We just have to guess that Debussy – who never used triple dots, even though Schubert, Schumann and Liszt did – expects us to understand his meaning from the context.

Even the ♩ ♩.. ♪ of bars 15–18 is not the whole story, since arithmetically that last note should come before the last of the accompanying triplets-within-triplets (a sixteenth of the half-bar as against an eighteenth). To impose that, though, would be musically nonsensical, and any other attempt to 'correct' the notation would be counterproductive: in practice the existing notation neatly conveys an inbuilt rubato across the voices that unobtrusively looks after itself. These understood overdottings – like the understood ♩ = ♩ in 'La Cathédrale engloutie' – link back through romantic practice to older habits already seen in Chapter 10.

Example 15.8. Debussy, 'Ce qu'a vu le Vent d'Ouest', bars 18–19

FAURÉ AND ORCHESTRAL THINKING

A frequent orchestral notation in piano music involves voices that meet in the course of tied notes. Example 15.9, for instance, shows the polyphonic sense rather than exactly how the two thumbs have to cope with the overlapping *d'♮*s. Other examples can be found throughout Fauré's Twelfth and Thirteenth Nocturnes as well as in the Passepied of Debussy's *Suite bergamasque* (bar 34) and the Prélude of Ravel's *Tombeau de Couperin* (bar 7). We can quickly guess why composers preferred this descriptive notation, suggesting the voicing to aim for. (Example 20.4 shows a rare exception, at bar 7 where Fauré marks the bass tie purely prescriptively across the voices.)

Example 15.9. Fauré, Seventh Nocturne, op. 74, bar 106

A further ambiguity arises when two voices converge on a partly tied note. In Example 15.10a the doubled left-hand sixteenth-note at beat 3 obviously needs sounding, whereas Example 15.10b suggests the opposite, a point Fauré neatly makes by sharing or not sharing the notehead. (Occasionally his logic comes unstuck: in old editions of the Third Barcarolle, for example, a few bars mix ties with shared noteheads that clearly need re-articulating.)

Example 15.10

a: Fauré, Twelfth Nocturne, op. 107, bar 67

b: Fauré, Sixth Nocturne, op. 63, bar 3

In passing, Example 15.10 illustrates Fauré's almost obsessive use of ties instead of longer or dotted notes (including the right hand in Example 15.10b). Had he used whole notes for the bass in Example 15.10, the question of re-sounding or not would be clear from the outset. His aim was doubtless to encourage pianists to stay in the keys, sometimes while re-pedalling. (The third of Debussy's *Images* [*oubliées*] of 1894 shows the same distinction, for exactly that physical reason, across the otherwise identical bass of bars 76 and 77.) Partly a legacy of his teacher Saint-Saëns, Fauré's tied notation may also have been a way of defining strict rhythmic division in an era when augmentation dots could still be rhythmically variable. As we've already seen (and will see again in Chapter 17), Debussy sometimes counted on this variability.

<h2 style="text-align:center">RAVEL'S ORCHESTRAL PIANO</h2>

Despite the amount of Ravel's piano output that exists in orchestral form (and vice versa), it's typical of his professionalism that his piano versions show virtually no evidence of orchestral reduction. This partly reflects that most of them were conceived for piano – though Chapter 19 has further comment on this regarding the *Pavane pour une Infante défunte*. Even his imitations of trombone slides and musical saw in the Concerto in G allow tactile enjoyment at the piano (as do similar slides in Chabrier's *Impromptu* and *Bourrée fantasque*).[21] While Ravel always envisaged *La valse* for orchestra, his solo and two-piano versions were completed first and have established an understandable place in the repertoire. If their primary purpose was for ballet rehearsal, Ravel, being Ravel, made them top quality from the outset.

Ironically, the strongest sense of orchestral reduction comes from the one piece – 'Une barque sur l'océan' – whose orchestration left Ravel dissatisfied. Two reasons can be seen. Orchestral though they seem, the piece's rolling arpeggios lose much of their dynamism when orchestrated (inevitably) with string tremolo. In addition, the piece's dynamics are pianistically conceived: waves that take the piano from *ppp* to *fff* and back over just a bar or two leave insufficient time to open up the dynamic range of an orchestra, even though Ravel lengthened bars 28 and 29 for that purpose in the orchestral score. As with Debussy's *L'isle joyeuse*, orchestral though it feels, the structure is essentially and skilfully pianistic.[22]

In a subtler way, Ravel's beloved *Valses nobles et sentimentales* pose problems because even the most detailed notation can't show all the subtle voicing the work needs. It can't play itself off the page in the way that even much of *Gaspard de la nuit* does once we've mastered its notes. This explains Ravel's exceptional fastidiousness when coaching pianists in the *Valses* (as recounted by both Vlado Perlemuter and Henriette Faure). If knowing the orchestral score helps, another key lies in the music's constant sense of stylized gesture (not for nothing did the work lend itself so soon to ballet).

For pianists, Ravel's most revealing transcription is probably the four movements he orchestrated of *Le tombeau de Couperin*: Alfred Cortot even insisted this was where the pieces found their definitive form.[23] In the Forlane particularly, the orchestral score shows more detailed voicing, phrasing and articulation, with shorter slurs and more rests and staccato. Indeed, Ravel's articulation in the piano score would spell disaster in orchestral performance. Although a rhythmic rationale can be read in his longer slurs in the piano score, reading his orchestral score at the piano prompts a lighter touch, articulation and pedal. Again a single notation is insufficient to convey all the music's information. Some important details of voicing visible only in the orchestral score include the cor anglais line from bar 1 of the Forlane (left hand $b\sharp$–$c'\sharp$–$e'\sharp$ in the piano version, passing to the right hand $e'\natural$–$d'\sharp$ etc.), the horn's rising fifth at bar 61 of the Prélude (as numbered in the London Peters edition), and – closely related – the way the Rigaudon's opening trumpet fanfare rises a fifth to e'', leaving the g'' above it as a descant.

One of Yvonne Lefébure's anecdotes bears on this. As a student in Cortot's class she played *Jeux d'eau* to Ravel, daring (despite the printed slurs) to start with a light staccato touch over the pedal: this prompted Ravel's immediate reply, 'That's it.'[24] His slurs thus primarily define the phrases, with the option of lively inner articulation where apt. We might imagine Debussy, in his place, adding dots under the slur; Ravel perhaps omitted them to avoid clutter that might slow the pianist. (A similar effect can actually be obtained by playing the passage lightly but legato right in the keybed, using the thumb notes as anchors.) Ravel's comments on editing Mendelssohn's piano music bear on all this, regarding the different ways of writing the equivalent articulation for piano or orchestra.[25]

MORE ON ORCHESTRAL REDUCTIONS

Playing *Pelléas et Mélisande* from Debussy's piano score is an unsurpassable way of sensing the orchestral composer at the piano.[26] It was the form in which he first played (and sang) the opera in order to have it taken up for performance, using a skill honed by years of playing (and singing) the likes of *Boris Godunov* and *Tristan und Isolde* at the piano. (He was in some demand for this in the 1890s and was known for managing the whole of *Tristan* from memory – no wonder those two operas echo through his music.) Chapter 7 has already noted Debussy's and Ravel's ability to play Chabrier operas by heart, recalling a mostly pre-gramophone era in which piano or duet reductions were the main way of learning – and sometimes performing – orchestral and operatic repertoire. After playing through any of those vocal scores, a piece like *L'isle joyeuse* or 'Une barque sur l'ocean' (even 'Poissons d'or' or 'Jardins sous la pluie') shows up in a very different light, just as hearing Debussy's orchestral 'Fêtes' can galvanize the climactic crescendos of *L'isle joyeuse* or 'Mouvement'.

Orchestral thinking also affects our treatment of dynamics. At bars 13–16 of Debussy's 'En bateau' (from *Petite suite*) *p* might seem an odd dynamic for what look like trumpet fanfares – until we imagine those muted trumpets in the long crescendo of 'Fêtes'. Debussy leaves it to our imagination and skill to find the distant but incisive colour; we can even try playing them out *forte* (just once, to banish feebleness) before finding the equivalent as heard from a distance. This was perhaps in Debussy's mind on those oft-reported occasions when he insisted on keeping the piano lid down.

A further slant comes from the pianist Gaby Casadesus who remembered, as a young girl, watching Debussy cover his ears as he listened to the pianists at the end-of-year Paris Conservatoire *concours* (where he was visiting examiner).[27] His orchestral climaxes in 'Fêtes' and *La mer* – probably louder than anything before in French repertoire, even Berlioz – suggest we read that anecdote, like his tactics with piano lids, as reflecting an intolerance of coarseness rather than of decibels *per se*. The very incisively marked main climaxes of 'Mouvement' and 'Poissons d'or' – those rare moments where Debussy's tiger unsheathes its claws – support taking his dynamics at his word: without the weight of bass strings they need stronger attack than the full *fortissimi* of 'Reflets dans l'eau', 'La Cathédrale engloutie' (with its admonitory *sans dureté* [without hardness]) and *L'isle joyeuse*, whose textures virtually hand us the *fortissimo* without any need to push.

CHAPTER 16

EDITIONS AND WHAT THEY CAN'T QUITE TELL US

A FIRST confession here has to be that urtext, in its literal meaning of 'original text', is rarely the aim of a critical edition. We hardly want to undo revisions that composers made to their original texts at proof or in the light of rehearsal and performing experience, sometimes over many years. In practice the word 'urtext' has acquired a secondary meaning of a *Fassung letzter Hand* that includes all the composer's known revisions as well as addressing all known or suspect misprints, and using smaller print or square brackets to identify anything added by the editor, plus a commentary explaining what has come from where.[1] Even the most detailed editorial commentary, though, can't convey all that lies behind an edition, and a look behind the scenes can prompt us to read between the lines of a score, spot lurking problems and sometimes guess solutions.

We may wonder what need there is for new editions of composers whose music is still mostly available in 'original editions' which they proofread. One answer comes from the 'pools' of known problems and unpublished corrections that have long circulated among performers. Slips and misprints can arise in all sorts of ways. In modal or chromatic passages full of accidentals and cancellations, it's easy for the odd accidental to fall by the wayside either in a draft or in the course of recopying or printing. The danger also lurks of an engraver or in-house editor trying to correct something unorthodox that wasn't in fact wrong. As an example, the manuscript of Debussy's *Masques* shows, fully written out in both bars 27 and 296, the melodic motive [musical notation] (redolent of his orchestral *Nocturne* 'Fêtes'). Surviving proofs of *Masques* show this printed each time as [musical notation], with the middle ♯ corrected in Debussy's hand to ♮ at bar 27 but not at bar 296. The original edition accordingly prints G♮ at bar 27 but G♯ at bar 296. While we may guess

Debussy meant G♮ each time (the *Œuvres complètes* accordingly remove the ♯ from bar 296), we can't now be totally sure. On the other side, surviving manuscripts often show house editors – some of them friends of the composers, like Durand's Lucien Garban – doing their job well, correcting composers' errors and omissions with the composers' co-operation and approval: their written queries remain visible on many manuscripts and proofs.

Surviving manuscripts are just the tip of the creative iceberg. Once a piece is complete in rough draft the main creative work is done, and the aim of the fair copy is to make it intelligible to others. The exact notation of keys, clefs and accidentals is often decided only at this stage. Even then fair copies habitually leave out clefs and key signatures on new systems: numerous errors can be traced to these omissions. Recopying can also be a dreary chore, and a composer's imagination easily jumps ahead of a slow-moving nib. Franck and Fauré were especially prone to this.[2] A few passing cases can be seen in Debussy's *Études*. For example, in bar 38 of 'Pour les agréments' Debussy's autograph fair copy and the first edition show a rather anodyne left hand d''♯ where his early draft (reproduced in the Minkoff facsimile edition) has d''♮ (Ex. 16.1a), making a much more pleasing (and Chabrier-like) double appoggiatura across the hands (d''♮/g''♮ to d''♯/g''♯). His final reading here was surely a slip of the pen, his eye jumping ahead as he recopied.

A similar case, at bar 123 of Fauré's Fifth Nocturne, involves an odd-sounding a''♮ halfway up an arpeggio otherwise featuring A♯ (Ex. 16.1b). Some manuscript facsimiles in the London Peters edition show how this probably happened: Fauré first wrote the note (logically, it would seem) as a''♯ but then transcribed it as a''♮ when he recopied that whole passage. On the other hand, his early copy has an aberrant ♯ against the final b'' of bar 126 which he corrected to ♮ in the later copy; perhaps he had this already in view as he recopied bar 123, provoking a reciprocal slip of the pen. The 1924 re-edition of the piece (edited in part by Roger-Ducasse) complicated matters by not only maintaining the suspect a''♮ in bar 123 but adding a corresponding ♮ three notes later (as shown above Example 16.1b). Even if we regard that as a misunderstanding, a definitive answer is elusive since a case could be made for a''♮ as a passing note, or even for A♮ as a compositional option through the whole bar. A modal change in mid-bar, though, would cause pedal and textural problems abnormal for Fauré, suggesting that his earlier manuscript provides our best answer.

Example 16.1

a: Debussy, 'Pour les agréments', end of bar 38, autograph fair copy and first edition

(preparatory draft has ♮)

b: Fauré, Fifth Nocturne op. 37, bars 123–5, autograph and first edition (1884–5)

Ravel's *Jeux d'eau* has long been dogged by a similar chain reaction in its fifth last bar: the first edition's engraver forgot to put a ledger line through the last right-hand quarter-note *c‴♯*, whose note-head a subsequent re-engraver then misread as *b″*.

Composers also tend to use proofs as a last chance for revisions and improvements: the entirely different frame of mind needed for that easily explains why howling errors sometimes occur cheek by jowl with meticulous revisions. Awareness of that prompts us to think creatively of what might have caused some apparently aberrant readings. For example, older editions of Debussy's *Suite bergamasque* show implausible F♮s at bar 87 of the Menuet which (reading creatively between the lines) we might guess as being unintended remnants from a modally different earlier version of the passage. (We can only guess, for the piece's manuscript is long lost.) In all these ways a work's evolution – from sketch to draft to fair copy, then via proofs to a first edition and subsequent reprints – constantly risks mixing improvement with corruption: we just have to be alert.

'ORIGINAL' EDITIONS

Once a piece is in print, rehearsal can mercilessly expose errors that evaded the most careful proofing. The distractions of rehearsing, though, mean that such errors are often just noted on the wing, which explains why we sometimes see a composer hastily correcting the same error differently on different exemplars. Besides this, numerous corrections that Fauré, Debussy and Ravel noted over the years never found their way into reprints. We can only guess if they were overlooked at the moment of reprinting, decided against, or simply refused by the publisher on grounds of inconvenience or cost. Nor are reprints immune from new mishaps. Two important accidentals at bar 72 of Fauré's Second Nocturne appeared correctly in the first print of 1884 then mysteriously vanished from all reprints. The rogue element there, in the first print, was a misprinted accidental above them, which reprints corrected but at the expense of wrongly deleting the two underneath. (Fauré tried in vain to have that corrected: the London Peters edition does so.)

After a composer's death the term 'original edition', beloved of publishers, becomes more elastic again. Posthumous reprints of many 'original' Debussy editions continued to retouch them without saying on what basis. We have to guess if the sources were scores now lost that the composer had corrected, or corrections the composer had indicated to colleagues, or just someone's opinion. (Some of them make sense; a few are dubious.) In another terminological stretch, the 'original edition' of Debussy's First Book of Preludes sold from the 1960s onwards was in fact an entirely new engraving, made for reasons now unknown.

As for Fauré, the 'original edition' of his first eight Nocturnes and first six Barcarolles, as sold from the mid-1920s, is a somewhat botched rendering of a revision he prepared towards the end of his life with the help of his former student Roger-Ducasse. The marked-up copy used for it has mostly vanished, leaving us often guessing which changes were made by whom (Fauré was notoriously lax about this), and if many remaining errors plus some new ones are the result of oversight, misprint, or misinterpretation by Roger-Ducasse. (Among much else, the 1924 edition reversed a few sensible corrections incorporated in a 1918 re-engraving of the Sixth Nocturne.) Fauré saw a test print of the new edition two months before he died, and was so appalled that he tried, fruitlessly, to block it. The faults were never addressed: instead, the volumes were reissued in 1958 (as still sold in 2009) with added fingerings and hand rearrangements, some of them at odds with Fauré's indications, by the pianist Germaine Thyssens-Valentin.

Ravel is mostly less problematic: he usually polished new works carefully until they reached print, then let them go. Nonetheless his handexemplar of *Gaspard de la nuit* shows dozens of written corrections and retouches never incorporated in reprints; more are reported by pianists like Vlado Perlemuter who worked with Ravel. (All are incorporated in the London Peters edition.) Nor does the 'original edition' of *Le tombeau de Couperin*, as reprinted from the 1950s, tell us that its metronome indications were later additions, reportedly at the instigation of Marguerite Long.[3] As for Chabrier, from the early 1890s his publisher reissued the *Pièces pittoresques* one by one in re-engravings that incorporate important composer revisions in 'Paysage' and 'Mauresque'. His health poor, Chabrier failed to spot dozens of misprints in the new engravings (assuming he was shown proofs); subsequent reprints (such as International) revert to the original 1881 print (urtext in the over-literal sense), losing Chabrier's revisions. In addition, the standard editions of *Ronde champêtre* and *Impromptu* published after Chabrier's death were heavily edited, including a changed tempo for *Impromptu* (which Chabrier headed *Allegro* not *Allegretto*) and added pedalling in *Ronde champêtre*. (The Dover edition cleans this all up.)

All that said, we can generally take it that editions dating from the composers' lifetimes faithfully include their corrections and proof emenda-tions, despite all the misprints. For example, Debussy completely rewrote the last page of his prelude 'La terrasse des audiences du clair de lune' at proof – much to its musical benefit – leaving the manuscript reading obsolete. Surviving proofs of his First Book of Preludes similarly show that most of the differences between his autograph and the first edition are his deliberate revisions (contrary to the assumption of the current Wiener Urtext edition).

LIVING DANGEROUSLY

Given so many complications, the idea of a definitive text becomes a chimera: we can try to represent (or reconstruct) the composer's intentions as we can best ascertain them, but sometimes no definitive reading is possible, often because the composer wasn't sure either. It's fair to convey this in an edition, showing options on added staves or even with the occasional '[?]', provided it doesn't turn into page clutter or editorial abnegation; at best it can let the performer sense the composer's – and editor's – dilemma from within.

We certainly shouldn't fool ourselves that editing can be objective, an issue that James Grier confronts at the outset in his book *The Critical Editing of Music*: 'the central tenet of this book [is that] editing is an act of criticism.'[4] Indeed, nothing imposes subjectivity faster than any attempt to duck it. For example, if we leave unflagged or uncommented a reading that seems suspect but is not provably wrong, that decision to stand aloof is as subjective as any visible intervention.[5] Our one measure of objectivity is to observe our subjec-tivity and try to sense all that we can through the composer's eyes and ears, via what we know of their lives, letters, composing habits, manuscript sources and so forth. In the end no issue is more 'authentic' than the basic fact that the composer wanted the piece to work.

Like a performance, any edition is an interpretation of sources, even if it can leave more options open. Thus no two critical editions are ever likely to concur exactly. A well-researched edition can even be something of a virtuoso performance, particularly if it can extract idiomatic solutions from intractable source problems. Even performing a piece makes us the editor of our own performance, especially if the edition we use prompts a choice between viable variants.

Editing logic and procedures

Details of this often have to vary according to the composer's known habits, even if some general rules can be drawn. While editions proofed by the composers are a priority source, manuscripts are vital for checking innumerable details. This is clear from a plea Debussy made to his publisher Durand in 1907: 'Could you please beseech your engraver to respect the exact placing of dynamics – it's of extreme and pianistic importance.'[6] Comparison between Debussy's manuscripts and printed editions shows what was troubling him: dynamics, often attached to specific voices, were sometimes moved by the engraver to look neater on the page. Bars 244–8 of *L'isle joyeuse* thus become easier to play once we know Debussy wrote the crescendo hairpins under the system (for just the left hand: hence his mention 'of pianistic importance'), and in 'Des pas sur la neige' his voicing in bars 5–6 and from bar 22 makes quite different sense once we know he wrote the crescendo hairpins above the system, affecting just the top line. A few sudden *p* or *pp* markings in *L'isle joyeuse*, the Toccata of *Pour le piano* and the Menuet of *Petite suite* – also at bar 28 of Fauré's Seventh Nocturne – similarly make better sense once we know that the composer placed them just after the first note of the bar, rather than at the start of the bar as printed in older editions.

We can't entirely blame the engravers for believing they were just being helpful there by squaring things off, because it's exactly the sort of thing many composers expected them to tidy up. Fauré's writing, for example, was quite large, and the close spacing of manuscript staves obliged him (like many composers) to write most dynamics above or below the system, leaving the engraver to move them mid-system as appropriate, guessing which ones were meant for just one hand or staff. In that context it took Debussy's engravers (who were constantly deciphering different handwritings) some time to register that Debussy, in his unusually small and meticulous hand, marked dynamics exactly where he wanted them printed.[7]

Debussy's complaint probably involved another engravers' habit: by squaring off hairpin dynamics to make them look neater, they often made them start or end illogically. 'Jardins sous la pluie' shows an example that probably fuelled Debussy's plea to Durand: the first edition (Ex. 16.2a) makes bars 86 and 87 look innocuously similar but leaves the exact intent and relation of the two crescendos unclear. The autograph placing (Ex. 16.2b) immediately clarifies this, bringing up the left hand then both hands to the culminating *mf*. While the difference may look small on paper, the first edition's loss of dynamic focus can make that whole page flop like a half-heated soufflé, the architectural and expressive damage then spilling over to the following pages.

Example 16.2. Dynamics in Debussy's 'Jardins sous la pluie', bars 86–8

a: first edition (1903)

b: autograph dynamics (as in *Œuvres complètes*)

System or page breaks are high-risk points where composers easily forget to carry over slurs or hairpins. Though engravers sometimes dealt with this intelligently, a few cases fell prey to makeshift solutions. Example 16.3a shows a prime example, leaving an oddly incomplete crescendo and an equally senseless short slur at that fast tempo. Fauré's manuscript solves matters by showing that he forgot to complete a longer slur, doubtless along with the hairpin (Ex. 16.3b). Observing this can make similar occurrences elsewhere easy to spot and solve at a glance.

Example 16.3. Fauré, *Dolly*, 'Messieu Aoul', bars 17–21, primo part

a: first edition

b: autograph, presumed intention shown in broken lines

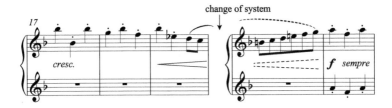

Debussy's open-ended reverberation ties suffered a similar fate when engravers cut them short in keeping with engraving rules stipulating that a tie must end on either a note or a barline. This led to a whole bar of tied-over reverberation from bar 6 being lost from the first edition of 'Les collines d'Anacapri'. A similar distortion at bar 9 of 'Et la lune descend sur le temple qui fut' left the bass a beat short in the original edition (it should enter at beat 3, as in the *Œuvres complètes*). One might argue – the engraver doubtless did – that the troublesome Monsieur Debussy should have filled those tied-over beats or bars with rests. From Debussy's descriptive habits, however, we can guess why he avoided doing that in places where he wanted reverberation, not silence. The pragmatic Ravel often compromised in such contexts (as in 'La vallée des cloches'), by adding rests over or inside reverberation ties to make the rhythmic totals explicit.

In defence of engravers it can be added that engraving, a slower task again than recopying, is so abstract from the music's real tempo that we can easily understand why engravers, however musically literate, sometimes lost all musical sense as they bashed out the copper plates. Among the more amazing results in standard old editions are *pp rubato* (instead of *pp subito*) at bar 294 of Franck's *Prélude, Choral et Fugue*, *f espress.* (instead of *f sempre*) at bar 99 of Fauré's 'Le pas espagnol' (from *Dolly*), and *p* instead of *sf* for a strongly accented note near the start of Debussy's 'Les collines d'Anacapri'.[8] The 1910 first print of 'La Cathédrale engloutie' even managed to render Debussy's *flottant et sourd* at bar 72 as *flottant et lourd*! These known examples prompt us to guess solutions in other cases where no manuscript survives.

ACHILLES' HEELS

Working with manuscripts soon reveals the types of slip to which composers are most prone. Miscounted ledger lines reflect not only the fatigue of recopying but also the way Fauré, Debussy and Ravel were all taught the use of antique clefs: visible in their student counterpoint exercises, these are sometimes centred a line above or below standard treble and bass clefs. As late as 1915–16 it took several prompts from Saint-Saëns to make the absent-minded Fauré aware of a repeated ledger line error near the end of his Second *Valse-caprice* of 1884; even then the error persisted in subsequent reprints.[9]

Octave transpositions are a standard hazard, especially at page or system changes. Both Ravel (bar 73 of 'Ondine') and Debussy (final chord of 'Hommage à S. Pickwick' and elsewhere) noticed missing *8va* signs only after the pieces were in print. We may surmise some others involving either hand (bar 31 of Ravel's 'Une barque sur l'océan', possibly even the last two notes in bar 73 of 'Ondine', plus a few in *Ma mère l'Oye* ('Laideronnette') and the finale of his Piano Trio).[10] An eccentric octave lurch across bars 257–8 of Debussy's *Masques* (corrected in the *Œuvres complètes*) can probably be attributed to incomplete proof emendations made over a system break. After publication of his *Études* Debussy indicated a similar correction to the pianist Walter Rummel: in 'Pour les octaves' the last left-hand dyad of bars 4 and similar should be an octave lower than in the first edition (Example 7.19d follows his correction). Unfortunately he omitted to clarify whether this also applies to the following right-hand dyad; the example of *Masques* and the passage's sequential logic suggest it probably should.

As for Fauré, a duplicate manuscript page of his Fifth Nocturne shows how an improbable octave lurch in bar 121 arose as he revised a complex arpeggio texture. (Example 15.3c corrects it as in the London Peters Edition: the fair copy and original edition give the last two dyads of bar 121 an octave lower.) Three bars later another octave dislocation occurs, the accented melody rising by a fourth at the end of bar 124 (Ex. 16.1b) instead of falling by a fifth as happens at every other occurrence of the theme (as in Example 15.3b, then again at bars 60 and 190). This case could be read as a compositional compromise since the melody is forced into a higher register anyway from bar 125: the quandary here is between losing the expressive effect of a falling fifth and being obliged to leap up an octave and a half just after it. I've seen composers decide such cases virtually on the toss of a coin in the course of rehearsal.

A recurring ambiguity from Fauré's era is the use of '8' under bass notes to signify either simple transposition or *coll'8ᵃ bassa*. When a passage mixes written-out bass octaves with single low notes marked '8', we can often assume *coll'8ᵃ*, as in parts of Fauré's Sixth and Seventh Nocturnes or the third of

Chabrier's *Valses romantiques* (though not in the opening section of Fauré's Fifth Barcarolle). It takes a closer look to spot the same issue in Variation X of Fauré's *Thème et variations* (bars 102, 108, 120 and 124 by analogy with bar 112), followed confusingly by '*8*' signs across bars 128–34 that can only mean simple transposition. Debussy's notation is more precise, and his piano roll of 'La Cathédrale engloutie' confirms just a single low bass *C′* from bar 28. (The complication there is that on smaller pianos this can sound so puny as to necessitate surreptitious upper-octave resonance – a private sin for pianists to decide, beyond the remit of urtext editing.)

For repeated beats, bars or phrases in manuscripts, or even for longer recapitulations, Debussy and Ravel often saved time by using shorthand ranging from *✗* to sequences of letters or numbers. Transitions in or out of such recapitulated passages risk the occasional non-sequitur: for example, bar 97 of the Prélude in *Pour le piano* – also perhaps bars 94–5 of 'Golliwogg's cake walk' – suggest *sempre pp* rather than the printed *p* carried over from the earlier passage. On a smaller scale, *✗* signs sometimes raise confusion over whether they repeat a beat or a bar: this can account for oft-discussed missing accidentals in bar 71 of Ravel's 'Ondine' and a cacophonous final beat in bar 102 of 'Une barque sur l'océan' (both corrected in the London Peters edition). Related problems of whether repeated beats are meant to include articulations or double stems (some of which may have been added later than the *✗* signs) affect passages in Debussy's *Études* and *En blanc et noir*.

Fauré tended to avoid such shorthands and recopy repeated or parallel passages in full, leaving myriad small variants. Many of them do no harm (variety in performance is always worth encouraging), and the London Peters editions adjust only a few that lie so awkwardly as to suggest a slip of the pen. Some cases clearly resulted from Fauré's eye or ear jumping a bar, hearing the music faster than the pen could write. Obvious examples are a rogue left-hand D♭ bass octave on the penultimate page of the third *Valse-caprice* and – corrected in the London Peters edition – an oddly jarring *a♭* towards the end of bar 63 in the Sixth Nocturne; in each case the oddity makes sense not there but in the next bar.

Chapter 5 has already noted a repeated bar in 'Jardins sous la pluie', added by Debussy at proof but missing from his manuscript at a change of page. His manuscripts of *Pour le piano* and *Children's Corner* shows similar slips at page changes which again he corrected before they went to print. He may have missed one case, though, in the prelude 'Les tierces alternées' where bar 31 jolts, without any obvious purpose, a sequence of otherwise paired bars. In his autograph this bar again coincides with a page change, and the context similarly suggests he may have meant the bar to be repeated (as flagged in the *Œuvres complètes*).[11]

Modality has equivalent hazards. The manuscript and first edition of Debussy's *L'isle joyeuse* leave its main theme (Ex. 1.3a) without the ♮ to the *g″* in bars 9, 15, 16 and 66, but supply it at the theme's returns in bars 64 and 65; they similarly flatten the seventh degree whenever the theme returns in any other key (bars 107, 147, 204 and 212). Reprints from 1910 onwards add the corresponding ♮ in bar 66, but we have only the word of Bernardino Molinari – who orchestrated the piece with Debussy's help – and the pianist Marguerite Long that Debussy did intend *g″*♮ in bars 9, 15 and 16.[12] (Later Durand prints added the ♮ to bars 9, 15 and 16, perhaps at the prompting of Mme Long.) Doubtless the natural-sounding 'overtone' scale involved – plus the tactile way *g″*♮ lies under the hand – lulled Debussy into overlooking the discrepancy with the key signature.

This can alert us to other possible cases, two of which are addressed in the *Œuvres complètes*: at bar 16 of "*Les fées sont d'exquises danseuses*" modal and harmonic factors again suggest a natural is needed to *g″* and *g‴* (maintaining an octatonic sequence), and similarly ♯ to the *e′* at bars 16 and 66 of 'Pagodes' (Ex. 1.5). As in *L'isle joyeuse* the note involved is on the cusp of the key signature and the assumed inflection lets the hand fall naturally, avoiding an obtrusive arpeggiation in 'Pagodes'.[13]

One case in Ravel involves a harmonic-cadential gesture common to many of his works (Ex. 16.4a), with a characteristic sharp on the answering chord's ninth degree (as shown by the arrow in Example 16.4a). The one exception in all his output – Example 16.4b, recapitulating Example 16.4a – leaves a strong feeling that the corresponding sharp (to *c′*) must have been intended there too; Example 16.4c is just one of dozens of parallel passages that support this.[14]

Example 16.4. Ravel cadential gesture (arrows indicate the notes at issue)

a: Concerto in G, first movement, from 8 bars before figure 9, solo part

b: from 6½ bars before figure 27, solo part

c: *Le tombeau de Couperin*, Menuet, bars 19–20

A subtler case affects bar 27 of Debussy's *Étude* 'Pour les agréments': analogy with bar 17 suggests that Debussy inadvertently omitted an intended ♯ to both the *b* and the *d* of the last chord (no present edition observes this). Anybody worried about such apparent liberties need only look at bars 25 and 139 of 'Les tierces alternées', where Debussy absentmindedly omitted one of an intended pair of sharps (to the *d′*). Although he spotted the slip soon after publication, his written correction lay unpublished for over seventy years and would have been lost had a colleague not carefully preserved it.[15]

An equally telling slip occurs eight and nine bars before the end of the first of the *Images* [*oubliées*] of 1894, where Debussy – twice – wrote a natural at beat 3 without noticing it was needed two chords earlier. Fauré did the same at bar 45 of his First Nocturne (the ♮ to the right-hand *b′*), a lapsus that most performers correct without even noticing anything amiss. The mishap-strewn central episode of Debussy's *Nocturne* of 1892 (Ex. 9.4) is one of the strongest reminders to read always with a wary eye and ear. The repeated moral is that any composer's attention or pen can slip: Poulenc once admitted to having absentmindedly written *pp* where he meant *ff* and discovered the error only at rehearsal, with an understandable jolt.[16] Ravel's Concerto in G suggests a similar slip near the end of the first movement (rehearsal figure 35): reading the piano's printed *f* as an intended *p* makes better sense of the ensuing crescendo and crucially lets the bassoon and horn solos through.

Fatigue was probably at the root of a whole cluster of semi-visible slips at bars 58–9 of Debussy's 'Pour les notes répétées'. Example 16.5a shows the first edition's apparently plausible reading (apart from Debussy's mangled Italian for *un pochettino*): only the crescendo hairpin seems odd, implying a continuity over the barline at odds with the left hand's phrase break and harmonic disjunction. Debussy's fair copy (Ex. 16.5b) adds support to the continuity by showing a phrasing contradiction over a system break, plus bass ties in bar 58 that might be read as pointing past the barline. His preparatory draft completes the picture: in the midst of some messy revision the final reading of bar 58 shows three essential accidentals missing from the later sources (Ex. 16.5c). Put it all together and everything falls into line musically with that initially suspect crescendo.

Example 16.5. Debussy, 'Pour les notes répétées', bars 58–9

a: first edition

b: autograph fair copy, lower staff (dynamics as above)

c: the same with additional accidentals as in Debussy's preparatory draft (more roughly written with numerous messy erasures)

Composer's drafts come into their own in such cases, sometimes showing revisions entered in the course of making the fair copy, the pen shuttling back and forth between the two sources. Accidents or oversights occasionally make the draft a later or more reliable source than the fair copy: Chapter 17 shows an example in Debussy's 'Pour les quartes'. A similar relationship exists, rather exceptionally, across the autograph and surviving proofs of Debussy's First Book of Preludes: only after the plates were engraved did Debussy add final details to the autograph, then copy them to proof. A few of them, however, eluded his eye or jumped a bar or two, notably in 'Minstrels' and 'Ce qu'a vu le Vent d'Ouest' (as noted in the *Œuvres complètes*). One late addition he made to 'Voiles' appears to have jumped a bar even on the autograph: musical logic suggests that the entire indication *Cédez - - - - // a Tempo* across bars 26–8 should be a bar earlier – probably the leap of a fatigued eye across two similar-looking triplet groups a bar apart.

These queries are now impossible to answer definitively, along with one in Debussy's 'Ondine' of whether the initial grace-note flurry of bar 13 was meant to be repeated in mid-bar.[17] We can also only guess if some printed 𝄐 signs in his *Études* are, as several of his Preludes might suggest, misprints for 𝄑. In the autographs of the two collections the symbols look identical and thus would suggest reading 𝄑 each time – were it not for a 𝄐 in Debussy's early draft of 'Pour les cinq doigts' at bar 110, which his fair copy and first edition replace by an unequivocal ·?̂. Whatever we conclude, raising these queries at least prompts us to explore the music's logic.

EDITORIAL ADVENTURES

Debussy's polyphonic thinking in his piano music often emerges vividly from his manuscript stemming. 'Mouvement' from *Images* is particularly revealing in the way its bass line points down throughout the piece, visually projecting the large-scale architecture. The *Œuvres complètes* reproduce this – or rather restore it, because the first edition inverted many of the bass stems in keeping with engraving norms, fracturing visual continuity and misrelating voices, as Example 16.6 shows. Debussy's manuscripts are remarkably consistent about this over the years, suggesting his clear intentions, even if he knew that engraving conventions would often prohibit them from being printed exactly.

Example 16.6. Debussy, 'Mouvement' (*Images*), bars 46–8, auxiliary staff as in autograph and *Œuvres complètes,* main reading as in all other editions (which also misprint the *arpa*)

Experience with the *Œuvres complètes* often proved what had gone awry in the first editions: in several passages where Debussy's autograph notation was carefully restored and sent off for the new engraving, back came proofs identical with the first edition, the same engraving rules having been reimposed a century later. A memorable victory was snatched when third proofs for 'Poissons d'or' finally re-stemmed some treble notes upwards as they appear in Debussy's autograph (at bars 72–3: his notation is very graphic as the notes concerned are already high above the staff), with the engraver's annotation above in vivid green ink, 'Debussy, dans son paradis, doit être soulagé!!!' ('Debussy, in his paradise, must be feeling relieved!!!').

Fortunately the *Œuvres complètes* were able to print some hairpins in the same open-angled way as they appear in the manuscripts of pieces like *L'isle joyeuse*, visually indicating bold crescendos and diminuendos that should have listeners on the edge of the seat. The house style of many publishers still forbids this (I wish I were kidding), printing such hairpins with lines nearly parallel as dictated by rules of printed graphics, and readers have to guess from musical sense (or editorial commentary) that a similar openness of dynamics pervades works like Fauré's *Dolly*, sometimes taking dynamics across extremes in just a few beats.

Fauré's usage of stem directions is almost contrary to Debussy's. Probably because of his larger writing, he often directed them just to take best advantage of space available: the voices shown at one point by respective up-stems and down-stems thus can suddenly become inverted a bar or even beat later. Ravel sometimes does the same. This lets the sounding result speak for itself, not unreasonably since the sense of Fauré's part-writing tends to be obvious. Sometimes Fauré's layout works less well in print, causing congestion and voicing dislocation: Example 16.7 shows an example in the *Pièces brèves* (ending a sequential passage), which the Peters edition renotates as on the auxiliary staff.

Example 16.7. Fauré, *Pièces brèves* op. 84, no. II, bars 27–9, main reading as in sources, editorially re-stemmed on auxiliary staff

It's a quirk of editing to find oneself thus treating two composers in opposite ways in order to obtain the same goal of polyphonic continuity and clarity on the page. A few cases of Fauré's humpty-dumpty stemming can be traced to his having double-stemmed main bass notes for emphasis after the figurations were already written: some surviving proofs catch him literally red-handed at this, the stems added in red ink. Even then we have to balance idealism with pragmatism, as it's important not to over-sanitize a composer's notation to the point of masking its character. A few cases also require editorial caution when Fauré's stemming indicates hand distribution, as we'll see in Chapter 20.

RISKY SOURCES

The *Œuvres complètes de Claude Debussy* are probably the first critical edition to have treated a composer's recordings seriously as a source, taking corrections and viable variants from the piano rolls Debussy recorded around 1912 (see Appendix 3). As with Fauré's and Ravel's piano rolls (consulted for London Peters editions), these entail hazards even beyond the primary one that a roll can't guarantee original dynamics or tempo. The editor's quandary is illustrated by the way a roll often confirms a detail like an accidental missing in other sources: to take this on board, though, immediately obliges consideration of all variants on the roll, however indifferent or even troublesome they may seem.

The practical question there is where to draw lines and how to justify them. For the Debussy *Œuvres complètes* and the London Peters Fauré, this prompted four editorial categories: 1) variants that clearly correct errors in other sources (these were directly incorporated in the new musical text); 2) musically viable variants (these are shown on auxiliary staves); 3) indifferent or less than useful variants (relegated to the list of readings); and 4) obvious fluffs (ignored, to avoid overloading the commentary). The very existence of the rolls forces us into this unavoidable subjectivity, of which we have to make the best musically. Categories 1–2 may also reflect what the composers had marked in handexemplars now lost.

One of the most telling details imported from Debussy's piano rolls into the *Œuvres complètes* is a sequence of left-hand off-beat dyads on the first page of 'Danseuses de Delphes', filling odd-sounding gaps in the first edition's texture and more closely matching a similar texture on the next page. Their musical logic suggests that Debussy left them out of the fair copy and first edition by mere oversight. It was especially gratifying to launch the *Œuvres complètes* with some chords never printed before on the first page of the first Prelude: the risk of doing this was later vindicated when it emerged that Debussy had indicated the same correction to Ricardo Viñes. This prompted the *Œuvres complètes* and the London Peters Fauré edition to propose added notes or chords (in small notes or brackets) at similarly suspicious gaps in Debussy's 'Ce qu'a vu le Vent d'Ouest' and two of Fauré's Nocturnes.

This activity is most obvious in Debussy's, Fauré's and Ravel's wartime editions of Chopin, Schumann and Mendelssohn (which follow norms of the era rather than those of modern critical editing). Chapter 15 has already touched on Ravel's views, resulting from that project, on the marking of articulation. More interesting again is to observe composers editing their own music. Surviving proofs show Debussy, in 1905, editing his *Suite bergamasque* originally composed in 1890. His retouches comprise added counterpoints and heightened modal colour (by means of deftly placed added accidentals), balanced by the excision of weaker passages, notably between the present bars 72 and 73 of the Menuet. The result shows him skilfully stepping back into the shoes of the composer he had been in 1890. If he brought off the task with considerable aplomb, it reminds us that revisiting music written years earlier has its hazards. This emerges from Fauré's revision, late in life, of piano pieces he'd composed up to forty years before. Chapter 18 shows a few places where his revisions raise problems that make the normal editorial practice of *Fassung letzter Hand* unworkable.

Fauré's revisions also tend to nudge up the dynamics, usually in ways that clarify the music's outlines. This might raise an instant suspicion of being the result of his increasing deafness, were it not a known habit of his earlier years, almost whenever he revised or recopied anything. In general his later adjustments imply renotation rather than musical rethinking, often in apparent reaction to precious or tentative performance – hence his habit of repeating or duplicating *f*, *sempre f*, *crescendo* and ⤙ signs; this shows him battling even during his lifetime against understated performance of his music.

Another role often hidden is that of composers' colleagues in helping a work to its final form. Alfred Cortot's editing role in Fauré's *Fantaisie* op. 111 is known from letters and evidence on manuscripts. The autograph of Fauré's Tenth Barcarolle equally shows Cortot's intervention (with Fauré's blessing) in renotating bars 30 and 32 more playably by transferring notes from left to right hand.[18] Editorial quandaries can arise, though, when useful non-autograph annotations of that sort don't show the composer's imprimatur. Who can now tell which of them might have been made at the piano with the composer alongside ('you're right, that should be a sharp not a natural', or 'oh, that ought to be a beat earlier', or even 'ignore that metronome mark, it's nonsense'). I've often witnessed this at rehearsal. While editors have to play safe with such markings, editions can usefully alert readers to important cases.

The first edition of Debussy's *L'isle joyeuse* contains a revealing piece of editing (whether in-house or by Debussy is unknown). Example 16.8 shows bars 7–8 according to Debussy's autograph (the *ossia* reading) and the first edition (the main reading), the latter doubtless adjusted to prevent a hand collision. French piano music, however, is full of such voice or hand overlaps (for example, bar 10 of 'Bruyères'), and the autograph reading in Example 16.8 frankly offers two advantages. First, it shows the longer-term polyphony more clearly (cf. the continued sustained notes in Ex. 1.3a). Secondly, it can easily be managed with some sleight of hand, allowing the *a* to be held through any desired pedal aeration at beat 3. The *Œuvres complètes* show both readings; the 'critical act' (to use James Grier's term) underlying this could be read as the implied question 'Might it have been better left unchanged?'

Example 16.8. Debussy, *L'isle joyeuse*, bars 7–8

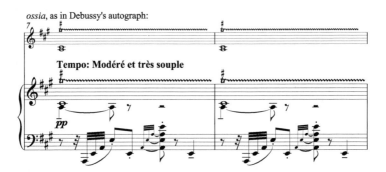

'Pour les arpèges composés' shows another late 'edit', definitely by Debussy, that raises a more practical problem. Example 16.9 shows the first edition's odd rhythmic alignment at the end of bars 7 and 9. A part-explanation emerges from Debussy's fair copy, which shows that the bass rhythm for beat 3 in each bar was originally ♩, the latter note correctly aligned under the upper staff's final ♪; in this form the notation makes overall sense. For reasons unknown Debussy then amended each ♩ to ♩, scratching out the dot and the end beam but leaving the last note's alignment unchanged. (Why the first edition moved it farther right again is an added mystery: was the engraver perhaps asked to move it left but accidentally moved it the wrong way on the mirror-image plate? I've seen exactly that mistake occur on other proofs.) To make sense of Debussy's revision, either the bass *B'♭* has to be realigned under the top *c'* and the *m.g.* indication removed, or the arpeggio has to be sped up and followed by a longer rest. If most critical editions, including the *Œuvres complètes*, opt for the latter solution, my sympathy is more with the former (to avoid a scramble) – or even just that of regarding Debussy's revision as a possible aberration and reverting to his original dotted bass rhythm (which frankly appears to make just as good musical sense if not better). In sum, this passage is another that defies definitive solution.[19]

Example 16.9. Debussy, 'Pour les arpèges composés', first edition (1916), bars 7 and 9

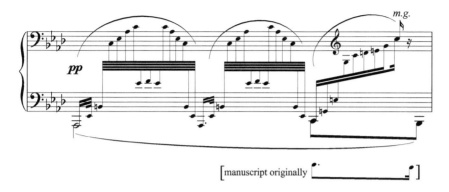

It's also pertinent to wonder how Debussy played (for example) his *Berceuse héroïque* at the piano after he had orchestrated it: his orchestral version arguably enlivens a rather static ending in the piano version by adding some extra melodic echoes. Debussy's piano roll of *La plus que lente*, recorded after he orchestrated the piece, differs sufficiently from the printed piano score to have justified transcribing it in the *Œuvres complètes* (1/4, Appendix).

CHOOSING AN EDITION

Appendix 4 provides some documentation on the matter of choosing editions. Devotees can ideally compare critical editions – libraries are there to help them – for what they can learn from their differing approaches and conclusions. Facsimiles are always worth acquiring: no printed edition, however well prepared, can recreate the sense of playing from the composer's writing. If they show some less-than-definitive readings, these can be all the more illuminating for those who know the music well.

CHAPTER 17

Rhythm, tempo, dance and humour

The pitiless, mournful despotism of the metronome   – D.-E. Inghelbrecht

Every time we let ourselves go with unmarked speed fluctuations, we give proof that
we have failed to meet the composer's intentions, and that we are using a trick to
save ourselves.   – D.-E. Inghelbrecht

INGHELBRECHT'S contrasted remarks sum up the quandaries of playing 'in
time' without stiffness, sogginess or preciousness. This must be the hardest
element of music to notate, allowing for internal fluidity and differing
acoustics, instruments and performers' touch. French repertoire often
demands more concentration again to hold a steady tempo underneath the
ornamented rhythmic surface and to bind the structure coherently. If it can be
tempting in performance to let effects like *cédez, rit., serrez* or *rubato* prolif-
erate, their very presence in print implies a default of stricter tempo than in
most Germanic music, one that reflects the historic importance of dance in
French music.

Many fluctuations marked by the composers also have a structural function: to exaggerate or compound them risks structural damage in pieces like
Debussy's Preludes where structures that can look segmented on the page rely
on rhythmic continuity for integration into larger spans. Over-attention to
the surface can risk caricaturing the music, like viewing a large Impressionist
painting only from close up, without moving back enough to see its brush
strokes coalesce into larger shapes.

A scarcely notatable French way of letting the music breathe between
phrases, especially in Fauré or Ravel, is sometimes a momentary wait on the
last note of a sentence or paragraph, inaudible as such to the listener, and
without any slowing before. Ravel's extreme aversion to preparatory or

sentimental slowing is repeatedly documented by his colleagues Gaby Casadesus, Vlado Perlemuter, Hélène Jourdan-Morhange and Jacques Février; Perlemuter revealingly recalled that Ravel wanted the Menuet of his *Sonatine* 'supple' yet 'above all with absolute rhythmic strictness'.[1]

Fauré in turn is reported as insisting on conveying 'les nuances' without tempo change (the word in French refers primarily to dynamics). Fauré's son Emmanuel recalled that his father played his works 'avec une régularité de métronome', a view corroborated by the violinist Hélène Jourdan-Morhange and the singer Claire Croiza ('a metronome incarnate' was Croiza's term). The tenor of their remarks suggests that, for Fauré, indulgent lingering (or any kind of rhythmic sloppiness) was a *bête noire* tantamount to dressing his music in frills and pink ribbons.[2] If Croiza's own recordings (and Fauré's piano rolls, as we'll see) are less metronomic than that might suggest, we can still read her as meaning 'rhythmically taut', with all it implies about the surrounding norms with which they had to contend.

As for Debussy, pianists Maurice Dumesnil, Marguerite Long, Paul Loyonnet and E. Robert Schmitz all recall his insistence on exact rhythm; Pierre Monteux, who conducted the première of *Jeux*, remembered, 'And he wanted everything exactly in time.'[3] Marguerite Long adds that even for the opening swirls of 'Feux d'artifice' Debussy insisted on four in the bar, while his indicated *sans rigueur* in 'Hommage à Rameau' demanded 'nulle infraction rythmique' (no rhythmic liberties) and practice with the metronome.[4] Jane Bathori, one of Debussy's favourite singers who was also a fine pianist, enlarged on this in terms of Debussy's insistence on exact rhythmic observation without pedantry – hence his *sans rigueur* instructions.[5] (The *sans rigueur* indication in 'Hommage à Rameau', going by Debussy's notational habits already seen, might be read as covering the piece's occasional departures from $\frac{3}{2}$ metre.) Paul Loyonnet recalled playing 'Danseuses de Delphes' to Debussy, who immediately remarked that 'some eighth-notes weren't exactly in time. I replayed the piece while Debussy tapped a merciless beat [*une mesure impitoyable*] with his foot.'[6] This mirrors Debussy's initial reaction when Dumesnil started to play him 'Hommage à Rameau': 'I do not hear the triplets in time' – complicated by his then finding the triplets 'too strictly in time' when Dumesnil played him 'Clair de lune' (possibly the section marked *rubato*).[7] Debussy's habit of tying over main beats is often a part of the music's rhythmic architecture, as at the start of his *Image* 'Et la lune descend': playing the opening phrase in strict time directs the phrase aptly to the first sounding main beat at bar 3.

Experiment at the piano shows how surprisingly close Debussy can often be played to the metronome. The inbuilt textural variety assures flexibility (assuming suppleness of touch and voicing), and nearly all the passages recalcitrant to a mechanical beat are those indicated with the necessary fluctuations.

A typical case, the indicated *rubato* at the start of 'Reflets dans l'eau', essentially calls for space at the start and end of each two-bar group (*à la* Brahms) with a compensatory pull into the middle. Much the same applies across the longer eight-bar *rubato* phrases from bar 67 of *L'isle joyeuse*, the crux being to keep a sense of waltz. (A slight lingering on the second chord of bars 67 and 68 essentially does the trick and avoids the danger of sounding like two-in-the-bar). This matches Debussy's advice to Maurice Dumesnil to apply rubato 'within the entire phrase, never on a single beat'.[8] (This reflects the general point that rubato intrinsically draws attention to the notes affected, a warning not to highlight subsidiary figurations at the expense of broader themes.) On a larger scale all this relates to the larger-scale architectonic rubato marked by Debussy across *L'isle joyeuse* and 'Hommage à Rameau' (as discussed in Chapter 4). In sum, his rubato indications – always carefully cancelled afterwards – usually suggest rhythmic intensification, sometimes a surge rather than slowing which, well managed, draws attention away from itself. As with pedal, we can often sense how much is needed by first trying the passage without. (Besides which, local indications like *un pochettino rubato* at bar 58 of Debussy's *Étude* 'Pour les notes répétées' obviously indicate a surrounding default of less, not more.)

Claire Croiza recalled Henri Duparc once telling her, 'If I had known what some singers do with them I would never have put any rallentandi in my songs.'[9] This helps explain why Fauré later cut some similar indications from his scores, with mixed results as we'll see in Chapter 18. In Chabrier and early Debussy an older Schumannesque rule sometimes holds of a local *rit.* applying just to the end of the bar or short phrase, with *a tempo* then tacitly assumed.[10] (See for example the second page of Chabrier's 'Paysage' in the Dover edition.) This must apply in the closing bars of Fauré's Fifth and Eleventh Barcarolles: in the case of the Fifth – where his manuscript places *poco rit.* a bar earlier than the first edition – musical sense suggests reading it as barely more than a tenuto lingering on the left thumb's *b*.

Sometimes ostinato patterns across transitions serve as a warning against slowing, for example in Example 15.1, in bars 18–19 of the first movement in Ravel's *Sonatine* (the repeated $f'\sharp$–e'), over the repeated a–$b\flat$ linking the recapitulation to the cadenza in 'Oiseaux tristes', and across the main transitions (bars 23–4 and 39–40) of Debussy's 'Cloches à travers les feuilles'.

A distinction also emerges between *Rit.* and the progressive *Rall.*, notably in Fauré where the latter often gently winds down the end of a long span. Alfred Cortot reports Chabrier's strictness over the distinction (see p. 319 below) and, from his own experience, extends the same rule to Dukas and Ravel. The *Rit.* before the recapitulation of Debussy's 'Hommage à Rameau' makes the point: as Jacques Février observed in his teaching, the tempo there, if anything, has to ease forward again through the final triplets of bar 56 into *Au mouv*[t] at bar 57. The same can be sensed – despite the *molto rall.* this time – in the two-note upbeat to the recapitulation of Fauré's Fifth Nocturne. Gaby Casadesus neatly defined the distinction relative to Ravel's indicated *Rit.* at bar 28 of *Jeux d'eau*: 'without slowing down, Ravel wanted only a very slight ritenuto before the return to *a tempo.*'[11] This helps us negotiate delicate turns like the end of bar 6 in *Jeux d'eau*, which certainly can't be played to the metronome yet daren't slow audibly (hence doubtless Ravel's avoidance of any marking).

It's important to know that the sign // in later Debussy scores (for example, as in *Cédez _ _ _ _ //*) never means a hiatus: it merely defines the end of *Cédez, Serrez* or whatever. Again the very fact that Debussy didn't foresee the danger of confusion implies his default assumption of continuity – as with his unmarked sounding metrical equivalences in 'La Cathédrale engloutie' and the infamously redundant *Le double plus lent* near the end of *Pour le piano* (both discussed in Chapter 15). Reading Debussy this way makes consistent sense of his notation and bears out Messiaen's oft-reported description of him as 'one of the greatest rhythmists of all time'.[12] In effect Debussy's music swarms with rubato at many levels, mostly written into the notation, and his indicated fluctuations – the visible tip of the iceberg – mostly warn us where he couldn't notate it completely.

Of Debussy's twelve *Études*, six contain the marking *scherzando* (joking, playful), besides one marking *ballabile* (dance-like). This reflects not just the constant wit in Debussy's writings and letters (often in the form of untranslatable puns, even in his blacker moods) but also the occasional gag written into his piano music, notably from *Children's Corner* on, an element probably inspired by his infant daughter Chouchou. The opening page of his *Études* might be read as revenge on Chouchou's piano practice, while telling us what the coming *Études* are *not* about. A century later we easily risk a false perspective by viewing such music through a modernist mid-twentieth century the composers never knew, rather than in the dance-like wake of Chabrier, Massenet, Delibes and even Gounod, never mind Chopin.

If Debussy's dance sources are clearest in his early works, later textures veil them only lightly, especially when titles or tempo headings specify sarabande, menuet, habanera or waltz. Robert Godet recalled how Debussy admired the paintings of Degas 'for the unique grace of his rhythms in dance movements'.[13] Besides his explicit ballet compositions, Debussy saw his orchestral *Nocturnes* – plus possibly some of his Preludes and *Children's Corner* in orchestral form – danced to by Isadora Duncan, Loïe Fuller and others, to the extent that Fuller's dancing may have inspired one of his Preludes (see Appendix 2).

Ravel, in addition to his original ballets, orchestrated several of his piano works for ballet performance, along with works by Chabrier, Schumann and Chopin. In 1913 he defended the stage adaptation of Fauré's *Dolly* (in Henri

Rabaud's orchestration), saying that 'every musical work may undergo [such transcription] on condition that good taste presides'.[14] Most telling is Ravel's letter of February 1906 to Jean Marnold outlining what eventually became *La valse*, 'a grand waltz, a sort of homage to the memory of the great Strauss – not Richard, the other one, Johann. You know of my deep sympathy for these wonderful rhythms, and that I value the joie de vivre expressed by the dance far more deeply than the Franckist puritanism.'[15] (Ravel's disdain here was for the Franckist school rather than Franck himself, of whose *Variations symphoniques* he was very fond.)

<h2 style="text-align:center">DANCE GESTURES</h2>

Émile Vuillermoz recalled how Debussy played the Sarabande of *Pour le piano* 'with the easy simplicity of a good dancer from the sixteenth century' in a way that 'recaptured, bar by bar, the feel of a vanished civilisation'.[16] This probably involved several gestures that slightly bend musical notation. Vlado Perlemuter advised marginal rhythmic compression of the piece's repeated pattern ♫, dynamically falling away from the first note (the classical meaning of a slur). Debussy's stepdaughter Dolly de Tinan added her memory of Debussy making a characteristic 'sarabande lift' before the long chord in bars 2 and similar of that piece and at bars 8 and similar of 'Hommage à Rameau'. She also recalled that Debussy kept 'Hommage à Rameau' firmly in three (not six).[17] If the scores don't show these gestures more explicitly than by a few dots and dashes, Debussy's concern was probably to avoid any risk of caricature. For those familiar with dance the gestures are inherent in the mention 'sarabande' in the title or tempo heading; if that seems to us indirect, the fault is with our era for losing the relevant dance awareness. The same goes for Debussy's heading *mouv^t de habanera* in 'La soirée dans Grenade' and 'La Puerta del Vino': Marcel Ciampi reported that Debussy wanted their dotted rhythms sometimes stretched towards sextuplet value, the same sort of natural elasticity as in Mozart's siciliana rhythms.[18]

Ravel's *Miroirs* show two rhythms that defy notation, as Ravel confided to Gaby Casadesus and Vlado Perlemuter. For bars 2 and similar of 'Oiseaux tristes' the triplets of the bird-call have to be slightly compressed – calling for discreet sleight of hand when the figure returns over the left hand ostinato – and in 'Alborada del gracioso' the 32nd-note turns at bars 126–9 and 157–60 conversely have to be slightly stretched.[19] Compressed triplets are a frequent French and Spanish dance gesture (as opposed to Brahmsian stretching): Fauré's reported insistence on distinguishing audibly between the duplets and triplets in Variation III of his *Thème et variations* can suggest light laughter, moving through the triplets then easing back the duplets.[20] Debussy's reply in

1907 to the young Manuel de Falla sums up the composer's dilemma: 'What you ask is rather hard to give a definite answer to! It's not possible to write down the exact form of a rhythm, any more than it is to explain the different effects of a single phrase!'[21]

WALTZ

As with Chopin, waltz tends to be endemic in French triple metre when the texture doesn't suggest sarabande or minuet. Ravel illustrated this by warning Henriette Faure not to turn the Menuet of his *Sonatine* into a waltz by hurrying or misinflecting it.[22] Sarabande often makes itself felt through a dissonant or marked second beat, as in Ravel's 'Le jardin féerique', Debussy's 'Danseuses de Delphes' or Fauré's Thirteenth Nocturne. The 'lift' already observed in two Debussy sarabandes is a gestural variant of that.

We may thus read numerous unlabelled contexts in the manner of Fauré's advice to Vlado Perlemuter for Variation V of his *Thème et variations*: to let it waltz.[23] Besides pervading Fauré's Barcarolles, waltz can be heard variously in Chabrier's exuberant *Impromptu* and his slower 'Mélancolie', in the alluring central section then the wild coda of Debussy's *L'isle joyeuse*, and again in Debussy's *Étude* 'Pour les octaves' and the first movement of *En blanc et noir*. One of Debussy's treasured *objets d'art* was a cast of Camille Claudel's sculpture *La Valse* (reproduced in Roberts, *Images*, p. 309, and Nectoux, *Harmonie en bleu et or*, pp. 173–4).

All this affects French musical usage of the word *lent* in triple metre, often assuming an underlying slow waltz as in Debussy's prelude 'La terrasse des audiences du clair de lune' or – slower again – 'Feuilles mortes' and 'La Cathédrale engloutie'. These are admittedly slow beyond the norms of danced waltz, like the Épilogue of Ravel's *Valses nobles et sentimentales*.

Context for this comes from the start of Ravel's *Valses nobles et sentimentales*, headed *Modéré* along with a vigorous but judicious ♩ = 176. (Read this as ♩. = 58 and the *modéré* becomes clearer.) In the music of Johann Strauss II, so admired by Ravel, a moderately slow waltz (*The Blue Danube*) and moderately fast waltz (*Die Fledermaus* – Ex. 17.1a) often differ mostly through internal articulation. Example 17.1b allows the amusing experiment of playing from Strauss straight into Ravel. This possible pun (he may well have meant it) also embraces Schubert's *Valses nobles*, whose opening rhythm ♫ ♩ ♩ ♫ ♩ ♩ ♫ ♩ ♩ Ravel deftly shifts a beat sideways. Beyond waltz, French tempo markings tend to reflect underlying structure rather than surface figurations: this vitally affects the long opening melodies that launch Fauré's *Dolly* suite and Debussy's *Petite suite*.

Example 17.1

a: From Johann Strauss II,
Die Fledermaus, Overture

b: Ravel, *Valses nobles et
sentimentales*, bars 1–2

Ravel reportedly liked to repeat an anecdote of Brahms writing a few bars of *The Blue Danube* into an autograph album and signing it 'Alas, not by Johannes Brahms'.[24] A counterpart comes from Debussy's prelude *"Les fées sont d'exquises danseuses"*, whose lingering central episode twice echoes a famous Brahms waltz (Ex. 17.2: the Brahms, from op. 39, is shown above it). Debussy's preference for Brahms's alto line is in character: in Mallarméan style it tickles the ear with something evocatively familiar rather than instantly identifiable. This follows a witty tradition (from days of laxer copyright laws) in which, for example, the Mazurka in Delibes's *Coppélia* cheekily recycles the Can-can from Offenbach's *Orphée aux enfers* in waltz time. (Try it and see.)

Example 17.2. Debussy, *"Les fées sont d'exquises danseuses"*, bars 79–80 (likewise bars 96–7)

Debussy's *La plus que lente* of 1910 is somewhat *sui generis*, a riposte to the *valse lente* fad already parodied by Massenet's *Valse très lente* (Really slow waltz) as well as Satie's song *Je te veux*. In reality it isn't a particularly slow piece, and Debussy's title – a deft blend of Massenet and Couperin – can only be approximated in translation as 'The slow waltz outwaltzed'. The violinist Arthur Hartmann recalled Debussy proudly playing him the newly completed piece in summer 1910, in the face of Hartmann's puzzlement and Emma

Debussy's embarrassment: neither of them understood the piece, which Hartmann thought was a failed attempt at a best-seller.[25] Debussy's violinistic inspiration for it leaves the question of why he set it in the most unviolinistic of keys (F♯) and made no violin version. Perhaps Hartmann's incomprehension discouraged him, though Debussy later arranged it for *brasserie* orchestra (as Satie did with *Je te veux*), starting with an added cimbalom cadenza. The piece's rondo sequence is punctuated by two very leisurely cadences, producing almost the sense of a suite of waltzes. The final page teasingly draws out the same cadence, repeatedly making wrong turns like an over-adhesive guest who doesn't want to leave. As with Ravel and the *Valses nobles*, Debussy had a special fondness for *La plus que lente*, whose apparently rampaging sentiment veils some highly sophisticated wit.

Fauré's *Valses-caprices*, again *sui generis*, lie somewhere between *La plus que lente* and forebears ranging from Chopin to Liszt's *Valses-caprices* based on Schubert. All too easily dismissed in northern climes as frivolous, they deserve the consideration of Alfred Cortot's appraisal:

> One couldn't have suspected, before [Fauré] wrote the four pieces that make up the *Valses-caprices* and which are among the most characteristic of his output, that he could have contained, without in the least denying their worldly, facile and brilliant characteristics, so much sensuous grace, such perfect distinction and passionate tenderness.[26]

Fauré's own tenderness for them emerges from a letter he wrote in 1919, years after their composition, to one of his favourite pianists, Robert Lortat:

> May I ask you – how tedious composers are! – to take the opening theme of each of the *Valses-caprices* more slowly? The justification, as I see it, of the title *Valses-caprices*, is <u>variety of tempo</u>. They're always played too fast and too <u>uniformly fast</u>.[27]

In fact the first two *Valses-caprices* show these intentions fairly clearly: in the first one the opening tempo can be set broadly enough to allow for Fauré's *accelerando molto* from bar 15 and the grace note at bar 35, yet lively enough to allow for *Meno mosso* from bar 47. Fauré's plea to Lortat, however, raises enough questions to justify devoting Chapter 18 to him.

DEBUSSY, DANCE AND THE METRONOME

For all Debussy's distrust at times of metronome markings – notably his famous remark of October 1915 observing that 'they work for a bar', like '*les roses, l'espace d'un matin*[28] – his scores show him supplying them more often than not from 1907 onwards. His exceptionally detailed ones throughout the *Image* 'Et la lune descend sur le temple qui fut' – ignored by most performers – are entirely practicable, hold the piece together and provide, just once in Debussy's piano output, a detailed graph of how tempo can breathe with the texture without drawing undue attention.[29]

Metronome markings also head nine out of twelve Preludes in Book 1. In 'Danseuses de Delphes' Debussy's sarabande-like ♩ = 44 guards against sagging in the middle of the piece. For 'La fille aux cheveux de lin' his ♩ = 66 suggests a gentle minuet, especially at the lilting rhythm ♫♩♫♫♫ in bars 24 and 26. This rhythm returns in the second of his three Mallarmé songs of 1913, explicitly headed *Dans le mouvt d'un Menuet lent*, an ironic serenade to a shepherdess on a porcelain teacup. The allusion is highly relevant to 'La fille aux cheveux de lin' with its shepherd's-pipe-like opening, for the prelude's title refers back, via Leconte de Lisle's eponymous poem, to Robert Burns's 'Lassie wi' the lint-white locks', a shepherd's love song to a shepherdess. Debussy's prelude seems as near in spirit (if not nearer) to Burns's poem as to de Lisle's, prompting us to wonder if he knew it too. 'Bruyères', the only prelude in Book 2 with a metronome marking, again shows ♩ = 66 in combination with the same rhythm, ♫♩♫♫♫ (from bar 6). The more flowing tempo in this piece's middle section is easily managed if the top-line arabesques are kept very light above the more sustained lines in mid-texture.

Debussy's indications ♪ = 88 for 'Voiles' and ♩ = 84 for "*Les sons et les parfums*" are arguably a notch on the cautious side and work best near the end of each piece. (Note the 𝟤/𝟦 time signature in 'Voiles' as opposed to 𝟦/𝟪 in 'Reflets dans l'eau', 'Brouillards' and even 'Feux d'artifice'.) In "*Les sons et les parfums*" this affects what Cortot called the 'valse bleue', the café violin of Baudelaire's poem. In that context bars 30 and 49 suggest a sudden whiff of tango, the initial bass note really an upbeat to the ♫♫♩♩ ♩ that follows. Musical sense suggests that the *cédez* marking in these bars be read gesturally rather than denoting a slower pulse: at bar 30 the marking answers an earlier *en animant*, and at bar 49 it follows a complex mixture of tempo fluctuations.

Apart from the notational ambiguities discussed in Chapters 15–16, seriously problematic tempo markings are mercifully rare in Debussy. The fairly exceptional case of *Masques* is discussed in Chapter 14. Debussy's 𝟨/𝟪 indication for this piece is a simplification, for in reality it alternates 𝟨/𝟪 patterns (bars 1–2) with fast 𝟥/𝟦 ones (bars 3–4). *Danse* of fourteen years earlier does the same in converse order, to the extent that its original title *Tarentelle styrienne* makes curious sense if read almost in crossword fashion, *styrienne* across bars 1–2 and *tarentelle* across bars 3–4.

Besides the sarabandes, habaneras, minuets and waltzes already noted, Debussy's Preludes suggest a somewhat pendular veil dance in 'Voiles' (see Appendix 2), a Spanish *polo* in 'La sérénade interrompue', fast *saltarello* in 'Les collines d'Anacapri', Chopinesque scherzo in some of 'Feux d'artifice', a more moderate duple-time scherzo for 'La danse de Puck' (echoing *L'isle joyeuse* and 'The little Shepherd'), a similar scherzo blended with a somewhat flatfooted saraband for the benignly inane Mr Pickwick ('Hommage à S. Pickwick Esq.'), and a few ragtimes.

The pianist Jacques Février taught 'Minstrels' as he said Poulenc had 'revealed' it to him in moderate, strict cakewalk tempo, doubtless a legacy from Poulenc's teacher Ricardo Viñes who premièred the piece with Debussy practically at his shoulder. ('Minstrels' figured in Poulenc's first piano lesson with Viñes in 1916.) This matches Scott Joplin's repeated exhortations never to play ragtime fast. The sung element of most cakewalks, and their comically exaggerated off-beats, warn against rushing: various American songs in the genre, along with Satie's song *La diva de l' 'Empire'*, are a useful tempo guide for Debussy's 'Golliwogg's cake walk'. The bracketed additions above Example 17.3 show how another evergreen cakewalk song, Stephen Foster's *Camptown Races*, echoes amusingly across two of Debussy's cakewalks.

Example 17.3

a: Debussy, 'General Lavine – excentric', bars 51–2

b: Debussy, 'Golliwogg's cake walk', bars 30–1

Recognizing these helps us spot much of the dance in Debussy's *Études*. 'Pour les octaves' revisits textures from Debussy's earlier *Valse romantique* and the second of Chabrier's *Valses romantiques*, while a much slower waltz emerges from the middle of 'Pour les accords'.[30] Sarabande is suggested by 'Pour les sixtes' and parts of 'Pour les arpèges composés' and 'Pour les quartes', especially in their Rameau-like dotted rhythms, while 'Pour les sonorités opposées' mixes elements of sarabande and barcarolle in a manner that recalls 'Clair de lune'. In 'Pour les cinq doigts' the indication *mouv^t de gigue* cautions against haste by suggesting analogy with Debussy's orchestral *Image* 'Gigues'.

'Pour les huit doigts' and 'Pour les degrés chromatiques', like the finale of *En blanc et noir*, suggest the same *scherzando* dance as much of 'La danse de Puck' – a useful warning since the opening tempo of 'Pour les huit doigts' has to allow for the later triplets and the final accelerando, in a piece that suggests woodwind runs and flurries. (Debussy's *sans ralentir* on the last page of *Masques* is a similar alert not to start too fast – see p. 201 above – just as *plus lent* towards the end of 'La terrasse des audiences' conversely warns against starting it too slowly.)

If we pace the start of 'Pour les notes répétées' to allow for its fast triplets from bar 49, a moderate ragtime emerges, similar to 'Minstrels' and the central movements of Debussy's Cello and Violin Sonatas (all of them in G). Even Debussy's songs *Pantomime* and 'Chevaux de bois' of the 1880s smack of cakewalk, suggesting that the rhythm was intuitive to him before it crossed the Atlantic (it's generally assumed to have reached France in the 1890s). The inherent humour of his cakewalks becomes affectionately elephantine in 'Jumbo's Lullaby' from *Children's Corner*.

'Pour les quartes' contains the most complex mix, with a waltz-like §̆ from bar 1, a saraband-like ¾ from bar 29 and even a touch of cakewalk (bar 49). The resulting alternations may have made even Debussy a touch dizzy, for they spawn a serious notational problem on the piece's second page. Debussy originally notated bars 25–36 in half their printed values (Ex. 17.4a), before noticing that this left the eighth-note much slower than on the piece's first page.[31] His revised fair copy (Ex. 17.4b) repairs this from bar 25, but at the expense of rhythmic continuity over bars 24–5. We can see him trying to massage this with his added *poco rit.* and *L'istesso tempo* – the latter ambiguously readable, by Debussy's norms already seen, as either a literal ♪ = ♪ or a sounding continuity of triple time.

Example 17.4. Debussy, 'Pour les quartes', bars 23–6

a: abandoned page of fair copy

b: final fair copy and first edition

We might wonder why Debussy didn't double the note values in bar 24 too. In fact his early draft (as reproduced in the Minkoff facsimile volume) shows exactly this, the triplets of beat 1 amended in pencil to sixteenths (like the *stretto* triplets of bar 7). This was probably a very late revision, for it makes sense only relative to Example 17.4b; perhaps fatigue distracted him from carrying it over to his final fair copy. Since it necessitates adjusting the rest of bar 24, Example 17.5 shows two possible ways of applying it.

Example 17.5. Debussy, 'Pour les quartes', possible editorial renotations of bar 24 to allow for Debussy's unpublished correction to beat 1

a: maintaining the original bar length

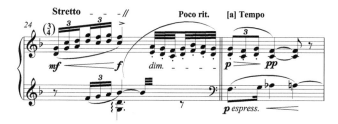

b: restoring the original rhythmic relationship to bar 25

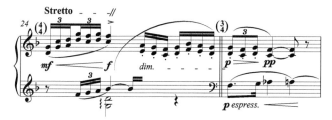

In practice the problem extends several bars further back (Ex. 17.6), raising the query of why Debussy didn't double the note values from bar 18. (Compare bar 18 with bars 24–5 in the examples above; even if doubled in value, the bar 18 triplets still play twice as fast as their answer in bar 25, possibly a deliberate compositional ploy.) Bars 20–1 and 23, however, militate against any renotation since they already match the opening tempo well.

Example 17.6. Debussy, 'Pour les quartes', bars 17–22

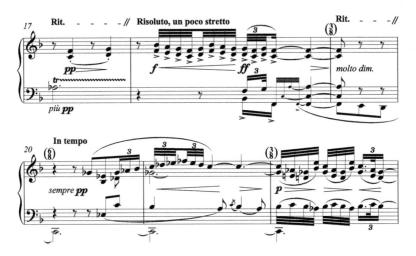

If the density of tempo indications over bars 17–20 betrays Debussy again massaging the problem, an alternative solution might be to augment the values of bar 18 into two bars of $\frac{3}{4}$ (retaining *stretto*, possibly without the preceding *rit.*), possibly augment bar 19 into $\frac{3}{4}$ (again removing the *rit.*, thus matching bar 25), and either add a calming *rubato* above bar 22 or augment it into $\frac{3}{4}$ with an added *stretto*. I go into such detail because this page has long raised problems at the piano and suggests a knife-edge between two possible metric notations. No single solution solves everything, evoking Stravinsky's famed remark that the 'Danse sacrale' of his *Rite of Spring* was clear in his mind long before he found a way of notating it.

CHABRIER, AUVERGNAT CLOGS AND THE METRONOME(S)

Chabrier's *Bourrée fantasque* features the same clog-stamping *bourrée d'Auvergne* that opens *Joyeuse marche* and permeates several of the *Pièces pittoresques*, all typifying Chabrier's reported remark that 'my music rings with the stamp of my Auvergnat clogs'. [32] (The flamenco heel-stamps in *España* might be seen as close cousins.) However, the printed ♩ = 152 and ♩ = 160 in

Bourrée fantasque, 'Danse villageoise' and the central section of 'Paysage' raise immediate problems of articulation and breathing on instruments of any era, as well as longer-term problems of line and continuity – not least when the central section of *Bourrée fantasque* instructs *istesso tempo* (same speed) and simultaneously *molto espressivo*. Chabrier's unfinished orchestration of *Bourrée fantasque*, containing no metronome marking, answers this by showing artic- ulation that's unplayable in practice above ♩ = c. 132 (for example the repeated down-bows in bars 1 and 3, given the *f* dynamic). Further analogy comes from *Joyeuse marche* where Chabrier indicates a judiciously manageable but still exhilarating ♩ = 126 for similar rhythmic patterns, and from his ♩. = 80–88 in *España* (equivalent to ♩ = 120–132).[33] In practice, if we take most of *Bourrée fantasque*, 'Danse villageoise' and the central part of 'Paysage' around a more manageable ♩ = c. 138, they still emerge pretty boisterously, a vital point being that excitement depends directly on vigour of articulation. The same holds for the outer sections of 'Menuet pompeux'.

By contrast, Chabrier's metronome markings make immediate sense in 'Mélancolie', 'Sous bois', 'Idylle' and (at least the start of) 'Tourbillon' – plus *Joyeuse marche* and *España* as already seen. Two such opposed camps in Chabrier's markings suggest they may derive from different metronomes, perhaps one of them at his composing bolt-hole in the Touraine. We also easily forget how inaccurate clockwork metronomes could be: almost every one I've checked over the years has proved to be anything from one to four notches out. Consideration of this can be vital in pieces like the enchanting 'Mauresque', whose spell is promptly lost if it rushes. The preface of the Dover Chabrier edition offers some remedial suggestions; Poulenc also usefully quotes Ricardo Viñes's recommendation of ♪ = 192 for 'Scherzo-valse', the one *Pièce pittoresque* Chabrier left metronomically unspecified.

RAVEL

Ravel's metronome indications can be surprisingly variable, from the meticu- lously reliable ♪ = 144 of *Jeux d'eau* (reduced at proof from 152) to an implausibly scrambled 120 in his early *Sérénade grotesque* (unpublished during his life) and an oddly ponderous ♩ = 60 for his lone *Prélude* of 1913 (perhaps a reflection of its origin as a sight-reading test). Anarchy has dogged the *Pavane pour une Infante défunte*: although Ravel famously didn't want it to become 'une Pavane défunte', the opening marking on different editions from his lifetime veers dizzily from ♩ = 80 to 54.[34] Chapter 16 has already noted some dubiety about the metronome markings added to post-1950 prints of *Le tombeau de Couperin*: improbably slow in the Fugue and Menuet, they conversely push the outer movements rather hard, risking (in particular) a rattly Toccata in which the player is inevitably forced to slow at inappropriate moments.[35] Despite his reputation for precision – or perhaps even in keeping with it – Ravel is reported by Manuel Rosenthal as once admitting that metronome markings are at best 'a safeguard [*un garde-fou*] . . . If I put ♩ = 92, it means "not 120" and equally "not 72".[36]

As with Debussy, Ravel's most varied rhythmic surfaces are the ones that need most effort to hold the underlying pulse. One trap lies across bars 67–8 of 'Ondine', where the changing surface speed of the figurations can throw the pulse unless we're alert (and don't slow too much at bar 66). In 'Une barque sur l'océan' this needs slight discretion: in practice the ¾ and ⁴⁄₄ episodes can slightly move on to avoid squareness. Ravel's ♩ = 58, added to the piece's orchestral version, is still a useful guide for the piece's start and reprises. His opening markings for 'Noctuelles' and 'Oiseaux tristes' are similarly most practicable at the start and end. For the seventh of the *Valses nobles et sentimentales* – the only one lacking a clear tempo marking – the rhythmically similar 'Danse des Rainettes' from *L'Enfant et les sortilèges* provides a useful ♩ = 208.

Ravel's advice to pace the Menuet of his *Sonatine* like that of Beethoven's Sonata op. 31 no. 3 (in E♭) raises another aspect of his notation: the short phrases that let the piece breathe and dance in classical manner, a matter that can be helped by supple wrists and an alert right foot.[37] Similar alertness in *Le tombeau* helps keep the Fugue dancing, notably when the phrasing marks a complete break in texture. (This happens after the first chord of bar 40 and in beat 2 of bar 51 – quieter but just as decisive breaks as the more obvious ones at the climax of 'Petit Poucet' in *Ma mère l'Oye*). Besides 'Le jardin féerique', his most intense sarabande emerges from his Concerto for Left Hand (along with the Passacaille movement of his Piano Trio).

Ravel's rhythm again can reflect language. The title *Pavane pour une Infante défunte* – never intended as tragic, possibly a take on Gounod's *Funeral March of a Marionette* or Alkan's more facetious *Marcia funebre sulla morte d'un papagallo* – follows the verbal rhythm of a truncated alexandrine starting in mid-phrase, with each mute 'e' unpronounced as in the texts of Ravel's *Histoires naturelles*. (Compare with Debussy's alexandrine 'Et la lun*e* descend sur le templ*e* qui fut' with its pronounced 'e's: from 'descend' onwards the two titles metrically match.)[38] Ravel's *Pavane* opens similarly with a two-bar phrase that sounds more like the tail end of a consequent relative to the five-bar phrase that follows. Besides the arguable mid-phrase start already seen in Example 17.1b, the opening in both 'Ondine' and 'Le gibet' essentially conveys that the piece has started rather than is starting. (Any lingering on the first note is therefore counterproductive.) The clashing sevenths or semitones that launch many of Ravel's pieces (even the early *Menuet antique*) again have an air of starting in mid-phrase. (As always, these matters are context-sensitive:

the start of Debussy's *Children's Corner*, for example, suggests easing into tempo over the opening beat, and the composer's stepdaughter Mme de Tinan recalled hearing Debussy do so.)[39]

Another prosodic trait is Ravel's habit of added asides, as it were, in the form of grace-note figurations between bars in *Jeux d'eau*, 'Noctuelles', 'Alborada' and 'Ondine' (and throughout the first movement of his Trio): they need to be played outside the measured beat yet without slowing before. (The one at bar 18 of *Jeux d'eau* adds almost exactly an eighth-note in value; the one at bar 37 defies such measurement.) This might relate to descriptions by Ravel's friends of his characteristic gestures while pronouncing witty asides.[40]

A few careful notational details are worth observing in Ravel's Concerto in G. In the 'Adagio' his left-hand beaming (maintaining $\frac{3}{4}$) warns against bumping the half-bar with the apparent syncopations. In the first movement, conversely, syncopations like the *de facto* $\frac{3}{4}$ sequence before figure 17 and around figure 34 warn against racing the $\frac{3}{2}$ tempo, especially in the run into the recapitulation. The very short rest that launches this run is just enough to let the hands drop to the bass and make the start audible, followed by effective $\frac{3}{2}$ units, initially in hyper-groups of three, an augmentation of the sounding $\frac{3}{4}$ beforehand. I pedantically say this because of a helter-skelter tradition there established by Marguerite Long: unsupported by Ravel's notation or the surrounding metrical patterns, it may have caused Ravel considerable annoyance.[41]

ADDENDA AND A FEW BLIPS OF NOTATION

Research has shown that tempi in performances of Debussy tended to slow through the twentieth century.[42] Chapter 21 returns to this, along with a few caveats about piano rolls. Franck's metronome markings can jolt us in that respect, not least the alarmingly breezy $\downarrow$ = 116 for the *maestoso* start of his *Prélude, Aria et Final*. Even allowing for inaccuracy in Franck's metronome (or his way of using it), his markings suggest that habits in the late nineteenth century were anything but laggardly; his music also shares too many gestures, structural and notational, with Fauré, Chabrier and Saint-Saëns, and even Debussy and Ravel, to suggest a different tempo mentality from theirs.[43]

Although Franck's *Prélude, Choral et Fugue* has no metronome markings, we may jump again on seeing Franck writing (in 1888) that the work 'lasts 13 minutes': most recordings take between seventeen and twenty.[44] Even if his estimate was off the cuff, it prompts re-examination of an opening *moderato* that precedes a *Choral* marked *poco più lento*. A revealing exercise is to work centrifugally (as it were), first finding a comfortably flowing tempo for the central *Choral*, then letting the other parts settle around it (the *Prélude* thus has to start slightly faster). Treated thus the work can be managed without undue haste in fourteen minutes, breathes with an excitement comparable to Franck's Violin Sonata, and all markings (ritardandi, etc.) make instant sense.

Other pieces that can benefit from reading backwards to the opening include the Prélude of Debussy's *Pour le piano*, whose introductory five bars yield their sense only once we've seen see how the rest of the movement effectively unfurls them and retrospectively suggests a suitable opening tempo. Tempo headings, usually one of the last items to be written on a completed score (or even added at proof), often relate to broader aspects than just an opening phrase and sometimes can suggest a cautionary element, as if preceded by the word 'nevertheless'.

Notation thus poses constant challenges of *relative* accuracy. The more a composer tries to cover every eventuality (Debussy springs to mind), the more relatively misleading any lapse in notational clarity can be. Chapter 3 showed a problematic case in Ravel's 'Scarbo', a tempo equivalence at bar 430 that can be related to either bar 395 or bar 429 but not to both because of a tacit accelerando between them. (Had the first edition numbered the bars, this could have been solved with a formula like ♩ = ♩. *de la mesure 395*.) A similar case affects Debussy's *Hommage à Haydn*, whose manuscript indicates *Le double plus vite* at the change from slow-waltz 3/4 to *scherzando* 3/8, an effect already assured by the notation. The first edition replaces this with ♩. = ♩ *precedente* (bar = preceding beat). Although this better defines the nimble tempo needed for the 3/8, the original indication allows a more elegant and practical local continuity of ♪ = ♪ over the double bar. Moving on slightly just before the double bar can yield the best of both worlds, combining an immediate ♪ = ♪ over the barline with ♩. = ♩ relative to two bars earlier. (Far from planning that in advance, I found myself doing it at the piano and only then became aware of why.) Again the score tells us the simplest part of what can otherwise defy easy verbal explanation. Something converse affects the transition into the slower middle section of Debussy's 'Pour les accords', where musical sense tells us his indicated ♪ = ♩. *precedente* is more a matter of feeling (with even a degree of local eighth-note continuity across the double-bar) than an instantaneous change of measured unit.

Such remaining ambiguities are more than understandable in pieces whose composers successfully negotiated numerous complexities. Awareness of this issue can help us spot remaining cases that probably need some reading between the lines. For example, *Mouv^t* at bar 18 of 'La danse de Puck' can more realistically be read as *Mouv^t* [*un peu plus allant*] relative to the opening ♪ = 138 (like Debussy's marking at bar 9 of 'Minstrels'); the same goes for bar 48 of 'Reflets dans l'eau'. Conversely, the second page onwards of Debussy's 'Ondine' can doubtless be read as settling into a slightly steadier tempo than the opening *scherzando* page, even if both need strict tempo within their own terms.

CHAPTER 18

A fresh look at Gabriel Fauré

His physique immediately betrays his southern origins: short, stocky, brown-skinned and dark-eyed, his hair white since he was twenty-five, and endowed with an extraordinarily youthful manner, Gabriel Fauré has always been and always will be ageless . . . His colourful, impulsive speech has a particular appeal of its own, and its sparkling witticisms are all the more effective for appearing involuntary

– Camille Saint-Saëns

The main problem with masterpieces is that they are surrounded by excessive respect and this ends up making them boring   – Gabriel Fauré

Fauré's earliest piano pieces date from the years 1862 to 1875, the years in which Debussy and Ravel were born; his last ones postdate both Debussy's death and the completion of Ravel's solo piano output. For all the bold development this generous output shows over its six decades, it can be moving to see Fauré's handwriting largely unchanged from his early to his late manuscripts, suggesting coherence all the way through – not for nothing do some of his last works rework material from his early years. Above all, his later works show undimmed passion and vigour far from the rambling introspection with which they are often cloaked. For all his aversion to crassness or blatancy, nothing in Fauré's music or writings supports any idea that he wanted his music understated: his son Philippe insisted repeatedly on the importance of 'playing out the drama' in it.[1]

MARKING THE BEAT

This is a notoriously debatable, context-sensitive matter, in which we have to be ever alert for hemiolas and cross-rhythms, whose impact is lost if we don't convey the default metre around them. Fauré's reported insistence on marking the beat can immediately be related to textures like the start of his

Second Barcarolle, whose first note, if not strongly marked, will sound to listeners like an upbeat, leaving the music flatfooted.[2] Similarly, at the start of his Fourth, Eleventh and Thirteenth Nocturnes or the first of the Preludes the rhythmically offset bass or accompaniment necessitates marking the melodic beat if the listener is to grasp the basic metre. Compare the opening of the Fourth Nocturne (its bass offset) with the melodically similar start of the duet 'Ketty-Valse' from *Dolly* (the bass on the beat), and the compensatory voicing needed in the Nocturne can quickly be sensed. In sum, any music embodying dance naturally needs to mark the beat, depending on how much it's already written into the texture.[3]

Fauré's equal insistence on marking the bass adds to the challenge. One useful technique is to sound offset bass notes as near the beat as one reasonably dares, while ensuring the melody is well voiced. (Low dynamics can still be assured by keeping intermediate figurations and voices very light.) Whatever the dynamic, Fauré's music is particularly intolerant of tentative rhythm or touch in melody or bass – doubtless one reason why his later revisions tend to mark dynamics up. A reciprocal context to these offset basses is the climactic Variation X in the *Thème et variations*, where the bass – and later the rising scales – need marking on the beat, even in *pp*, to give the off-beat right-hand chords something to kick against. (This can be done with a sense of $\frac{6}{8}$ rather than $\frac{3}{8}$ to avoid lumpiness.) Marguerite Long quotes Fauré as wanting a particularly strong bass accent at the *fortissimo* bar 85, to launch the variation's peroration.[4] The effect is a sort of Lombardic ostinato, a perennial Fauré favourite (a short-long pair in triplet rhythm, the short note on the beat): as in the rhythmically similar opening of the Seventh Nocturne or Eighth Barcarolle, omitting to mark the beat can sink the piece at launch. The pianist Eric Heidsieck observes that this norm of marking the beat in French music was for so long taken as read that Poulenc was really the first composer who felt compelled to mark accents consistently on main beats.[5]

In Fauré's Sixth, Seventh, Eleventh and Thirteenth Nocturnes the sarabande-like three-in-the-bar equally needs to be gently projected, with the added challenge of the long upbeat that starts the Sixth Nocturne. Bar 11 in both the Sixth and the Seventh Nocturnes reveals the close relationship between the two pieces, with identical melodic rhythm: the different metric notation of the Seventh merely reflects the Lombardic ostinato within the broader sarabande. In that respect we can usefully read the Sixth Nocturne's opening ♩ = 76 as ♩ = 38 (just off the scale of clockwork metronomes), and the Seventh Nocturne's ♩. = 66 as ♩. = 33. It also helps to know that the manuscript of the Sixth Nocturne is headed *Andante* rather than the printed *Adagio*, and that for the Seventh Nocturne Roger-Ducasse's preface to the 1924 edition hints that ♩. = 66 is really a minimum (likewise ♩. = 72 for *un poco più mosso* at bar 11).

Fauré virtually admits as much in the latter piece's coda by marking ♩ = 96 at bar 111 for just *un poco più mosso* (again) after the preceding ♩. = 66. The discreet fluidity needed within all this can be seen from details like the way bars 24–7 pick up and nourish the slightly faster theme from bars 15–18 before the same theme eventually returns, at bar 99, for the piece's main climax in the *allegro* tempo.

NOTATIONAL QUIRKS

The reprise of the Fifth Nocturne shares a notational curiosity with several passages in Mendelssohn and Schumann (as well as Brahms): Example 18.1 shows how both the autograph and the first edition are inconsistent about exactly how the triplets and duplets interact. When they coincide on one note (end of bar 151), we can safely assume that the triplets (which have to be quieter anyway) bend discreetly to maintain the rhythmic value of the duplets, as in the similar figurations of Mendelssohn's *Lied ohne Worte* op. 85 no. 1 or Schumann's *Fantasiestücke* op. 73 for clarinet and piano. Fauré's rather absentminded notation in bar 152 suggests a matching treatment without audible pedantry, a matter he probably solved in performance without even noticing.

Example 18.1. Fauré, Fifth Nocturne op. 37, bars 151–2 (alignment as in sources)

The start of the Sixth Nocturne raises a similar dichotomy (Ex. 18.2a). Played strictly, the accompanying triplets force the melody into triplet time, risking a false impression of $\frac{9}{4}$ metre and mismatching the answering bar 11 where the melody takes its trūe value, as again at the climactic bar 111 (Ex. 18.2b–c).[6] The issue becomes clear if we try the opening bars in the simplified form ♪♩ ♪ ♪; again this prompts the option of quietly bending the triplets to allow the melody its true value. As with Example 18.1, were the passage orchestrated the matter would look after itself. The syndrome is not uncommon in that era: similar examples (with ♪♩ ♪♪♪♪) can be found in

Saint-Saëns's song *La cloche* and Debussy's *En blanc et noir* (first movement, B♭ episode), in each case answering another voice without triplets.

Example 18.2. Fauré, Sixth Nocturne op. 63

a: bars 4–5

b: bars 11–12 (rhythmic alignment as in sources)

c: bar 111

TEMPO ARCHES

Examples like these – besides reminding us that any musical score is a transcription of sorts – show that, for all the rhythmic clarity Fauré's music demands, its notation can sometimes be a nettle-bed in ways that can easily discourage performers. The worst problems combine suspect metronome markings with a subtle arching of tempo in many of his musical spans. Tempo arching can be sensed from the way some of Fauré's larger paragraphs or spans need a more flowing tempo at the middle than at the beginning, without audible fluctuation. How does one notate this? Besides his explicit comment about it in the *Valses-caprices* (see p. 253), Fauré acknowledged the problem in his *Fantaisie* op. 111 for piano and orchestra, when he advised the young Robert Casadesus (whose playing he admired) to 'get back to a more spacious feeling with each return of the principal theme. Since one *inevitably lets oneself speed up during developments*, one must take advantage of returns of the theme in order to re-establish the tempo.'[7] (The emphasis is mine.) The same goes – often imperceptibly to the hearer – for slow movements in much of his chamber music: in the barcarolle second movement of the First Violin Sonata, his strategic *poco rall. e dim.* indications ease us back at the end of each tacit surge. Indeed any *rall.* indication in Fauré tends to be a retrospective signpost for this – occasionally even *poco rit.* as at bar 27 of the Seventh Barcarolle. This habit of letting the tempo move on can be heard in a wide repertoire on many early twentieth-century recordings (which generally show livelier norms of tempo than in later decades, even allowing for the timing constraints of early recording discs or cylinders).

In Fauré's case the habit might even be related to his famed sluggishness at waking up in the morning (a lifelong source of mirth to his family and friends). A few frisky-seeming metronome markings make sense when read as reflecting the 'woken-up' tempo, as in the Fifth Barcarolle (it works by the second page). Another hint of this personal rhythm of Fauré's comes from the unusual way his triple metres often start with a hemiola (how many other composers do this?), for example the first full bar of his Sixth Nocturne and of its *allegretto* section, or the final Variation XI of his *Thème et variations*. The sounding effect is of the music gathering momentum as it then glides into the indicated triple metre, an acceleration of structure over a constant tactus.

This large-scale elasticity has left some editorial problems, not least in the First Nocturne whose first edition indicated *un poco più mosso ma non tanto* at bar 21, before Fauré deleted the indication on his handexemplar and had it omitted from the 1924 re-edition. His deletion may have been a reaction to pianists who suddenly raced off: a 1925 Welte piano roll of the piece played by Magdeleine Brard – whom Fauré knew – does exactly that, after slowing indulgently though bar 20.[8] While we may guess that he wanted a sense of continuity over the transition, his deletion leaves us with a score that improbably appears to indicate *Lento* ♩ = 52 for the entire nocturne. If instinct tells us that the dramatic middle section needs to move discreetly faster, Fauré's presumed hope that it would happen by itself was ill-founded: by 1957 his son Philippe was asking in puzzlement why pianists didn't move this piece on from the second page as his father had done.[9] The reprise at bar 94 throws in another wild card with Fauré's sudden indication *Tempo 1°*, something we can doubtless read as an easing back to the main tempo (wherever we may have been meanwhile) after the virtuoso climax. But to which main tempo? That of bar 1 or the quietly more mobile one from bar 21? The dancing texture here, with the repeated notes, suggests something nearer the latter, especially since the material from bar 21 is about to return at bar 114.[10] Tellingly, this would still tend to sound to listeners like a return to *Tempo I.*

The autograph of Debussy's *Children's Corner* provides revealing comparison here, in that it omits many of the performing indications printed in the first edition. From this we may infer that in 'Jumbo's Lullaby' the printed *un peu plus mouvementé* at bar 39, then the reciprocal *retenu* and *1° Tempo* (bars 61–3), absent from the manuscript and obviously added at proof, convey discreet information more for the pianist than for the listener. What Debussy eventually decided to add there shines a torch on what Fauré decided to veil, each for understandable reasons.[11]

Fauré's rationale emerges from a wry remark he wrote to Roger-Ducasse in February 1923 while revising his *Valses-caprices* for a re-edition: 'I've taken out a lot of *pianissimi* and *accelerandi*. [Pianists] will always put in enough of them.'[12] A century on, his well-meant pruning has become a self-fulfilling prophecy by sometimes forcing pianists to intervene in the absence of vital instructions. Among the smaller indications that fell to Fauré's revising axe (shades of his Conservatoire nickname 'Robespierre') is a printed *Rit.* in early editions of the First Barcarolle over the second half of bars 17 and 19, clearly audible on his 1912 piano roll recording (as a gentle stretching out of the notes marked with staccato dots).[13] Several similar cases can justify the restoration in modern editions of such indications, suitably flagged.

A variant of the tempo arch is the open-ended surge. (Ravel's 'Scarbo' is an extreme example.) Explicitly marked in Fauré's Twelfth Nocturne, this progressive tightening of tempo can be tacitly sensed in the Ninth Nocturne, whose last page really has to move considerably faster than its opening. (The process, which arguably starts as early as bar 5, needs to avoid being obvious to the listener in this Nocturne; Fauré doubtless left it unmarked for that reason.) The climactic Variation X of the *Thème et variations* suggests a similarly imperceptible gathering of speed: Fauré's metronome marking, viable at the start, is several notches below what we need by the last page. (Conversely, Variations V and VII invite a gentle expressive easing in the middle, at the marking *espressivo*, perhaps explaining the latter variation's rather cautious metronome marking.)

Structurally the most curious tacit tempo surge involves the central part of Fauré's *Fantaisie* op. 111. In practice this lively $\frac{3}{4}$ section needs to end somewhat faster than it started, not only because its dramatic culmination will otherwise fall flat, but also because the music virtually forces us to, despite the lack of explicit indication. This can be sensed from the way the central $\frac{3}{4}$ section starts with half-note hemiolas that audibly take over the quarter-note pulse from the opening $\frac{4}{4}$ section – an exact notational doubling. Fauré's metronome marks basically support that sounding continuity.[14] The climactic closing bars of the central section, however, are so strongly articulated by the $\frac{3}{4}$ bar momentum (the final loud orchestral chords) that the quarter-note of the returning $\frac{4}{4}$ metre has little option but to carry over the pulse as ♩ = ♩. *precedente* – now a reciprocal factor of three. (To impose ♩ = ♩ *precedente* there would risk loss of ensemble as well as an overfast recapitulation, the very danger outlined by Fauré to Casadesus.) The music's texture supports the gradual tempo increase towards the end of the $\frac{3}{4}$ section, partly by the way the texture lightens between figures 13 and 14 (after the dotted ostinato finishes), and partly by the way the central section gradually weaves in the themes from the opening $\frac{4}{4}$ section, their original quarter-note pulse now filling a $\frac{3}{4}$ bar. At first this makes them sound slightly slower than in the opening section, before the texture encourages us to speed them slightly on to their initial sounding tempo, a sort of stretched elastic effect that spans the $\frac{3}{4}$ section. In practice the tempo increase easily happens by itself (as Fauré's advice implies) provided we don't obstruct it by being too literal at the wrong moment.

Fauré's final comment in that letter reveals – in his usual absentminded way – what he intuitively knew but didn't make explicit in the score: 'One last suggestion: the $\frac{3}{4}$ tempo in the middle struck me as a little too lively. It doesn't leave time to perceive the relationship that exists between this section, the section that precedes it, and the section that follows.'[15] This remark can make sense only in terms of the relationships just outlined: note how his wording avoids defining the same relationship across each side of the middle section. In sum, his tempo advice makes sense if read as 'Don't *start* the middle section too fast'. We might even guess that if Casadesus had started it too fast, it was with the end of the section in mind.

Should this appear heretical incitement, the issue and its importance quickly become clear on rehearsing the work. We have to be constantly alert to spot which pieces conversely work best at a steadily maintained tempo: trying the steady tempo approach usually settles the question fairly quickly.

FAURÉ AND THE METRONOME (INCARNATE)

While many of Fauré's metronome markings are salutary (as in the Fifth Nocturne, a piece that needs no tacit surges), a few are clearly wayward, as Fauré himself sometimes admitted. This affects several of the *Pièces brèves* and the Ninth, Tenth and Twelfth Nocturnes, whose indicated opening tempi feel unsustainably slow beyond the first bar or two. The closing pages of the Twelfth Nocturne then show two metronome markings so improbably scrambled as to suggest that Fauré absentmindedly set them against the undotted instead of dotted quarter-note – easily done there because of the hemiolas. (The London Peters edition addresses these issues.) The problem clears, though, in the judiciously indicated Thirteenth Nocturne, and doesn't affect the intermediate Barcarolles[16] or the op. 103 Preludes (except that the second page of the first Prelude tends to invite a more flowing tempo).

What can we deduce from all this? Had the onset of deafness in the 1900s temporarily affected Fauré's perception of attack and articulation? Or did he just set some markings too early in the morning? The problematic ones also mostly follow the arrival in Fauré's life of Marguerite Hasselmans, involving some discreet domestic reorganization that may have brought a different metronome into play. (Roger-Ducasse's preface to the 1924 edition of Nocturnes 1–8 draws attention to the endemic problem of inaccuracy in clockwork metronomes.) Nor, alas, do we have any recordings of Marguerite Hasselmans playing: it's feasible that Fauré, as his hearing problems set in, may have partly relied on her for metronomic reference. (The generally more viable metronome markings in his late chamber works were set with the help of colleagues who premièred them, such as Cortot.)

One reference comes from a list of corrections for Fauré's *Ballade* op. 19, noted by Pierre Auclert from studying the work with Marguerite Hasselmans.[17] Among his notes are metronome revisions, possibly indicated by Fauré to Hasselmans or worked out by the two of them when they took the work on tour (Fauré playing orchestra on a second piano). Even these – besides the discrepancies across the two original editions – leave enough problems in practice to prompt my own alternative suggestions, based on performing experience and shown below Table 18.1.

Another possible angle is suggested by a curious syndrome in several post-1900 scores. The fifth of the *Pièces brèves*, indicated $\downarrow$ = 72 by Fauré, in practice calls for a tempo of around $\downarrow$ = 92.[18] In the Sixth Nocturne the *allegretto* section from bar 19 similarly implies a tempo of $\downarrow$ = c. 96, rather than 76 as printed in the 1924 edition. For the start of the Fourth Nocturne Marguerite Long argued that Fauré intended $\downarrow$ = c. 66 rather than the 56 shown in post-1900 prints.[19] In the *Thème et variations* various factors (of which more below) suggest an opening tempo around $\downarrow$ = 60 rather than the 50 shown in post-1910 prints. All these markings date from Fauré's mid-fifties onwards, raising the query of whether middle-aged eyesight led him to misread the small digits on his metronome, possibly lulled by the identical second digit in each case.[20] However we regard that, the issue needs to be addressed, for its consequences have now dogged the works concerned for a century.

Table 18.1. Metronome sources for Fauré's *Ballade* op. 19

	Andante cantabile (bar 1)	Allegretto moderato (E♭ minor)	Andante (transition)	Allegro (B major)	Andante (transition)	Allegro moderato
solo piano edition (Hamelle, 1881)	♩ = 66	♩ = 100	♩. = 66	♩ = 120	♩. = 66	Allegro moderato ♩. = 72
full score (Hamelle 1902) and 2-piano score arr. Isidor Philipp	♩ = 66	♩ = 76	♩. = 66	♩ = 108	♩. = 66	Allegro molto moderato ♩. = 66
Marguerite Hasselmans (via Pierre Auclert)	♩ = 54		♩. = 58	♩ = 100		
Roy Howat's suggestions	♩ = 60	♩ = 88–92	♩. = 52	♩ = 100	♩. = 52	♩. = 52–58

A related hazard is visible from revisions Fauré made to his Fifth Nocturne almost forty years after writing it: for the 1924 re-edition he added an upper octave to each last left-hand note of bars 113–118. Logical though this may look, at full tempo it becomes near-unplayable. (His original reading facilitates access to each following bass note while completing the preceding chord's texture, an ingenious effect that relies on a very nimble tempo.) The obvious inference is that by the 1920s he had lost his original sense of the piece's tempo, whose dramatic and structural importance we saw in Chapter 15. Relevant comparison comes from two recordings of Poulenc playing his Piano Trio, one made thirty years after the other. The earlier one, from 1928 (two years after the work appeared), plays close to the printed tempi, whereas the 1958 recording slows everything several notches and even shows Poulenc blithely pedalling through his own *senza pedale* indications, which his earlier recording had respected.

STRUCTURE AND TEMPO

Almost everything we've seen so far hinges on delicate balances between structure and tempo: in performance we want to ensure that the music's architectural spans arch rather than sag, while the music both breathes and dances. Fauré's many sequences and ostinati, especially in later pieces, leave vital hints: judiciously paced they build intensity; too slow and they can obscure their goal by taking over the audible musical span. The thematic repetitions across bars 26–7 or 28–9 in the Ninth Nocturne, for example, need to be sensed within the larger sequence of bars 26–9 against bars 30–3, a warning against heaviness of tempo. Similarly in the fourth of the *Pièces brèves* the rhythmic ostinati need to support but not obscure the broader melodic spans, while the *poco rit.* at bars 15–16 implies a sufficiently flowing entry tempo to give it a *raison d'être.* (Again indicated ♩ = 72, this piece in practice can easily move on towards ♩ = 92, making clearer sense of its sequences, ostinati and *poco rit.* punctuations.)

A refreshing sidelight on all this is shed by the conductor Sir Adrian Boult, who recalled having heard Fauré on several occasions play his *Pavane* op. 50 'no slower than ♩ = 100!' and 'with no sign of rallentando even at the very end of the piece'. This compares interestingly with the printed ♩ = 84 in the *Pavane*'s orchestral score, plus the pause in the orchestral score's penultimate bar, both of which can be seen as allowing for the slower articulation of orchestra with *ad libitum* choir. It also suggests that the pause is just the briefest of lingerings – something that has multiple resonances for Fauré's piano music. Sir Adrian sums up by urging that Fauré's *Pavane* is not 'a piece of German romanticism . . . The words are obviously a leg-pull, and the scene is a number of young people dancing and chaffing each other.'[21] This relates directly to Fauré's dance conception of the piece as described in Chapter 10.

Something similar emerges from the original 1897 English edition of the *Dolly* suite, which marks the opening 'Berceuse' ♩ = 92 (an indication Fauré was unable to add to the French edition). If this tempo at first seems startling, it becomes immediately viable if we keep the accompaniment very light as marked: Fauré's pedal markings then make sense, the *allegretto* heading relates aptly to the melodic line, the sequences in the middle section flow easily, and the piece's affinity to the Sixth Barcarolle becomes apparent.

Fauré's indications for a single piece can sometimes vary almost vertiginously from source to source. For the *Pavane* just mentioned (another of his multi-purpose pieces), his various versions (piano solo, piano with voices, orchestra with or without voices) sport tempo headings ranging from *Allegro moderato* to *Andante molto moderato* – an apparent indecisiveness that brought him repeated teasing over the years.[22] This equally afflicts the eighth of his *Pièces brèves* (alias the Eighth Nocturne), which all French prints since 1924 have headed *Quasi adagio* ♩. = 58. Earlier prints, however, indicate *Andante* ♩. = 58, and Fauré's autograph tips the scales further with '*Andante* ~~*quasi allegretto*~~' – but always with the same ♩. = 58, suggesting that the verbal variants primarily refer to different structural layers. (*Quasi adagio* makes sense relative to the long melody, provided we don't impose the instruction on the running figurations.) In practice the piece's tempo tends to be capped by its bell-like bars 11–14 (otherwise it could easily turn into an *allegretto* barcarolle), and Fauré's ♩. = 58 acts mostly as a marker for the main nodal points rather than impeding its long sweeping phrases.

In the light of that, we may laugh on seeing that Fauré's *Romance* op. 69 for cello and piano was originally headed *Adagio*, before Fauré amended it first to *Andante*, then finally to *Andante quasi allegretto*! The subtle levels of structure involved in all this are particular visible in his song 'La fleur qui va sur l'eau' (op. 85 no. 2), whose tempo heading *Allegretto molto moderato* has an appended ♩ = 60 which relates the heading decisively to the long note values of the vocal line but demands a positively *allegro* launch of the piano's figurations. This shows the same under-the-surface thinking as Chabrier's *calme* indication in 'Paysage' (see pp. 189–90 above).

THÈME ET VARIATIONS OP. 73

If Fauré's *adagio* (literally 'at ease') can sometimes be practically equivalent to *andante*, this becomes crucial in his *Thème et variations* op. 73. Although French prints since 1910 or so have headed the theme *Quasi adagio* ♩ = 50 (and carry this through explicitly into Variation I), it may not be such a surprise now to read that the original respective Paris and London editions of 1897 indicate *Andante* ♩ = 66 and *Allegro molto moderato* ♩ = 69. (Note the single metronome notch separating such apparently contrasted headings.)

So what *did* he mean, and when, and what do we do now? An editorial priority is undoubtedly to show the full context. This can aptly include the work's close links to Schumann's *Etudes symphoniques*. Schumann's *Thema*, marked ♩ = 52, lasts sixteen bars, often changes harmony by the eighth-note, and involves only three bars of thematic repetition (apart from its first bar) before Variation I steps up the tempo. Fauré's thème by contrast lasts twenty bars with considerable internal repetition, its harmonies move at fastest by the quarter-note, and Variation I continues the same tempo until the basic opening theme has been heard verbatim at least six times. Contrary analogy could then be suggested with the processional opening of Franck's *Prélude, Aria et Final*, a passage with a comparable rate of harmonic motion and degree of repetition but marked (albeit improbably) ♩ = 116![23] Other factors that come into play with Fauré's *thème* include the off-beat accents that lend the accompaniment a pleasing swing – even swagger – but lose any clear purpose below c. ♩ = 60 (as does *poco rit.* at bar 20). Yvonne Lefébure recalled

Fauré complaining that 'for his taste the slower tempi [in his music] –
including the *thème* of the *Variations* – were always taken too slow'.[24]

Our focus clarifies again if we observe that Fauré's original 1897 markings
of ♩ = 66–69 make the most instantly vivid sense in Variation I. This might
imply a marginal degree of tacit leeway between it and the *Thème* (as across
the first two pages of his First Nocturne – or as between Debussy's first two
Preludes from Book 1). Another crucial hint comes from the ensuing transition into Variation II (*più mosso*, ♩ = 88), whose opening right-hand notes
complete the figuration from Variation I. A lurch at this point from ♩ = 50 to
♩ = 88 not only disrupts a clearly intended melodic continuity but risks misrelating the new quarter-note to the preceding eighth-note (at ♪ = 100),
causing a false sense of slowing in the audible underlying tactus. A possible
answer to all this might be that Fauré, around 1910, decided to ease the *thème*
itself back to ♩ = 60 (perhaps to allow for the necessary degree of 'give' at the
repeated cadences), and that this was misrendered in print as 50.

Added context comes from Variation VI, which post-1910 prints head
Molto adagio (♩ = 40). This marking, which replaces *Moderato* and *Molto più
moderato* (respectively) in the original French and English prints, suggests
verbal overreaction to the consequences of the somewhat inadequate earlier
heading *Moderato*. As it is, ♩ = 40 there guards against sluggishness and aptly
matches the London edition's *Molto più moderato* heading (arguably the best
option of the three). The work's remaining metronome markings, all added
for the 1910 reprint, suggest varying degrees of reliability: again the *poco rit.*
at the end of Variation VII (plus its staccato articulation) implies a preceding
nimbleness above the metronome marking.

However we negotiate this maze, full contextual awareness can let us clear
decades of dust, in particular by letting Variation II dance gracefully out of
Variation I instead of sounding, as it all too often does, like a desperate escape
bid. A lighter-footed view is equally prompted by D.-E. Inghelbrecht's orchestration of the *Thème et variations*, staged as a ballet in 1928 as *Rayon de lune*
(Moonbeam) – a concept by one of Fauré's own colleagues that reminds us
never to let this music plod. We may equally remember the incisive humour
of Fauré's many caricatures (see note 21 to Chapter 1), a trait that never faded
with age. A violin sight-reading test piece he wrote at the age of nearly sixty
mischievously ties a C♯ to a D♭ (just after the leap down from a tricky upward
scale), and in his late seventies he recalled in print, with undisguised glee,
some of the pranks he and his classmates used to perpetrate as young boys at
the École Niedermeyer.[25]

TACTUS IN THE SIXTH NOCTURNE

Chapter 15 traced a disguised yet strict tactus running throughout the Fifth Nocturne. A similar view of the Sixth Nocturne has sometimes been posited in view of the printed ♩ = 76 at each of its two opening sections. As we saw above, though, this is dubious: since the accompaniment slows from triplets to duplets across bars 18–19, such an equivalence could even make the *allegretto* from bar 19 seem slower than the preceding *adagio*. Some source evidence suggests that the intended tempo from bar 19 is ♩ = 96 (like the outer sections of the Fifth Nocturne) or even a touch faster. Read thus, a broader tactus comes into play, relating the ¾ bar unit of *allegretto* more to the half-note beat of the preceding *adagio*, each unit articulated by six eighth-notes.[26]

This metrical thread becomes increasingly interesting from bar 57, with the *subito* return of the *adagio* material, followed at bar 63 by the *allegro* tempo. The new *allegro* whole-note slightly notches up the preceding tactus (♩= 84 following on from ♩ = 76, the numeric difference being more theoretical than real since both the *adagio* and *allegretto* sections allow for some discreet moving on). Later alternations between the *allegro* material and *allegretto* 'flashbacks' exploit these equivalences (again allowing a notch or two of necessary leeway in some passages), until the climax (from bar 111, as in Ex. 18.2c) explicitly locks the *allegro* tactus into that of the returning *adagio*. Interestingly, Fauré omitted to mark the necessary *Tempo I* at bar 57, and his manuscript omits the necessary tempo modifications at bars 84, 86 and 111. Although editions over his lifetime added most of them, the manuscript exudes a striking sense of visual continuity throughout the piece, despite all the surface adjustments of tempo that the pianist has to observe. Awareness of this can help attune us to the piece's hidden but extremely taut rhythmic core, along with some interesting consequent architectural balance.[27]

MORE ON HYPERMETRE AND CROSS-RHYTHM

Marking the beat sometimes extends importantly to finding and articulating the hypermetre in later works, in ways not always immediately visible on the page. For example, the opening section of the Thirteenth Nocturne easily loses direction or shape in the short phrase juxtapositions from bar 10 unless we understand (and convey) four-bar articulation all through bars 1–16, until bar 21 retroactively extends bars 17–20 into a 2+3 group. This opens the way for more three-bar sequences (notably bars 26–31 and 34–39), each of which either compresses the larger hypermetre (a group of three bars against surrounding ones of four) or expands it (2+3 as across bars 17–21).

In that respect bars 26–8 suggest some structural guile, for the hemiola across bars 27–8 makes bars 26–8 act as a four-unit group (one $\frac{3}{2}$ unit plus three sounding ones of $\frac{2}{2}$). This anticipates the link into the central section, where a well-marked four-bar sequence straddles the double bar (two bars of *andante* $\frac{3}{2}$ plus two of *allegro* $\frac{2}{2}$). Unlikely though it may look on paper (with the change of metre and the *rall.* in bar 52), this four-bar group is so strongly marked at its start and end as to convey itself audibly as such, alerting us to carry the musical flow through the double bar, and carrying through a longer four-bar momentum that continues past the central section's main theme from bar 55. More dramatic intensity comes from the central section's subsequent play on four-, five-bar and (eventually) three-bar phrases. From bar 100 this last ternary element augments itself through rising levels of hypermetre, comprising three groups of paired bars of $\frac{2}{2}$, then three larger groups again of $\frac{3}{2}$ bars grouped in threes (that is, three times three times three half-note beats). Finally this metrical stretching releases itself into four-bar phrases from bar 115, which carry the music through the climax to the recapitulation, and thence through to the final bar.

That four-bar group straddling the transition into the central section is nothing new, for much the same can be seen in the Sixth and Seventh Nocturnes, whose *allegro* sections both start with a long hypermetric anacrusis before the new theme enters (two bars of $\frac{4}{2}$ in the Sixth Nocturne and a corresponding four bars of $\frac{4}{4}$ in the Seventh). Even bars 1–2 of the Sixth Nocturne, plus their own long anacrusis, give the piece an air of starting in mid-phrase, anticipating Ravel's similar habit.

The interesting (and initially hidden) duality of $\frac{3}{2}$ and $\frac{2}{2}$ patterns in the Thirteenth Nocturne reaches back more than forty years to the Scherzo of Fauré's First Violin Sonata, and finds a counterpart in several of his Barcarolles, involving endemic hemiola play between $\frac{3}{4}$ and $\frac{6}{8}$. The middle part of the First Barcarolle constantly opposes the two metres across the hands, before the Third Barcarolle makes a syncopated ostinato of the self-augmenting sequence ♪♪♪ ♪. ♪, which it later softens to right-hand $\frac{3}{4}$ over left-hand $\frac{6}{8}$.

After the Fourth Barcarolle's systematic alternations of sounding $\frac{6}{8}$ and $\frac{3}{4}$ (and again in the Eleventh Barcarolle, sometimes across the hands), the Fifth Barcarolle goes a step further by articulating many of its $\frac{9}{8}$ bars as $\frac{3}{4}+\frac{3}{8}$, most explicitly in the second theme from bar 16. Consistently notated in the manuscript and first edition as ♩ ♩ ♩ ♫, this theme builds up a rhythmic ostinato before going into playful alternation with normally articulated $\frac{9}{8}$ bars across bars 24–7. This rhythmic ambiguity already underlies the start of the piece (Ex. 18.3a), even if musical sense tells us to respect normal $\frac{9}{8}$ articulation at that stage. From bar 37 Fauré lets the hemiola speak for itself (Ex. 18.3b), anticipating the piece's main climax where the bass hammers out the $\frac{3}{4}+\frac{3}{8}$

rhythm before superimposing the first theme on it (bars 102–9). This large-scale metrical sophistication suggests shades of Fauré's friend Chabrier (who died just as Fauré was completing this Barcarolle), in terms of the rhythmic techniques seen in Chapter 13.

Example 18.3. Fauré, Fifth Barcarolle, op. 66

a: bar 1   b: bars 36–7

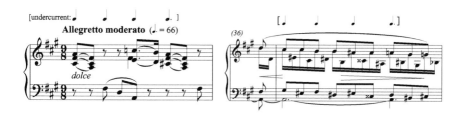

Nor does it stop there, for Fauré's Sixth Barcarolle, indicated in $\frac{6}{8}$, makes repeated play with barline-leaping hemiolas. From bar 24 these mark out two-bar groups effectively constituted $\frac{3}{8}+\frac{3}{4}+\frac{3}{8}$, alternating with 'normal' two-bar groups. The pattern, however, is already quietly active from the start, where the right hand kicks against the left hand's $\frac{6}{8}$ with a long $\frac{3}{4}$ sequence that starts midway through bar 1, turning the right hand's first half-bar into an effective upbeat (like Ravel's later Forlane). This incidentally makes sense of Fauré's mid-bar pedal releases in the opening three bars, coinciding with each right-hand accent.

Similar playfulness pervades the Seventh, Eighth and Tenth Barcarolles, pointing up their respectively sultry, playful and dramatic moods. The Eighth, the most scherzo-like of all Fauré's Barcarolles, again features $\frac{3}{4}+\frac{3}{8}$ patterns across bars 51–3, the left hand kicking against regular $\frac{9}{8}$ in the right hand in a way that invites some left-hand finger-pedal to mark the quarter-note cross-beats. An early manifestation of this playfulness comes in the 'Russian' episode of his early *Mazurka* (Ex. 9.3a) where each hand takes turns between marking the bar and playing hemiola hopscotch across the barline. Metrical play also ends the *Thème et variations*: a right-hand hemiola across bars 1–2 of Variation XI is imitated (in *stretto*) by a left-hand one across bars 2–3, before the melody in bars 10–13 articulates three units of $\frac{4}{4}$ (hyper-hemiola) over the left hand's $\frac{3}{2}$, and bars 20–3 mark out $\frac{3}{2}$ hemiolas across the $\frac{6}{8}$ diminution of the accompaniment in bar 23. As for the seascape-like Twelfth Nocturne (which may once have been envisaged as a barcarolle), readers can explore how much of it – or how little of it apart from the bass line – follows the indicated $\frac{12}{8}$ metre.

If such irrepressible rhythmic inventiveness and vitality hardly match long-held views of a self-effacing, understating Fauré, a century or more after most of these pieces were published we can well remove some musty old mutes from music that never asked for them.

CHAPTER 19

ORCHESTRAL THINKING AND THE PEDALS

What are you looking at his hands for? Look at his feet!
— Safonov to his pupils at a recital by Skryabin

Let's not forget that pianists are quadrupeds — Poulenc

IF precise notation of pedalling has defeated most composers, a single chapter can hardly fill the gap. However, a montage of what our composers said on the topic, plus some glimpses between the lines, can usefully complement what the scores show. Poulenc's advice to 'use more pedal [but] play more cleanly' – and to 'put *butter* in the sauce!'[1] – echoes his teacher Ricardo Viñes who, between 1901 and 1913, gave more Debussy and Ravel premières than all other pianists put together. Since Poulenc constantly credits Viñes with very generous pedalling, it's the more telling that Debussy twice criticised Viñes's playing for being too dry.[2]

Nothing more graphically shows the orchestral nature of the pedal than the opening of Ravel's *Pavane pour une Infante défunte*, respectively in Ravel's piano and orchestral scores. Ironically his piano original, with its semi-staccato bass, leaves pedal unmentioned until bar 13 (as if too obvious for spelling out), while his orchestration, made a decade later, necessarily assures the equivalent resonance by adding bassoons to sustain the pizzicato bass notes. Ravel's piano score of the piece can even be regarded as a model of piano reduction, conveying the music's essentials with a minimum of clutter. If that appears to be taking matters in historical reverse, who knows how he first heard the piece in his imagination? Still a student in 1899, he had little prospect of an orchestral performance, and his piano version shows some awkward hand stretches that suggest thinking beyond the piano. (The same goes for at least the first half of Debussy's *Suite bergamasque*.)

At the start of *Gaspard de la nuit* Ravel more explicitly indicates both pedals but leaves it to the performer how long to hold either of them. Our challenge there is to let the melody breathe while keeping the texture fluid. Much of this involves the pedal's delicate slip point, something that largely defies notation, where the dampers discreetly touch without smothering. In 'Le gibet' (whose score tacitly takes damper pedalling completely as read), a revealing exercise is to check if the pedal can be changed at all between bar 29 beat 2 and bar 35 without losing an essential note in one voice or another. In practice it can stay down through the whole passage: the slow tempo and low dynamics let each new chord overlay the sonority without troublesome blurring. Ravel's writing often allows for this: in 'Oiseaux tristes' for example, most pianos can tolerate pedal right through bars 1–6, 10–16 (or even to bar 17 beat 2), 26–7, and from bar 24 right through to the cadenza's *pressez légèrement* (effectively ignoring the barline).[3]

Ravel's 'Une barque sur l'océan' (*Miroirs*) demands some will-power in this regard, in the teeth of textbook norms: in bars 38–43 (and again later) any pedal change at the top of each wave cuts the bass and accumulated resonance just as we're at the least resonant end of the piano. Ravel's orchestration of the piece (which holds the bass through each wave) confirms the advice of his colleagues Jacques Février and Vlado Perlemuter (in lessons and piano classes) to pedal right through each wave. A subtler point there is conversely to aerate the pedal towards the end of each wave, letting the dynamics subside as we regain the more resonant low register. This general issue of register also affects the approaches to the main climaxes of Ravel's *Jeux d'eau* and 'Ondine', where the pedal can help nourish the crescendo as the texture moves up to the less resonant shorter strings.

Sudden damping also has its role, for example to isolate the final hanging chord of Ravel's 'Ondine' or *À la manière de Chabrier*, the latter obviously echoing Chabrier's 'Mauresque'; the same can probably be read into the end of Debussy's *Étude retrouvée*. In the first of the *Valses nobles* Perlemuter taught a sophisticated sudden damping learnt from Ravel, involving pedal from beat 1 to midway through beat 2, then none on beat 3. (This calls for very free arms to hold beat 3 before falling easily to the next chord.) Perlemuter reported that Ravel spent almost a whole afternoon with him on just that page and pedalling. Why Ravel left it unmarked in the score is debatable: either he later became more demanding – perhaps after hearing it massacred – or unthinkingly pedalled it well from the outset without perceiving any need to notate it exactly.

Explicit pedal indications from Debussy are even rarer than from Ravel. Maurice Dumesnil quotes Debussy as explaining, 'Pedalling cannot be written down: it varies from one instrument to another, from one room, or one hall, to another . . . Trust your ear.'[4] This helps explain some of his descriptive pedal indications seen in Chapter 15. Dumesnil prefaces that quotation with his general recollection of Debussy pedalling in generous but clearly defined swathes.

Walter Gieseking's view was that 'often the pedal sign in Debussy is the bass note'.[5] This raises the question of exactly where to release, and how audibly, after open-ended reverberation ties. Such ties, exploiting the inbuilt decay of piano tone, are intrinsically pianistic (calling for more precise notation when orchestrating) yet with orchestral implications of resonance.

Ravel sometimes opts for the generic indication *Ped.* without defining the subsequent release point (as frequently happens in 'Ondine'); this usage, read-able as *con Ped.*, is traceable back to Schumann in particular.[6] We can guess that his aim is for the listener not to hear the dampers' subsequent descent too clearly. Sometimes an indicated release mark suggests more a sense of 'we need to start clearing the pedal from here' or, conversely, 'by here the pedal needs to have been quietly cleared'; either of these can be read, for example, into bar 30 of Debussy's 'Pagodes'. The uncancelled *2 Ped.* indication that opens old editions of 'Pagodes', incidentally, is a slight misprint: Debussy's autograph has '*(2 Ped.)*', a neat way of saying 'yes, do use both pedals'. (The *Œuvres complètes* accordingly restore Debussy's parentheses, whose importance the original engraver missed.)

In two places Ravel leaves confusing reverberation ties. At bar 83 of 'Ondine' (shortly before Ondine lets drop her sulking tear), the bass ties end in mid-bar (in the manuscript and first edition), technically adding nothing since the bass value already fills the bar. Do they then imply pedal *past* the barline? While Perlemuter couldn't remember Ravel being specific in that case, the manuscript shows a (rather scrawly) pedal release under beat 4 (after the pause); although this slightly contradicts the notated bass value, it makes musical sense if released gently. The other case affects bars 19 and similar in the seventh of the *Valses nobles*: experiment suggests that pedalling the chord over the barline is not what the reverberation ties mean. (Ravel's orchestral score omits the ties.) These usages seem primarily visual, warning against intrusive damping: in the case of the *Valse* they suggest more the gesture of the chord left in the air, implying perhaps some half-pedal.

PERSPECTIVE VIA CHOPIN

Chopin's unusually thorough pedal markings provide background to all this, partly through the influence of his students and partly because of how few pianists pay them any attention even now. In fact they prompt many questions, not least of how instrument- or acoustic-specific some of them may be. Beyond that they suggest a mix of the cautionary (confirming what common sense suggests) and the more originally prescriptive for less obvious effects.

One of Chopin's most probable aims in showing such detail must have been to define norms for his music. Even that prompts questions when no pedal is marked. In 1910 Saint-Saëns insisted that 'if Chopin indicated the pedal [often], it's because he wanted it used where he marked and nowhere else'.[7] While this can sometimes be telling – we have to be alert for the places – blanket imposition of such a rule makes no sense (and certainly not in Saint-Saëns's own music).[8] Even composers who marked *senza pedale* didn't always practise what they preached, as we've already seen (p. 271) and will see again. Debussy's comments in 1915 about pedalling in Chopin (see p. 68) were a reaction to Saint-Saëns's rigid stance, and become more interesting again as Debussy's commentary continues:

> Chopin advised practising without pedal, and, with only rare exceptions, never to hold it on. It was also this art of using the pedal as a kind of *respiration* that I remember from Liszt's playing, when I had the chance of hearing him in Rome.
>
> The calm truth is perhaps that abuse of the pedal is merely a way of disguising lack of technique, and that one then has to make a lot of noise to succeed in drowning the music one's disgorging! Theoretically it ought to be possible to find some graphic way of showing this 'breathing' . . . it can't be impossible, and in fact I think there's a book by Mme Marie Jaëll, who treated pianos without indulgence, on the topic?[9]

Debussy's wording 'never to hold it on' ('*on ne la conservât point*') can make sense if read as not to hold through rests and phrase ends (of which more below). His qualification 'with only rare exceptions' would then relate to those of Chopin's markings that do pedal through rests, explaining their cautionary presence. Carried over to Chopin – as Debussy's wording implies – we might see the equivalent *respiration* in the (rarely observed) off-beat pedal releases in the second theme of Chopin's Third Ballade, bringing out the theme's forlane-like lilt. Debussy's descriptive pedal notation at the start of 'Les collines d'Anacapri' (see p. 210) also relates to this, both through his phrase *en laissant vibrer* and the subsequent *respiration* indicated by his breathing comma in bar 2.

If orchestral thinking encourages generous pedalling, it can also caution the other way, especially where the texture or melodic line suggests breathing. Debussy's Preludes show numerous such breathing points at phrase ends, notably at bars 2 and 9 of 'La fille aux cheveux de lin' (the shepherd's pipe tune), bars 25–6 of 'Danseuses de Delphes', and bars 8, 10 and similar of 'Canope'. More dramatic again is the staccato lift at the climactic bar 22 of 'La fille aux cheveux de lin' (like the climactic bars 33–4 of 'Petit Poucet' in Ravel's *Ma mère l'Oye*). Are these again what Debussy meant by *respiration*? If we read him orchestrally (or vocally) enough not to pedal lazily through these breathing points, our challenge is to aerate without any thud of dampers, like a singer breathing without gasping. That crucial slip-point of light damper contact is perhaps what Debussy would have liked to be able to notate.

This applies again to the many tailed-off short phrases in the Menuet of Ravel's *Sonatine* and the sudden rests in its first movement: at bar 3 beat 2 every pianist who worked with Ravel has vouched for Ravel's insistence on an audible break there (as can be heard on his piano roll recording). Marguerite Long quotes Fauré as wanting a similar breath at the end of bars 38 and 41 in his Sixth Nocturne.[10] In 'Danseuses de Delphes' and 'La fille aux cheveux de lin' this breathing articulation bears on Debussy's metronome indications, making them easier to follow and encouraging the inherent gentle dance.

A more dramatic example is the rests at the climax of Debussy's prelude 'Brouillards' (bars 29–30, after each upward arpeggio): with *subito* damping they can catch our breath as sharply as the many sudden rests in Ravel's 'Scarbo'. One of Debussy's very few explicit pedal markings is a sudden release in the last bar of 'Voiles'; his piano roll recording of 'Le vent dans la plaine' does exactly the same for its last bar (leaving the left hand B♭ resonating on its own, something the first edition doesn't show explicitly).

The start of Debussy's *"Les fées sont d'exquises danseuses"* invites special care with pedal, a sparkling texture whose simple prescriptive notation for the pianist masks a contrapuntal texture. (The slurs here can confidently be read as just defining the harmonic units.) Example 19.1, showing a transcription into quasi-orchestral *particelle*, suggests what the piano will do for us if we let it. However we view the exact colours, this passage yields best musical sense if played practically (or even completely) *senza pedale* up to the bass entry at bar 5.

Example 19.1. Debussy, "*Les fées sont d'exquises danseuses*", possible orchestration of bars 1–2 (cf. Ex. 2.4a)

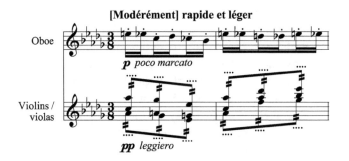

Such passages suggest a fastidiousness of pedalling peculiar to Debussy (and arguably Chabrier) concerning the polyphony between active and silent voices, or between legato and non-legato ones. 'General Lavine – excentric' shows an example at bars 47–50 (from the second full bar of the central episode): Debussy's careful notation lets us avoid fogging by catching the bass on pedal at the second eighth-note of bars 47 and 49, before a sudden release at the start of bars 48 and 50 (as the notation indicates) yields the appropriately comic effect. A debatable case is the start of 'Feux d'artifice', which can be read either *sec*, as if evoking sparklers or Catherine wheels, or with a discreet mask of half-pedal like a haze of cordite; the main concern, either way, is to avoid either drowning or clatter.

<h2 style="text-align:center">PORTATO</h2>

Not to be confused with *portamento* in singing or string playing, *portato* ('carried') is a gentle articulation usually shown by staccato dots under slurs. Each of Debussy's two books of Preludes opens with it (Ex. 1.9 and 2.3). On string instruments it signifies gentle breaks in a single bow stroke, on wind instruments a gentler articulation than normal tonguing. Any blanket legato-pedalling of Example 1.9 or 2.3 loses Debussy's written distinction between legato and portato voices, and it's probably most useful to imagine them orchestrated, the former perhaps with cor anglais for the rising legato line against portamento strings, and the latter on horns, harp and woodwind.

Naturally the piano's intrinsic percussiveness produces some automatic portato, even with pedal down, something we rely on when portato appears over pedalled bass notes. At the pedalled opening of 'Les collines d'Anacapri' the dots can also suggest light accents, such variation in meaning being just one of the vagaries of notation. As with the epigraph to Chapter 15, context usually clarifies: if the portato dots in bars 20 and 26 of 'Les collines' (as numbered in the *Œuvres complètes*) suggest aeration to avoid being mere legato, bar 35 of 'La fille aux cheveux de lin' conversely needs pedal to avoid sounding staccato (Debussy's phrase break suggests a judicious re-pedal at beat 3). The same can go for Fauré's *Thème et variations* at bar 3 of Variation IX (left hand) where the sauce needs all available butter for the right hand's legato. The fifth of Fauré's *Pièces brèves* has several portato figurations whose aeration is carefully allowed for by Fauré's written pedal releases (misaligned in old editions: the Peters edition corrects them).

Like staccato dots, rests in piano music can be fickle. Some suggest abrupt silence for dramatic or comic effect; others merely show where a voice is no longer active, requiring no sudden cut or perhaps a gently gradual one to let the texture breathe (as at bars 9 and 30 of Debussy's 'Hommage à Rameau'). Some are merely there to prepare an anacrusic entry, as in bars 2 and 6 of 'Reflets dans l'eau' where Debussy keeps rests to the minimum needed for defining the tenor re-entry.[11] While taste and acoustic largely determine how much discreet pedal clearance is wanted there, Debussy's notation suggests he intended no clearance at the start of bar 2 or 4 – as opposed to bar 9, where his opening rest marks an important structural breathing point.

Other passive rests can be found at the end of 'Danseuses de Delphes' (Ex. 19.2), where the staccato bass suggests a light and gently reverberant timpani stroke or bass pizzicato without an abrupt cut.[12] (On Debussy's own Blüthner – of which more in Chapter 21 – that bass note has more the effect of warming the existing chord than of adding obvious new pitch.) Debussy obviously loved this pizzicato-like effect, one that can be traced to the end of Chabrier's *Ballabile*: in this drier form it also ends Debussy's *Hommage à Haydn*, *La plus que lente* and 'Pour les quartes'. In 'Pour les accords', bars 96 and 98 combine a *pp* bass with a staccato wedge (unambiguous in his manuscript), suggesting a *dolcissimo* timpani-like stroke without dryness.

Example 19.2. Debussy, 'Danseuses de Delphes', bars 30–1

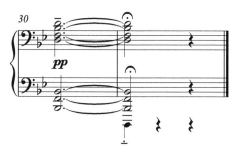

The closing bars of 'La fille aux cheveux de lin' almost exactly invert the texture of Example 19.2 (the rests now at the top), suggesting we read the arpeggiated quarter-note octaves at the top as reverberating, bell-like, through the final rests. This bears on bars 42–5 of 'La Cathédrale engloutie', where the presence of rests in just some of the voices is often read as calling for selective sustaining or damping. While Debussy's notation prompts reflection about voicing and breathing, highlighting these rests serves no clear musical purpose; it could be even argued that his notation was specifically intended to *avoid* any audible cut in sonority either at beat 3 or on the barline.[13] Anybody worried about this need only look at the closing system of *Pour le piano*, or the climactic passages of its Prélude, where a *secco* reading of Debussy's staccato bass and rests would be laughable. Chopin marks pedal through rests in many similar contexts, as we'll soon see Fauré do.

Tempo also has its say. In the lively opening of Debussy's early *Mazurka* any pedal on beat 1 (beyond a minimal dab) risks obscuring the bass timpani effect. And despite what has just been argued for the end of 'Danseuses de Delphes', the end of 'La Puerta del Vino' strongly suggests following Debussy to the letter by cutting the bass before the longer chord above it. A vital hint there is the bass tenuto dash, plus the similarly differentiated endings across the voices in the three surrounding preludes of Book 2 (nos. I, II and IV). These suggest Debussy's interest at just that time in exploring polyphonic differentiation, perhaps prompted by the end of the Scherzo in Chopin's B♭ minor Sonata.

Several of these issues combine in 'Voiles', a piece often pedalled through in a whole-tone haze because of its long unchanging harmonies. In fact the drum-like B♭ bass that sounds through bars 5–20, in contrast to the sustained bass B♭ from bar 21 onwards, invites aeration and a more polyphonic or orchestral reading of the voices and rests above it (a sense of woodwind and horns over gently resonating timpani). While pedal is clearly needed to hold essential notes and warm the texture, this is already far from blanket pedalling, something that can appropriately take over from bar 21, transforming the colour. Similar polyphony on the piece's last page, with all its aerating rests and staccato dots, then makes contextual sense of Debussy's sudden pedal indication in the final bars.

We return where we started: pedal is often our main orchestral colour, whether generous (Ravel's *Pavane pour une Infante défunte* and 'Une barque') or discreet, as in the Prélude of Ravel's *Tombeau de Couperin* where it can mediate between the brief resonance of Ravel's string pizzicati and the quiet but penetrating clarity of his oboe. Ravel's orchestration of that suite is often our key.

It's intriguing to see how often orchestral thinking encourages bolder pedalling in Ravel (and arguably Fauré) as against more careful aeration in

Debussy – probably because clarity in Ravel is often more visibly on the music's surface. Bar 45 of Debussy's 'Pour les arpèges composés' (Ex. 19.3) shows – besides an obvious lift midway through beat 2 – a delicate example on the final A♯s, where the suddenly thinned texture can tempt pedalling through from the chord before. Apart from causing an ungainly harmonic clash, this upsets the harmonic rhythm by robbing the hanging A♯s of their pivotal harmonic role.

Example 19.3. Debussy, 'Pour les arpèges composés', bars 45–6

UNA CORDA (SOURDINE)

While normal ideals warn against automatic soft pedal in lieu of skilful touch at low dynamics, the voicing of individual pianos often decides the issue. Vlado Perlemuter sometimes recommended using soft pedal at higher dynamics for dry or muffled colours like the start of 'Alborada del gracioso' (always subject to the instrument). As with damper pedal, Ravel sometimes leaves to our discretion where to end a *sourdine* indication. (*Sourdine* in French means soft pedal, contrary to older classical usage of *sordini* for dampers, perhaps because by the later nineteenth century *una corda* was no longer exactly that.) Both Ravel and Debussy specify *sourdine* through one entire piece ('Le gibet' and 'Serenade for the Doll') – though Debussy's piano roll recording of *Children's Corner* releases it for the loudest moments in 'Serenade for the Doll', and uses it just as much in the following 'The snow is dancing'.[14]

SOSTENUTO PEDAL

This can be contentious since many pianos have none, and concerns are sometimes raised about its legitimacy in music that doesn't mention it. As perspective against such a timid stance, we may immediately observe not only that sostenuto pedal was initially a French invention (of which more below) but also that most of Debussy's piano works – never mind Ravel's 'Le gibet' – don't mention damper pedal either. One obvious commercial reason for leaving sostenuto pedal unmentioned in musical scores would be to avoid deterring buyers whose pianos didn't have one. The main climax of Debussy's 'Hommage à Rameau', with its chromatic progressions over carefully tied-over bass octaves (Ex. 7.24b), is just one of many notations in this repertoire that effectively say 'Here's what I really want if you can manage it: get as near as you can.' It's what our composers had to do at home where they mostly had no sostenuto pedal.

They did, however, have access to sostenuto pedals, a device invented in France as early as the 1840s before being taken up by Steinway in the mid-1870s,[15] apparently with Liszt's blessing if not his prompting, some years before Liszt met Fauré and Debussy. Ravel must have known the three-pedal Pleyel grand that Ricardo Viñes owned in the first half of 1895.[16] Fauré and Ravel (and Viñes) certainly played the Steinway grand acquired in 1896 by Mme de Saint-Marceaux for her famous musical salon (Debussy may have played it too); they would also have played on the three-pedal Steinway full concert grand bought by Winnaretta de Polignac in 1906.[17] They also knew René de Castéra, whose much-admired three-pedal Steinway was bought in Paris in 1900 on the advice of Albéniz (and partly Viñes).[18]

Given that background, we can focus more on musical concerns: the main one here, as with any mechanical device, is clearly to avoid blatancy, as can happen in (say) the *fortissimo* chord sequence of 'La Cathédrale engloutie' if sostenuto pedal is offset by over-fussy damper pedalling. In practice this aquatic passage calls for such generous pedalling as to make sostenuto pedal immaterial: we can try using both, but listeners are unlikely to hear any difference unless the pedalling is drawing unwelcome attention to itself.

Another passage often associated with sostenuto pedal, the Prélude of *Pour le piano*, can be a borderline case on bright-toned pianos if the left foot is needed for the *sourdine*. Some pianists manage to cover two pedals with one foot, though the bass decay and low dynamics there are such that sostenuto pedal often makes little difference. More important is probably to voice the long bass notes strongly enough to let them last: as Debussy and Fauré would have known well, the stronger the bass, the more blurring is possible above it. A related texture can be found at bars 10–11 of Fauré's Fourth Nocturne (where the *pp* indication is obviously meant for the inside voices).

A few more passages where only sostenuto pedal can ensure the effect indicated in the score include bars 43–4 of Debussy's 'General Lavine', bars 110–15 of 'Jardins sous la pluie', bars 33–5 of 'Pour les quartes' (for the dance-like articulation above the tied bass), bars 17–20 of *"Les soirs illuminés par l'ardeur du charbon"* and, in *Children's Corner*, bar 43 of 'Doctor Gradus' along with the passages of piquant staccato against sustained chords in 'Golliwogg's cake walk' (notably bars 63, 67, 85–6 and 88–9). Examples in Ravel include bar 578 of 'Scarbo' (the last *ff* on the penultimate page) to clarify the abruptly alternating E major and G minor chords, bars 59–60 of the Menuet in *Le tombeau de Couperin* (to clarify the phrase break in bar 60, as happens by default in the orchestral version) and the last two bars of the *Sonatine*'s Menuet.[19] The 'Épilogue' of the *Valses nobles* is specially interesting because the passages that invite sostenuto pedal alternate conveniently with Ravel's *sourdine* indications, letting the left foot fill each role in turn if we so wish. The same happens at the start of the finale of his Piano Trio, a work that repeatedly invites recourse to sostenuto pedal in all four movements.

Even Chabrier's *Habanera* of 1885 prompts sostenuto pedal at bar 40, if the staccato articulation is to keep breathing as he obviously intended in the two preceding bars. In *Bourrée fantasque* the many staccatissimo two-hand articulations above sustained bass notes at least invite experiment, matching the contrasts that Chabrier wrote into his *Valses romantiques* of staccato on one piano against sustained pedal on the other. *Bourrée fantasque* generally is a challenging study for feet and hands alike (as Cortot observed),[20] almost a pedalling manual for Chabrier, including juxtapositions of pedalled and unpedalled staccato. Several visible erasures in the piece's manuscript show how much care Chabrier took over the exact placing of pedal markings. This piece is orchestral with a vengeance: indeed it would have become an orchestral rhapsody to match *España* had Chabrier's failing health not prevented him from completing its orchestration.

Study of pedal appears to have preoccupied Chabrier's later years, for his 1891 re-edition of 'Mauresque' (*Pièces pittoresques*) adds detailed pedalling with some surprise effects. (The Dover edition shows these and clarifies the sudden clearance he probably intended at the end: other reprints lose it all by reproducing the 1881 edition.) Despite its lack of pedal markings, 'Sous bois' demands a particularly delicate blend of pedal with Liszt-type *respiration* through the rests and phrase-ends (while always keeping it moving). This doubtless prompted Georges Falkenberg's close attention to the piece:[21] he judiciously recommends retaking pedal (with respiratory clearance just before) at notes 3 and 7 of bars 1 and similar, as well as at the middle of bar 6, then at each eighth-note in bars 8 and 11–16 (except the first eighth of bar 11 and the third one of bar 16). I quote this in detail not only because it repays study but also because it relates interestingly to Chopin's oft-quoted but rarely followed pedalling for bar 7 onwards of his *Barcarolle*. Similar 'respiratory' pedal is suggested at the end of 'Idylle' by Chabrier's orchestration of the piece (in *Suite pastorale*), which releases the sustained chords exactly where the piano score does (obviously without any thud of dampers), letting the final high notes – if we dare – sign off by themselves.

FAURÉ

Chapter 15 has already touched on Fauré's sporadic pedal indications, implying a tacit norm of intelligently generous pedal. The piano rolls Fauré recorded in 1908 and around 1912 confirm this, though the heavier pedalling on the 1912 ones may reflect his growing deafness. A typical case closes the first section of his First Barcarolle: from bar 30 the score indicates pedal across the arpeggio in the second half of this and the next bar, leaving tacitly understood what Fauré's Welte roll then confirms: to pedal from midway through bar 32 until a release at the final rest of bar 34 (as any orchestration of the passage would assume).

Some *scherzando* contexts in Fauré can take minimal pedal: 'Messieu Aoul' (alias 'Mi-a-ou') from *Dolly* is one, along with the scherzos of his First Violin Sonata op. 13 and First Piano Quartet op. 15, and the staccato duplets of the *scherzando* Variation III in his *Thème et variations*. Much of the piano writing in the finales of opus 13 and opus 15 equally suits *secco* or light dabs, the string instruments providing a sustaining 'orchestra' against which the piano can sparkle. Ravel's Concertos show similar distinct contrasts between highly pedalled episodes, notably when the piano is unaccompanied, and sparkling passages against orchestra that invite minimal (if any) pedal.

Fauré's classical training from Saint-Saëns partly underlies his discreet, sometimes cautious pedal notation. Given his tendency to notate reactively against sloppy habits, some of this was probably a guard against over-pedalling.[22] His classical notation is most visible from the way he places releases at the end of beats or under barlines (meaningless in practical terms) when the context suggests – like any orchestral thinking – legato pedal to the next beat. (Georges Falkenberg's 1892 treatise *Les pédales du piano* makes this point about pedal notation in general.) Fauré's piano rolls confirm this, and sometimes stretch the pedal past the onset of the next beat, avoiding sudden cuts of sonority on main beats – specially important when the bass is off the beat. Debussy is quoted by Maurice Dumesnil as advising the same thing.[23]

This involves a larger structural scale in Fauré's Sixth Nocturne, where the pedal release ending each of the first two main sections (bars 18 and 62) comes *after* the pause, thus maintaining pedal through the rests and pause. (Fauré's manuscript confirms this.) Any break across the sections is thus minimal – the pauses don't want to be too long either – avoiding fragmentation of the piece's long arched structure. Fauré's piano roll of the Seventh Nocturne supports this by holding the pedal through bar 38 (ending the opening slow section) until the first *allegro* note of bar 39. Should any of this appear to be inciting unwarranted liberties, we need only listen to Fauré's two piano roll recordings of the Third Nocturne (from 1908 and 1912), which pedal judiciously from bar 28 in the teeth of his own *senza Ped.* indication. Even bearing in mind Fauré's growing deafness in the years he made those piano rolls, experiment suggests that his *senza Ped.* in the Third Nocturne can probably be read descriptively – perhaps even a touch reactively – as 'keep it transparent'.

Fauré's notation supports that in another way – especially in his songs and chamber music – through his habit of tying the last note of a melodic phrase over to a final added eighth- or quarter-note, to avoid cutting the sound on a main beat.[24] Debussy echoed this concern by advising gentleness with pedal changes to avoid unwanted dips in sonority; for the start of 'Clair de lune' he suggested pedal down before the first note (a technique often advocated by Cortot). Heinrich Neuhaus's definition of this technique as 'opening up all the piano's pores beforehand' speaks for itself at the start of Chabrier's *Valses romantiques*, where the indicated pedal adds the resonance of all the lower strings to the opening high arpeggios.[25] It can be revealing to try the opening of 'La fille aux cheveux de lin', 'Oiseaux tristes' or Fauré's Fourth Nocturne in different acoustics with pedal applied variously before, as or just after the first note is sounded.

The main climax of the Thirteenth Nocturne (bars 123–6) merits mention here. Comparison with several analogous passages, including the pedalled-through climax of the Sixth Nocturne, suggests that whatever our pedal treat-ment here, Fauré's rests between the left-hand arpeggio groups are not intended to signify abrupt pedal cuts. His default usage elsewhere generally suggest he would more probably have marked such an exceptional usage explicitly. His through-pedal marking at the climax of the Sixth Nocturne is doubtless marked explicitly because the pedal there, very unusually, is to be held through a long paused rest for *both* hands, an assumption we would otherwise hardly make by default.

A degree of cautious exaggeration can be read into Fauré's pedalling at the fourth last bar of his Fourth Nocturne (Ex. 19.4): his release necessarily signals the change of harmony while leaving it to us to find possible ways of main-taining the longer notes. Georges Falkenberg notes a similar challenge, treatable only by half-pedal, at the half-notes of the arpeggiated *Choral* theme in Franck's *Prélude, Choral et Fugue.*[26]

Example 19.4. Fauré, Fourth Nocturne, bars 94–5, first edition and reprints

For the Fourth Nocturne we also have the emphatic word of Roger-Ducasse (in his 1924 preface to Nocturnes 1–8) that Fauré intended each ¾ passage in the closing pages (the sustained chords with rising scales above) to blend as an entity on the pedal, without any clever effects like retaking or using sostenuto pedal at the rests. In orchestral terms this suggests the resonance of an undamped harp for the upward runs in sixths. Anybody still worried about pedalling though the last bar of 'Danseuses de Delphes' or bars 42–5 of 'La Cathédrale engloutie' can take comfort from this.

Since the manuscript of Fauré's Fourth Nocturne has vanished, the pedalling at its final reprise raises a more unusual problem: as printed in the original edition it serves no visible purpose in bars 65, 67 and 69 (Ex. 19.5) and seems gracelessly abrupt in bars 66 and 68. An immediate solution (as in the London Peters edition) is to delay the releases – possibly misaligned by the first edition's engraver – until each half-bar. This leaves the question of the staccato bass eighth-notes. If read orchestrally as quasi-pizzicato, they need at least a discreet touch of pedal. Alternatively it's possible that the printed *Ped.* indications were simply intended farther left, under the bass notes (though this may seem somewhat tame after trying the quasi-pizzicato effect).

Example 19.5. Fauré, Fourth Nocturne, bars 65–6 as in the first edition (bars 67 and 69 repeat the pedalling of bar 65)

This last possibility is prompted by an engraving habit from that era which often placed pedal indications after, rather than under, low-lying bass notes or grace notes, to save space between systems. (Thus the original edition of Fauré's First Nocturne prints the piece's final pedal indication under the main chord, making it pointless unless it includes the preceding grace notes.) Surviving manuscripts usually clarify this.

A passing detail in Fauré's Fifth Nocturne throws extra light on the ever-shifting sands of pedalling and its orchestral implications. In 1922–3, nearly forty years after the piece first appeared in 1884, Fauré lengthened the bass note of bars 5 and 14, as shown in Example 19.6 (and the London Peters edition). This raises several questions. How much pedal did he assume in bars 1–4, and was it the same in 1884 as in 1922–3? If only light pedalling, was his original intention for bar 5 to increase the bass sustenance just a fraction? Did he then decide later to increase the contrast at bar 5? Or did he always envisage generous pedal from the start (reading the bass eighth-notes as shorthand to avoid the clutter of double voicing)? If the latter, do we read his later amendment to bar 5 as a clarification to allow for necessary pedal changes within bar 5?

Example 19.6. Fauré, Fifth Nocturne, bars 1–6 (likewise bars 9–15), first edition, with *ossia* reading showing Fauré's amendment in 1922–3

All the questions interact, and various answers are viable. Whatever we decide, they arguably affect bars 49 onward of the same piece (Ex. 15.3b) where Fauré's short pedal dabs can retrospectively imply equally light pedalling for bars 1–4. If definitive answers are impossible, a consideration at least of the options helps us always avoid the danger of mindless autopedalling.

CHAPTER 20

BODY LANGUAGE
AND THE PIANO

Why do I attach so much importance to this 'trifle'? Because [Liszt's] fingering . . .
brings the whole of Liszt before me. I see his hands, his gestures, his eagle manner,
I feel the breath of this demon in monk's habit.

– Heinrich Neuhaus[1]

Even if no two pianists ever fit themselves identically to the same piece, an
enjoyable secret of pianism lies in sensing and flexibly adjusting to the
composer's own natural ways of moving. At best this helps the music play us
as much as vice versa. Any osteopath or chiropractor will confirm that our
posture and muscle use even affect how we – like the composer – hear.

As actors know, much of our body language follows national or regional
habits (think of the famous French shrug). I once watched Jacques Février in
a piano class demonstrate part of a Brahms Intermezzo just after teaching
some Poulenc: for a few seconds the Brahms sounded bemusingly like Poulenc
– Février's posture still set for stricter French rhythm, articulation and voicing
– until he instinctively adjusted, transforming the sound and rhythm. Even
within a tradition it can be tricky to jump straight from playing (say) Ravel
into Debussy or vice versa. One reason is Debussy's love of having main lines
in mid-texture, against Fauré's and Ravel's tendency to think more in melody
and bass, something that tends to move the arm and hand differently. While
there are obvious exceptions to these general tendencies, they help explain
Debussy's reported description of the virtuoso's fifth finger as a 'scourge'.[2] (As
Debussy might have said, who would want an orchestra in which a trumpet
constantly blares out the top line?) His lighter top-line arabesques also reflect
a musical surface texturally, analytically and notationally more porous than
Ravel's. Bodily alertness to these innate voicing balances can help keep

textures clear and flowing, for example with light inner figurations in Fauré and lightly nimble top lines in Debussy.

THE PREHENSILE HAND AND THUMB

An early photograph of Debussy (see Plate 4) shows him aged five astride a tricycle. For handlebars think keyboard and we have the hand layout for his early *Mazurka* (from bar 3), the prehensile thumbs forming anchors for each bar's figurations. Three bars into his *Suite bergamasque* the same can be sensed again. The habit is still there in the 1900s, the thumb anchoring the right hand from bar 3 of 'Pagodes' (two notes together) and from bar 9 of *L'isle joyeuse* –

Plate 4. Debussy aged five, preparing for 'Chevaux de bois' and *L'isle joyeuse*

including the latter's left hand if we read the rising arpeggios as fingered 5–3–2–1. (Cf. Liszt's corresponding fingering in Ex. 11.2.) With thumb as supporting pivot, the top-line arabesques can easily be kept light (they'll always be heard), favouring the longer lines underneath that bind the structure (see Appendix 1). As late as 'Bruyères' of 1913, natural thumb weight helps the dissonant *d'♭* and *f* of bar 4 resonate through to their resolutions in bar 5. Small wonder that Debussy took so easily to gamelan sonorities, their layered weighting matching what was already innate.

Pivotal thumbs again make pianistic sense of the otherwise orchestral-looking opening of *D'un cahier d'esquisses,* the implied fingering shown editorially in Example 20.1. (While Debussy leaves fingering to us, no other option permits the indicated legato, especially at the fairly flowing barcarolle tempo discussed on page 201.)

Example 20.1. Debussy, *D'un cahier d'esquisses,* bars 1–3 (fingering editorial)

This supports the observations by various musicians that Debussy's hands stayed in the keys (see p. 72 and note 18 to Chapter 21). If bar 7 of 'Canope' (Ex. 20.2) appears to contradict that by specifying left hand for a *c'♯* within easy reach of the right hand, a closer look shows the similar physical intelligence involved, not just for preparing bar 9 (where the hand shift becomes obligatory) but also in avoiding a weak finger on the *c'♯*. The practical outcome each time is in voicing and rhythm, combining light dynamics and textures with clear voicing without slowing or arm tightening.

Example 20.2. Debussy, 'Canope', bars 7–9

Was Debussy left-handed? The query was raised by Joan Thackray, who observed that photos invariably show Debussy's sempiternal hand-rolled ciga-rette in his left hand.[3] (Ravel's sempiternal *caporal* by contrast always appears in his right hand if not in his mouth.) Debussy's handwriting betrays no defi-nite clue, and other photos show him variously gardening right-handed and punting left-handed. This suggests some ambidexterity, perhaps even a natural left-handedness retrained in childhood (as was then customary). The same query regarding Fauré's known ambidexterity might be related to his insistence on strong bass lines at the piano.

Whatever the case, Paul Vidal observed that Debussy, even in early years, 'had a left hand of extraordinary agility and capacity for extension'.[4] The piano parts of Debussy's *Proses lyriques* and 'Il pleure dans mon cœur' (from the *Ariettes oubliées*) call for wide but very quick bass leaps and arpeggiations, suggesting a sort of 'shoplifter's left hand' to match Ravel's 'strangler's thumbs' (of which more below). A naturally strong left hand is equally suggested by melodic bass or tenor lines in Debussy's early *Arabesques*, *Suite bergamasque* and *Valse romantique*, such as the descending left-hand scale over bars 15–22 of *Valse romantique*: starting from *c'* (most easily on left thumb), it invites bold voicing under a much lighter right hand (which will always be heard). The left hand again is the natural leading one in the rising lines from bar 43 of 'Reflets dans l'eau' and on the last page of *L'isle joyeuse*, and explicitly so at the start of the prelude 'Brouillards'. Debussy sometimes also makes strong demands of the left fifth finger, notably at bars 43–6 of 'Jardins sous la pluie' and in *L'isle joyeuse* at bars 152–5 and similar.

Fauré's version of handlebars often entails Thalberg-style melodies passing from hand to hand (or thumb to thumb), as in the First and Fourth Barcarolles, the last of the *Pièces brèves*, the *fortissimo* Variation IV of the

Thème et variations, and almost throughout his *Valses-caprices* which can be argued as texturally the most original (and virtuoso) of all his piano works. His natural thumb weight emerges from the implicit left-thumb tenor lines towards the end of the Fifth and Sixth Nocturnes (bars 194–200 and 129–30 respectively); although Fauré didn't bother to mark them with double stems, Roger-Ducasse's preface to the 1924 edition draws attention to them. A shoplifter's left hand to rival Debussy's is also suggested by some of Fauré's rapid leaps in the Fifth Nocturne, Fifth Barcarolle and *Thème et variations*.

Ravel's 'strangler's thumbs', as his friends dubbed them, appear to have been less a matter of size than squareness and strength; Jacques Février called them 'très développés' and quoted Ravel as wanting pianists to 'use them as lot'.[5] This can be sensed at the start of the *Valses nobles* (the right thumb taking two notes on the chordal ricochets), or in the final three bass bells of 'La vallée des cloches' where natural thumb weight assures the bell-like sonority. Example 20.3 implies a revealing hand layout combining a naturally falling thumb, lateral wrist flexibility and a nimbly accented 4 (of all fingers) to mark the theme. (One can admittedly split the arpeggio across the hands, but taking it in a single hand fall suggests a vivid sense of Ravel at the keyboard and also sets up the hand optimally for bar 8.) The pattern recurs at the end of bars 170 and 171 of 'Alborada del gracioso', again suggesting well-developed fourth and fifth fingers.

Example 20.3. Ravel, *Pavane pour une Infante défunte*, bars 7–8 (fingering editorial)

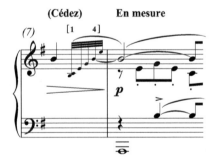

Ravel's other thumb games include the chromatic slides in the fifth of the *Valses nobles* and – most famously – thumb dyads for the slithering seconds in 'Scarbo' from bar 448. Example 12.7 shows more examples of thumb dyads, one of which neatly has the left thumb chromatically surrounding the index finger. Debussy meanwhile indicates right thumb and index finger to cover four notes at bar 26 of 'La Cathédrale engloutie'. These can be sensed as elaborations of other implicitly thumb-centric figurations like bars 95–108 in the third of Debussy's *Images* [*oubliées*] of 1894 (right thumb starting on *d″/e″*) and bars 137–40 of *L'isle joyeuse* (left thumb on *a′/b′*), sometimes involving both thumbs together or in playful alternation (as in Example 8.6 across bars 17–18, or 'Minstrels' from bar 9 onwards).

Curiously enough Ravel, who most openly admitted to composing at the piano, often produces the trickiest patterns, perhaps because the keyboard allowed him to test hand patterns to the limit for sonorous exploration. His professionalism in notation often conceals how orchestrally his piano writing is conceived: imagine, for example, the experimentation needed to arrive at the orchestral (or string quartet-like) polyphony of overlapping hands in 'Ondine' and the first movement of the *Sonatine*. This relates to similar layouts in Schumann which again betray orchestral thinking, as Debussy observed (p. 160 above). A more abstruse reverse-prehensility informs the Toccata of *Le tombeau de Couperin*, each half-bar launched from the weak end of the hand towards the thumb, requiring conscious effort from the pianist to keep releasing the wrist and avoid elbow tightening.

LIGHTNESS AND ESCAPEMENT

A particular lightness in the keys is suggested by the way Fauré's music often holds a low dynamic, even with very nimble figurations, before a brief but vigorous crescendo to climactic points: comparison between his manuscripts and editions shows him often compressing these crescendos even more in the course of revision or recopying. Similar fingertip lightness can be sensed in Ravel's toccata figurations in *Le tombeau de Couperin* and 'Scarbo' (the challenge being to keep textures light and the tempo steady without unmarked lurches or hiatus), as well as in the climactic crescendo of 'Une barque sur l'océan', whose right-hand ostinato can engender a sense of just skimming the keys. This suggests a tactile distinction from Debussy who more usually offers optimum dynamic control at the keybed, the keys hardly needing to rise beyond the point of double escapement (the opening trill of *L'isle joyeuse* or tremolos of 'Poissons d'or' – though this can apply equally to the start of Ravel's 'Ondine'). Experimenting higher or lower in the keys with these passages can be revealing for avoiding any 'rattle of pebbles'.

Ravel's enjoyment of the double escapement point can be sensed in his fast repetitions, or in the slower *Bebung* effect of the repeated B♭s in 'Oiseaux tristes' where a gentle drop-lift wrist action (plus arguably some oblique finger slippage in and out, *à la* Debussy) can catch the echo note just off the keybed. This standard wrist gesture for two-note phrases – the classical 'sigh' gesture taught by Chopin and Liszt[6] – might equally be read in classical pastiche contexts like the Menuet of Ravel's *Sonatine*. Ravel's colleague Robert Casadesus took this as axiomatic at the sight of any two-note slur,[7] something he doubtless learnt from his historically minded teacher Louis Diémer. A rare piece of film footage shows Ravel using the wrist very flexibly at the piano; he implicitly reads this as a norm elsewhere by signalling exceptions such as the Fugue of *Le tombeau* where he warned against too much wrist motion, doubtless because it would risk exaggerating already mannered gestures and weakening the piece's rhythmic crispness.[8]

Chromatic scales

A standard technique of the era is charted by Saint-Saëns who sometimes indicates four-fingered chromatic scales (e.g. right hand *1–2–3–4–1–2–3– 1–2–3–4* upwards from C), facilitating fast runs by reducing thumb passing. This can even be extended to include *4–5* (on either G–Ab or Bb–B♮, as Heinrich Neuhaus recommended for Liszt), which lets the pattern repeat itself by the octave instead of every two octaves.[9] Despite Debussy's deliberate omission of printed fingering in his *Études*, the obvious four-finger groups that open 'Pour les degrés chromatiques' suggest four- or five-fingered chromatics for the longer runs that ensue. His early draft of 'Pour les notes répétées' shows a physically similar *4–3–2–1* (visible in the Minkoff facsimile edition) written across the *Campanella*-like repeated notes from bar 49.

Fauré's hand stretches

Fauré's similar penchant for open-handed spreads (rather than frequent thumb passing) can be seen in his first *Valse-caprice*, through his *1–2–3–4–5* and *1–2–4–5* fingering for the wide right-hand arpeggios at bars 168–9 (sixth page). This piece is especially revealing about hand patterns: the fourth bar of its *meno mosso* second theme – like the related second bar of the legato motive two pages later – implies a thumb slide from black to white keys, and his printed left-hand fingering on the last page specifies a descending left-hand legato thumb under *5* (implying lateral wrist suppleness – see also his fingering at bar 11 of the Second Nocturne and bars 60–1 of the Fifth Impromptu).

Fauré tends to show fingering (like pedalling) only where something specific or unusual is needed. While nobody is obliged to follow him, it usefully shows how his hands worked, even in his imagination when (as often) he wrote away from the piano. On the basis of the examples just seen, Variation I of his *Thème et variations* suggests an intuitive sense of right thumb under *5* for notes 9–10 (*a″♯–b″*) in bars 2 and 10 (after thumb on the note 5 *e″♯*), perhaps also *1–2–3–4–5* for the spread-out notes 1–5 of bar 9.

Although a few of Fauré's textures – like the Third and Fourth Nocturnes – follow a Chopin-nocturne norm of left hand taking bass plus harmonic infilling, his fondness for rich lower textures sometimes involves a contrary pattern of manually holding the bass while the right hand takes both tune and harmony. In the Tenth Nocturne (bar 9 onwards) and Twelfth Nocturne (bar 2 onwards) this is the only viable option, and it bears on the oft-debated first page of the Sixth Nocturne (Ex. 20.4), where Fauré's stemming similarly suggests he envisaged the triplets generally taken by right hand except for those stemmed downward on the lower staff in bars 3, 5, 7 and 10. Above Example 20.4 is shown, editorially, the sort of fingering he may have had in mind: with a supple wrist and arm it can be sensuously enjoyable even under a medium-sized hand like Fauré's. (The postulated *5–2–1* in bar 7 is no wider than many stretches indicated by Chopin, even if the odd bit of left-hand takeover is a viable option.) While Fauré was never dogmatic about such matters, his reported preference here for right-hand spreads (according to Vlado Perlemuter) is worth noting, because French prints of the Sixth Nocturne since 1958 have editorially indicated a contrary disposition with a leaping left hand, a difference that markedly affects voicing.[10]

Example 20.4. Fauré, Sixth Nocturne, bars 6–8 (stemming as in autograph, fingering editorial)

Internal polyphony has its say. Imagine bars 8–9 of the Sixth Nocturne set for voices or instrumental quartet (Ex. 20.5), and the mirroring tenor line immediately suggests we highlight more than just the top line. (It also encourages respecting the melody's exact rhythm, as discussed on pages 265–6.) Fauré's piano texture adds enchantment by the way the triplets rhythmically offset the tenor reflections like ripples in water: not for nothing, perhaps, does the piece date from 1894, the year of Monet's first serious studies in water reflection. Sifting out the polyphony in this manner can be very useful for discerning the harmonic logic through the myriad arpeggios and suspensions of Fauré's later pieces like the Twelfth Nocturne and the late chamber works. Often these late textures aren't so far removed from early works: the opening layout of the First Nocturne, for example, returns almost verbatim forty years later in the Andante of his Second Violin Sonata. Pure string quartet textures can be sensed in parts of the Eleventh Nocturne (with a particularly bold cello line from bar 19, following the viola–cello dialogue from bar 13), the fourth of the *Pièces brèves*, the Thirteenth Nocturne and, perhaps most beautifully of all, the closing epilogue of his *Thème et variations* where he repeatedly plays at bringing in successive voices an eighth-note apart, crowning the process at bar 20.

Example 20.5. Fauré, Sixth Nocturne, bars 8–9 in polyphonic reduction

Much of the physical impetus of Fauré's piano writing emerges from passing details of layout, some of which have long been obscured by misprints. In the Seventh Nocturne his manuscript beaming in bar 54 shows how to divide an awkward-looking arpeggio figuration easily across the hands (a detail first printed in the London Peters edition). A similar case in the *Thème et variations* (again clarified in the Peters edition) introduces a technically inessential but enjoyable arm swing in the penultimate system of Variation X, one that keeps the torso supple and the music dancing. A related sense of swing drives the bell-like alternations in Example 19.4; a subtle version of it can be felt in the rather pendular alternation of hands marking the successive quarter-note beats in Variation VIII of the *Thème et variations*.

Fauré's use of [brackets across chords is sometimes puzzling. The sign is often taught as signifying non-arpeggiando as well as showing hand layout, but some of Fauré's brackets cover unstretchable spans in places where the hands are too far apart to allow redistribution (for example in the fourth of the *Pièces brèves*). With his smallish build Fauré appears to have had no more than average-sized hands, and his piano roll recordings (of which more in Chapter 21) show him often breaking ninths and tenths as well as anything larger. His [brackets appear mostly in post-1900 scores, often in similar places to where his earlier scores show normal *arpa* squiggles: compare for example ⎣ in the fourth *Pièce brève* of 1902 with ⁍ at bars 54–5 of the First Nocturne of the 1870s or – more exceptionally for a late work – his ⁍ at bar 4 of the Ninth Nocturne of 1908.

It might be argued that Fauré's ⎣ brackets are a quasi-replacement for the earlier squiggles, perhaps with the added proviso 'keep any arpeggiation crisp' (as his piano rolls do). This would explain his rare juxtaposition of the two signs in the final bars of the *Pièces brèves*, as a subtle piece of colour differentiation. (The piece's manuscript confirms the distinction.) Evidence suggests that we treat these signs with common sense free of dogmatism, an approach supported by Fauré's piano roll recordings. It's thus reasonable to infer, in the Seventh Barcarolle, that Fauré's bell-like printed *arpas* in bars 29–36 can continue in bars 37, 39 and 41; we can certainly assume with safety that he broke the wide left-hand dyads in bars 68 and 72. His Fifth Barcarolle rather absentmindedly supports this by supplying a tied bass grace note in bar 6 whose equivalent we really needed in bar 5.

RHYTHMIC OFFSETTING

The habit of gratuitous rhythmic dislocation between hands, beloved of romantic virtuosi, found little official sympathy with our composers – bearing in mind the relative nature of such things. (Parisian lore has it that Saint-Saëns, after listening to Paderewski rehearse one of his concertos, mischievously asked the conductor, 'Which of his hands have you decided to follow?') Some technical reasons have already been seen, such as the dislocation across voices written into particular passages. Some dislocation is obviously unavoidable across large bass stretches like the above-mentioned bar 5 in Fauré's Fifth Barcarolle or bar 48 of Debussy's 'Mouvement' (Ex. 16.6). Another standard written-in dislocation is Fauré's way of lightening piano textures by sounding the bass after the beat (as in Chopin's op. 45 Prelude). The converse, when a top line marks out the melody just after the beat, can be inferred right across bars 52–70 of 'Jardins sous la pluie' (Ex. 20.6) – a rare case where Debussy ironically needs to be 'top-lined' in a passage that doesn't even mark the top line as an independent voice (it's the only real melody there, vitally balancing the bass). Other examples are the start of Franck's *Prélude, Choral et Fugue* and the climactic bar 111 of Fauré's Sixth Nocturne (Ex. 18.2c) whose top *f‴* completes the melody from the preceding bars. As with the first of Chopin's op. 28 Preludes, these offset melodies can sound to the listener equally like the main beat (the bass anticipating it), an inbuilt ambiguity that still respects the bar's sounding length.

Example 20.6. Debussy, 'Jardins sous la pluie', bars 56–9

A variant of this involves some 'double-struck' beats where Debussy effectively sounds the same beat twice, linked by a fast arpeggio or strum across the hands. Examples occur in the third last bar of 'Jardins sous la pluie' (Ex. 20.8, bar 155) and the very similar penultimate bar of 'Les collines d'Anacapri'. In bars 50–1, 53–4 and 58 of 'La Puerta del Vino' similar offset rhythms were originally printed as in Example 20.7a, all notes full size. For reprints Debussy had each of the bars renotated as in Example 20.7b, the note sizes and beams now directing emphasis to the bass and matching bars 2–4 (Ex. 20.7c). His *Études* show two more such passages, one in full-size notes ('Pour les agréments' bars 5–6 and 45–6), the other in small notes ('Pour les arpèges composés' bars 62–3). These rhythms relate somewhat to Ravel's prosodic metrical 'asides' discussed on page 261.

Example 20.7. Debussy, 'La Puerta del Vino'

a: bar 50 (bar 51 identical), first   **b: the same bars, reprint of later**
edition of 1913   **1913**

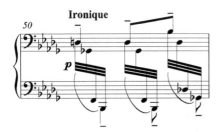

c: bars 2–4 (as in all editions)

The syndrome also involves the opening *gruppetti* of 'Minstrels', where Debussy's *sur le temps* demands a very crisp strum to let both the initial attack and the melodic *d* mark the beat, rather like bars 2–4 of 'La Puerta del Vino'. Ravel's *très serré* arpeggiations in bars 1–5 of 'Alborada del gracioso' (Ex. 12.7 motive *a*) are similar: for melodic reasons each *e'♭* has to mark the beat as much as the top of the strum does. All this relates to a more discreet element of pianistic attack, that imperceptibly quick arpeggiation that can soften the impact of a chord at any dynamic: at the quiet end this sort of quick arpeggiation can enhance the suggestions of harp (literally *arpa*) that open Debussy's 'Canope' or those from bar 4 of 'Danseuses de Delphes'.

A more hidden moment of offset polyphony across the hands can be sensed on the last page of Ravel's 'Ondine' at bar 89, where the left thumb's *e♯* quietly completes the *c♯–d♯* melodic line emerging from the preceding cadenza. Exactly the same *do-re-mi* progression can be sensed completing itself with the left hand's *g'♯* in the closing bars of 'Jardins sous la pluie' (Ex. 20.8), after the previous bar's *e'–f'♯*. I confess to sometimes rearranging hand layout here to let the left thumb mark the *g'♯* and to give the *ff* top *d'''♯* more securely to left hand, like Debussy's layout at the end of 'Les collines d'Anacapri'. The

resultant dialogue of *do-re-mi* against *si-la-sol* ( ) matches the

equivalent contrapuntal dialogue in the climactic coda of

L'isle joyeuse, evocatively redolent of Chabrier (see the brackets in Ex. 7.17 and the theme in Ex. 7.8b).

Example 20.8. Debussy, 'Jardins sous la pluie', bars 154–5

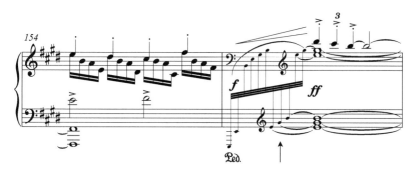

In this rich context the topic of rhythmic offsets refuses dogmatic treatment beyond what Ravel would doubtless have deemed 'good taste': our best rule is to be alert to how any tempting dislocation might react with what's already inbuilt. Chabrier's metrical cross-hand syncopations discussed in Chapter 13 help explain his reported extreme aversion to any further gratuitous disloca-tion.[11] Variation II of Fauré's *Thème et variations* specifically features disloca-tion across two-octave unisons, but within a strict rhythm that gives it a Schumannesque air of overtone echoes; his G minor Prelude from op. 103 reciprocates the texture (right hand before left). A final salutary tale emerges from the unison piano figurations ♪♪♪ that dominate the first movement of Fauré's Second Piano Quintet op. 115: his first draft shows these notated as ♪♪, relating the movement's textural mood instantly to that of his Second Piano Quartet. While his revision doubtless aims at avoiding physical congestion, awareness of the original – quite playable if one doesn't think too hard – can vitally affect our conception of the piece.

FISH FINGERS TO CAT'S PAWS

While any debate about rounded versus flat fingers inevitably involves indi-vidual technique, unusually flat fingers are suggested by two necessary cases of *m.d. dessous* (right hand under) in Debussy's 'Les tierces alternées' (from bar 11) and 'Ondine' (bars 1–3 and 5, reverting to curved fingers in bars 4 and 6). These implicit exceptions contrast with the rounder fingers needed for starting (say) Ravel's 'Ondine'. The semitone clashes that launch many of Ravel's pieces suggest more consistently rounded fingers; his oft-reported low posture at the piano, whether one favours it or not, tends to assure this auto-matically. Individual physiques and techniques vary so much that composers can be understood for leaving this mostly to performers. Gaby Casadesus recalled Ravel's advice for the infamous 'cheesegrater' glissandi in 'Alborada del gracioso': 'I don't care how you play them. Play them in single notes, or with your nose if you want.'[12] Yves Nat, who worked with Debussy, reportedly answered queries about permissible fingerings with an earthily French 'Vous avez deux mains, dix doigts : démerdez-vous.'[13]

This somewhat echoes Chabrier's indication for a *subito ff* bass cluster in his piano solo and duet versions of *Joyeuse marche*: '*écraser cet accord avec la paume de la main gauche*' ('whack this chord down with the palm of the left hand'). Chabrier's orchestral score, incidentally, replaces the cluster with a cymbal. In a slight refinement of this technique, Perlemuter used to recom-mend relaxedly dropping the underside of the fist on the sudden *ff* bass B♭ at bar 30 of Ravel's 'Alborada del gracioso'. This can also serve usefully for the *sff* bass *C'♯* at bar 57 of Debussy's 'Poissons d'or'.

It goes almost as read that constant freedom of arms and shoulders is effec-tively written into the music. The sense of easy hand and arm motion in Debussy's 'Danseuses de Delphes' (from bar 6) or 'Pour les accords', with their rapid transfer of arm weight across the keyboard – along with the fast chord leaps in the middle of 'Le vent dans la plaine' – imply Debussy's ease in this technique. His unobtrusively quick left-hand leaps at very low dynamics in 'Et la lune descend' support this, to the extent that absolutely free arms are obligatory for the piece's viability at his indicated tempi (along with firm fingers for dynamic control low in the keys).

Debussy's famed 'massaging' of the keys has a simple scientific basis: his reported oblique finger stroke at low dynamics, as observed by Maurice Dumesnil (moving towards the key edge as the key descends), ensures optimum control in simple terms of gearing. This was matched by Debussy's insistence on a certain finger firmness: 'but it must be the firmness of rubber, without any stiffness whatsoever [to ensure that] in pianissimo chords, for instance . . . the notes will sound together'.[14] Illustration comes from Yvonne Lefébure's almost lurid childhood recollection of Debussy playing the last two pages of 'Jardins sous la pluie', his 'large hand arched like a vault, fingers flexed to the tip of the last phalanx, knead[ing] the keys close in with a sound that was softly mellow yet powerful and radiant'.[15]

Oblique attack again suggests itself in the cat's-paw-like figurations that launch *"Les fées sont d'exquises danseuses"*, keeping each hand out of the other's way. A similar action informs the final crescendo bars of Ravel's Concerto in G, irresistibly evoking images of Ravel dangling string at his beloved Siamese cats. (It also can be sensed, perhaps with feline irony, in his indicated black-to-white index-finger slides for the bird calls in 'Petit Poucet' from *Ma mère l'Oye*.)

OTHER SLIPPERY NOTATIONS

Example 15.4b from Debussy's 'Feux d'artifice', with its 'faked' bass continuity, can be related to some other layouts best not taken too literally, certainly not at the expense of fluidity. Debussy's piano roll recording of 'La Cathédrale engloutie' avoids an awkward leap to a printed bass grace note at the end of bar 60 by simply tying it over from earlier in the bar (as shown in the *Œuvres complètes*). This may encourage us, midway through bar 46 of *D'un cahier d'esquisses*, to do the same with an awkward bass D♭ under an *f*, avoiding an intrusive arpeggiation. Similarly in the Prélude of *Pour le piano* at bar 56, it's frankly less obtrusive to omit the left hand's off-beat chord repetitions in beats 2–3 than to clog the action by pedantically squashing them in. Another case, texturally very similar, occurs at bar 40 of Debussy's song 'Il pleure dans mon cœur': again his notation maps out ideal polyphony rather than two-handed practicality.

Support for pragmatic *bon goût* in these cases comes from bars 41–4 of 'Les collines d'Anacapri', whose inner rising scale omits the notes *e'–f'♯* in bar 43 for obvious physical reasons. (It would thus make sense to consider 'restoring' them in any orchestration.) Marguerite Long reports Debussy's advice for small hands at bar 5 of 'Hommage à Rameau': to avoid intrusive right-hand arpeggiation at beats 2 and 3 by tying over the top b''. In 'La terrasse des audiences' Debussy adopts an alternative solution in the somewhat comparable texture of bars 29 and 31 by omitting what would be an awkward $c''\sharp$ in the third chord (cf. the surrounding chords). On that basis we might also read his initial right-hand $g''\natural$ at bar 52 of 'Et la lune descend' as polyphonically descriptive rather than technically obligatory – unless we adopt the alternative solution of breaking the chord (plus the surrounding two) in the same manner as bars 25–6.

Appendix 1 relates to all this with some more prescriptive technical observations.

CHAPTER 21

THE COMPOSER AS PIANIST

[Debussy] played the piano as only a composer can   – Hélène Jourdan-Morhange

Above all, no affectation!   – Claude Debussy

THIS chapter amplifies many accounts already available of composers' habits at the piano (for example in Nichols, *Debussy Remembered* and *Ravel Remembered*, and Nectoux, *Gabriel Fauré: A Musical Life*). One characteristic that repeatedly emerges is the composer playing primarily as a composer. This can account for Debussy's displeasure with Ricardo Viñes's over-pianistic tremolos (see p. 219), as opposed probably to something more like the soft woodwind or string flurries that characterize orchestral scores like 'Jeux de vagues' or *Jeux*. A related stance emerges from Ravel's reaction on hearing Robert Casadesus play 'Le gibet': 'You bring out harmonies which pianists usually don't do; I can see you are a composer.'[1] (So much for not wanting his music interpreted.) A counterpart to that comes from reports of Debussy's and Fauré's sympathetic playing of Schumann, Chopin and Bach (see Chapters 6, 10 and 11).

Our composers also shared skills in vocal coaching and accompanying. Fauré's work with church choirs occupied more than half his working life, and he was a constant song accompanist at what we can justifiably call the 'cutting edge' Parisian salons. Chabrier – like Debussy a rarer visitor to the salon, never mind the church – was chorus master for the Lamoureux Concerts through the 1880s: one of France's top vocal coaches, he prepared many singers for major Wagner roles, including Ernst van Dyck for Bayreuth. Ravel regularly coached and accompanied such singers as Jane Bathori, Marcelle Gérar and Madeleine Grey in his own songs, and played in most of their concert premières. (Bathori's husband, the tenor Émile Engel, to whom Ravel dedicated one of the *Histoires naturelles* in 1906, was also a close friend of Chabrier.)

Debussy worked closely with singers all his life: besides training the original *Pelléas* cast (and later Maggie Teyte, the second Mélisande), up to the last months of his life he coached and accompanied the likes of Bathori, Rose Féart and Ninon Vallin.[2] The violinist Arthur Hartmann, who performed with Debussy in 1914, recalled Debussy at home singing and playing *Le promenoir des deux amants*, as well as 'flawlessly' sight-reading difficult songs by Loeffler while he 'solfègged' the vocal line. (Hartmann's most amazing account is of Debussy in 1910 accompanying his four-year-old daughter Chouchou in fluent renderings of Fauré's *Les roses d'Ispahan* and songs by Chausson and Duparc!)[3]

Pianos

The historic rivalry between Erard and Pleyel extends past France's borders here. Debussy's taste in pianos was happily polygamous, unlike Fauré's and Ravel's ostensible preference – albeit never restrictive – for Erard. (In 1908 Fauré recorded piano rolls using a Grotrian-Steinweg; in 1912–13 he, Debussy and Ravel recorded more of them probably on a Steinway model B, or just possibly a Feurich.)[4]

Ravel and Debussy were fairly quick to exploit the 88-note keyboard range up to top c'''' (predominant after 1900, though first tried by Erard as early as the 1820s), using $a''''\sharp$ in *Jeux d'eau* (1901) and 'Reflets dans l'eau' (1905). Ironically, $a''''\sharp$ is not on Ravel's 1908 straight-strung Erard grand (Erard continued to offer these older options until the late 1920s: see Appendix 3 for details of this piano). Debussy in turn advised Marcel Ciampi, when playing 85-note pianos, to replace the printed $a''''\sharp$ at the end of 'Les collines d'Anacapri' with $d''''\sharp$ (rather than a bluesy $a''''\natural$).[5]

Less known is that a few late nineteenth-century Erards took the bass down to G', a range first tried as early as the 1850s.[6] This can put a fresh complexion on some low $G''\sharp$s in Ravel's 'Une barque sur l'océan' (bar 44, also bar 92 in the piece's manuscript). The failure of this compass to become standard doubtless explains why Ravel settled for A'' in place of implied $G''\sharp$s or $G''\natural$s in bars 39 and 41 of the same piece and in *Jeux d'eau* (bars 49–50 and 59), 'Scarbo' (bars 15, 334 and 395–409), the finale of his Piano Trio (just before rehearsal figure 9) and the end of the Concerto in G. (On one autograph of *Jeux d'eau* the A''s in question appear to have been written first as $G''\sharp$). In practice the compromise sounds less disturbing on straight-strung Erards, though Ravel's friend Lucien Garban advised using the 'real' lower notes implied by these passages on any piano that has them.[7] Ravel's Concerto for Left Hand implies the occasional low F'', perhaps with Bösendorfer in mind for the work's Austrian dedicatee Paul Wittgenstein.

Ravel equally responded to what his favourite pianos offered. The straight stringing on most Erards of the time tends to characterize each register, giving a distinct tang for example to the tenor-register sequences of minor sevenths in the opening lines of *Jeux d'eau* and the Menuet of the *Sonatine*, or to the various layers of bells in 'La vallée des cloches'. (Overstrung – that is, cross-strung – pianos tend to sound more homogeneous across their range because more of the strings cross the middle of the soundboard.) Straight stringing likewise often has more clarity in the upper bass range, allowing lines such as the F–E♮ bass alternations on the second page of Chabrier's 'Paysage' to be marked out without becoming thick or heavy. Some Fauré bass lines, like the main climax of the Fifth Barcarolle or bar 9 onwards in the Sixth Barcarolle, sound marvellous in this respect on his own surviving Erard of 1914. That same relative clarity also allows bold through-pedalling without disagreeable smudging in parts of Ravel's 'Oiseaux tristes' and 'La vallée des cloches', while the Erard's woodier treble range responds pleasingly to castanet effects like bar 12 onwards in 'Alborada del gracioso'. Although Erards are also sometimes credited with a lighter and shallower touch facilitating glissandi, Ravel's and Fauré's – at least in their present condition – have a normal modern key drop and weight.

Debussy, somewhat *à la* Chopin, favoured his various Bechstein, Blüthner and Pleyel instruments, all overstrung and usually brand new. He was especially proud of the 'aliquot' resonating treble strings on his Blüthner medium grand of 1904 (see Appendix 3). This suggests his penchant for a singing treble (as on Bechsteins), and indeed Debussy's Blüthner still sustains beautifully: he famously liked to open its lid to show visitors the extra strings, shutting it again before it was played! We can probably thank its unusually pure bass (characteristic of Blüthner grands) for the final low *A″*s in *"Les sons et les parfums"*, and the more coalescent bass of Bechstein uprights for the gong-like clusters that open or close 'Pagodes', *Masques*, 'Reflets dans l'eau' and 'La Cathédrale engloutie', or that appear on the second page of 'Et la lune descend sur le temple qui fut'. Debussy's Blüthner has a light touch (like most Bechstein uprights) that would have let him extract considerable tonal range with little visible effort.

Jane Bathori recounts that Debussy wrote the accompaniment of his 1904 song 'Le Faune' specifically for the Erard 'in whose bass range he found the muffled but incisive sonority of the tambourine'.[8] He also chose a particular Erard – admittedly for a concert in the Salle Erard – to première his preludes 'Danseuses de Delphes', 'Voiles', 'La Cathédrale engloutie' and 'La danse de Puck' on 25 May 1910.[9] This was probably straight-strung (as most Erards then were: a review of the event by Paul Landormy described it as 'un modèle un peu ancien'), raising the question of how its varying registral colours may have reacted to some of Debussy's very wide-spaced chords. This characteristic of his writing tends to match his predilection for overstrung pianos, and may in passing add a gloss to the way Ravel tends to keeps both hands closer together at the keyboard.

For much of his adult life Debussy appears to have had Pleyel uprights on complimentary loan from the firm. Narcisse Lebeau (alias Vital Hocquet) recalled seeing a 'splendid' Pleyel in Debussy's otherwise modest rue de Londres apartment in the early 1890s, and Victor Segalen and George Copeland mention an upright Pleyel in his study (at the Avenue du Bois de Boulogne) in 1907 and 1911.[10] Three different instruments may have been involved: besides the 1890s one, Louis Laloy noted that Debussy loved the mahogany case of the Pleyel he was offered shortly after 1902, whereas two visitors to Debussy's house in 1911 described the upright as small (or 'tiny') and black.[11] Distinct from these again was the curio of a 'dismountable piano' that Pleyel sent to Pourville in 1915 for the summer holiday during which Debussy completed his *Études*.[12]

Although Debussy's fondness for Bechsteins is well known, exact dates are uncertain. We can only guess if his first one was the rosewood upright that Laloy saw in his Rue Cardinet apartment late in 1902 (which, Laloy writes, was replaced shortly thereafter by the mahogany Pleyel).[13] Again there may have been several: Gino Zuccala is quoted as having seen a Bechstein *chez* Debussy in 1910, and in a letter of March 1913 Debussy refers enthusiastically to 'a new Bechstein' – an instrument that Alfredo Casella remembered being moved in 1914 from Debussy's study to the salon to let the two of them rehearse *Ibéria* (in Caplet's two-piano transcription).[14]

Debussy's playing

Our most salutary account is probably the report of a Brussels house concert in 1914 in which Debussy played the last two *Estampes*, the first two *Images* of 1905 plus 'Danseuses de Delphes' and 'La fille aux cheveux de lin' from Preludes Book 1, and accompanied Ninon Vallin in his *Proses lyriques* and *Chansons de Bilitis*:

> Debussy's playing is devoid of all mannerism, and surprises by its simplicity. No underlining of harmonic subtleties: the melodic lines are drawn in fine traits; absolutely no distortions of rhythm or vain effects. This great simplicity, at first disconcerting, quickly captivates, and every page we hear leaves a penetrating impression of clarity.[15]

This usefully balances the many accounts that emphasize Debussy's 'caressing', even 'massaging' of the keys (see p. 307): finesse of touch clearly never became precious or interfered with line. Most of his remarks and reported habits at the piano exude professional common sense, and his oft-quoted exhortation to 'make me forget the piano has hammers', far from implying anything insipid, can be balanced with Manuel de Falla's recollection of him saying he wanted 'just the hammers to sound and not the fingers to become hammers'.[16] If such playing earned Debussy a reputation far from arm-whirling virtuosity, this is tempered by Stravinsky's memories of him in 1912 or 1913 playing *Jeux* in piano reduction ('How well that man played!'), and sight-reading *The Rite of Spring* in duet form:

> What most impressed me and what is still most memorable from the occasion of the sight-reading of *Le Sacre* was Debussy's brilliant piano playing. Recently, while listening to his *En blanc et noir* . . . I was struck by the way in which the extraordinary quality of this pianism had directed the thought of Debussy the composer.[17]

From one detail of notation in *L'isle joyeuse* we can infer several of Debussy's pianistic habits. In Example 16.8 his shortened right-hand *a* in the first edition shows a compensatory dash that effectively says 'Voice this nevertheless as if it were a whole-note'. This not only typifies Debussy's use of dashes as light *marcato* accents (as he meticulously explains in 'Mouvement' and 'Les tierces alternées') but also assumes the pianistic rule of voicing long note values to allow for tonal decay. Elsewhere Louis Laloy describes Debussy's tenuto dashes as signifying a 'transparent sonority . . . which is prolonged by the pedal, with the finger leaving the key immediately' (the literal opposite of *tenuto*).[18] While this doesn't always make sense – bars 29–30 of 'Pour les arpèges composés', for example, need more literal *tenuto* treatment – Laloy's description is sometimes apt, as in bars 11 onwards of 'Les tierces alternées'. (Laloy may have been thinking rather of the marking $\bar{-}$, to which that treatment is entirely apt.) For the opening left-hand tenuto notes of 'Reflets dans l'eau' Debussy's Chopinesque instruction – 'keep your left hand hanging loosely from your wrist . . . then let it drop' – assures the colour while guarding against tightness or jabbing.[19] This accords again with accounts of Debussy's hands generally staying in the keys. Probably nothing sums up his pianistic professionalism better than a story that Alfred Cortot told against himself: after performing some Debussy at a recital, he gallantly asked twelve-year-old Chouchou if his playing had been faithful to her father's intentions, only to be felled by her innocently frank reply, 'Oui . . . mais Papa *écoutait* davantage' ('Papa used to *listen* more').[20]

DEBUSSY'S RECORDINGS

Our most immediate witness of Debussy's playing is the series of audio discs of him accompanying Mary Garden in 1904 in three of the *Ariettes oubliées* and the tower song ('Mes longs cheveux') from *Pelléas et Mélisande*. Despite the background noise and some pitch flutter, we hear exactly what they sang and played, the basic pitch confirming the original tempi. Nothing takes us more vividly into the studio than hearing Garden clear her throat in the introductory bar of 'L'ombre des arbres' before coming in off pitch (a tricky chromatic entry). Like any good répétiteur Debussy adds the needed note and she quickly recovers.

One probably needs to have played 'Green' to appreciate the virtuosity of Debussy's opening flying octaves and subsequent arpeggios, taken with apparent quiet ease at a dizzying ♩. = 126–132. He plays all the songs essentially in time as printed, except that his printed *poco stringendo* in 'L'ombre des arbres' becomes *molto* (possibly a matter of Garden's breathing), his opening ♩ = c. 40 pretty well doubled by bar 19. Equally striking is his treatment of the short piano postlude in 'L'ombre des arbres', shown in curly brackets ({ }) in Example 21.1: his sudden effective return to a faster quarter-note in bar 30 makes beat 2 sound more like a continuation of the preceding off-beats than a sudden augmentation. This effect matches what we saw in Example 15.2; something similar can be heard on Debussy's piano roll of 'La Cathédrale engloutie' across bars 85–6.

Example 21.1. 'L'ombre des arbres' (*Ariettes oubliées*), bars 27–31 (voice tacet); indications in brackets taken from Debussy's 1904 recording

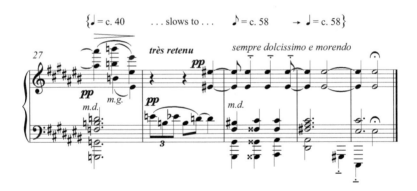

Debussy's hands nearly always sound together on these recordings. If brief untidiness can be heard in the opening figurations of 'Il pleure dans mon cœur', studio nerves there are understandable from anyone: after starting around ♩ = 144, Debussy eases back at Garden's entry to around 126. With apparent effortlessness he keeps almost exact time through the left-hand 'shoplifter' stretches at bars 19 and 23 – a feat we can best appreciate by trying it, and one that bears out Paul Vidal's observation about his supple, agile left hand (see p. 297). Elsewhere we hear him gently keeping Garden moving, sometimes with a classical rubato that keeps time under her rhythmic stretching and judicious portamenti. In bar 53 of 'Il pleure' Debussy treats his own *Revenez au 1ᵉʳ mouvᵗ* as a smooth but almost instantaneous return to tempo (in practice this guards against the ensuing vocal entry being under tempo). A page later his quietly instantaneous *a tempo* under Garden's long-held final word ('*peine*') supports her graceful portamento down to the final *d′ ♯*, while conveying a structural sense of *a tempo* at the piano's subsequent re-entry (which is where the original 1888 edition indicates *a tempo*).

Surprising though the nimble tempi in 'Green' and 'Il pleure' may now seem, we can almost certainly discount any theory that Garden and Debussy hurried to fit them on 78rpm sides: each original side has time to spare, and the longest one, 'L'ombre des arbres', enjoys much the most leisurely tempo. Indeed, Garden later specifically endorsed these tempi.[21] If studio nerves might partly explain Debussy ignoring his own *rit.* at bars 11–12 of 'Green' – and his scrambling of the treacherous arpeggio into bar 32 – all those details suggest an assumed norm of forward motion unless otherwise marked, an implication we've also seen in Fauré's scores. Unfortunately the scratchy 1904 recording conveys few dynamics, masking much of the sheer excitement in these highly virtuoso performances. Try emulating them, though, and we can quickly appreciate what went into them.

These recordings reveal four basic rubato layers: first, within the beat (stretching augmentation dots or compressing short notes as discussed in Chapter 17); secondly, over whole phrases (as we saw Debussy recommend to Maurice Dumesnil in 'Clair de lune', or at the start of 'Reflets dans l'eau'); thirdly, indicated tempo arches over larger spans ('L'ombre des arbres', relating to the marked tempo layering over 'Hommage à Rameau' and the latter part of *L'isle joyeuse*); and finally the more classical melody-versus-accompaniment rubato across voices for which Chopin was famous. While this last type is mostly written into Debussy's piano notation, a vivid description of its practical nature comes from Émile Jaques-Dalcroze (a friend of Fauré), who related how Ysaÿe (a friend of Fauré and Debussy) wanted him as accompanist to keep strict time under Ysaÿe's rubato – which Ysaÿe practised on trains against the steady rhythm of the train wheels over the track joints, ensuring he was back with the beat by each passing telegraph pole.[22]

Debussy's other recordings comprise fourteen of his piano pieces on Welte-Mignon reproducing piano rolls (see Appendix 3), a system that encodes the relative durations of each key and pedal depression in the original performance, plus at least some degree of the original dynamics. (This type of recording is distinct from ordinary pianola rolls whose notes are cut straight from the score, leaving all expressive elements to be controlled by the 'pianolist' as the roll plays back.) It's not surprising that pianists in the early twentieth century preferred to record rolls rather than 78rpm discs, given the primitive quality of audio recording in that pre-microphone era: at their best reproducing rolls could play back from a real piano with vivid immediacy and dramatic seeming fidelity. Their disadvantages are that dynamics and voicing unavoidably vary on each playback instrument, subtleties like extreme *pianissimo* and half-pedal are at the mercy of different pianos' thresholds of hammer throw and damper engagement, and exact tempi can't be guaranteed since playback speed leaves pitch unaffected. Although the mechanisms of reproducing pianos are calibrated for accurate playback speed, a degree of irrecoverable latitude remains.[23]

Recorded apparently in 1912 and issued late in 1913, Debussy's rolls leave an impression of less tidy playing than his audio recordings, even if most of the rubato is concentrated – logically enough – in *La plus que lente*, which incidentally works up to some lively tempi. The main problems lie in some oddly ragged dynamics, local rhythm and coordination across hands or chords that contrast oddly not just with Debussy's audio recordings but also with rolls by other virtuosi of the era.

Some explanations are worth spelling out (with particular thanks to Rex Lawson, Denis Hall and Kenneth Caswell for illuminating discussions) because of widespread misconceptions of exactly what reproducing piano rolls can and can't do. First, they work by constantly defining whether any note or pedal is up or down. While this serves many virtuosi well, the system could easily be confused by Debussy's mostly low dynamics and any tendency to work at points of escapement and half-pedal – even before replaying such delicate mechanical data on a different instrument. Secondly, even the best reproducing systems differentiate dynamics only across the two halves of the keyboard.[24] For all its sophistication, the system thus can't reliably show exactly how Debussy may have voiced or half-pedalled delicate passages like the start of 'Danseuses de Delphes' with its indicated mix of legato and portato.

Thirdly, even different exemplars of the same roll often reveal disparities of attack or spread on the same chord, the result of inexact factory copying.[25] Some perceived hand separations or chord-spreads on Debussy's rolls are thus certainly not original. Fourthly, despite some claims over the years, nobody knows exactly how or to what extent Welte was able to record dynamics from a performance, even before we consider the physical impossibility of reproducing them exactly on another instrument. Regardless of how such data were obtained, Welte's editors then had to convert them all into rows of edge perforations on a replay master; in doing so they had to judge not only how much of what and where but also how far in advance to place each perforation affecting dynamics (and likewise pedalling), to allow the playback pneumatics just the right amount of time to act.[26]

Last but far from least comes tempo. For all the inbuilt safeguards, two expertly set Welte machines recently produced such variant timings from Debussy's 'Cathédrale engloutie' roll as 5′01″ (on Kenneth Caswell's Pierian CD) versus 5′35″ (on Denis Condon's),[27] or conversely Condon's 12′53″ for the *Children's Corner* roll versus Caswell's 13′30″. This latitude can result from marginal variation in the setting or calibration of playback instruments, or in paper thickness between different copies of a roll. (Since playback speed is set by the take-up spool, the more paper that winds around it, the faster the paper moves over the suction bar.)[28]

A multitude of hidden variables thus affects what we hear from rolls, probably dominated above all by the condition and fine-tuning of the replaying instrument and mechanism. Rex Lawson has opined (in conversation) that Edwin Welte's ideal was possibly to produce an optimal playback master, after which the quality of copies sold to the public may have interested him less. This would explain Debussy's oft-quoted panegyric to Welte (reproduced in facsimile in Caswell's CD booklet for Pierian 001) dated 1 November 1913: '*Cher monsieur*, It is impossible to attain more perfect reproduction than that of the Welte apparatus. What I have heard leaves me marvelling, as I am happy to affirm to you with these words.' We can probably assume Debussy heard carefully prepared production masters, and his unusually stilted wording suggests that his happiness may also have been related to a dangling cheque, given his ever-precarious finances. Even such replayable masters would have taken time to prepare from the original ink-and-roller marks; the recordings appear to have been made in 1912 (rather than 1913 as often assumed), when Welte reportedly took his equipment and technicians to Paris for the purpose.[29] (Besides, had Debussy recorded in 1913 he would surely have included Preludes from Book 2.)

Allowing for all that, some skilled recent playbacks from the rolls have yielded remarkably convincing results in 'Le vent dans la plaine', 'La danse de Puck' and 'La Cathédrale engloutie'. Since the heavy flywheels of the Welte mechanism guard against sudden fluctuations in spool playback speed, we can safely take the sounding tempo equivalences on the roll of 'La Cathédrale' as what Debussy played. (Most playbacks of this roll yield an opening tempo of around ♩ = 60–66, similar to Henri Busser's indication quoted in note 4 to Chapter 15.) Despite the caveats mentioned above about articulation, this roll does suggest something of Debussy's habits in chordal attack: the first chord of bars 1, 3 and 5 sounds *plaqué* (together) as opposed to an audible degree of upward *arpa* in the following chords, and again in the right-hand chords from bar 16. Debussy's roll of 'La soirée dans Grenade' reveals a larger-scale fluidity of tempo matching his printed indications, along with some elasticity in the dotted ostinato rhythm. In bars 33–6 the printed rhythms ♫♪ and ♪. are slightly snapped towards the values ♪.♪ and ♪.♪, while ♫♪ is reciprocally stretched towards ♫. In *La plus que lente* the most audible problem on Debussy's roll is some scrappy local rhythm, though larger rubato and tempo range seem convincing. 'Danseuses de Delphes' plays considerably below Debussy's printed tempo marking: though this may indeed be what happened on the day, it perhaps invites some circumspection. The same goes for a rather laborious *D'un cahier d'esquisses*, given the tempo issue discussed on page 201.

At the other extreme comes *Children's Corner*, originally all on a single roll that yields breathless tempi quite at odds with Debussy's moderate printed tempi, such as ♩ = c. 176–192 for *modérément animé* in 'Doctor Gradus ad Parnassum' and a dizzying ♩ = 208 or more for *allegretto ma non troppo* in 'Serenade for the Doll'. The lively tempi on Debussy's 1904 audio recordings don't have this sort of cramped breathlessness, and when we read Maurice Dumesnil's recollection that Debussy wanted 'Doctor Gradus' and 'The snow is dancing' to sound 'not too fast' – the latter 'not fast at all' – and 'Serenade for the Doll' to sound 'délicat et gracieux',[30] it suggests something is amiss with the roll. Interestingly, a 1920s reissue of this roll (in 'licencee' format for American machines) spreads the six pieces over three rolls with perforations proportionately farther apart, yielding much more spacious tempi when played back at the specified settings. Besides taking the breathlessness out of the three pieces just mentioned, this pulls back the outer sections of 'Golliwogg's cake walk' to around ♩ = 80 (instead of 112 on the 1913 issue), close to Debussy's metronome markings for related ragtime movements in his Cello Sonata and Violin Sonata. Some dance-like snapping of the ♫ rhythms now becomes audible (as on the roll of 'La soirée'), and the off-beat *sforzati* have time to register properly.

A technical element has its say here: on playback, the 1913 issue of the *Children's Corner* roll is prone to a repeated problem whereby dynamics fail to take proper effect and the pedal fails to catch bass notes, because the pneumatics have insufficient time to act. On the more spaced-out 1920s reissue the problem solves itself. The obvious implication is that someone in-house made adjustments to redress a perceived fault.[31] However, neither is the 1920s reissue above suspicion, for 'Jumbo's lullaby' and 'The little shepherd' now emerge suspiciously slow, and the percentage tempo difference from the 1913 roll varies slightly from piece to piece. Whatever the answers, the problems refuse to be explained in terms that allow blind trust in the rolls.

A final word about tempo in 'La Cathédrale engloutie' comes via some witness accounts. Paul Roberts, recounting that his teacher Vivian Langrish always played and taught 'La Cathédrale' as it sounds on Debussy's Welte roll, suggests that the issue of tempo equivalence may have been known to British pianists who had heard Debussy play the piece on one of his London visits. It was certainly known in Budapest, where an elderly piano teacher in 1987 recounted that his own teacher, after hearing Debussy play 'La Cathédrale' in Paris, conveyed the relevant information to his pupils over the ensuing decades.[32] Most vivid of all for me is the memory of playing the piece around 1980 to Mme de Tinan, tacitly following the tempo continuity of Debussy's roll: as the piece progressed her bearing and expression visibly changed, by the last page she was gently singing along, and when it ended she exclaimed, '*That's* how he used to play it! Why do people play the piece so slowly nowadays? Tell your fellow-pianists!'

CHABRIER

If stories are legion of Chabrier leaving pianos – including Renoir's on one occasion – unplayable after his solo renditions of *España*,[33] they can be tempered with awareness that many of the instruments were decades old in an era when that made a serious difference. (One wonders in passing how their Russian cousins withstood Balakirev's *Islamey*.) Some accounts from Chabrier's colleagues clarify our focus. Alfred Cortot recounts what he heard from his fellow-student Édouard Risler, dedicatee of the *Bourrée fantasque*:

> [Chabrier] insisted on meticulous observation of tempo and accentuation. He refused to allow a *sforzando* to be softened, a *forte* to be taken for a *fortissimo* or for a diminuendo to *p* be misread as a diminuendo to *pp*. He even insisted on the fine difference between *ritenuto* and *rallentando* and refused to accept their being confused. He was also utterly strict about both hands playing together.[34]

Chabrier's friend Paul Lacome described a soirée in 1883 when Chabrier and a renowned visiting Polish virtuoso, Lewita, took to the piano in turn after dinner (Lacome's piano having already withstood *España*): 'how much better Chabrier [plays than Lewita], who is prodigiously accurate but without personality!'[35] After Chabrier's death Lacome reacted thus on hearing Francis Planté play some of the *Pièces pittoresques*: 'He plays [Chabrier] really badly, like a romantic . . . with little coquetries and affectations which don't suit Chabrier . . . That's not it at all; and had Chabrier heard him he wouldn't have failed to give him a lesson by taking over at the piano.'[36] What might have ensued is suggested by Vincent d'Indy's account of rehearsing the two-piano *Valses romantiques* with Chabrier in January 1887 (exactly a year after Debussy and Paul Vidal played the same pieces to Liszt):

> So I practised the three waltzes *con amore*, making a point of carefully observing all the markings – of which there are plenty! At the rehearsal . . . Chabrier cut me short halfway through the first waltz and, with a look both

astonished and facetious, erupted, 'But, *mon p'tit*, it's nothing like that at all!' – When, a bit taken aback, I asked him to explain, he riposted, 'You're playing it as if it were by a member of the *Institut!*' – Then followed a wonderful lesson in playing *alla Chabrier*: contrary accents, pianissimos to nothing, sudden detonations in the middle of the most exquisite tenderness, and also obbligato miming, lending the whole body to the musical interpretation.[37]

On another occasion d'Indy related, 'With his stubby arms, fat fingers and a certain clumsiness of motion, [Chabrier] nonetheless could attain extreme finesse and a maximum of expression which very few great pianists – hardly even Liszt and [Anton] Rubinstein – have surpassed.'[38] In earlier years Chabrier used to amuse habitués of his Parisian Auvergnat club *La Soupe aux Choux* (Cabbage soup) with police-chase improvisations while his companions read out newspaper crime reports.[39] Even with his health failing in early 1892, his impromptu play-through of much of his piano music – after a generous dinner – left the conductor Georges-Martin Witkowski astounded at Chabrier's 'dazzling virtuosity . . . his left hand in particular defied the fiercest difficulties'.[40] The lively musical gatherings at Chabrier's home – which housed an extraordinary organ with varied percussion effects apparently bought from one of the Expositions universelles – were something of a Paris institution that regularly brought in Manet and Renoir and their wives (both good pianists: Chabrier's *Impromptu* is dedicated to Mme Manet) plus the likes of Fauré, Chausson, Duparc, d'Indy, Messager, Saint-Saëns and Massenet (the last two possibly not together, given their sometimes strained relations).

RAVEL

Ravel's distaste for practising was no secret, although we should remember how highly trained he was (see p. 161, for example). Natural talent seemed to have endowed him with skills including – according to Robert and Gaby Casadesus – great agility in virtuoso techniques like the fast repeated notes and double glissandi of 'Alborada del gracioso', which he apparently managed better than they could.[41] Gaby Casadesus also mentioned a stiffness of wrist and fingers: this might be linked with his low seating position, though it may have facilitated his frequent hand overlaps. In 1907 Louis Laloy noted that despite Ravel's stiff-looking manner at the piano accompanying the première of his *Histoires naturelles*, 'his fingers were able to find the sonorities – enveloped and veiled, or light and sparkling – which were in his mind.'[42] Asked in 1910 to give Mikhail Fokine an idea of his music, Ravel reportedly played 'Ondine' well enough – on an upright, too – that Fokine immediately wanted to set the piece as a ballet.[43] If Ravel later balked at the idea of recording *Gaspard* himself, his reason for co-opting Robert Casadesus rather than Viñes to record 'Le gibet' emerges from a letter of March 1922 in which he indignantly explains that Viñes had always insisted on playing the piece too fast, for fear of boring the audience.[44]

According to Émile Vuillermoz, Ravel created his most magical moments in private, 'brushing the keys, making magical sounds flow between his hands. He loved long solitary conversations with the instrument, collecting sonorous harmonies like butterflies.'[45] Differences of individual and national style from performers left him unworried: many are the stories of him (and likewise Debussy) endorsing performances quite different from his own conception so long as they showed musical intelligence and coherence.[46]

Ravel's solo piano recordings, all on reproducing rolls, are documented in *A Ravel Reader* and Appendix 3 here; the 1922 rolls attributed to him of 'Le gibet' and the Toccata from *Le tombeau* were apparently played by Robert Casadesus after Ravel found his own technique (or stretch in 'Le gibet') inadequate. This might explain why Ravel's earlier roll of the *Sonatine* omits the finale. His roll of the *Valses nobles* can vividly evoke the purposeful if imperfect pianist Ravel knew he was (as his letters over the years wryly attest). The second *valse* shows a generous degree of cross-hand dislocation, along with some chord rolling in the second and fifth *valses* and the Épilogue. Some of this, along with his rather breathless opening *valse*, might be attributable to nerves, a supposition supported by Harry Adaskin's memory of Ravel, on his 1928 American tour, haring off so fast in the finale of his Violin Sonata that Joseph Szigeti's bow ended up hopelessly tangled in his violin strings.[47]

Nerves might also explain a few moments of mild anarchy between the hands on the first page of 'La vallée des cloches' in Ravel's 1928 roll: musically quasi-viable in terms of the hands' (and bells') intrinsic independence there, this perhaps raises a darker shade of the ataxia (inability to co-ordinate motions) that progressively afflicted his last years. One striking detail from that roll is how rapidly and crisply he arpeggiates the piece's final three low bells. His 1922 roll of 'Oiseaux tristes' confirms his advice to Gaby Casadesus by slightly compressing the triplet group in bars 2 and similar. Inasmuch as playback speed can be relied on, his 1922 roll of the *Pavane pour une Infante défunte* moves mostly in the range ♩ = 63–69.[48]

FAURÉ

Virtuosity leaps from the piano parts of the chamber works which Fauré premièred and regularly toured until deafness stopped him, plus his *Ballade* which he premièred in its orchestral form. Both his son Philippe and

Marguerite Long remarked on his weighty hands and the full tone they produced; Philippe adds that while his father's hands 'looked heavy . . . in fact they were supple and light [and] he hardly raised them above the keys but was still able to obtain any effect he wanted. . . . There's no doubt he could have had a brilliant career as a virtuoso if he'd been more ambitious and more concerned with the plaudits of the crowd.'[49] Add Long's view (equally revealing of her own habits) that Fauré's playing 'lacked the impact and brilliance Fauré himself used to demand from his interpreters', along with Philippe's observation that 'He had a horror of virtuosity, of rubato and effects aimed at making the audience swoon', and we better understand exactly what connotations of virtuosity bored Fauré. On the other side we have Marguerite de Saint-Marceaux's remark in 1907 that Édouard Risler had played Fauré's piano music 'without charm . . . I'm too used to hearing it played by Fauré who pours his soul into the keyboard.'[50]

Fauré's recordings, all on reproducing rolls, mix solo pieces with piano reductions of his violin *Berceuse* op. 16 and *Pavane* op. 50. Of his Welte rolls (probably recorded in 1912), the Third Nocturne in particular suggests his gently forward-moving way of playing, with strong melodic lines and generous but judicious pedalling. That of the *Pavane*, played back at the stipulated setting, confirms Sir Adrian Boult's reminiscences quoted in Chapter 18 by maintaining a minimum $\downarrow$ = 100. A telling moment on Fauré's Welte roll of the First Barcarolle is a timely spurt of tempo, as indicated in the score, that gives brilliance to the quiet yet climactic run at bars 77–8; it suggests we needn't be shy about the quietly scintillating runs at bars 104–5 of the Sixth Nocturne or bars 80–5 of the Seventh, or the more prolonged one at the main climax of the First Nocturne.

The less sophisticated Hupfeld rolls Fauré recorded in 1908 give a more basic idea of the same sense of rhythm, melodic line and pedalling, but leave questions open of nuance, articulation and overall tempi. His Hupfeld roll of the *Thème et variations*, however, appears to confirm an issue discussed in Chapter 18 by speeding up marginally into Variation I, then again through the climactic Variation X. Both his Welte and Hupfeld rolls of the Third Nocturne linger slightly in the second half of bar 42, like his Welte roll of the First Barcarolle in bars 17 and 19. His Welte roll of the Third Nocturne also shows a consistent and highly localized rubato in bars 17–22 (and the similar bars 84–9), in the form of a momentary lingering on each second beat before immediately moving on again. At bars 22 and 89 this tellingly results in a slight delay before, then a quickening *through* the cadence at the end of the bar. In the Seventh Nocturne his Hupfeld roll eases back through the second half of bar 18 into the printed *Tempo I* at bar 19, a detail he perhaps left unmarked in the score for fear of overcooking. A rarer rhetorical *ritenuto* can be heard on his roll of the Second *Valse-caprice* over bars 404–5 (tenth and ninth last bars of the piece), plus an added bass octave in the piece's last three unison D♭s (each hand plays octaves).

Fauré's pupils could sometimes be overly pious on his behalf. Roger-Ducasse, in his preface to the 1924 edition of Fauré's first eight Nocturnes, advises taking the initial *d'♮* at bar 73 in the Seventh Nocturne with left hand to avoid arpeggiating a particular chord – which Fauré's Hupfeld roll of the piece unabashedly arpeggiates. Fauré's roll of the *Thème et variations* even shows him breaking the wide left-hand dyads in bars 4, 7 and 12 of Variation VIII, something most of us would now avoid by taking the upper note with right hand. In Variation III his roll nimbly breaks some wide left-hand chords 2+1, 3+1 or 1+2. In general his usage seems pragmatic and decisive: both his rolls of the Third Nocturne arpeggiate the otherwise slightly awkward first right-hand chord in bars 24 and 91, while his roll of the Seventh Nocturne plays bar 5 beat 1, bars 37–8 and the piece's three final chords absolutely *plaqué* but breaks the first chord in bar 73 (as mentioned above), likewise the left hand at beats 1 and 2 of bars 29–30 and 104–5. (The *arpas* always complete themselves on the beat, not after, and are never languid.) Fauré's arpeggiated final chord on his roll of the *Thème et variations* suggests a pretext – in the teeth of some existing doctrine – for breaking the unstretchable last chord of the Sixth Nocturne. (The only other practical option, tying the bass to free the hand for the notes above, can risk an uneasy sense of ending on a second inversion.)

Amusing snapshots of how both Debussy and Fauré were perceived at the piano (and doubtless sent up at parties or by Conservatoire students) emerge from Alfredo Casella's first series of *À la manière* parodies published in 1911. 'À la manière de Gabriel Fauré', a purported *Romance sans paroles*, starts *andante, quasi allegretto*, pedantically ties notes instead of dotting them, mixes ⁞ with ⸦ on the same chord along with the command *sans arpéger*, and of course ends *senza rallentare*. 'À la manière de Claude Debussy', after opening *avec une sonorité molle et diffuse*, features bass tremolos with diminuendo from **ppp** followed by unstretchable left-hand chords marked *sans arpéger*, the top note parenthesized as if to say omit rather than arpeggiate. Casella here may have been guying public perception more than the composer himself, whom he knew quite well. Revealingly, the one pastiche in which Casella fails (quite dismally) to capture the victim's idiom is 'À la manière de Maurice Ravel' (from the second *À la manière* series of 1913, which includes Ravel's own two offerings). In the context of his more successful Fauré and Debussy pastiches, this is suggestive of the extreme sophistication of Ravel's musical syntax, quietly masked as ever by a transparent-looking surface.

In piano music there's no room for padding, one has to pay cash and make it constantly interesting. It's perhaps the most difficult medium of all, if one wants to do it as satisfyingly as possible.   – Gabriel Fauré

How much one first has to discover, then discard, to reach the bare flesh of emotion.   – Claude Debussy

When I say my music *annoys* me, I'm being quite logical: it *annoys* me because I chide myself for not doing better and because I always compare it with the most beautiful works, depreciating it in my eyes; but don't get me wrong, I find it very nice indeed when I compare it to a lot of commercially successful *saloperies*.   – Emmanuel Chabrier

My objective, therefore, is technical perfection. I can strive unceasingly to this end, since I am certain of never being able to attain it. The important thing is to get nearer to it all the time.   – Maurice Ravel[51]

APPENDICES

'FACILEMENT, FACILEMENT':
FINDING TECHNICAL EASE

Even allowing for pianists' differing techniques, the last few chapters can usefully be followed through here by briefly addressing a few notorious passages on the basis of practical experience, in ways that can easily be extended to other pieces.

DEBUSSY'S ÉTUDES, PRELUDES AND IMAGES

'*Facilement, facilement*' was one of Chopin's favourite phrases for encouraging students not to get in their own way. Coupled with another radical Chopin line, 'Let the hand fall',[1] it eases Debussy's 'Pour les accords', where our main clue is to know not to pull in the upper arms after the far-flung second chord of each bar, but to release them slightly outwards again (just as after the previous chord), then let the hands drop on prepared fingers to the third chord, with arguably a touch of pivotal help from the thumbs. The same, with no sideways arm pulling, can easily assure the left hand's bass leap to bar 70 of 'Pour les cinq doigts', avoiding hiatus; the same goes for the right hand in the middle of bars 44 and 47.

Gesturally related to these is the climax of 'Le vent dans la plaine' (bars 28–34), which becomes relatively easy if we let the upper arm weight drop just once for each beat, with free-moving but prepared hands and lower arm bouncing through the chords like skipping stones on water. (A source variant shown in the *Œuvres complètes* can also ease matters.) The contrary-motion arpeggios that launch the coda of 'Jardins sous la pluie' are a variant of this, the chords now quickly rolled before each hand vaults over the thumb and drops to the next one. This technique pervades 'Feux d'artifice', a much easier piece than it looks once we've learnt where the hands fall. From the end of bar 2 common sense invites us to let the left hand take over the last three notes to avoid a right-hand splash or hiatus. (I mention this only after hearing several pianists defeat their own objective there in well-meant attempts at being true to the score.)

'Danseuses de Delphes' uses the chordal technique of 'Pour les accords' at quieter levels in a way that sometimes suggests Debussy almost thinking of two pianos, like Poulenc's later *Élégie*. In the *Image* 'Et la lune descend' this extends once more to quiet but vital left-arm agility. The piece's daringly muted dynamics, following those of 'Cloches à travers les feuilles', are finally released in the long dynamic accumulation of 'Poissons d'or'. Seeing the three pieces thus together helps us understand their linked expressive architecture, an issue clearly on Debussy's mind when he wrote the letter quoted on page 42 above. It can be noted in passing that '*faites vibrer*' near the end of 'Et la lune descend' merely confirms that Debussy wants the note re-sounded, not tied. For the repeated *sff e″–d″* fanfares at bars 84–5 of 'Poissons d'or', dropping the full hand (and arm) weight to a strong *4–3* or even *2–1* (then over to *4*) can be useful for trumpet-like incisiveness. In other pieces the fourth finger's greater length (relative to the fifth) can be useful for relaxed control in delicate passages, for example by passing *4* over *5* for the top *a″♭* in bars 48 and 50 of 'Brouillards' (likewise in bars 46–8 of Ravel's 'Ondine'), or conversely *5* under *4* for the sustained *f′* in bars 57 and 59 of 'La sérénade interrompue' (after the *g′♭* grace-note).

GASPARD DE LA NUIT

Ravel's advice not to make the opening figurations of 'Ondine' too clear (see p. 221 above) can be met by practising just the first half of each four-note group, the hand gently falling into each first note or chord (always on prepared curved fingers) and the wrist swinging slightly up and respectively outwards and inwards for the second one. The remaining half of each group can then happen virtually by itself. Besides averting arm tightness, this also guards against the groups rhythmically misaccentuating. For the Thalberg-type texture of bars 52–4 (Ex. A.1) a key to pitfall-free traversal is to let each thumb act as a pivot over which the hand easily vaults and falls to the next melody note, avoiding any pulling in of arms. The right thumb thus briefly holds down the last *a″* of each beat in a similar anchoring role to that of the left middle finger in the last of Chopin's op. 28 Preludes. Although fingering inevitably varies with hand shape, from bar 14 it's worth at least trying *3/2* (rather than *4/2*) on the first right-hand dyad along with some of the following ones.

Example A.1. Ravel, 'Ondine', bar 52 (fingering editorial)

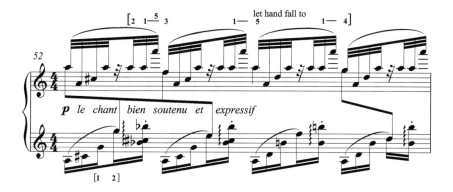

The cadenza of 'Ondine' becomes easier once we identify the vital left-hand notes in each descending group as the first two: this spares effort (and helps voicing) by letting the following two (for fourth and fifth fingers) virtually look after themselves. Likewise from bar 32 of 'Scarbo', clarity in the upward crescendo arpeggios is more vital than in the downward diminuendo ones, the thumb again acting as pivot and marker at the top. In bar 36 the physical awkwardness of suddenly having to drive away from the strong end of the hand can be eased by giving the first six or seven notes to the right hand.

A large-scale key to 'Scarbo' is to remember that its *jota*-like material from bar 52, far from being a speed test, continues the bar pulse of bars 32–6: any tempo dislocation across the two motives shreds the piece's structure, forcing us to slow later when the music least wants it. (As we saw in Chapter 3, this piece's entire structure and drama depend on never slowing down – not even easing back – apart from its instantaneous metrical equivalences which maintain an unslowed pulse underneath.) If the wild waltz motive from bar 32 resembles the fourth of the *Valses nobles et sentimentales* (marked $\bullet. = 80$), the later material from bar 52 equally relates to Chabrier's *España* – which Chabrier also marked $\bullet. = 80$. A basic tempo of $\bullet. = $ c. 80–84 from bar 32 of 'Scarbo' can accommodate it all (give or take a notch), including the flamenco-like episode from bar 256, and makes Ravel's low dynamics possible without turning into clatter. The resulting *subito* $\bullet = $ c. 80–84 at bar 395 can logically be inferred back to bar 1. This analogy with *España* becomes specially telling from bar 478, where 'Scarbo' takes up exactly the same bass ostinato as the equivalent culminating crescendo of *España* (in Chabrier's two-piano version: see pp. 86–7 above), at which point Chabrier nudges the tempo up to $\bullet. = 88$.[2]

Given the pianistic intricacies of 'Scarbo', we can easily forgive Ravel for leaving one impractical bit of layout over bars 503 and 509–10: Vlado Perlemuter's suggested solution was to take the successive eighth-note beats of each bar in the hand sequence RRL rather than the score's original implied RLR (impossible across bars 509–10), which Ravel later amended in bar 510, with limited success, to LRL (as shown in the London Peters edition). A related awkwardness in the seventh of the *Valses nobles et sentimentales*, at the fast right-hand leaps of bars 31 and 34, can be solved by transferring $f'\sharp$ to the left hand (along with d' in bar 34, launched from a preceding 5 on $f\sharp$), the right thumb taking each b', like the a' in bars 19 and 22.

Debussy again

A textural forerunner of Example A.1 above, involving similar thumb-vaults, is the recap of Debussy's early *Rêverie*, a piece whose most vital indication is the ¢ time signature in its first print, corrupted in later editions to C (see the commentary in *Œuvres complètes* 1/1). A decade later the Toccata of *Pour le piano* calls again for alternating thumb-vaults from each hand from bar 9, the left hand at the half-bar, the right hand ending each bar on thumb to start the following one on 2. (This fingering, arguably traceable to Debussy, is shown in the *Œuvres complètes*: cf. Chopin's F major Prelude from op. 28. The Finale of Ravel's Piano Trio needs the same treatment in bars 22–3.) Bars 43 and 45 of Debussy's Toccata again suggest his leonine left hand: small hands can ease this by taking $d''\sharp/c''\sharp$ with the right thumb.

L'isle joyeuse

Ravel's apt description of *L'isle joyeuse* as 'an orchestral reduction for the piano'[3] serves as an astute piece of performing advice, one that encourages us to avoid fatigue by reading the busier figurations as background filling not to be over-articulated. The hand is often physically supported (if we allow it) by slower-moving lines, like the one shown schematically in Example A.2: from bar 7 to beyond bar 30 most of this line falls most easily under the thumb. (The first place where it doesn't, bar 11, nicely frees up the right thumb for possible use on each triplet e', a good way of avoiding hand tightening.)

Example A.2. *L'isle joyeuse*, **bars 7–33, underlying melodic line, schematic notation**

Particularly interesting here is the implicit thumb line [musical notation] in bars 25 and 27: if we let the surrounding figurations virtually happen by themselves around this, the passage becomes instantly easier to play and keep in time, setting off the dramatic rest at beat 2 (surely a candidate for sudden pedal release). It also leads effortlessly into bar 28 (both hands) as well as aptly echoing bars 12–13. It then equally anticipates the transition across bars 66–7 where the thumb marks out a matching *b–bb–a* into the piece's central section. Thumb voicing this passage in turn helps to avoid overslowing in bar 66 and, from bar 67, offers a warmer, more orchestral texture than melodic top-lining would.

In the E major episode from bar 99, fatigue can be avoided if we ease our way (slow practice at first) through the figurations as broken chords, finding the key notes on which the hand can fall and letting the other notes roll from and to them. The B major episode from bar 36 equally benefits from this, in terms of letting the figurations roll lightly around the supporting melody. Equally dramatic under the hand is how much easier (and more sonorous) the piece's last twelve bars are if physically led from the left hand, letting the right hand almost play itself. Debussy's manuscript placing of dynamics supports this (see p. 232 above).

The *5–3–2–1* finger mnemonic already noted for bars 7 and 67 (p. 72 above) is equally helpful for the right hand from bar 19, holding the long note on pedal: avoiding fourth-finger fatigue, it allows easy quieter voicing. (It may have come from Debussy and was taught by pianists including Perlemuter and Marcel Ciampi, the latter of whom worked with Debussy.) The same figuration later in the piece (from bar 166) implies editorial ties across some of the long notes (also for musical reasons), as suggested in the *Œuvres complètes*. As a related matter of finger reach, Vlado Perlemuter advised left thumb (surrounded by 5 and 2) for the middle E♯ of each C♯ triad in bars 52–9. Once those combined issues of voicing and layout are dealt with, many of this piece's technical problems melt away, and it can become as sensual a romp (if always a challenging one) for the pianist as for the listener. Debussy's dynamics help us avoid tightness or pushing by repeatedly showing us where we can drop the accumulated dynamics, as in the cumulative crescendo sequence stretching across bars 133–219.

Debussy's careful tempo markings in *L'isle joyeuse* suggest, as with Ravel's 'Scarbo', a structurally anchored basic tempo from bar 7 (I suggest ♩ = c. 76): this then provides reliable reference (sometimes at the equivalent ♪ = c. 152) for bars 28, 64 and 99 and probably 220, as well as a baseline against which we can read Debussy's meticulously defined departures from it at bars 67, 145, 160 and 244. The piece can then flow symphonically without forced slowing or hiatus at inappropriate places. Even the opening quasi-cadenza needs little intervention: the notation (including some corrected dynamics in the *Œuvres complètes*) mostly tells us what to do to ensure the sense of freedom. Again a pivotal thumb mostly near the keybed from the opening *c″♯* onwards can launch the piece with an aptly spiralling motion through the hand and wrist (this pays off handsomely from bar 244). Immediately before the coda, at bar 219 smaller hands can facilitate the awkward leap to a left-hand ninth by letting the thumb play *c′* along with the printed *d′*: the difference is virtually undetectable and does no musical damage.

'LA TERRASSE DES AUDIENCES DU CLAIR DE LUNE'

The problems posed by this piece are less ones of audible virtuosity than perceptual ones of sensing its polyphonic continuity – indeed its underlying diatonic simplicity – through all the surface false relations, key shifts and double bars. A schematic reduction to polyphonic stepwise motion (Ex. A.3) can help clarify this under the hand. It relates directly to the stepwise motions already seen within or across Examples 1.2–5 and 2.2, plus the polyphonic reductions shown above Example 1.4 and under Examples 9.5 and 15.7. Example A.3 charts up to the point where the piece's pervasive dominant presence completes its first 'looping of the loop'. It can be surprising at first to note that only five bass notes underlie this passage, three of them short drones: C♯, D♯, C♯, B♭ and the final C♯ from bar 16 which, in a curious yet effortless way, retrospectively underpins bars 14–15.

Example A.3. Polyphonic reduction of 'La terrasse des audiences du clair de lune', bars 1–16 (note values polyphonically schematic)

APPENDIX 2

GLOSSES ON TITLES AND
MUSICAL ALLUSIONS

REGARDING two French children's songs repeatedly alluded to in French music, 'Dodo, l'enfant do' and 'Nous n'irons plus au bois', see pages 5, 153 and 199 above and the Foreword to *Œuvres complètes de Claude Debussy* 1/2, p. xix. The title 'Jumbo's Lullaby' follows (like the *Œuvres complètes*) a correction made during Debussy's lifetime to the peculiar original spelling 'Jimbo' (a confusion engendered by pronunciation issues).

Debussy's preludes 'Voiles' and 'General Lavine' are possibly remnants of never-completed music for the stage acts of two Americans, the dancer Loïe Fuller and the clown Edward Lavine. A caricature portrait of Lavine with grotesque epaulettes and outsize flappy shoes is reproduced in Schmitz, *The Piano Works of Debussy*, p. 42. The Loïe Fuller connection is reported by two of Debussy's acquaintances, Edgard Varèse and Yvonne Lefébure.[1] Other title sources for Debussy's Preludes are listed in *Œuvres complètes* 1/5 and the volume's budget offprint. A forerunner to 'Hommage à S. Pickwick Esq.' can be found in César Franck's humorous treatment of the same opening tune in his *1er Duo (4 mains) op. 4 sur le GOD SAVE THE KING*, dedicated to the English sisters Anne and Emmeline Stratton.

APPENDIX 3

COMPOSERS' SURVIVING INSTRUMENTS AND RECORDINGS

Dᴇʙᴜssʏ's Blüthner grand, now in the Musée Labenche, Brive-la-Gaillarde:

> no. 65614, made in 1904, 192 cm long, 88-note, overstrung (i.e. cross-strung), overdampers plus 'aliquot' resonating strings in the treble range; bought by Debussy probably in Eastbourne in 1905, acquired by the Musée Labenche in November 1989, restored in 2000 retaining original materials.[1] A photo of it can be seen on http://www.musee-labenche.com/Anglais/pianode1.htm (accessed in 2007). What became of Debussy's Pleyel and Bechstein uprights (which he mostly had on loan or on hire) is unknown.

Ravel's Erard grand, conserved at 'Le Belvédère' (Ravel's former home, now the Musée Maurice Ravel), Montfort l'Amaury:

> no. 96117, made in 1908, 215 cm long, 85-note, straight-strung, under-dampers; restored in 1985 and 2007. Ravel probably acquired it after 1910: a photo taken by Roland-Manuel in 1912 shows him seated at what appears to be the same piano in his Avenue Carnot home (Roland-Manuel, *Maurice Ravel*, facing p. 64). It replaced a modest upright which Manuel de Falla and Mikhail Fokine remembered seeing there until at least 1910 (Nichols, *Ravel Remembered*, pp. 41 and 81). A colour photo of the Erard can be seen in Milon et al., *Maurice Ravel à Montfort l'Amaury*, pp. 30–1; it also features (twice) on the present dust jacket.

Fauré's Erard grand, now in the Musée de la musique, Paris:

> no. 104960, made in 1914, 185.5 cm long, 85-note, straight-strung, under-dampers; bequest of the composer's daughter-in-law Blanche Fauré-Fremiet in 1984, no restoration known since Fauré's lifetime. Its tone is pleasingly clear and mellow. No trace remains of his previous pianos (some of which may have been on complimentary loan from Erard).

None of Chabrier's instruments has been traced. A celebrated drawing of 1873 by Detaille (reproduced on p. 127 of Delage, *Chabrier* (Iconographie musicale)) shows Chabrier playing a Pleyel but without identifying whose or where.

RECORDINGS

For a comprehensive list of LPs recorded from the reproducing rolls listed below see Hall, 'The player piano on record'; for a comprehensive list of reproducing rolls see Sitsky, *The Classical Reproducing Piano Roll*.

DEBUSSY

Audio recordings, Debussy accompanying Mary Garden, Gramophone & Typewriter Co., recorded in 1904:

> 'Mes longs cheveux descendent' (*Pelléas et Mélisande* Act 3 Scene 1): G&T 33447, matrix 3078F
> 'Il pleure dans mon cœur' (*Ariettes oubliées*), G&T 33449, matrix 3075F
> 'L'ombre des arbres' (*Ariettes oubliées*), G&T 33450, matrix 3076F
> 'Green' (*Ariettes oubliées*), G&T 33451, matrix 3077F

CD transfers from these include the EMI box set with the 1941 Désormière recording of *Pelléas et Mélisande* (7 61038 2 (1988), transfers by Keith Hardwick, reissued in 2006 as 3 45770 2, remastered by Andrew Walter) and Pierian 0001 (2000, transfer by Kenneth Caswell). A Ward Marston transfer of 2008 (Marston 52054–2) electronically removes the wow and flutter from the originals.

Welte-Mignon piano rolls, recorded 1912, issued 1913:[2]

> 2733: *Children's Corner* (complete)
> 2734: *D'un cahier d'esquisses*
> 2735: 'La soirée dans Grenade' (*Estampes*)
> 2736: *La plus que lente*

2738: 'Danseuses de Delphes', 'La Cathédrale engloutie', 'La danse de Puck' (Preludes, Book 1)

2739: 'Le vent dans la plaine', 'Minstrels' (Preludes, Book 1)

(No listings are known under 2737 or 2740–1.)

Recordings to CD include The Caswell Collection vol. 1 (Pierian 0001, 2000, realized by Kenneth Caswell) and The Condon Collection (Australian RCA, 1991, reissued on Dal Segno, realized by Denis Condon). The earliest recording to LP was on USA Columbia, 1950 (reportedly realised in Germany in 1948 by Richard Simonton with the help of Edwin Welte).[3]

Around 1910 Aeolian-Orchestrelle 'Themodist' pianola rolls appeared of several Debussy pieces, all labelled 'Interpretation by the Composer' with a facsimile of Debussy's writing at the start of each roll: 'La ligne de style marquée dans ce rouleau a été dirigée par moi [the style line marked on this roll was directed by me]. / Claude Debussy / 16.VI.09.' Unlike true repro-ducing rolls, these are factory-prepared pianola rolls (following the score) which were then played back in the presence of the composer who – doubt-less after some briefing – guided 'interpretation' controls in each hand to adjust dynamics and tempo. These traced 'style lines' on the roll which could be followed on subsequent replaying.[4]

RAVEL

Welte-Mignon rolls recorded in 1912 or 1913, issued in 1913 or 1914:

2887: *Sonatine*, movements 1 & 2
2888: *Valses nobles et sentimentales*

Duo-Art rolls recorded on 30 June 1922, issued in 1922:

084: *Pavane pour une Infante défunte*
082: 'Oiseaux tristes' (*Miroirs*)

Duo-Art roll recorded and issued in 1928:

72750: 'La vallée des cloches' (*Miroirs*)

For more documentation see *A Ravel Reader*, appendices E and F, pp. 524–34, where Jean Touzelet clarifies who recorded what (see p. 321 above). CD realizations include The Caswell Collection vol. 4 (Pierian 0013, 2002) and The Condon Collection (Dal Segno DSPRCD004). The earliest LP realization of the Welte rolls was USA Columbia ML4291 (1950), prepared in the same way as the Columbia Debussy one listed above.

FaURÉ

Hupfeld rolls, recorded in May 1908:

  53081: *Berceuse* op. 16, arr. Benfeld
  53082: Third Nocturne
  53083: *Romance sans paroles* no. 3; later reissued under licence as Ampico
    66531
  53084: Third *Valse-caprice*
  55905: First Barcarolle
  55906: 'Fileuse' from *Pelléas et Mélisande*, arr. Cortot
  55908: Third Impromptu
  55909: *Mazurka* op. 32
  55910: Fourth Nocturne
  55911: Seventh Nocturne
  55912: *Pavane*
  55916: *Sicilienne* op. 78
  55917–18: *Thème et variations* (some exemplars contain the whole work on
    one roll)
  55919: First *Valse-caprice*
  55920: Second *Valse-caprice*

(No listings are known under 55907 or 55913–15.)

No sound recordings are currently available of these rolls, from which it is now almost impossible to ascertain exact original tempi and dynamics; they also show technical problems including faulty octave doublings (see the London Peters edition commentaries to the Nocturnes and *Thème et variations*).

Welte-Mignon rolls recorded 1912, issued 1913:

  2772: *Pavane* op. 50
  2773: First Barcarolle
  2774: Third Prelude (from op. 103)
  2775: Third Nocturne
  2777: *Sicilienne* op. 78

(No listing is known under 2776.)

Chabrier, like Franck, died too early to leave any recordings. Recordings by the composers' associates are beyond the present scope of this appendix, though see p. 92 above (and the associated note 12) regarding Risler's recording of Chabrier's 'Idylle', and pp. 214 and 219 regarding Viñes's of Debussy's 'Poissons d'or' (along with 'La soirée dans Grenade'). Incomplete Viñes recordings also survive of 'Pour les sonorités opposées' (which he probably didn't study with Debussy – he occasionally misreads the bass) and 'Hommage à Rameau' (taken at a surprisingly nimble pace). Cortot recorded one solo piano piece by Fauré, the composer he worked with most closely (the third of the *Romances sans paroles*, recorded in 1928); he knew Debussy and Ravel less well. Marguerite Long's recordings, though of obvious interest, prompt queries about how closely they represent the composers' wishes (see note 3 to Chapter 16 and note 41 to Chapter 17).

CRITICAL EDITIONS: A BRIEF SUMMARY

The end of Chapter 16 has already broached the topic of choosing an edition. The present list excludes non-urtexts, even if marked up and fingered by specialists; while often interesting, the additions are less essential than the composers' markings, and corrupt readings tend to be left uncorrected. Surviving proofs of *Le tombeau de Couperin*, incidentally, show that Ravel fingered some of the Prélude then deleted it before the suite went to print.

CHABRIER

Pièces pittoresques: Éditions du Marais, Paris (now Jobert), Collection Patrimoine vol. 1, ed. Roger Delage (1990)
[First critical edition, well documented, suffers from a high incidence of misprints]

Emmanuel Chabrier, Works for solo piano, ed. Roy Howat, Dover (1995)
[Critical edition of all Chabrier's mature completed piano works (including *Pièces pittoresques*), reprinted from early prints with corrections touched in]

DEBUSSY

For facsimile editions of the piano *Images*, *Études* and first book of Preludes see Bibliography under Debussy.

Durand: *Œuvres complètes de Claude Debussy*, series 1 vols 1–8 (1986–2009), complete piano music, ed. Roy Howat, Christophe Grabowski, Claude Helffer and Noël Lee

[Detailed critical editions, no editorial fingering; individual works from these volumes are now available separately in budget offprints, with a shorter commentary]

Other critical or part-critical editions include Henle (reprints of which take some account of and refer to the above *Œuvres complètes*), Peters, Wiener Urtext and Bärenreiter. All except Peters add editorial fingering. See also note 1 to Chapter 16.

FAURÉ

Peters Edition, London, ed. Roy Howat, including the complete Nocturnes (EP 7659), *Pièces brèves* (EP 7601), *Romances sans paroles* (EP 7711), *Thème et variations* (EP 7956), and *Dolly* (EP 7430)
[Critical edition, not editorially fingered; editions of the Barcarolles in press (2009: EP 71904) and *Mazurka* and *Valses-caprices* in preparation]

Also in preparation is a planned full Fauré critical edition from Bärenreiter (editorial board presided over by Jean-Michel Nectoux). A Henle edition of the *Thème et variations* is meticulously edited but misses some important sources including the true first French edition.

FRANCK

Prélude, Choral et Fugue and *Prélude, Aria et Final,* ed. Joël-Marie Fauquet, vols 12 and 5 of Collection Patrimoine, Éditions du Marais (now Éditions Jobert), 1991 and 1990

RAVEL

Peters Edition, London, ed. Roger Nichols, complete works for solo piano
[Thoroughly researched critical edition, replaces an older Leipzig Peters series]

A new Durand critical edition is now in planning, under the general direction of Denis Herlin.

Regarding the clavecinistes, non-critical editions or cheap reprints are best discarded and replaced with the likes of Kenneth Gilbert's Le Pupitre editions (Heugel) or the more recent Bärenreiter; they transform how the music looks and sounds. Also worth signalling is an excellent and informative Henle edition of Balakirev's *Islamey* (2004, ed. Norbert Gertsch).

APPENDIX 5

LOCATIONS OF MUSICAL MANUSCRIPTS DISCUSSED

US-NYpm = Pierpont Morgan Library, New York

F OR reasons of space only manuscripts explicitly discussed in this book are listed here. More comprehensive lists can be found in Delage, *Emmanuel Chabrier*, Lesure, *Claude Debussy: biographie critique*, Orenstein, *Ravel, Man and Musician*, Philips, *Gabriel Fauré: A Research Guide*, and in the critical editions listed in Appendix 4. Although the list below is current in 2009, privately owned manuscripts sometimes change hands through sale or legacy.

CHABRIER

Aubade: Paris, Musée de la musique
Bourrée fantasque: *F-Pn* musique, Ms. 19201
Ronde champêtre: archives of Éditions Enoch, Paris

DEBUSSY

Children's Corner: *F-Pn* musique, Ms. 983
Estampes: *F-Pn* musique, Ms. 988
Études: *F-Pn* musique, Ms. 993 (fair copy); private collection (duplicate page quoted in Ex. 17.4a). Debussy's working draft is dispersed across various locations (mostly listed in the Minkoff facsimile edition: see Bibliography under Debussy)
Etude retrouvée: *US-NYpm*, D289.P877 (gift of Margaret G. Cobb)
L'isle joyeuse: *F-Pn* musique, Ms. 977

Hommage à Haydn: private collection, Paris

Images [oubliées] of 1894: *US-NYpm*, Robert O. Lehman deposit, D289.I.314

Images of 1905–7: *F-Pn* musique, Mss. 998–1000 (1re série), Ms. 1005 (2e série). See Bibliography under Debussy for facsimile editions, also note 19 to Chapter 8 regarding a related sketch

Lindaraja: *F-Pn* musique, Ms. 22948

Pour le piano: Paul Sacher Stiftung, Basle

Preludes, Book 1: *US-NYpm*, Robert O. Lehman deposit, D289.P922 (see Bibliography under Debussy for Dover facsimile edition)

'La Cathédrale engloutie', orchestration by Henri Busser: *F-Pn* musique, Ms. 18837 (Busser's manuscript), plus a copy (unidentified hand) in the Durand archives

Preludes, Book 2: *F-Pn* musique, Ms. 1006

Suite bergamasque, proofs corrected by Debussy: *F-Pn* musique, Rés. Vma 286

FAURÉ

Fifth Barcarolle: *US-NYpm*, Robert O. Lehman collection, F2655.C955

Eighth Barcarolle: *F-Pn* musique, Ms. 17742

Fifth Nocturne: Beinecke Rare Books and Manuscript Library, Yale University, F. Koch collection (FRKF Deposit #901c)

Sixth Nocturne: *US-NYpm*, Robert O. Lehman collection, F2655.N756

Seventh Nocturne: *F-Pn* musique, Ms. 17943

Eleventh Nocturne: *US-NYpm*, Robert O. Lehman collection, F2655.N7511

Pièces brèves :

no. I: Washington, Library of Congress, ML31.H43a / No. 64 Case (Music 1235)

no. V: Paris, Archives nationales, Aj^37 200, 2

no. VIII (also known as Eighth Nocturne): Bibliothèque François Lang, Royaumont, France, Réserve 23

First Violin Sonata, op. 13: *F-Pn* musique, Ms. 20298

Second Violin Sonata, op. 108: *F-Pn* musique, Ms. 22144

First (C minor) Piano Quartet, op. 15: *F-Pn* musique, Ms. 17770 (finale only)

Second Piano Quintet, op. 115, preparatory draft: *F-Pn* musique, Ms. 17773

RAVEL

Gaspard de la nuit: Harry Ransom Center, University of Texas at Austin

Jeux d'eau (3 autographs in all): preparatory draft, *F-Pn* musique, Ms. 15198; first fair copy, *US-NYpm*, Robert O. Lehman deposit, R252.J58; second fair copy (*Stichvorlage* for first edition) sold at Sotheby's London on 7 December 2004 (lot 113)

'Une barque sur l'océan' (*Miroirs*): *F-Pn* musique, Ms. 13453 (non-autograph copy marked up by Ravel, *Stichvorlage* for first edition)

[*Menuet*] (unpublished): *F-Pn* musique, Ms. 17650

Le tombeau de Couperin, corrected proofs (annotations not in Ravel's hand but obviously copied from his corrections): Paris, Durand archives

NOTES

CHAPTER 1

1. Late in life he wrote to Émile Vuillermoz, 'You do me a great honour by calling me a pupil of Claude Monet' (*Debussy Letters*, p. 313); see also Lépine, *La vie de Claude Debussy*, p. 84, and Romilly, 'Debussy professeur', p. 5.
2. English translation in Bretell, *Impressionism*, pp. 233–5. Besides Lockspeiser's surveys (*Debussy: His Life and Mind* and *Music and Painting*), documentation of Debussy and visual arts can be read in Nectoux, *Harmonie en bleu et or*, Simeone, 'Debussy and expression' and Botstein, 'Beyond the illusions of realism'.
3. See the reproductions in Delage, *Chabrier* (Iconographie musicale), pp. 57, 60–72 and 75, including now-famous canvases by Manet, Monet, Renoir, Sisley and Cézanne that once hung in Chabrier's home. Poulenc (*Emmanuel Chabrier*, pp. 185–7) lists those auctioned in 1896. Roger Delage devotes two chapters to Chabrier's links with painters and notes his acquisition of Goya etchings in 1883 (*Emmanuel Chabrier*, pp. 135–63 and 284).
4. Desboutin's portrait of Chabrier, along with his 1895 tribute to Manet and Chabrier, is reproduced in Delage, *Chabrier* (Iconographic musicale), pp. 70–1.
5. See for example Homer, *Seurat and the Science of Painting*, passim.
6. His alleged reply to Franck, 'Et pourquoi voulez-vous que je module si je me trouve très bien dans ce ton-là ?', sounds convincingly in character (Laloy, *La musique retrouvée*, p. 122).
7. Not a standard western mode, this is sometimes known as the overtone or acoustic scale because of the way the acoustic series's first two dissonant overtones approximate to the scale's mixolydian seventh and lydian fourth. Fauré, Ravel and Bartók also used it; its Indian origins are discussed in Chapter 8.
8. This tends to confirm that $g'\sharp$ is indeed meant in bar 10; Chapter 16 returns to Debussy's initially absentminded spelling of these bars. An early prompt for this analysis was Arnold Whittall's article 'Tonality and the whole-tone scale in the music of Debussy'.
9. *Debussy Letters*, p. 155, letter dated 19 August 1905. See Mark McFarland's article 'Transpositional combination and aggregate formation in Debussy' for related procedures in Chopin that link to Debussy and for references to studies of diatonic–chromatic contrasts in classical repertoire.

10. Bar 77 here marks the return of the tonic triad, anticipated but sidestepped in bars 73–5. A few editions misnumber the piece's bars by miscounting the cadenza-like bar 23 (split over two systems) as two bars; Debussy's manuscript confirms it as a single bar.

11. From Debussy's reported conversations in 1889–90 with Ernest Guiraud, translated in Lockspeiser, *Debussy: His Life and Mind*, vol. 1 p. 206.

12. See Poulenc, *Emmanuel Chabrier*, p. 62, Marnat, *Ravel: souvenirs de Manuel Rosenthal*, pp. 10–11, and Rosenthal, *Musique adorable*, p. 27. Roger Delage (*Emmanuel Chabrier*, pp. 217–18) discusses Chabrier's more radical, 'visceral' use of modality by comparison with the more locally picturesque modality of composers he admired including Berlioz, Gounod and Saint-Saëns. Ravel's student Roland-Manuel (*Maurice Ravel*, p. 112) similarly argues that Chabrier founded modern French modality.

13. See d'Almendra, 'Debussy et mouvement modal dans la musique du XXᵉ siècle'. Some biographical uncertainty remains: d'Almendra reports Debussy's sister Adèle as saying in 1948 that the young Achille-Claude had spent a good part of his infant years in Cannes with his aunt (who brought up his siblings Adèle and Alfred) and was trained in the musical liturgy of the cathedral. Debussy himself referred only to one stay in Cannes, from early 1870, which may have lasted some time because of the Franco-Prussian war and its Parisian aftermath (see Lesure, *Claude Debussy: biographie critique*, pp. 14–16). However long the young Achille's stay (or stays), Cannes was where he had his first piano lessons. Lesure (ibid., p. 461) corrects a likely error by d'Almendra, who said Debussy visited Solesmes in 1893 to hear Gregorian chant (probably confusing him with an Abbé de Bussy, curate of Saint-Gervais).

14. Some editions inexplicably omit the staccato dot, clear in the autograph and first edition. Regarding the title see Appendix 2.

15. *A Ravel Reader*, p. 350. Earlier usages (including Liszt) are traced in Taruskin, 'Chernomor to Kashchei', pp. 85–7.

16. This was doubtless the scale's origin, just as the whole-tone scale derives from two augmented chords a tone apart. Prominent diminished-seventh-based octatonic passages can be found as early as Weber and Hummel (e.g. the Largo of the latter's op. 87 Piano Quintet of 1822, at bars 20–3).

17. See Taruskin, 'Chernomor to Kashchei', regarding the scale's exploitation by Rimsky-Korsakov in the wake of Liszt and earlier Russian sources, and also Kahan, *Music's Modern Muse* (pp. 70–1) and '"Rien de la tonalité usuelle"' for Prince Edmond de Polignac's wholly independent explorations from the late 1870s (certainly known to Debussy, Fauré and Ravel and probably to Chabrier). Octatonic passages by Polignac's friend Fauré include the climax of his Second Nocturne and melodic lines in the Sixth Nocturne (bars 52–6) and the first of the *Pièces brèves* (bars 28–32). Ravel's widespread octatonic usage, noted in Howat, 'Modes and semitones in Debussy's Preludes and elsewhere', is linked particularly to Rimsky-Korsakov by Steven Baur ('Ravel's "Russian" period'); Chapter 6 returns to the topic.

18. See also the texturally similar bars 20–2 of 'Le tombeau des naïades' (1898) from Debussy's *Chansons de Bilitis*, which mixes whole-tone and octatonic fragments.

19. Jean-Michel Nectoux (*Harmonie en bleu et or*, p. 206), quoting this analogy presumably from Howat, 'Debussy et le piano', p. 37, adds a literary gloss involving descriptions of pagoda roof curves that Debussy may have read in Camille Mauclair's prose poem 'Pagode'.

20. *Debussy Letters*, p. 140, and *Debussy on Music*, p. 248.

21. Caricatures by Fauré of Saint-Saëns, André Messager, Verlaine and Dukas – including one depicting Saint-Saëns playing harp strings stretched from his grotesquely elongated nose – are reproduced in Nectoux, *Camille Saint-Saëns & Gabriel Fauré: correspondance*, plates 3, 6, 7 and 8, Nectoux, *Fauré*, 1972 edition p. 35 (also *Marguerite de Saint-Marceaux: Journal*, p. 1131), Nectoux, *Gabriel Fauré: His Life through his Letters*, p. 164, and the Hudry essay accompanying the Foster/Claves CD of Fauré's *Pelléas et*

Mélisande. More unpublished ones (including one of d'Indy) are in *F-Pn* musique (Est. Indy 010 bis and Est. Fauré G 146–9).

22. Nectoux, *Gabriel Fauré: A Musical Life*, p. 92
23. To that list Nectoux (ibid.) adds, perhaps more debatably, the start of the Second Nocturne and the middle of the Seventh Prelude, plus the writing in the Barcarolles generally.
24. Routley, '*Des pas sur la neige*: Debussy in Bilitis's footsteps'.
25. Jankélévitch, *Debussy et le mystère*, pp. 89–100, and Lockspeiser, *Debussy: His Life and Mind*, vol. 2 pp. 237–9.

CHAPTER 2

1. Such performances occurred quite soon: Jane Mortier played Book 1 complete on 3 May 1911, and Walter Rummel did the same for Book 2 on 12 June 1913 (see Timbrell, *Prince of Virtuosos*, p. 35). The extracts premièred by Debussy were nos. I, II, X and XI from Book 1 (5 May 1910), followed by IV, III, VI and XII on 29 March 1911; then nos. I–III from the still-unpublished Book 2 (5 March 1913) followed by VII, X and IX on 19 June 1913.
2. The one momentary departure from pure whole-tone in the outer sections is a repeated chromatic passing note in bar 31.
3. The tenuto dashes in bar 40, which most editions print against the f'♯s, may have been intended for the d's below (as in *Œuvres complètes* reprints: see the Dover autograph facsimile). Elliott Antokoletz (*The Music of Béla Bartók*, pp. 6–8) also draws attention to the G♯–D modal axis in 'Voiles'.
4. Roger Nichols ('The prosaic Debussy', p. 88) draws attention to a similar play on B♭ relative to B and A in the 1904 song 'Colloque sentimental', whose final A tonality relates similarly to the song's opening emphasis of B♭ and A♭.
5. In brief, the key sequence from no. IV onwards traces out a repeated expanding penta-tonic sequence of A–B–D–F♯/G♭, B♭–C–E♭–G. This is less essential to overall logic, and the pieces' intrinsic contrasts by then suffice to set them in relief.
6. Debussy's autograph records that preludes I, III and II were completed (in that order) between 7 and 12 December 1909 and nos. V, VI and IV between 26 December and 1 January 1910; three more are dated later and the remainder undated (see the Dover facsimile or the Foreword to *Œuvres complètes* 1/5).
7. See *Debussy Letters*, pp. 256–65 and 327.
8. The clearest octatonic occurrence in Book 1 of the Preludes is on the first page of 'Ce qu'a vu le Vent d'Ouest'; Chapter 9 returns to this passage relative to Musorgsky.
9. See in particular McFarland, 'Debussy and Stravinsky: another look at their musical relationship', and Baur, 'Ravel's "Russian" period', along with other sources of Stravinsky research and analysis to which they refer.
10. This overlay mirrors that of 'Des pas sur la neige', by starting with a complete dorian mode, then changing it to æolian by replacing the B♮ with B♭ (bar 2) before adding the remaining black keys in order of descending fifths.
11. Abbate, '*Tristan* in the composition of *Pelléas*'. Peter Platt's arguments, touched on in 'Debussy and the harmonic series', were explored in more detail in his lectures at the University of Sydney and in conversation.
12. Youens, 'Debussy's setting of Verlaine's "Colloque sentimentale"'.
13. *Debussy Letters*, p. 258. Stravinsky later recalled, 'Debussy was in close contact with me during the composition of *Jeux* and he frequently consulted me about problems of orchestration' (Stravinsky and Craft, *Conversations with Igor Stravinsky*, p. 50 n2). This would have been exactly while Debussy was completing Book 2 of the Preludes: his manuscripts of *Jeux* show that he orchestrated the work between autumn 1912 and April 1913.

14. Debussy's letter just quoted goes on to say, 'You'll progress beyond *Petrushka*, of course, but you can still be proud of what the work stands for' – the touch of evident petulance suggesting some inner turbulence. By January 1916 Debussy, admittedly ill and depressed, was describing Stravinsky to Robert Godet as 'a spoilt child who, from time to time, cocks a snook at music. . . . When he's old, he'll be intolerable . . . but, for the moment, he's amazing' (*Debussy Letters*, p. 312).
15. This was on 9 June 1912; it's not altogether certain if this was the occasion on which Debussy sight-read the work in piano duet with Stravinsky, a feat Stravinsky never forgot and which Laloy later ascribed to spring 1913 (see Walsh, *Stravinsky: A Creative Spring*, pp. 181 and 593 n63).
16. *Debussy Letters*, p. 265.
17. 'Les tierces alternées' was the last prelude composed, in January 1913: see *Debussy Letters*, p. 236, and the Foreword (p. xv) to *Œuvres complètes* 1/5. Robert Orledge has observed (in conversation) another passage from *The Rite* quoted verbatim at bars 59–60 of Debussy's *Berceuse héroïque* of 1914.
18. Scott, *My Years of Indiscretion*, pp. 104–5. (A variant paraphrase of this can be read in Scott's other memoirs, *Bone of Contention*, p. 128.)

CHAPTER 3

1. Quoted in Nichols, *Ravel Remembered*, p. 55. The relationship to painting techniques is a vivid one.
2. See *A Ravel Reader*, Appendix D on pp. 517–23, also Plate 16 facing p. 367. Similar techniques can be heard in the Adagio of his Concerto in G (bars 46–50 and 58–61).
3. Ravel possessed a score of these songs; one wonders if he noticed Berg's allusion, which must be deliberate: the final *fff* climax in Berg's song hammers out the B♭ ostinato from 'Le gibet' at the word *Stirb!* ['die!']). Debussy's *Épigraphes antiques* mostly rework his musical interludes of 1901 for Pierre Louÿs's *Chansons de Bilitis*, but this particular passage is one he added in 1914. Hans-Heinz Stuckenschmidt, a Ravel biographer, notes the Berg–Debussy concordance ('Debussy or Berg? The mystery of a chord progression') but surprisingly overlooks Ravel's originating role.
4. Perlemuter and Jourdan-Morhange, *Ravel according to Ravel*, p. 33.
5. The most characteristic relationship here is between the climaxes in F♯ and C; Ravel's Concerto for Left Hand repeats this in a work whose main keys are D and E.
6. Chromatic splitting pervades 'Scarbo' from bar 2 onwards; the habit audibly reaches back to Ravel's two-piano 'Habanera' of 1895.
7. This reading of tempo follows Roger Nichols's commentary to the London Peters edition in assuming ♩ = preceding bar at bar 430 (i.e. the listener hears no change in tempo), and that Ravel's indication there, '♩ = ♪ du mouv^t précédent', refers back to bar 395 (i.e. ♩ in bar 430 = ♪ in bar 395). This implies an inexorable speeding up through bars 411–29, something the music's textures make inevitable. (It's also propelled by an intrinsic tempo increase over bars 1 and 2, repeated over bars 395–6 etc.) On the page the continuity of pulse from bar 395 to bar 460 is surprisingly hard to track, mostly because Ravel notates it prescriptively for pianistic convenience: it becomes more visible if we imagine bars 430–59 notated in ⅜ and half its present note values. (Ravel's obvious reason for not doing that was to avoid quadruple beams from bar 430.)
8. The strong cadential endings of *La mer* and *L'isle joyeuse* are also more exceptional for Debussy. Conversely, the pieces where Ravel builds to a dissonant rather than cadential culmination tend to be those most Debussy-like in shape, like 'Oiseaux tristes', 'Une barque sur l'océan' or 'Ondine'.
9. Letter to Jean Marnold of May 1910, quoted in *A Ravel Reader*, p. 117.

CHAPTER 4

1. Rosen, 'Where Ravel ends and Debussy begins', pp. 32–3.
2. Since Ravel's Forlane in *Le tombeau* was closely modelled on one by Couperin (of which more in Chapter 10), Rosen's view might imply considerable foresight on Couperin's part.
3. One of Perlemuter's oft-repeated tenets (in classes and printed interviews) was that Ravel's music holds its place so well in the repertoire primarily because of its architectural strength.
4. *A Ravel Reader*, p. 421, and Nichols, *Ravel Remembered*, p. 101.
5. Debussy is less explicit about this last detail at bar 220 of *L'isle joyeuse*: in practice his *Un peu cédé* there brings the eighth-note tempo back to that of bar 28 or bar 7, just as bar 51 of 'Hommage' explicitly returns to the tempo of bars 1 and 38.
6. *Debussy on Music*, pp. 22–3, from a review written in April 1901.
7. See Howat, *Debussy in Proportion*, p. 133, regarding some Schumannesque elements of sonata form implicit across the totality of *La mer*; the sonata elements in Debussy's String Quartet also suggest Schumann and Franck.
8. Marie Rolf uses the term 'additive variation' for a similar pervasive process across Act 4 Scene 4 of *Pelléas et Mélisande* ('Symbolism as compositional agent in Act IV, Scene 4 of Debussy's *Pelléas et Mélisande*', pp. 123–7). Roderick Shaw first drew my interest to this process in 'Reflets dans l'eau' and 'Poissons d'or'.
9. Wenk, *Claude Debussy and the Poets*, p. 152.
10. Grayson, 'Bilitis and Tanagra', pp. 131–3.
11. *Marguerite de Saint-Marceaux: Journal*, p. 511. Viñes's diary notes that only 'Poissons d'or' had some success at its première on 21 February 1908; the other two *Images* were 'un véritable fiasco' (Gubisch, 'La vie musicale à Paris', p. 231).
12. *Claude Debussy: correspondance*, p. 1083; letter dated 10 April 1908. Louis Laloy's review of the première noted that Viñes's 'performance, interesting as always, nevertheless felt the effects of such a brief period [six weeks] of study' (Priest, *Louis Laloy*, p. 207).
13. Eigeldinger, *Chopin, Pianist and Teacher*, p. 66. Several questions arose when Jean-Jacques Eigeldinger and I tried emulating this on the Broadwood chosen by Chopin for his English recitals in 1848 (no. 17047 of 1847) plus two other instruments he used that same year (Pleyel no. 13819 of c.1847, kept by Chopin in his English lodgings in 1848, and Jane Stirling's 1843 Erard; all three instruments in the Cobbe Collection at Hatchlands). Was Hallé referring to the *f* reprise from bar 84 or the *ff* start of the coda from bar 93, or even just the last two pages? Did Chopin maintain *pp* or let the energy build again (hard to avoid, given the full textures and vigorous motion)? Or did he thin out the left-hand octaves? Such questions can now only remain open.
14. See Howat, 'Dramatic shape and form in "Jeux de vagues"'.
15. He also left a duet version of *Bourrée fantasque*.
16. Marguerite Long quotes Debussy remarking of Fauré, 'il ne sait pas finir' ('he doesn't know how to end') (*Au piano avec Gabriel Fauré*, p. 105). Robert Levin (in conversation) has also drawn attention to this characteristic.
17. *Gabriel Fauré: His Life through his Letters*, p. 94.
18. Ibid., n1.
19. Ibid., pp. 66–7, though this leaves a query about chronology: according to Fauré's letter the *Ballade* existed as separate solo pieces until 1879, and its integrated orchestral version was premièred in April 1881 (the date written on its manuscript), yet Liszt and Fauré are known to have met only in 1877 and 1882. Either they met again in the interim or Fauré took some time to act on advice given in 1877.
20. *A Ravel Reader*, p. 30.

21. Only after first presenting this analysis (in 'Ravel and the piano') did I become aware of Messiaen's related one (with a few variants of detail), published posthumously in Messiaen, *Analyse des œuvres pour piano de Maurice Ravel*, pp. 25–38.
22. Ravel also said this to Paul Loyonnet (Giraud, *Paul Loyonnet*, p. 322).
23. Debussy gives the same arching role to returning motives, for example in 'La soirée dans Grenade' (bars 61–6) and *L'isle joyeuse* (bars 64–6).

Chapter 5

1. The photograph (taken in 1911 by Satie) is reproduced in Nectoux, *Harmonie en bleu et or*, p. 194; a slightly trimmed version, with the Hokusai print just visible, appears in Lesure, *Claude Debussy* (Iconographie musicale), p. 135, and Nichols, *Debussy Remembered* (between pp. 134 and 135).
2. See note 10 to Chapter 1 regarding faulty bar numbering in some editions.
3. The exact value is decimally irrational: 0.618034 is often used as a good approximation, but the digits will go on for ever if we let them. Mathematically the exact value is $(1 \pm \sqrt{5}) \div 2$.
4. Gustav Fechner's 1876 findings on the aesthetics of golden section rectangles (*Vorschule der Aesthetik*) are still fuelling debate: see for example McManus, 'The aesthetics of simple figures' and Nagy, 'Golden section(ism)'.
5. For botanical examples ranging from snail shells to sunflowers, fir cones and catkins (and many others) see the present book's Bibliography under Church, Colman and Coan, Cook, Lendvai, and Thompson. For a brief survey of the golden section's role in art, see likewise under Ghyka and Hambidge. One of the most famous twentieth-century architectural applications was through the architect Le Corbusier's 'Modulor', following Zeising's and Fechner's theories on the proportions of the human body (again see Bibliography). Arguments for and against are rife regarding the role of golden section in edifices including the Parthenon in Athens and the Egyptian Pyramids.
6. For maximum arithmetical accuracy the first division would theoretically be after 22 rather than 23 bars. While the discrepancy is small (exact golden section of 58 lies between 22 and 23), it can be justified musically in terms of smaller phrase structure, and makes the vital point that the numbers are subservient to musical sense. We can also note that the irregular lengths of bars 11 and 23 partly cancel each other out, and their effect on overall proportions is too tiny to affect the logic of Figure 5.2.
7. Long (*Au piano avec Claude Debussy*, p. 45) quotes Debussy as referring here to bar 35 onwards; the image is equally relevant to bars 1–8.
8. *A Ravel Reader*, pp. 394, 433 and 454. In *Claude Debussy, rhétoricien français*, pp. 279–84, Neil Heyde analyses the finale of Debussy's Violin Sonata partly along Poe's lines.
9. For chronology of the piece's completion see *Claude Debussy: correspondance*, pp. 914–19.
10. In 'Cloches à travers les feuilles' each of the piece's $\frac{2}{4}$ bars counts as half a standard $\frac{4}{4}$ bar. All our measurements thus follow the score's articulation (the normal way of measuring metre or hypermetre) rather than clock time which varies unpredictably from one performance to another.
11. Besides Ernő Lendvai's Bartók analyses (listed in the Bibliography) see Howat, 'Bartók, Lendvai and the principles of proportional analysis', along with the correspondence it generated from Lendvai, Hans Keller and myself in *Music Analysis*, 2:3 (October 1983), pp. 299–300, 3:3 (October 1984), pp. 255–64, and 4:3 (October 1985), p. 337.
12. See Howat, *Debussy in Proportion*, pp. 189–91, for a complete proportional analysis.
13. Ibid., pp. 192–3.

14. Discussion of the topic with various composers suggests this issue can be something of a red herring, in that the activity of composing is often so intense that composers are later unable to recall exactly what elements were consciously designed or not.
15. *Debussy Letters*, p. 137.
16. See the analysis in Howat, *Debussy in Proportion*, pp. 136–8.
17. *Debussy on Music*, p. 255.
18. Two of them appeared in *La Revue Indépendante* (April–May 1888) when one of the magazine's subscribers was Debussy's brother Alfred. A skilled literary man (*inter alia* he translated Rossetti), Alfred was in close touch with Édouard Dujardin, the *Revue Indépendante*'s founder: their correspondence (now in the Harry Ransom Center, University of Texas at Austin) mentions meetings between Claude-Achille and Dujardin.
19. See Oudin, *Aristide Briand: la paix*, pp. 32–3, and Howat, *Debussy in Proportion*, pp. 164–7 and 229. The word *Hydropathes* puns on the name of their founder Émile Goudeau (= *goût d'eau*), whom Debussy knew.
20. See Lesure, *Claude Debussy*, pp. 98–101, and Lockspeiser, *Debussy: His Life and Mind*, vol. 1 pp. 141–5.
21. See Marnat, *Ravel: souvenirs de Manuel Rosenthal*, p. 157 [*recte* 'mère' for 'père'], Mercier, *Les sources ésotériques*, vol. 1, pp. 123ff, Michelet, *Les compagnons de la hiérophanie*, pp. 66–88 (especially p. 75), and Lockspeiser, *Debussy: His Life and Mind*, vol. 2 pp. 272–7 and vol. 1 passim. From the 1960s Debussy was bizarrely implicated in the *Prieuré de Sion* legends exploited by Dan Brown's novel *The Da Vinci Code*, based on a document now regarded as a hoax, the purported *Dossiers secrets d'Henri Lobineau* deposited in 1967 in the Bibliothèque nationale, Paris.
22. This pentacular property is directly reflected in the presence of $\sqrt{5}$ in the ratio's value.
23. Nagy, 'Golden section(ism)', part 2, pp. 94–8.
24. Studies on this topic include Siegele, *Bachs theologischer Formbegriff*, Rutter, *The Sonata Principle*, and Howat, 'Architecture as drama in late Schubert'.

CHAPTER 6

1. See Timbrell, *French Pianism* (passim).
2. See Eigeldinger, *Chopin, Pianist and Teacher*, pp. 129–30, 170, 188 and passim. Descombes's role is somewhat shadowy: his pupil Cortot admiringly but slightly guardedly defined him as 'guardian of a pianistic tradition within the ambit of the great example of the Polish Master' (Cortot, *Aspects de Chopin*, p. 177). Descombes was one of Ravel's teachers; Satie's included both Mathias and Descombes.
3. Fauré's first three Preludes of op. 103 also appeared in 1910; the remaining six, composed later that year, appeared in 1911 (another intended three were never written). Like Debussy's Preludes, Chopin's were first published in two books of twelve.
4. *Les écrits de Paul Dukas sur la musique*, pp. 514–15.
5. More of this in Chapter 9: Debussy's early *Mazurka* echoes both Tchaikovsky and the opening rhythm of Saint-Saëns's *1re Mazurka* op. 21, while Fauré's suggests Russian input (despite Nectoux's view of it as Chopin pastiche, in *Gabriel Fauré: A Musical Life*, p. 48). Fauré, according to his son, would have preferred non-picturesque titles for his piano works (Fauré-Fremiet, *Gabriel Fauré*, p. 139).
6. Along with her famous singer sister Maria Malibran, Viardot was daughter and sister of the singers Manuel García *père et fils*.
7. Some of Mme Viardot's Chopin reminiscences are incorporated in Saint-Saëns's 1910 article 'Quelques mots sur l'exécution des œuvres de Chopin'. These extracts are quoted in Eigeldinger, *Chopin, Pianist and Teacher*, pp. 49, 54, 58–9 and 65–6.
8. Nectoux, *Gabriel Fauré: A Musical Life*, p. 49.

9. It occurs dramatically as a half-close on the dominant ($E\flat^7$ over a bass D) in Bach's G minor organ Fantasia BWV 542, and more quietly in Beethoven's 'Moonlight' and op. 22 piano sonatas. Ravel, aware of the 'Moonlight' connection, once illustrated it to Arthur Hoérée with wry amusement, given his habitual disdain for 'le grand sourd' (recounted in conversation by the late Arthur Hoérée). Chopin's usage, like Paganini's, turns it into an elided Neapolitan cadence that skips the dominant, as also in Schumann's song 'In der Fremde' from the op. 39 *Liederkreis* of 1840 (in the same key as Example 6.3 and composed in the years between Chopin's op. 9 Nocturnes and *Barcarolle*).

10. For the slightly uncertain chronology of Debussy's stay or stays in Cannes around 1870–1 see Lesure, *Claude Debussy*, pp. 14–15, and Dietschy, *A Portrait of Claude Debussy*, pp. 11–13.

11. Although some, including Dietschy (ibid., p. 18), have ridiculed Mme Mauté's claim, Jean-Jacques Eigeldinger suggests an open verdict (*Chopin, Pianist and Teacher*, p. 129n), and has observed (in conversation) that there were undoubtedly many Chopin pupils for whom no documentation survives.

12. According to the often unreliable souvenirs of Mme Mauté's daughter Mathilde (the ill-fated bride of Verlaine), Debussy maintained contact until Mme Mauté's death in 1883; Dietschy suggests she may have continued coaching him after his Conservatoire admission (*A Portrait of Claude Debussy*, p. 20). Verlaine and Mathilde were living *chez* Mme Mauté when she taught Debussy, though he never mentioned having met Verlaine there.

13. *Claude Debussy: correspondance*, pp. 1871 and 1926–7 (also *Debussy Letters*, p. 301), letters of 27 January and 1 September 1915. Debussy's 'respect' for Saint-Saëns's 'great age' (rather than any other qualities) may have been partly facetious, given their famed antipathy. Parisian lore has it that Saint-Saëns, on hearing once that Debussy was suffering from a stomach upset, retorted, 'Il a dû manger de sa propre musique' ('he must have been eating his own music').

14. Eigeldinger, *Chopin, Pianist and Teacher*, p. 275.

15. Long, *Au piano avec Claude Debussy*, pp. 25–6 and 36–7. Louis Laloy related that Debussy's playing of Chopin first made him understand the latter (Priest, *Louis Laloy*, p. 49).

16. Austin (ed.), *Debussy: Prélude à l'après-midi d'un faune*, p. 73.

17. Debussy's perfect pitch and strong key sense are entertainingly described by René Peter (*Claude Debussy*, pp. 50–1).

18. See Long, *Au piano avec Claude Debussy*, p. 63, corroborated by pianists including Jacques Février quoting Emma Debussy.

19. Information kindly supplied by Carl Schachter, who was told by Kenton.

20. See Eigeldinger, *Chopin, Pianist and Teacher*, p. 32 and Carbou, *La leçon d'interprétation d'Yvonne Lefébure*, p. 145. The tradition appears to have filtered, via Georges Mathias and his student José Tragó, to Tragó's pupil Manuel de Falla, who used to deplore pianists playing 'as if the keyboard is on fire, raising their hands and not making the sound at the bottom of the key' (Harper, *Manuel de Falla*, p. 179).

21. Romilly, 'Debussy professeur', p. 6.

22. Eigeldinger, 'Twenty-four Preludes op. 28: genre, structure, significance', pp. 181–93.

23. See *Claude Debussy: correspondance*, pp. 1915, 1922–3 and 1925.

24. Long, *Au piano avec Claude Debussy*, p. 37.

25. *Claude Debussy: correspondance*, pp. 1870–1927. While Debussy's methods were not those of modern urtext practice, his letters show a scrupulous editorial intent. In Example 6.8b–c the staccato dots and hairpins, absent from more recent urtext editions, compare tellingly with Example 6.8a.

26. Eigeldinger, *Chopin, Pianist and Teacher*, p. 54.

27. 'tout cela, c'est pour arriver à la "simplicité"'; quoted in Herlin, 'Une œuvre inachevée: *La Saulaie*', p. 7.

28. Marnat, *Ravel: souvenirs de Manuel Rosenthal*, p. 10.

29. *A Ravel Reader*, pp. 335–6 (first printed in *Le courrier musical* of 1 January 1910); however, see also p. 337 n1 regarding Ravel's complaint that *Le courrier musical* had mangled his text.
30. Orenstein, *Ravel, Man and Musician*, p. 205.
31. Ibid., pp. 242–3. Ravel's version replaced Diaghilev's earlier *Les Sylphides*; unfortunately Ravel's score and parts were later lost (see Nijinska, *Early Memoirs*, p. 508).
32. The original *Gaspard de la nuit* poems by Aloysius Bertrand were approximately contemporary with these Chopin works (though published only in 1842), suggesting an element of *Zeitgeist* shared with Chopin's friend Delacroix. Deborah Crisp ('Between the sublime and the terrible') notes how Chopin and Delacroix were both criticized in their time for cultivating what was perceived as ugly and macabre at the expense of 'beauty'.
33. Moscheles's *Étude* features a similar texture to Chopin's except that it gives the chromatic runs to the stronger, prehensile end of the right hand.
34. Delage, *Emmanuel Chabrier*, p. 48.
35. *Les écrits de Paul Dukas sur la musique*, pp. 205 and 517.
36. For other modal-thematic links between the two pieces see the music examples in Samson et al., *Falla–Chopin, la música más pura*, pp. 65–6.

CHAPTER 7

1. Reported in Delage, 'Debussy et Chabrier', p. 62.
2. Poulenc, *Emmanuel Chabrier*. Regarding Ravel see *A Ravel Reader*, notably p. 394; Ravel's piano teacher Henri Ghys was a longstanding friend of Chabrier (Delage, *Emmanuel Chabrier*, p. 86).
3. Other prominent examples can be found in the second system of Ravel's 'Pavane de la Belle au bois dormant' (*Ma mère l'Oye*), the penultimate page of Debussy's Violin Sonata (figure 5), Franck's *Prélude, Choral et Fugue* (bars 35–8), Debussy's *Ballade* (bars 94–6) and *Valse romantique* (bars 59–62), and virtually throughout Poulenc's music. A chromatic pendulum in thirds remarkably similar to Example 7.4b occurs in the overture to Chabrier's *Une éducation manquée*.
4. The melodic line of Example 7.5a can also be heard in the first movement of Fauré's First Piano Quartet of 1879, which may just antedate 'Paysage' – though we can only guess what fragments and improvisations these friends might have played informally to each other.
5. Poulenc observes this Chabrier–Debussy link (*Emmanuel Chabrier*, pp. 63–4) but absentmindedly misattributes it to the latter's *Arabesques*; the Fauré–Debussy one was noted by Jean-Michel Nectoux in *Fauré*, p. 57 and 'Debussy et Fauré', p. 18.
6. Compare with the equivalent transition into the recapitulation in the seventh of Ravel's *Valses nobles et sentimentales*.
7. These dissonant appoggiaturas in Chabrier can suggest an equivalent colour to that of a stopped hand-horn; one of the expressive secrets of playing him is arguably to catch this, for example in 'Improvisation' from the *Pièces pittoresques*, with the left hand's opening B♮ and the recurring expressive c♯s at the top of the third page.
8. See bars 5 and similar of *Jane* and bars 61 and 68 of the Menuet. According to Chabrier's letters he composed the *Impromptu* (first published in 1873 as *1er Impromptu*) in either 1865 or 1868 (*Emmanuel Chabrier: correspondance*, pp. 1136–7 and 1143). Plans to reprint it in the early 1890s foundered when the original plates (riddled with errors) proved unusable. Ricardo Viñes had the 1873 edition (Korevaar and Sampsel, 'The Ricardo Viñes Piano Music Collection', pp. 372–3 and 387).
9. Cobb, *Debussy's Letters to Inghelbrecht*, p. 26.

10. Debussy was doubtless linking the 'Spleen' poem with Verlaine's ill-fated marriage to Mathilde Mauté, daughter of Debussy's childhood piano teacher. The motive recurs in Debussy's unfinished opera *Rodrigue et Chimène* whose libretto, like that of *Gwendoline*, was by Catulle Mendès.

11. The following Poulenc quotations come from Poulenc, *Emmanuel Chabrier*, pp. 57 and 60–2.

12. Poulenc's memory may have undergone some rubato here: Risler's Pathé recordings are normally listed as having been made in 1917, when Poulenc was eighteen.

13. The following Ravel quotations come from Bruyr, *Maurice Ravel*, p. 35, Poulenc, *Emmanuel Chabrier*, p. 96, *A Ravel Reader*, pp. 303 and 394 ('Memories of a lazy child') and Nichols, *Ravel Remembered*, p. 164. Roland-Manuel (*Maurice Ravel*, pp. 20 and 22) recounts Ravel's discovery, as a student, of Chabrier's song *Chanson pour Jeanne*, which he enthusiastically took along to his bemused composition teacher Pessard and later declared central to his own style. In 1893 the teenaged Ricardo Viñes and Ravel were coached by the ailing Chabrier in his *Valses romantiques* before performing them in a concert. Jean Françaix quotes an amusing reported aftermath of this meeting (*De la musique et des musiciens*, pp. 171–2, English translation of the anecdote in Nichols, *Maurice Ravel: A Biography*). Viñes's memories of the encounter must have influenced the later recording of the *Valses romantiques* in 1955 by Viñes's pupils Poulenc and Marcelle Meyer (reissued in 1982 on CD: EMI Références C 151 73.125/6).

14. Roger Delage (*Emmanuel Chabrier*, p. 681) notes that Chabrier was among the subscribers who bought Manet's *Olympia* for the Louvre in 1889. To Ravel's Manet–Chabrier analogies we might add 'Mauresque' from the *Pièces pittoresques* relative to Manet's *Polichinelle* lithograph, of which Manet dedicated a copy to Chabrier (reproduced in Delage, *Chabrier* (Iconographie musicale), p. 67, Plate 36).

15. The first three quotations come from Delage, 'Debussy et Chabrier', pp. 57–9, the following one from Poulenc, *Emmanuel Chabrier*, p. 44.

16. Poulenc, *Emmanuel Chabrier*, pp. 110–12, as recounted by Inghelbrecht. Debussy's pupil Mme de Romilly recalled Debussy's untiring love of Chabrier's *Valses romantiques* and *Ode à la musique* which he respectively played with her and taught to her choir ('Debussy professeur', p. 3).

17. Falla, *On Music and Musicians*, p. 95.

18. Remark made to the musicians of the New York Philharmonic in 1910, as recounted by the bassoonist Benjamin Kohon (La Grange, *Gustav Mahler: chronique d'une vie*, vol. 3, p. 867). Besides *España*, Mahler conducted several renowned New York performances of Chabrier's *Ode à la musique*.

19. Lambert, *Music ho!*, pp. 171–2.

18. Françaix, *De la musique et des musiciens*, pp. 63 and 58. The statement appears nowhere else in the Stravinsky literature; Françaix perhaps heard it directly from Stravinsky. *Petites suites* must mean Stravinsky's arrangements for small orchestra of piano duet pieces composed in 1914–17.

CHAPTER 8

1. An earlier (1994) version of this chapter ('Debussy and the Orient') extends beyond the piano, notably by viewing *La mer* in relation to Indian music and Japanese art. The present analogies concerning 'Pagodes' are taken from there; some are quoted or paraphrased in Nectoux, *Harmonie en bleu et or*, pp. 206–7.

2. Regarding questions of 'influence', Neil Sorrell observes: 'with Debussy a much more fruitful word would be confirmation. It seems far more plausible that what he heard in 1889 confirmed what he had, at least subconsciously, always felt about music, and this experience went far deeper than a desire to imitate something new and exotic' (*A Guide to the Gamelan*, p. 3, quoted also in Cooke, *Britten and the Far East*, p. 5).

3. Bailly's shop and its habitués are described in Michelet, *Les compagnons de la hiéro-phanie*, pp. 66–88. Laloy later recalled, on first meeting Debussy in 1903, 'his sinuous face which reminded me of the Far East, calm out of courtesy' (Priest, *Louis Laloy*, p. 48).

4. At Debussy's prompting, Laloy published Segalen's Polynesian study 'Voix mortes: musiques maori' (under Segalen's pseudonym Max-Anély) in 1907; Segalen dedicated it to Debussy, who encouraged him to follow it with a study of Indian music.

5. See Pierné and Vidal, 'Souvenirs d'Achille Debussy', p. 11.

6. The word 'gamelan' means 'orchestra'; see *New Grove*, 'Indonesia'.

7. See *New Grove*, 'India'.

8. Annegret Fauser discusses all the Asian theatrical genres Debussy experienced there (*Musical Encounters at the 1889 World's Fair*, pp. 165–215); Nectoux also provides numerous illustrations (*Harmonie en bleu et or*, pp. 184–207). Other discussion comes in Devries, 'Les musiques d'extrême-orient à l'Exposition Universelle de 1889', Boyd, 'Debussy and the Javanese gamelan' and Mueller, 'Javanese influence on Debussy's *Fantaisie* and beyond'.

9. See Cooke, *Britten and the Far East*, p. 15, for details of the Balinese gamelan Poulenc heard, generally more rumbustious than the Javanese genre.

10. Laloy, *Debussy*, p. 33, and Blanche, 'Souvenirs sur Manet et Debussy'.

11. Mervyn Cooke (*Britten and the Far East*, p. 7) also observes that pagodas are rarely found in Indonesia.

12. The dominating 8- and 16-bar periods can still be viewed as gamelan metaphors, as observed by Helen Kasztelan ('Debussy's *Estampes*: a new approach to Salzerian interpretations'). Although mobile bass lines are not characteristic of gamelan, the various gongs in a large gamelan allow for different gongs in different cycles.

13. *Debussy on Music*, p. 278.

14. Another gamelan was donated in February 1887 to the Paris Conservatoire, where Debussy could have examined it, though his primary interest doubtless lay in what he could hear in performance.

15. Romilly, 'Debussy professeur', p. 18.

16. *Claude Debussy: Monsieur Croche et autres écrits*, p. 229; see also his remarks about percussion quoted in Joly-Segalen and Schaeffner, *Segalen et Debussy*, p. 107.

17. See particularly pp. 16–18 of *Le son dans la nature*. Michelet (*Les compagnons de la hiérophanie*, pp. 66–75) mentions Debussy's almost daily conversations with Bailly about 'the esoteric aspects of oriental and occidental music'; more on this appears in Henri de Régnier's 'Souvenirs sur Debussy'.

18. De Jong-Keesing, *Inayat Khan*, p. 121.

19. Sketchbook in the Robert O. Lehman collection, Morgan Library and Museum, New York, call number D289.5464.

20. Nectoux, *Harmonie en bleu et or*, p. 200.

21. Laloy, *La musique retrouvée*, p. 177; the piece is dedicated to Laloy – who shortly before had championed Ravel's *Histoires naturelles*, somewhat to Debussy's chagrin! In *Debussy*, p. 95, Laloy describes the piece as 'farther away than *Pagodes*, in a Far East less torrid and more solemn'.

22. Peter Platt, 'Debussy and the harmonic series', explores this in pioneering detail.

23. Information kindly supplied by Dr Reis Flora.

24. See Rao, *Rāganidhi: A Comparative Study of Hindustani and Karnatak Rāgas*, vol. 4 p. 193, and Gervais, 'Étude comparée des langages harmoniques de Fauré et de Debussy', p. 41.

25. See Michelet, *Les compagnons de la hiérophanie*, p. 75, de Jong-Keesing, *Inayat Khan*, pp. 120–1, and Musharaff Khan, *Pages in the Life of a Sufi*, p. 111. In London and America the players achieved some celebrity as the Court Musicians of Baroda.

26. Quoted in de Jong-Keesing, *Inayat Khan*, pp. 120–1, and Timbrell, *Prince of Virtuosos*, p. 46.

27. De Jong-Keesing, *Inayat Khan*, pp. 121–2.
28. Information kindly supplied by Hakiem van Lohuizen; some of it appears in Visser, 'Een muzikale Oost-West-ontmoeting'. Helpful information was also supplied by Mrs H. Teunissen of the International Sufi Movement in The Hague. Despite a mention by de Jong-Keesing (*Inayat Khan*, p. 122), Lohuizen sees no connection between Inayat Khan's music and the 'Pas de l'éléphant' in *La boîte à joujoux*, which Debussy footnoted (obviously in fun): 'Old Hindu chant still used in the training of elephants; it is constructed on the scale of "5-in-the-morning" and is obligatorily in 5-in-a-bar.'
29. Information from Hakiem van Lohuizen, who was told this by Musharaff Khan. The fate of the vīna is unknown: Debussy died before the brothers were able to return to Paris.
30. Khan, *Music*, p. 1.
31. *Claude Debussy: Monsieur Croche et autres écrits*, p. 246.
32. Musharaff Khan, *Pages from the Life of a Sufi*, p. 111.
33. *Claude Debussy: correspondance*, p. 2030 (letter of 30 September 1916); cf. p. 28 regarding Cyril Scott's related memoir.
34. Arkel and Gwendoline now live in the Musée Claude Debussy at Saint Germain-en-Laye, Gwendoline's two smaller enamel infants (they fit inside one another like *matryoshka* dolls) at the Centre de Documentation Claude Debussy in Paris.
35. These are reproduced in Nectoux, *Harmonie en bleu et or*, pp. 195 and 189; see also Lockspeiser, *Debussy: His Life and Mind*, vol. 2 pp. 23–6.
36. Nectoux, *Harmonie en bleu et or*, pp. 198 and 241 n34 (quoting Debussy's friends Paul-Jean Toulet and Vallery-Radot), Vallas, *Claude Debussy et son temps*, p. 367 (quoting Henri Malherbe), and Nichols, *Debussy Remembered*, pp. 203 (quoting Vallery-Radot) and 165–6 (quoting George Copeland).
37. See reproductions in Nectoux, *Harmonie en bleu et or*, pp. 185, 192–3, 197 and 201; the 'Poissons d'or' plaque is also reproduced on the front slip-cover of Roberts, *Images*, in Lesure, *Claude Debussy* (Iconographie musicale), p. 181 (back to front), and in Schmitz, *The Piano Works of Claude Debussy*, p. 46 (the only reproduction that shows its ornate *karakusa* frame).
38. Pahissa, *Manuel de Falla: His Life and Works*, pp. 47.
39. The decorated *Pelléas* score is in the Harry Ransom Humanities Research Center, University of Texas at Austin; the first edition covers of *Estampes* and *La mer* are reproduced in Nectoux, *Harmonie en bleu et or*, pp. 191 and 206.
40. For example, in 1915 he wrote to Jacques Durand: 'Last night, at midnight, I copied out the last note of the *Études* . . . Phew!. . . The most intricate Japanese *estampe* is child's play beside the graphics of some pages' (*Claude Debussy: correspondance*, p. 1940).
41. Bromfield, 'Japanese art' pp. 27–8, and LaFarge, 'An Essay on Japanese Art'.
42. For more detail see the Foreword and source notes in *Œuvres complètes de Claude Debussy* 1/3.
43. *Debussy on Music*, p. 44.
44. Ibid., p. 130.
45. Long, *Au piano avec Claude Debussy*, p. 148.
46. Argüelles, *Charles Henry*, pp. 86n and 138–9n.
47. Shah, *The Sufis*, passim.
48. Ibid., p. 270.

CHAPTER 9

1. Falla, *On Music and Musicians*, pp. 11 and 20–1. Albéniz's 'Córdoba' (from *Cantos de España* op. 232) typifies this mix of church and Moorish chant (like Córdoba's cathedral, originally its mosque).

2. Steven Baur notes that Stravinsky heard *Rapsodie espagnole* in St Petersburg in December 1909 just as he was starting on *Firebird* ('Ravel's "Russian" period', pp. 578–9), but also quotes Richard Taruskin regarding Ravel's debt in *Rapsodie espagnole* to Rimsky-Korsakov.

3. Brody, 'The Russians in Paris', p. 160.

4. Schaeffner, 'Debussy et ses rapports avec la musique russe', pp. 171–2.

5. See Schaeffner, 'Debussy et ses rapports avec la musique russe', p. 174, and Priest, *Louis Laloy*, pp. 48 and 51 n6. De Brayer's sources of *Sunless* and *Boris Godunov* were apparently scores that Saint-Saëns brought back from Russia early in 1876.

6. These ostinati arguably owe a shared debt to Chopin, but with a much more restrained colour than Chopin's nearest usages.

7. Delage, *Emmanuel Chabrier*, pp. 398–9, with particular reference to the article 'Moussorgski et Chabrier' in which the composer Pierre-Octave Ferroud compared *Boris* with *Le Roi malgré lui* and Musorgsky's *Pictures from an Exhibition* with Chabrier's *Pièces pittoresques*.

8. The progression is characteristically over a drone, and the passing ♯5 step in the rising alto or tenor line (arrowed in Example 9.3) can support either a diminished or an augmented chord. Russian obsession with the gesture from Glinka onwards is charted by Gerald Abraham (*On Russian Music*, pp. 259–60), Garden ('Balakirev's influence on Musorgsky', pp. 15–17), Taruskin ('Entoiling the Falconet') and DeVoto ('The Russian submediant in the nineteenth century'), though they mostly overlook its Schubertian ancestry (for example in the first movement development sections of the G minor Violin Sonata D.408 and A major Piano Sonata D.959, and in the second *Suleika* song D.717): only DeVoto observes a passing instance (without the drone) in Schubert's 1825 *Ave Maria*. Less exotic sounding examples (because they form part of longer diatonic modulations) can be found in the middle of Chopin's C♯ minor Waltz op. 64 no. 2 and the first movement in each of Dvořák's two piano quintets. As Taruskin observes, the Russians habitually used the device for exotic evocations (hence *nega*, pronounced '*nyega*', a Russian term for the seductive effect of a perceivedly sensual Orient), as in Balakirev's *Islamey* and *Tamara* (both of which Taruskin leaves unmentioned), Borodin's *Prince Igor* and Rimsky-Korsakov's *Scheherazade*. Mark DeVoto's term 'Russian sixth' for the progression is memorable but conflicts slightly with Abraham's use of the same term (*On Russian Music*, pp. 259–60) for a different albeit associated Russian usage of German sixth over a tonic drone.

9. Balakirev's first two mazurkas (his only ones composed before Fauré's) contain nothing as Slavic-sounding as Example 9.3a. Borodin's only prominent *nega* progressions in print by 1880 were in duet reductions (1875 and 1877) of his first two symphonies. Mark DeVoto spots Debussy's use of the progression in *Danse* (bars 239–46) and the orchestral 'Fêtes' as well as at the start of his 1880 Piano Trio (suggesting that Debussy's duets with Mme von Meck that summer included Borodin symphonies).

10. Regarding Fauré's contact with Taneyev and the uncertain date of Fauré's *Mazurka* see Nectoux, *Gabriel Fauré: A Musical Life*, pp. 48, 278 and 532.

11. I am grateful to Anastasia Belina for helpful information about Taneyev and for providing copies of his music from those years.

12. See Steven Baur, 'Ravel's "Russian" period', which goes only as far as the *Rapsodie espagnole* but essentially defines the terms of Ravel's usage in works like *Gaspard de la nuit*.

13. See Orenstein, *Ravel, Man and Musician*, p. 58, also *A Ravel Reader*, p. 346 for Ravel's description of *Islamey* as 'a masterpiece'.

14. Regarding *les Apaches* (a group of forward-looking artists that met regularly from 1900 to 1914) see Orenstein, *Ravel, Man and Musician*, pp. 28–9.

15. Stravinsky as quoted in Nichols, *Debussy Remembered*, p. 108.

16. Personal communication from Bennett Lerner. The relationship becomes amusingly graphic if we try starting Debussy's piece with the right hand an eighth-note early.

17. Maurice Dumesnil reported that his enthusiasm for 'Reflets dans l'eau' once caused his eviction from Philipp's Conservatoire class (Moldenhauer, 'From the library of a forgotten pioneer', p. 4).

18. See Schaeffner, 'Debussy et ses rapports avec la musique russe', pp. 164–5 and 173–4; as Schaeffner remarks, the fable hangs on Robert Godet's assumption that Debussy had nothing on his piano stand for several weeks except the neglected *Boris* score, open at the same page. The score originally came from Saint-Saëns (see note 5 to this chapter) and was lent by de Brayer to Debussy via Godet. François Lesure (*Claude Debussy: biographie critique*, p. 139) updates some details of Schaeffner's arguments, which raised considerable heat on first publication in 1953.

19. The first of Fauré's *Romances sans paroles* has a sequence of non-neapolitan Ab^7–D^7 alternations (bars 33–7; cf. also Ex. 1.4) that possibly anticipates Musorgsky's usage: although published in 1881, Fauré's piece appears to date from 1864, when he was still in his teens (Nectoux, *Gabriel Fauré: A Musical Life*, p. 527). For more on the history of Musorgsky's sequence see Taruskin, 'Chernomor to Kashchei', pp. 110–12 and 140.

20. *Debussy on Music*, pp. 200–1, '"La chambre d'enfants" de Moussorgsky'; some French sources translate the songs' title as *Enfantines*.

21. Debussy's own comments link *En blanc et noir* to Velázquez and Goya (*Claude Debussy: correspondance*, pp. 1905, 1909 and 1972), again implying Goya vis-à-vis Musorgsky.

22. Inghelbrecht, *Mouvement contraire*, pp. 190–2. The first Parisian staging of *Boris* (in Russian) was in 1908.

23. Mme de Romilly recalls obtaining every available Belaïeff duet edition of the 'Five' plus Glazunov to play at lessons with Debussy, who also taught her *Islamey* (Romilly, 'Debussy professeur', pp. 5–6).

24. Falla, *On Music and Musicians*, p. 95.

25. For documentation of the folkloric roots of *España* see Delage, *Emmanuel Chabrier*, pp. 287–93.

26. See Falla's essays on Debussy and Ravel, in *On Music and Musicians*, pp. 41–5 and 93–7, particularly p. 45.

27. For examples of this see Clark, *Isaac Albéniz: A Guide to Research*, p. 27.

28. Ibid., p. 13.

29. Falla, *On Music and Musicians*, p. 42. Several of the connections quoted in this paragraph come from Michael Christoforidis's paper 'The Moor's last sigh: Paris, symbolism and the Alhambra'.

30. Information from Michael Christoforidis and Elizabeth Kertesz. See also Fauser, *Musical Encounters at the 1889 Paris World Fair*, pp. 261–7, and Laurent, 'Andalousie au temps des Maures' (website).

31. Lockspeiser suggests this was Pedrell's 1906 Catalan collection *La Cançó popular catalana* (*Debussy: His Life and Mind*, vol. 2 p. 260n); Pedrell was mentor to Albéniz, Falla and Granados.

32. Brody, 'Viñes in Paris', pp. 50–1; less convincingly she includes *Pour le piano* in that assessment, a work Debussy wrote before he knew Viñes.

33. Mark DeVoto shows one (*Debussy and the Veil of Tonality*, p. 42) linking bars 95–8 of 'La sérénade interrompue' to bars 33–6 of 'El Albaicín' (and also to Example 9.8b here).

34. Pahissa, *Manuel de Falla: His Life and Works*, p. 48. In a written tribute to Albéniz (*Debussy on Music*, pp. 301–2) Debussy singles out 'El Albaicín' and 'Eritaña' from *Iberia*; he also observes Basque, Catalan and Andalusian distinctions in Albéniz's music while noting French influence on it. In conversation Michael Christoforidis has observed how close Debussy's (and Falla's) evocative treatment of Granada and the Alhambra often comes to that of Washington Irving's famous *Tales of the Alhambra* of 1832, a book Debussy could easily have known in French translation.

35. See Christoforidis, 'Manuel de Falla, Debussy and *La vida breve*'. It was mainly through Debussy's intervention that Durand published Falla's *Quatre pièces espagnoles* for piano in 1909.

36. Gubisch, 'La vie musicale à Paris', p. 224.
37. Ravel's 'Habanera' eventually appeared in both orchestral and two-piano form in 1908, as the third movement of his *Rapsodie espagnole*. Its original two-piano version, as the first of the two *Sites auriculaires*, was published by Éditions Salabert in 1975. The same blend of D♭^{7} and G^7 can be heard in Borodin's *Prince Igor* overture.
38. Entry for 24 March 1902 (Gubisch, *Le journal de Ricardo Viñes*). In personal correspondence Nina Gubisch suggests that the 'Valle' reference is to the village of San Carlos del Valle.
39. Nectoux, 'Albéniz et Fauré (correspondance inédite)'.
40. Koechlin, *Gabriel Fauré*, p. 71; Nectoux, *Camille Saint-Saëns & Gabriel Fauré: correspondance*, p. 139; Long, *Au piano avec Gabriel Fauré*, p. 35 (even if we treat as possible fancy her phrase 'Some trace of Arab blood must have run in Fauré's veins . . .').
41. Wallace, *Nationalism and Identity in the Solo Piano Music of Gabriel Fauré and Isaac Albéniz*. Jean-Michel Nectoux also observes this affinity (*Gabriel Fauré: A Musical Life*, p. 381).
42. Roland-Manuel, *Maurice Ravel*, p. 14, and Narbaïtz, *Maurice Ravel, un orfèvre basque*, p. 85. Ravel *père* had been appointed by Gustave Eiffel as engineer in charge of building the railway from Madrid to Irún, a main line that negotiates some very challenging terrain and still runs successfully today.
43. See *A Ravel Reader*, pp. 126–8. Ravel's fluency in Basque is endorsed by Narbaïtz (*Maurice Ravel, un orfèvre basque*) and Rousseau-Plotto (*Ravel: portraits basques*); it was apparently Mme Ravel's first language (and Spanish her second). Her name also appears as Maria Deluarte, even 'de Huarte': see Narbaïtz, *Maurice Ravel, un orfèvre basque*, pp. 85–8.
44. Falla, *On Music and Musicians*, pp. 96–7.
45. Roland-Manuel, *Maurice Ravel*, pp. 14–15 and 122. Regarding Ravel's Spanish heritage see also Le Bordays, 'L'Espagne ravélienne', and 'Pour Ravel' by Ravel's friend André Suarès.
46. Diary entry for 23 November 1888, in Gubisch, 'La vie musicale à Paris ', p. 12.
47. Maurice Dumesnil, quoted in Moldenhauer, 'From the library of a forgotten pioneer', p. 4, a claim that receives implicit support from Viñes's diaries. Viñes's one fall from grace with Ravel, over the tempo of 'Le gibet', came long after Ravel's solo piano output was complete (see p. 321).
48. A specific Basque link to these is the bandas tradition of village bands with brass and percussion all blaring full blast (it has to be heard to be believed).
49. Falla, *On Music and Musicians*, pp. 96–7.

CHAPTER 10

1. I quote in particular the harpsichordist Nicholas Parle and the violist Lucy Robinson. Like many practitioners of this repertoire I prefer to call this French era classical (as Debussy's contemporaries did) rather than baroque, inspired as it was more by ancient Greece than by rococo Italy.
2. Recounted by Paul Poujaud (to whom Franck addressed the remark) to Alfred Cortot, who quotes it in *La musique française de piano*, vol. 1 p. 188. Debussy may well have been at that concert (of the Société nationale de musique) on 9 April 1881, in which Marie Poitevin performed 'Idylle', 'Improvisation', 'Danse villageoise', 'Menuet pompeux', 'Sous bois' and 'Scherzo-valse'.
3. Although not published complete until 1982, *Les Boréades* was already something of a *cause* in the nineteenth century: the excerpts performed by Diémer's Société des instruments anciens in two concerts of May 1896 and another of May 1899 (Becker-Derex, *Louis Diémer et le clavecin*, pp. 46, 78 and 81) were not necessarily first hearings.
4. Roger Delage (*Emmanuel Chabrier*, p. 252) notes that Chabrier's library included Rameau's *Les surprises de l'amour* (in what must have been the first edition of 1757)

and three volumes of Scarlatti sonatas but not Couperin (to which, though, he could easily have had access).

5. Ellis, *Interpreting the Musical Past*, p. 90.

6. See Becker-Derex, *Louis Diémer et le clavecin*, pp. 49–50, 53–4 and 59, and Eigeldinger, *L'univers musical de Chopin*, p. 95, who also list editions from the 1840s onwards by Méreaux (an associate of Chopin), Laurens and Farrenc.

7. The instrument, now in the Russell Collection, Edinburgh, is shown on pp. 18 and 28 of Becker-Derex, *Louis Diémer et le clavecin*. As pianist Diémer (already encountered in Chapter 9 with *Islamey*) premièred many new works including Franck's *Variations symphoniques* of 1885 and Fauré's Twelfth Nocturne and Twelfth Barcarolle of 1915–16.

8. For programme details see Becker-Derex, *Louis Diémer et le clavecin*, pp. 40–1, and Fauser, *Musical Encounters at the 1889 Paris World's Fair*, pp. 27–42 and 317–19.

9. Ibid., p. 30.

10. Becker-Derex, *Louis Diémer et le clavecin*, pp. 46, 75 and 77.

11. Diémer's edition is quoted here and in Example 10.2 as the one Fauré and Debussy would have known; Diémer's only additions in each case are the phrasing and dynamics.

12. The pianist Sébastien Risler kindly supplied copies of his grandfather's audio recordings, now mostly obtainable on CD.

13. Some circumspection is in order here since a surviving manuscript of *Aubade* shows the variant title *Sérénade* (and other deleted headings possibly not intended for the piece, as Roger Delage notes in *Emmanuel Chabrier*, p. 333). The title 'Aubade' probably comes from another manuscript of the piece now unlocated (see the commentary to the Dover edition).

14. See Jourdan-Morhange, 'Ravel à Montfort-l'Amaury', pp. 165–6, and Marnat, *Ravel: souvenirs de Manuel Rosenthal*, pp. 178–9.

15. *A Ravel Reader*, p. 32.

16. Ibid., pp. 155–6, and Roger Nichols's preface to the London Peters edition of *Le tombeau*.

17. The latter is doubtless unlabelled because its role as part of the Prélude avoids normal gigue periodicity; it also precedes the suite's 'official' Gigue in $\frac{6}{4}$ dotted rhythm. Its $\frac{12}{8}$ rhythm and natural tempo match most of Bach's gigues and the '2me Gigue en Rondeau' from Rameau's *Pièces de clavecin* of 1724.

18. The Italians, having had a Parisian base for several decades, were expelled by Louis XIV in 1697 after they lampooned his powerful mistress Mme de Maintenon. They were brought back a year after his death. See also Anya Suschitzky's discussion in 'Debussy's Rameau', pp. 405–8.

19. *Debussy on Music*, p. 217.

20. For more discussion of this relative to Debussy, including the *bergamasque* (a danced *commedia* derivative whose name puns on the town of Bergamo), see Roberts, *Images*, pp. 87–112.

21. See the last facsimile page in the Presser edition of *Étude retrouvée* and Orledge, *Debussy and the Theatre*, pp. 206–16. Orledge observes French overture rhythms in Debussy's sketches for this project. The topic of harlequinade was also fresh in Debussy's mind then from his ballet *La boîte à joujoux*.

22. Tunley, *François Couperin and 'The Perfection of Music'*, p. 8.

23. Ibid., p. 7, quoting Le Sieur Faret, *L'Honneste-Homme, ou, l'Art de plaire à la cour*, p. 34.

24. Quoted in Nichols, *Debussy Remembered*, p. 161.

25. *François Couperin and 'The Perfection of Music'*, pp. 8–11; see also Okamoto, *Between the Ancient and the Modern*, passim.

26. See Lesure, *Claude Debussy: biographie critique*, p. 482; Debussy miswrote 'IXV' for 'XIV'.

27. For more on Watteau's use of arabesque decoration – the '*style moderne*' of his time that directly inspired turn-of-the-century *Art nouveau* – see Okamoto, *Between the*

Ancient and the Modern, especially p. 90, and Suschitzky, 'Debussy's Rameau', pp. 408 and 412.

28. *Claude Debussy: correspondance*, p. 1835. Debussy's last phrase relates interestingly to the view argued many years later by Michael Levey ('The real theme of Watteau's *Embarkation for Cythera*', p. 180, quoted in Roberts, *Images*, p. 104) that Watteau's painting depicts not an excited embarkation but a more jaded departure from the island (Watteau left the painting untitled). In an article of January 1913 Debussy similarly referred to the 'plaintive figures' of Watteau's landscapes (*Debussy on Music*, p. 273).

29. See the Foreword to the *Œuvres complètes* 1/3, p. xvii. Viñes's diary entry refers back to another one for 13 June which names 'L'Ile [*sic*] joyeuse', a detail overlooked by François Lesure who associated the July event with the first series of *Images* (*Claude Debussy: biographie critique*, p. 243). The gallery in question is now the Clore Gallery at Tate Britain, London.

30. *Debussy Letters*, p. 188.

31. Debussy's fondness for Couperin's lower tessituras suggests explorations independent of Diémer's editions and performances which, as Katharine Ellis notes (*Interpreting the Musical Past*, p. 91), tended to avoid lower registers in favour of bird evocations and the higher reaches of the keyboard.

32. The printed title pages of Debussy's three completed sonatas of 1915–17 are particularly similar in style to the eighteenth-century title pages of Leclair's violin sonatas. Debussy's never-completed plan was for six sonatas, of which the fourth and sixth were to use a harpsichord. For some discussion of Debussy's Sonatas relative to Rameau and Couperin see Messing, *Neoclassicism in Music*, pp. 45–9.

33. Couperin's slightly different meaning of the symbol – a fractionally delayed attack – reads interestingly against Debussy's usage, normally readable as a breathing point.

34. Official title *Variations, Interlude et Finale pour piano, sur un thème de J.-Ph. Rameau*.

35. *Debussy on Music*, pp. 110–13.

36. For more discussion see Suschitzky, 'Debussy's Rameau', and François Lesure, *Claude Debussy: biographie critique*, p. 237.

37. An odd note emerges from Ravel's expressed view of Rameau as too dry (or 'trop raisonnable') beside Couperin or Lully (*A Ravel Reader*, p. 363, also Marnat, *Ravel: souvenirs de Manuel Rosenthal*, p. 172) – a puzzling charge against one who orchestrated so boldly or produced the almost Ravelian 'L'enharmonique'. If Ravel was perhaps tilting at Rameau's appropriation by the Schola Cantorum, it may also reflect some literally stuffy performances: d'Indy used to pad out Rameau's orchestral textures in performances that increasingly irked Debussy (see Suschitzky, 'Debussy's Rameau', p. 437, and *Debussy Letters*, p. 306). Couperin *le grand*, part of Louis XIV's court, was also more at the heart of Ravel's idealized *vieille France*. Nonetheless, Marcel Marnat (*Maurice Ravel*, p. 424) opines that *Le tombeau de Couperin* echoes Rameau more than Couperin, and Ravel's own library was well stocked with Rameau operas (Nectoux, 'Maurice Ravel et sa bibliothèque musicale', p. 53).

38. Robinson, 'Forqueray *Pièces de Viole*', pp. 262, 264–5 and 269.

39. See Eigeldinger, *L'univers musical de Chopin*, pp. 85–98, regarding Chopin's possible knowledge of Couperin's music. Several of the affinities Eigeldinger lists leave Chopin in a pivotal position between Couperin and Debussy.

40. Priest, *Louis Laloy*, pp. 23, 49 and 228.

41. Eigeldinger, *L'univers musical de Chopin*, p. 139.

42. See p. 155 below, also Nectoux, 'Debussy and Fauré', pp. 20–1, *Gabriel Fauré: His Life through his Letters*, pp. 176–7, and Fauré's reference to Watteau in *Gabriel Fauré: A Life in Letters*, p. 181. Durand may again have had a hand in the title *Masques et bergamasques*, one Debussy had planned to use; see Orledge, *Debussy and the Theatre*, pp. 151–5.

43. Nichols, *Ravel Remembered*, p. 141.
44. Fauquet, *César Franck*, p. 607; composed in 1884, the work was premièred and published in 1885 (cf. Chapter 6 above regarding Debussy's First Book of Preludes in relation to the 1910 Chopin centenary).
45. 'J'étais, au fond, tellement féru de *père* Bach'; letter from Chabrier to Hermann Levi dated 6 November 1890, in *Emmanuel Chabrier: correspondance*, p. 831.
46. Joly-Segalen and Schaeffner, *Segalen et Debussy*, p. 107, and Lesure, *Claude Debussy: biographie critique*, p. 156.
47. Nectoux, *Gabriel Fauré: A Musical Life*, p. 42.
48. See Fauré, 'Souvenirs', p. 7. The adolescent works include the opening 'Berceuse' of *Dolly* and the two fugues in the *Pièces brèves*.

CHAPTER 11

1. Perlemuter and Jourdan-Morhange, *Ravel according to Ravel*, p. 35.
2. The traditional French guild of jugglers, acrobats, magicians, bear- and monkey-trainers, minstrels and other entertainers, whose attempts to control the musicians of Louis XIV in the 1690s and 1700s were legally thwarted by Couperin and his colleagues (see Tunley, *François Couperin and 'The Perfection of Music'*, p. 110). The last part of Couperin's *11ᵉ Ordre* lampoons the guild in a mock five-act mini-farce, *Les Fastes de la grande et ancienne Mxnxstrxndxsx* [Ménestrandise].
3. Romilly, *Debussy professeur*, p. 4.
4. Scott, *Bone of Contention*, p. 128, and Marcel Ciampi in conversation in 1976.
5. Issued respectively by Fromont and Durand. Durand's catalogue already included a duet transcription by Bizet of Schumann's op. 56 *Sechs Stücke*; Bizet's own *Jeux d'enfants* echo Schumann as strongly as anything in the French repertoire.
6. Priest, *Louis Laloy*, p. 49.
7. Delage, *Emmanuel Chabrier*, p. 255.
8. Now in the Fogg Art Museum, Cambridge, Mass., this is the second of Manet's two oil portraits of Chabrier, both reproduced in Delage, *Chabrier* (Iconographie musicale), pp. 63–4 (plates 32–3).
9. Nichols, *Ravel Remembered*, pp. 16 and 116, as recounted by Jacques-Émile Blanche around 1900 and Poulenc in 1917: both mention the inherent 'contrary' or 'paradoxical' element in his *boutades*.
10. Roland-Manuel, *Maurice Ravel*, p. 18.
11. See Orenstein, *Ravel, Man and Musician*, p. 241; only parts of Ravel's orchestration survive.
12. Marnat, *Ravel: souvenirs de Manuel Rosenthal*, pp. 8–9. Rosenthal adds, 'It was amazing to hear this man so often considered cold, even glacial, express himself thus' and recalls Ravel's special fondness for Schumann's *Das Paradies und die Peri*.
13. *A Ravel Reader*, pp. 386–7.
14. Orenstein, *Ravel, Man and Musician*, p. 124.
15. Long, *Au piano avec Gabriel Fauré*, p. 158; the affinity with 'Pour les sixtes' was pointed out by Roger Nichols (in conversation).
16. A common possible source here is the first movement coda in Beethoven's 'Eroica' Symphony, though Fauré's usage more closely echoes Schumann's.
17. Recounted by Fauré in his 1922 obituary of Saint-Saëns, quoted in Nectoux, *Camille Saint-Saëns & Gabriel Fauré: correspondance*, p. 142.
18. See *Gabriel Fauré: His Life through his Letters*, p. 72.
19. Nectoux, *Gabriel Fauré: A Musical Life*, p. 43.
20. Marnat, *Ravel: souvenirs de Manuel Rosenthal*, p. 8. A miniature silhouette of Weber still hangs next to the music-room door in Ravel's house at Montfort l'Amaury.

21. *Emmanuel Chabrier: correspondance*, pp. 411–13, letter to his publisher Georges Costallat.
22. *Debussy on Music*, pp. 100–8; a mention of 'the wonderful *Freischütz* overture' just a week later (ibid., p. 113) forms a postscript to Debussy's first Rameau panegyric.
23. Nectoux, 'Maurice Ravel et sa bibliothèque musicale', p. 55; these scores are now mostly housed in *F-Pn* musique.
24. 'Conseils pour interpréter Ravel', pp. 89–91; Merlet also compares 'Scarbo' to Liszt's 'Feux-follets' and first Mephisto Waltz, and links Ravel generally with elements of *Mazeppa*.
25. Cortot, *La musique française de piano*, vol. 1 p. 73.
26. Walker, *Franz Liszt: The Final Years*, pp. 475–6, and Lesure, *Claude Debussy: biographie critique*, pp. 83–4.
27. Published by Breitkopf, the *Trauermarsch* follows on from a 30-bar *Trauervorspiel*. The *Portraits* first appeared complete in 1956. Liszt's ostinato of Example 11.3a is taken in turn from Mihály Mosonyi's Elegy for István Széchenyi (1860), a piece Debussy is unlikely to have known. I am grateful to Alan Walker for helpful information on this topic.
28. Four years earlier Fauré recounted in a letter how Liszt had spontaneously played him his new piano version of *Cantico del sol di San Francesco*: 'He was like a humble child showing you a piece of homework!' (*Gabriel Fauré: His Life through his Letters*, p. 105).
29. The brackets above Example 11.5a also mark out the opening bass line of *Tristan* (Ex. 11.5b), as does the main first movement theme in Franck's Symphony (D–C♯–F–E–A, then F–E–A♭–G–C). The Symphony's orchestration – not least the cor anglais and bass clarinet solos – strongly echoes that of *Tristan*.
30. For which Wagner never forgave Offenbach, whose title resonates again in Saint-Saëns's *Carnaval des animaux*. A similar fate has so far eluded (dare I say it?) *Pelléas et Mélisande*, except for an amusing spoof on its libretto by Proust; a burlesque of César Franck's Symphony can be found ('The old geezer') in Peter Warlock's *Two Codpieces* for piano duet.
31. Observed in conversation by Robert Orledge.
32. Quoted in *Emmanuel Chabrier: correspondance*, p. xii. Chabrier's song *Ruy Blas* from the 1870s could easily pass for Wolf.
33. Watson, *Bruckner*, p. 27. Might Chabrier and Fauré have heard this event too?
34. Other examples include 'Fêtes' from the orchestral *Nocturnes* (bar 23, *ff*, *le double plus lent*), the song 'Chevaux de bois' of the 1880s and the *ff* ostinato in the Toccata of *Pour le piano*.
35. Phillips, 'Viennese fundamental bass tradition', p. 402.

CHAPTER 12

1. For a comparative study of the song and the prelude in relation to the poem's form see Routley, 'Debussy and Baudelaire's *Harmonie du soir*'. One of Debussy's very first song settings, of Gautier's 'Les papillons' in 1881, follows a simpler type of *pantoum*: Debussy carefully includes the word on his manuscript (see Rolf, 'Debussy, Gautier, and "Les papillons"', p. 104).
2. Newbould, 'Ravel's *Pantoum*'.
3. Poulenc, *Emmanuel Chabrier*, pp. 24–5.
4. Ravel's earlier *Menuet antique* does something similar but without the same degree of compaction, following the combined themes with a more standard recapitulation.
5. The London Peters edition counts first- and second-time bars separately: with concurrent bar-counting Examples 12.3b–12.5 count as bars 153–4, 64–9, 89–94 and 153–9.
6. James, *Ravel*, p. 46.

7. This goes aptly with Baudelaire's line, 'That which is not slightly distorted lacks sensible appeal', quoted in Orenstein, *Ravel, Man and Musician*, p. 123n.
8. *A Ravel Reader*, p. 393. Ravel's orchestral version, which allows more space for orchestral crescendo, is carefully tailored to make up an alternative, equally viable set of large-scale proportions: in brief, the two climaxes of the central section mark the respective halfway points from the start to the end of the piece and from the start of the central section to the end of the piece.
9. Stuckenschmidt, *Maurice Ravel: Variations on his Life and Work*, p. 149.

Chapter 13

1. This adds weight to Poulenc's linking of the *Pièces pittoresques* with Debussy's Preludes: like each book of Preludes the *Pièces pittoresques* form a coherent 40-minute cycle if performed complete. Surviving manuscript fragments suggest that Chabrier initially headed each piece just with a roman numeral, as Debussy later did with his Preludes.
2. Cortot, *La musique française de piano*, vol. 2 p. 49.
3. For related hyper- and hypometric structures in Schubert see Howat, 'Architecture as drama in late Schubert' and 'Reading between the lines of tempo and rhythm in the B-flat Sonata, D.960'.

Chapter 14

1. Dumesnil's recollections of his teacher Ricardo Viñes and his resultant introduction to Debussy are quoted in Moldenhauer, 'From the library of a forgotten pioneer', pp. 3–4.
2. This may well be the coal merchant Debussy met through the impresario Gabriel Astruc during an earlier fuel shortage: according to Astruc the coal merchant 'had a pretty wife who was also an excellent musician', and some anthracite was duly supplied 'in return for an inscription on her copy of *Pelléas*' (Nichols, *Debussy Remembered*, p. 109).
3. For fuller details see the preface to *Œuvres complètes* 1/3, Howat, 'En route for *L'isle joyeuse*', and Vanhulst, 'L'éditeur bruxellois Schott frères et *D'un cahier d'esquisses* de Claude Debussy'.
4. 'Hommage à Rameau' figures on the contract for the *Images* that Debussy signed with Durand in July 1903.
5. See *Claude Debussy: correspondance*, p. 813.
6. Robert Orledge has suggested (in conversation) that the central piece could alternatively have been 'Clair de lune', also in D♭ and the most musically modern piece in the four-movement *Suite bergamasque* eventually published in 1905. Early announcements (around 1904–5) for this *Suite bergamasque* listed its third piece as 'Promenade sentimentale' (again a poem by Verlaine) instead of 'Clair de lune', raising the query of whether the latter was just a change of title or a change of piece.
7. Choudens rather irrelevantly added a no. 4, the duet *Marche écossaise* which he had bought separately.
8. Giraud, *Paul Loyonnet*, p. 231 ('Je ne me souvenais pas que c'était si joli!').
9. See Nectoux, *Gabriel Fauré: A Musical Life*, pp. 336–9 and 556–7: the ballet used Fauré's orchestrations of *Madrigal* and *Clair de lune* and one by Marcel Samuel-Rousseau of *Le plus doux chemin*.
10. See *A Ravel Reader*, pp. 245–6, and Zank, *Maurice Ravel: A Guide to Research*, pp. 367–8.
11. The piece may originally date from 1899 or 1901 (see Howat, '"Un tas de petites choses" et de petits mystères pour quatre mains').

CHAPTER 15

1. 'This rhythm must have the sonorous sense of a sad and frozen background landscape.'
2. See notably Long, *Au piano avec Maurice Ravel*, p. 22.
3. Long, *Au piano avec Claude Debussy*, p. 43. The *Œuvres complètes* omit the indication but explain its source background.
4. See Burkhart, 'Debussy plays "La Cathédrale engloutie" and solves metrical mystery', also Debussy *Œuvres complètes* 1/5, the Dover Preludes facsimile, and *Debussy in Proportion*, pp. 159–62. Acquaintances of Debussy who recorded the piece in this manner include Alfred Cortot, George Copeland and Yvonne Lefébure. Lefébure disarmingly said she'd never thought of playing it any other way (information from Tamás Vesmas; see also Carbou, *La leçon de musique d'Yvonne Lefébure*, p. 140). Henri Busser's orchestration, reportedly commissioned in 1917, indicates *battez les noires* at bars 1 and 13, *battez les blanches* at bars 7 and 22, *Mouvt du début* at bar 84, ♩ = 66 at bar 1, and ♩ = 53 [*sic*] at bar 7. In *De Pelléas aux Indes galantes*, p. 204, Busser recalls letting Debussy check his orchestration in 1917 (his manuscript leaves some ambiguity of date).
5. For possible explanations see the Dover facsimile (which shows Debussy at one point treating the two notations as equivalent) and the commentary to *Œuvres complètes* 1/5. The equivalence also follows a usage from Rameau's time: in setting French speech $\frac{2}{4}$ metre was always avoided and written instead as $\frac{2}{2}$, the ♩ tacitly equal to ♩ in surrounding $\frac{3}{4}$ or $\frac{4}{4}$ bars (see Tunley, 'The union of words and music in seventeenth-century French song'). Rameau's *Les fêtes de Polymnie*, edited by Debussy just before he composed his Preludes, shows examples of this in the opening recitative.
6. See bars 26–30 in the second of the *Nuits blanches*, first published by Durand in 2000; a duplicate autograph fragment confirms the equivalence.
7. Walter Gieseking advised counting bar 81 onwards in six to maintain 'absolutely strict time' under the notated crossbeats (Elder, *Pianists at Play*, p. 227).
8. Long, *Au piano avec Claude Debussy*, p. 103.
9. Columbia LF41, recorded 1930, reissued since on various LP or CD transfers.
10. The piece's autograph shows that bars 64–7 were an afterthought: bar 63 originally led straight to the present bar 68, which had the same chord as the present bar 64.
11. See the last page of 'Hommage à S. Pickwick'. Debussy's never-completed operetta on Poe's *The Devil in the Belfry* was intended to include a whistled part for the Devil. At the start of 'Le matin d'un jour de fête' in his orchestral *Ibéria* (just after the introductory passage which the piece shares with the prelude 'La sérénade intérrompue') Debussy had in mind 'urchins whistling' (*Debussy Letters*, p. 217).
12. And perhaps even the wooden leg of a night-watchman, in the second interruption in 'La sérénade interrompue' (Schmitz, *The Piano Works of Claude Debussy*, p. 7).
13. Durand, *Souvenirs d'un éditeur de musique*, p. 74.
14. A vocal reading is supported by Routley, '*Des pas sur la neige*: Debussy in Bilitis's footsteps'.
15. Neil Heyde (*Claude Debussy, rhétoricien français*, p. 295) observes the unavoidable compromise this entails at the piano, whether or not one re-sounds the Es at that point.
16. Nichols, *Debussy Remembered*, p. 160.
17. *Debussy Letters*, p. 274.
18. The matter of grace notes versus measured notation is further affected by a performing habit of the era – a remnant of French overture practice – in which short note groups were often understood as compressed or compressible (along with overdotting), in ways that later twentieth-century practice came to outlaw. Robert Philip (*Early Recordings and Musical Style*, p. 92) observes that recordings of Poulenc's piano playing right up to the 1950s show this sort of compression.
19. Giraud, *Paul Loyonnet*, p. 322.

20. Example 15.8 shows the spatial problem already starting to impinge at bar 18 beat 2 (the bass octave). Some editions rebeam the rising scales from bar 19 as a means of correcting the values within each beat, leaving the larger disparity across the ostinato unaddressed.

21. Regarding the musical saw (the solo cadenza trills in the Concerto in G) see Perlemuter and Jourdan-Morhange, *Ravel according to Ravel*, p. 91. Debussy is similarly reported as imitating the musical saw in his Violin Sonata (first movement, around rehearsal figure 3: see Poulet, note to Arion CD ARN68228).

22. Ravel's later orchestration of 'Alborada del gracioso' answers that by almost doubling the length of the piece's final crescendo (bars 213–18 in the piano version).

23. Thieffry, *Alfred Cortot, Cours d'interprétation*, p. 85.

24. 'C'est ça'; quoted in Roger Nichols's preface to the London Peters edition of *Jeux d'eau* and in *A Ravel Reader*, p. 571; Ravel apparently later prompted her, 'half-serious, half-joking, "transmit the tradition".'

25. These are quoted in *A Ravel Reader*, pp. 515–16 (Appendix C).

26. Fascinating echoes of *Pelléas* can be heard in Debussy's *Images [oubliées]* of 1894, notably the end of the first piece (cf. the end of Act 1), then the sequential descents at the central climax of the central Sarabande, which can be heard again in Act 2 Scene 1 – not long before Mélisande's ring falls into the well accompanied by exactly the arpeggio that launches the central climax of the third *Image*. Other echoes of *Pelléas* can be heard in the Prélude of *Pour le piano* (just before the main recapitulation: cf. Act 3 Scene 2); *Masques* (again just before the main recapitulation: cf. various of Golaud's appearances from Act 3 Scene 2 on); 'Reflets dans l'eau' and 'Pour les arpèges composés' (interlude into Act 3 Scene 3); 'Serenade for the Doll' (Act 4 Scene 3) and the *Berceuse héroïque* (end of Act 1 Scene 2).

27. Information from Philip Lasser. In a letter of 1917 to Robert Godet, Debussy mentions his 'low tolerance of noise' (*Debussy Letters*, p. 325).

CHAPTER 16

1. Some older critical editions, notably Henle, use parentheses for editorial additions, causing confusion with Debussy's own use of parentheses. For a summary of sensible editorial practice see Grier, *The Critical Editing of Music*.

2. See the commentary in Joël-Marie Fauquet's Éditions du Marais editions of Franck's two piano triptychs.

3. Information from Vlado Perlemuter. Mme Long's claims to authority take something of a dent from Ravel's reported reference to her in his last few years, when he was often unable to recall names, as 'celle qui ne joue pas si bien du piano' (Marnat, *Ravel: souvenirs de Manuel Rosenthal*, pp. 184–5).

4. Grier, *The Critical Editing of Music*, p. xiii and passim.

5. I once saw this point made unforgettably if inadvertently by an editor who banged the table with his fist to emphasize the statement 'We must be scientifically objective about this!'

6. See *Œuvres complètes* 1/3, p. XII: Debussy uses the word *nuances* there in the normal French sense of dynamics and articulation rather than fluctuations of tempo.

7. The engravers in question were among the best: Charles Douin engraved most of Debussy's and Ravel's mature works and Fauré's late works for Durand; Fauré's earlier music was mostly engraved by the renowned Leipzig firm of C. G. Röder.

8. See *A Ravel Reader*, p. 218, for Ravel's correction of a printed *Andante* ♩ = 68 to *Animé* ♩ = 168 in the piano score of *Daphnis et Chloé* (starting the final $\frac{5}{4}$ dance): the misprint remains uncorrected today.

9. See *Camille Saint-Saëns & Gabriel Fauré: correspondance*, pp. 115–18: in bars 376, 378 and 382 left hand beat 2 should be as in bars 372 and 373 (the third and fourth bars of the final *allegro* section). Fauré even recopied the passage for Saint-Saëns without at first noticing anything amiss (ibid., p. 117); his 1908 Hupfeld piano roll corrects it, probably unconsciously.

10. The 'Ondine' example was noted by Ravel's friend Lucien Garban; see Roger Nichols's commentary in the London Peters edition.

11. This issue, along with ambiguous readings of ⁒ signs, famously arises in several Schubert manuscripts and original editions.

12. See Long, *Au piano avec Claude Debussy*, pp. 63–4, and the commentary to *Œuvres complètes* 1/3. Molinari's orchestration, dated 1917, was published by Durand in 1923.

13. The manuscript of *"Les fées"* omits to repeat the key signature on new systems; that of 'Pagodes' indicates bar 66 merely as a repetition of bar 16.

14. See for example *Ma mère l'Oye* ('Les entretiens de la Belle et de la Bête' and 'Le jardin féerique'), the piano *Prélude* of 1913, the Passacaille of the Piano Trio, *Berceuse sur le nom de Gabriel Fauré*, the Concerto for Left Hand (rehearsal figures 9 and 10 and the final cadenza) and all through *Daphnis et Chloé*.

15. See the commentary to *Œuvres complètes* 1/5. In the manuscript the passage is written out only once.

16. It happened in his Sonata for Two Pianos: see Schmidt, *The Music of Francis Poulenc*, p. 428.

17. The autograph has a system change exactly there in mid-bar, leaving a small amount of space at the start of the new system but fully notating the rest of the bar.

18. In this process of recopying, Fauré's autograph *cresc.* from the last beat of bar 31 was lost.

19. Later reprints of the first edition joined up the double beam at the final *c″*, perhaps mostly for visual reasons that overlooked – and masked – the underlying musical problem.

CHAPTER 17

1. Elder, *Pianists at Play*, p. 74, and Perlemuter and Jourdan-Morhange, *Ravel d'après Ravel*, p. 18 (Hélène Jourdan-Morhange then replies, 'The great difficulty in Ravel is to *jouer souple* without being dragged into rubato').

2. Nectoux, 'Entretien avec Emmanuel Fauré-Fremiet', p. 17, Jourdan-Morhange, *Mes amis musiciens*, pp. 22–3, and H. Abraham, *Un art de l'interprétation*, p. 212. See also Long, *Au piano avec Gabriel Fauré*, p. 103 and Nectoux, *Gabriel Fauré, a musical life*, pp. 43, 45 & 294.

3. Nichols, *Debussy Remembered*, pp. 158–9, 161 and 186, Giraud, *Paul Loyonnet*, pp. 229–31, Long, *Au piano avec Claude Debussy*, pp. 38 and 41–2, and Schmitz, *The Piano Music of Claude Debussy*, pp. 37–8. Walter Gieseking (who didn't know the composers personally) observes tellingly that in this repertoire 'The indications *"cédez"* and *"serrez"* must be played with great discretion. They signify no more change than the moderate rubato of the romantic German style' (Elder, *Pianists at Play*, p. 249).

4. Long, *Au piano avec Claude Debussy*, pp. 46–7, 74 and 115. While Mme Long's books famously tend to inflate her role and importance, her musical gist here is supported by others' accounts, and alertness to her prose often lets us distinguish her own opinions from memories of what the composers said.

5. Bathori, *On the Interpretation of the Mélodies of Claude Debussy*, p. 28. Her recordings, in which she accompanies herself, reveal (like Croiza's) occasional judicious rubato that intensifies the normally taut rhythmic rein she keeps on the music – for example

by compressing the opening upward run in Debussy's *Chansons de Bilitis* (something she may have picked up directly from Debussy).

6. Giraud, *Paul Loyonnet*, p. 230. 'Avis à ceux qui croient aux œuvres floues de Debussy!', Loyonnet adds.

7. Nichols, *Debussy Remembered*, pp. 158–9. Dumesnil gave the première of 'Hommage à Rameau' in December 1905.

8. Ibid., p. 159, referring to 'Clair de lune'.

9. Bannerman, *The Singer as Interpreter*, p. 95.

10. Some manuscripts show broken lines (left unprinted in early editions) that define the extent of the *rit.*; the Debussy *Œuvres complètes* restore such cases.

11. Notes to the Schirmer 1985 edition of *Jeux d'eau*, ed. Robert [Gaby] Casadesus (the English text there slightly mistranslates the phrase).

12. Williams, *The Theories of Olivier Messiaen*, vol. 1 p. 261, and Samuel, *Entretiens avec Olivier Messiaen*, p. 71 ('Debussy . . . fut un des plus grands rythmiciens de tous les temps'). In conversation Graham Williams recalls Messiaen repeatedly saying this.

13. Godet in interview with Georges Jean-Aubry (*Claude Debussy: lettres à deux amis*, p. 43).

14. *A Ravel Reader*, p. 363. For detailed discussion of Ravel's ballets see Mawer, *The Ballets of Maurice Ravel*, particularly p. 259 regarding this aspect of his music generally.

15. *A Ravel Reader*, p. 80.

16. Quoted in Nichols, *Debussy Remembered*, p. 156.

17. Information from Mme de Tinan (1892–1985) when I played the pieces to her in the late 1970s. The infant dedicatee of Fauré's *Dolly* suite in the mid-1890s, she grew up from the age of twelve (from 1904) in the Debussy household. An accomplished singer like her mother, she performed in private with accompanists including Poulenc and Reynaldo Hahn.

18. Information kindly supplied by Ciampi's pupil Julia Hennig.

19. Reported by Vlado Perlemuter and Gaby Casadesus in *Ravel according to Ravel*, p. 21, and Elder, *Pianists at Play*, p. 75. Ravel's orchestral score of 'Alborada' pushes the compromise the other way by renotating the turns in sixteenth-notes.

20. Marguerite Long reports Fauré's exasperation whenever he heard this contrast underplayed or mismanaged (*Au piano avec Gabriel Fauré*, p. 157).

21. *Debussy Letters*, p. 176.

22. Faure, *Mon maître Maurice Ravel*, p. 83.

23. See the Preface to Peters edition EP 7956 of the *Thème et variations*.

24. Nichols, *Ravel Remembered*, p. 62.

25. Hartmann, '*Claude Debussy as I Knew him*' and Other Writings, pp. 79–81.

26. *La musique française de piano*, vol. 1 p. 146.

27. Quoted in Nectoux, *Gabriel Fauré: A Musical Life*, p. 471.

28. *Claude Debussy: correspondance*, p. 1944. The work in question is his Cello Sonata (which was published with metronome markings), not, as is often assumed, his *Études*, which appeared only in 1916. His remark has often been misconstrued through mistranslation of the rest of the sentence (misreading his word *manque* as *marque*): in fact he's elegantly explaining to Durand why he nonetheless *does* want to add metronome markings, and the range he indicates at the start of the Cello Sonata neatly answers his '*l'espace d'un matin*'. In 1914, asked about metronome markings for *L'isle joyeuse*, he replied that they would be 'useful only as *points de départ*' (ibid., p. 1835), a matter addressed by his detailed tempo indications in that piece.

29. See also the detailed metronome markings Debussy added around the same time to his exemplar of *Prélude à l'après-midi d'un faune*, starting at a flowing ♩. = 44 (like 'Danseuses de Delphes'); they are reproduced in the Norton Critical Score edited by William Austin.

30. A description by Debussy of 'Pour les agréments' as taking 'the form of a barcarolle on a somewhat Italian sea' (*Claude Debussy: correspondance*, p. 1920) hardly suits the piece, and is perhaps a slip for 'Pour les sonorités opposées'.
31. See facsimiles in the Minkoff *Études* volume and the *Œuvres complètes* 1/6, p. 116.
32. 'Je rythme ma musique avec mes sabots d'auvergnat'; quoted in Delage, *Chabrier* (Iconographie musicale), pp. 12 and 14–15.
33. The markings for *Joyeuse marche* and *España* come respectively from Chabrier's piano duet and duo versions.
34. See also note 48 to Chapter 21. Page 217 of *A Ravel Reader* quotes Ravel's corrections, still not implemented in print, of a spate of faulty tempo indications in *Daphnis et Chloé* including inadvertent doublings and halvings of note values.
35. See note 3 to Chapter 16. Two of these markings (for the Prélude and Forlane) also appear in the 1919 orchestral score along with an implausible-seeming 120 for both Menuet and Rigaudon, suggesting they came, for better or worse, from Ravel – though that doesn't exclude input from Long who had just premièred the piano version. See Perlemuter and Jourdan-Morhange, *Ravel according to Ravel*, pp. 78–80 and the commentary to the London Peters edition of *Le tombeau* for alternative tempi from associates of Ravel; Perlemuter's suggestions (in his teaching) included ♩ = c. 108 for the Rigaudon and 126–132 for the Toccata.
36. Marnat, *Ravel: souvenirs de Manuel Rosenthal*, pp. 147–8.
37. Regarding the link to Beethoven, see Roger Nichols's preface to the London Peters edition of the *Sonatine*.
38. Roland-Manuel quotes Ravel as repeatedly insisting, 'When I put together the words which make up this title, my only thought was the pleasure of alliteration' (Roland-Manuel, *Maurice Ravel*, p. 29).
39. Information from Mme de Tinan (late 1970s, in conversation around the piano).
40. See Nichols, *Ravel Remembered*, p. 140.
41. Felix Aprahamian, who heard Ravel and Long rehearse the Concerto in 1932 in the Queen's Hall, London, recalled (in conversation) overhearing furious arguments between them. Mme Long's 1932 recording of the work accelerates *poco a poco* to c. ♩ = 152 through the first movement's two build-ups, leaving the orchestra sometimes panting behind, and with an ungainly hiatus at the recap.
42. See in particular Chapters 4 and 7 by James Briscoe and Brooks Toliver in Briscoe, *Debussy in Performance*.
43. See van Eck, 'César Franck's metronome markings reconsidered', and Whitehead's discussion of this in 'New perspectives in Franck studies'.
44. See Fauquet, *César Franck: correspondance*, p. 175, plus the list of comparative timings in Whitehead, 'New perspectives in Franck studies', p. 56.

CHAPTER 18

1. Philippe Fauré-Fremiet, *Gabriel Fauré*, pp. 158–62.
2. Regarding Fauré's marking of the beat and bass lines see Roger-Ducasse's preface to the 1924 edition of Nocturnes 1–8 (paragraphs 4–5) and Marguerite Long, *Au piano avec Gabriel Fauré*, pp. 103–4. The Second Nocturne shows Fauré adding accents (after the piece's publication) specifically to mark out the beat against melodic syncopations (from bar 24: see the commentary to the London Peters edition). The present chapter's observations join explorations of Fauré's rhythmic sophistication in Robin Tait's *The Musical Language of Gabriel Fauré* and Carlo Caballero's *Fauré and French Musical Aesthetics*.
3. It's nevertheless clear why Ravel reportedly told Ricardo Viñes, in the Menuet of his *Sonatine*, to 'avoid emphasising the first beat; that would be vulgar' (Perlemuter and

Jourdan-Morhange, *Ravel according to Ravel*, p. 13). The texture there already makes the beat clear, particularly if kept in time as Ravel insisted.

4. Long, *Au piano avec Gabriel Fauré*, p. 161. Compare the similar offsets across the hands in the finale of Fauré's First Violin Sonata, where he marks bass accents more consistently.

5. Remarks made in conversation and at piano masterclasses. In the Lombard-dominated first movement of Fauré's Second Violin Sonata op. 108, Fauré's autograph shows he initially marked accents mainly on the Lombardic offbeats, before adding compensatory ones to the main beats at proof, doubtless the fruit of rehearsal experience.

6. Robin Tait and Robert Philip note this rhythmic dichotomy, without drawing firm conclusions (*The Musical Language of Gabriel Fauré*, pp. 193–4, and *Early Recordings and Musical Style*, pp. 74–5).

7. *Gabriel Fauré: His Life through his Letters*, p. 312 (letter of 26 February 1921 to Henri Casadesus, uncle of Robert).

8. Welte roll 7057, issued in 1925 (but doubtless following a pre-1924 edition).

9. Philippe Fauré-Fremiet, *Gabriel Fauré*, p. 158. Vlado Perlemuter, who played this piece several times to Fauré, marked progressive tempo increases from bar 21, reaching ♩ = 72 by bar 79.

10. Over the years Fauré tinkered in various ways with the marking at bar 94 (*Tempo I. Lento* in the 1883 first edition, reduced to *Tempo I* in the 1924 print, the entire indication scored through in Fauré's handexemplar); the London Peters edition adjusts it to *A tempo* with a cautionary footnote.

11. Such tempo arches relate to Debussy's large-scale shaping of tempo in 'Hommage à Rameau' and *L'isle joyeuse*, as discussed in Chapter 4. The notational problem is an old one: regarding Schubert's approach to it see Howat, 'Architecture as drama in late Schubert' and 'Reading between the lines of tempo and rhythm in the B-flat Sonata, D. 960'.

12. *Gabriel Fauré: His Life through his Letters*, p. 327. His comment might seem self-defeating after his complaint four years earlier to Robert Lortat (see p. 253 above) that pianists played those same pieces at too uniform a tempo! In fact his revisions to the *Valses-caprices* appear to have been mostly lost, for the consequent Hamelle re-edition (issued only in 1930) leaves the first three unchanged.

13. Vlado Perlemuter reported a brief *poco calando* that Fauré discreetly recommended (but never marked, probably for fear of exaggeration) in the last bar or so of trill on the penultimate page of his Second Impromptu (information from Peter Norris).

14. The printed ♩ in the orchestral score's two metronome markings (at bar 1, then starting the ¾ section) is an obvious twofold error (*recte* ♩ and ♩. respectively); the orchestral score's opening 86 [*sic*] conversely makes better sense than the two-piano score's printed 80. (In practice this section can comfortably move up to around 92.)

15. *Gabriel Fauré: correspondance*, p. 310.

16. If anything Fauré's metronome markings for the Seventh to Ninth Barcarolles appear a touch on the fast side.

17. Auclert, 'La Ballade op. 19 de Fauré'. Though not stated outright, the implication of his article, printed shortly after his death, is that his corrections came from her.

18. The third and fourth of the *Pièces brèves* can arguably be viewed similarly; their *poco rall.* and *allargando* indications then make sense. The issue is addressed in the Peters edition.

19. Long, *Au piano avec Gabriel Fauré*, p. 130. The piece's earliest prints indicate ♩ = 72.

20. Fauré had reading glasses (see *Gabriel Fauré: A Life in Letters*, pp. 101–2) but was self-confessedly absentminded with them; they almost never appear on photographs. In his last years his correspondence attests to serious eyesight problems, which might explain why the problem eases in his last works: he may by then have needed someone else to read from the metronome.

21. Boult's comments, written to Robert Orledge (1975) and *The Musical Times* (June 1976), are quoted in various Peters editions of the *Pavane* (solo piano, flute and piano, and flute with piano and two voices). Chapter 21 corroborates his comments from an independent source.

22. In a letter of July 1888, Fauré confesses to being regarded by his colleagues as 'devoid of common sense when it comes to indicating a tempo' (*Gabriel Fauré: His Life through his Letters*, p. 141).

23. See p. 261 above with note 43. Fauré and Franck were in frequent contact at that time through the Société nationale de musique, where Fauré helped organize the premières of Franck's two triptychs.

24. Carbou, *La leçon de musique d'Yvonne Lefébure*, p. 123. This is corroborated by others who worked with Fauré; according to various of Nadia Boulanger's students (in conversation), one of her perennial complaints was that Fauré was usually played too slowly.

25. Fauré, 'Souvenirs', pp. 8–9. The violin piece can be found in Peters Edition EP 7515.

26. Source evidence for this is listed in the London Peters edition. The tactus equivalences mooted here across bars 18–19 and 62–3 are supported by the *rallentando* at bar 18 and the lack of one at bar 62.

27. Counting the opening half-note as the tactus equivalent of a bar of *allegretto* and a whole-note of *allegro*, the first two sections almost exactly balance (55 + 56 units), the crux of the first climax (bar 17) lies almost exactly halfway to its reiteration at bar 59 (49:50 units), and the latter lies exactly halfway to the crux of the main culmination at bar 113 (99:99 units).

CHAPTER 19

1. Quoted by Grant Johannesen in Timbrell, *French Pianism*, p. 217. Elsewhere Poulenc recalled, 'Nobody taught the art of pedalling better than Viñes. Thus he paradoxically managed to play clearly in a sea of pedal' (*Entretiens avec Claude Rostand*, p. 30).

2. See *Debussy Letters*, pp. 222 n2 and 274.

3. See the comments of Ravel's colleague Henri Gil-Marchex in 1925 ('La technique du piano', p. 43): 'In general the pedal [in Ravel] isn't difficult to manage, but since it often needs to be held down for a long time, a large variety of touch is needed to avoid fogging the harmonies.'

4. Nichols, *Debussy Remembered*, p. 163.

5. Elder, *Pianists at Play*, p. 12.

6. See Falkenberg, *Les pédales du piano*, pp. 80–1.

7. Saint-Saëns, 'Quelques mots sur l'exécution des oeuvres de Chopin', p. 387.

8. Regarding source-supported *secco* effects in Chopin see Rosenblum, 'Some enigmas of Chopin's pedal indications', and Crisp, 'Between the sublime and the terrible'.

9. See note 13 to Chapter 6 for the source of this quotation. Marie Jaëll's published writings include nothing detailed about pedalling, and Edward Lockspeiser (*Debussy: His Life and Mind*, vol. 2 pp. 46–7) was probably right in opining that what Debussy had in mind was the treatise *Les pédales du piano* of 1892 by Georges Falkenberg, a student of Chopin's pupil Mathias.

10. Fauré's autograph confirms this: the slur in bar 38 originally continued to the next bar before Fauré cut it back to allow a breath over the barline.

11. At the reprise in bar 40 the first edition added a half-bar rest at beat 1; absent from the manuscript, it is removed in the *Œuvres complètes*.

12. Debussy's piano roll of 'Danseuses de Delphes' pedals through, but with no final low $B''\flat$ because the Welte reproducing mechanism plays no lower than bass C'.

13. The Dover autograph facsimile volume shows several rests and augmentation dots missing in these bars, suggesting that Debussy's aim was not pedantically literal. The impossibility of consistency emerges from Dean Elder's recommendation ('Gieseking's pedaling in Debussy and Ravel', pp. 233–4, 251, 270 and 283) to mark these rests by retaking or sostenuto pedal – likewise in the closing bars of *"Les sons et les parfums"* – but conversely to pedal through all the rests in Example 16.8, in bars 48 and 50 of 'General Lavine' and on the first page of 'Voiles'.
14. The player piano specialist Rex Lawson suggests (in conversation) that the occasional pedal detail on these rolls may have been affected by in-house editing (while editing in dynamics from the original rubber or roller traces), involving possible added touches of *una corda* or vice versa.
15. Banowetz (*The Pianist's Guide to Pedaling*, p. 4) mentions examples produced in 1844, 1860 and 1862 by the now-forgotten makers Boisselot, Debain and Montal.
16. See Brody, *Paris: The Musical Kaleidoscope*, pp. 181–2. Viñes's diary entry for 12 January 1895 confirms the nature of its middle pedal ('to sustain whichever notes one wants').
17. Hamburg-built Steinway model D no. 124129, now in the collection of Henri-Louis de La Grange. Model and number details of the Saint-Marceaux Steinway are untraced, but sostenuto pedal was standard on all Hamburg and New York Steinways from model A (6'3") upwards well before 1900 (contrary to the assertion in Banowetz, *The Pianist's Guide to Pedaling*, p. 4). On some other makes middle pedals had different functions, for example lifting all the dampers of just one register.
18. See de Beaupuy et al., *René de Castéra*, p. 95 and the photo between pp. 192 and 193 showing the piano's three pedals.
19. This last case, like many others, still suggests generous damper pedal to avoid blatancy; Vlado Perlemuter (whose own Steinway was a model O with no sostenuto pedal) recommended flutter-pedalling here (*Ravel according to Ravel*, p. 14), echoing Falkenberg's advice for similar contexts.
20. Cortot, *La musique française de piano*, vol. 1 p. 205.
21. *Les pédales du piano*, p. 99.
22. The foggy pedalling for the second movement in old editions of Fauré's A major Violin Sonata is probably a misprint (see the commentary in Peters edition EP 7487).
23. Cited in Nichols, *Debussy Remembered*, p. 160.
24. A secondary aim may have been to avoid performers cutting long notes short: now considered sloppy, this was once standard classical practice.
25. Nichols, *Debussy Remembered*, pp. 159–60 (quoting Maurice Dumesnil), and Neuhaus, *The Art of Piano Playing*, p. 158.
26. *Les pédales du piano*, p. 87.

CHAPTER 20

1. Neuhaus, *The Art of Piano Playing*, p. 143. (Neuhaus was born in 1888, just two years after Liszt's death.)
2. '*Quelle plaie!*'; Long, *Au piano avec Claude Debussy*, p. 26.
3. Personal communication from Joan Thackray. Debate with several colleagues suggests that the matter of cigarette holding is inconclusive in itself of hand dominance.
4. Lesure, *Claude Debussy: biographie critique*, p. 33.
5. Février, 'Les exigencies de Ravel', p. 892, and Elder, *Pianists at Play*, pp. 73 and 75.
6. See for example Eigeldinger, *Chopin, Pianist and Teacher*, p. 42. Liszt's teaching of the gesture was continued by his pupils Marie Jaëll, Rudolf Breithaupt and Martin Krause (the teacher of Edwin Fischer, Wilhelm Kempff and Claudio Arrau).
7. Elder, *Pianists at Play*, p. 31.

8. Faure, *Mon maître Maurice Ravel*, p. 88; quoted in the preface of the London Peters edition of *Le tombeau de Couperin*. The film footage of Ravel appears in the Fichman–Weinstein film *Ravel*.

9. Neuhaus, *The Art of Piano Playing*, pp. 142–3; pp. 150–1 refer to eight possible chromatic scale fingerings, including those for Chopin's *Études* op. 10 no. 2 and op. 25 no. 6.

10. For Perlemuter's recollections on this topic see Bosch, 'Fauré, Ravel, Perlemuter', pp. 25–6.

11. Cortot, *La musique française de piano*, vol. 1 p. 202.

12. Elder, *Pianists at Play*, p. 75.

13. A more pungent version of *débrouillez-vous* (literally 'unmuddle yourself'); reported in conversation by Eric Heidsieck. Kenneth van Barthold recalls (personal communication) once asking Nat rather insistently about using thumb on a particular note, only to be told, 'mon cher ami, si ça t'arrange tu mets le cul dessus.'

14. Dumesnil as quoted in Nichols, *Debussy Remembered*, pp. 159–60 and 162–3.

15. Carbou, *La leçon d'interprétation d'Yvonne Lefébure*, p. 145. Lefébure's recollection, seventy years after the event, starts, 'His *HAND*! Debussy's hand at the piano!'

CHAPTER 21

1. Elder, *Pianists at Play*, p. 33.

2. See Schmitz, *The Piano Music of Claude Debussy*, p. 35, and Lesure, *Claude Debussy: biographie critique*, pp. 49–50 and 171, regarding Debussy's coaching of singers and choirs: Mme de Romilly described him as 'a marvellous choral director, angelically patient, taking us all in turn to let us master the different parts, and he succeeded in turning a bunch of vague, rather bumbling amateurs into a small, melodious, disciplined group.'

3. Hartmann, *'Claude Debussy as I Knew him' and Other Writings*, pp. 68, 63 and 104.

4. See the photograph of Fauré in Fontana, *Namhafte Pianisten im Aufnahmesalon Hupfeld*, p. 64, and Kenneth Caswell's booklet to his CD realizations (Pierian 001) of Debussy's piano rolls. Fauré's loyalty to Erard is documented in various letters: 'mon admirable Erard' (in 1910: Fauré-Fremiet, *Gabriel Fauré: lettres intimes*, p. 185), 'cher petit Erard' (summer 1919: Bodin, *Les Autographes* sale catalogue 117, April 2006, item 107), and in an unpublished letter of 5 February 1916 to his brother Amand (collection of H. Garus): '. . . c'est pardessus tout, un Erard que je recommande à tes amis pour la qualité et la durée.'

5. Information from Julia Hennig.

6. In the 1840s the young César Franck gave dramatic demonstrations on a piano by Henri Pape with an eight-octave *F″* to *f″″*, as wide a compass (a fourth higher) as the current Bösendorfer Imperial. Such large compasses were short-lived because of poor tone and overstrain on wooden frames.

7. Noted by Garban on his Ravel exemplars now in the library of Bakersfield College, California.

8. Bathori, *On the Interpretation of the Mélodies of Claude Debussy*, p. 62.

9. Lesure, *Debussy*, p. 322.

10. Nichols, *Debussy Remembered*, pp. 40 and 166 (quoting Lebeau and Copeland), and Joly-Segalen and Schaeffner, *Segalen and Debussy*, p. 85. (Why Narcissus the Handsome should wish to be known instead as Vital Hiccough remains one of the more inscrutable mysteries of the Belle Époque.)

11. Priest, *Louis Laloy*, p. 48, Nichols, *Debussy Remembered*, p. 203 (quoting Vallery-Radot), and Vallas, *Claude Debussy et son temps*, p. 367 (quoting Henri Malherbe).

12. *Claude Debussy: correspondance*, p. 1912.

13. Priest, *Louis Laloy*, p. 48.
14. Lesure, *Claude Debussy: biographie critique*, p. 317 (quoting Zuccala), *Claude Debussy: correspondance*, p. 1590, and Nichols, *Debussy Remembered*, p. 172 (quoting Casella). It is possible the Zuccala report of a Bechstein was a confusion with the Blüthner grand, otherwise it oddly implies a simultaneity or rapid succession of Pleyel and Bechstein uprights *chez* Debussy, in addition to the Blüthner grand.

    The relative absence of Steinway from this *catalogage* is probably explicable by Paul Loyonnet's description of it as 'le piano des riches' (Giraud, *Paul Loyonnet*, p. 230), as page 288 above tends to corroborate. René de Castéra, as it happens, was persuaded by Albéniz and Viñes to buy his Steinway in preference to an Erard; it soon became a favourite of de Castéra's friends, notably Blanche Selva who teasingly contrasted its malleable colours with Albéniz's and d'Indy's 'rattly' or 'clanky' old Erards (de Beaupuy et al., *René de Castéra*, pp. 100, 184 & 186).
15. Review signed X.X. in *Le guide musical*, 60:19–20 (10 and 17 May 1914), p. 410; quoted in Lesure, *Claude Debussy: biographie critique*, p. 382. The review corroborates Manuel de Falla's memory that Debussy's piano 'technique was exact and precise, and he would not deviate from the interpretation indicated in the original score' (Pahissa, *Manuel de Falla: His Life and Works*, p. 170).
16. Durand, *Quelques souvenirs d'un éditeur de musique*, p. 74, and Demarquez, *Manuel de Falla*, p. 195 (quoting Jaime Pahissa).
17. Stravinsky, *An Autobiography*, p. 49; Stravinsky and Craft, *Conversations with Igor Stravinsky*, p. 50.
18. Priest, *Louis Laloy*, pp. 108–9. Elsewhere Laloy – whose wife took piano lessons from Debussy – recalls Debussy's 'supple, living touch, with the hands always on the keys' (ibid., p. 23).
19. Maurice Dumesnil as quoted in Nichols, *Debussy Remembered*, pp. 162–3.
20. Recounted in conversation by Mme de Tinan (who probably overheard the exchange), and quoted (from Cortot) in Lockspeiser, *Debussy: His Life and Mind*, vol. 2 p. 199; English wording as in Dolly Bardac (Mme de Tinan), 'Memories of Debussy and his circle', p. 163.
21. Mary Garden's lurid verbal reminiscences of half a century later (*The Mary Garden Story*, pp. 216–17) give a wry account of the primitive recording conditions (playing and singing into an acoustic horn), but single out the tempi as the one reliable element for singers to follow.
22. See Philip, *Early Recordings and Musical Style*, pp. 43–4.
23. Robert Philip emphasizes some of these points, observing that the musical sense of many subtle agogics is reliant on the associated dynamics, impossible to render exactly on piano rolls (*Performing Music in the Age of Recording*, pp. 31–3). Angela Turner's appraisal of Ravel's rolls of the *Valses nobles* and *Pavane* (*Maurice Ravel's Performances of his own Piano Compositions*) includes an amusingly vivid illustration of how differently the same roll can play back from differently set instruments.
24. A frequent way of bringing out a single note in a chord was for house editors later to offset it from the rest of the chord (usually by marginally advancing it), adding quick dynamic adjustment before and after. Apparently Welte rolls rarely if ever engage in this (information from Denis Hall). For a detailed account of all these mechanical issues see Denis Hall's article 'The reproducing piano: what can it really do?'.
25. See ibid., p. 22 for some facsimile illustrations of this. The oldest surviving Welte source material consists of some 'second masters', already a phase or two on from the original recording.
26. See Lawson, 'On the roll', p. 33, and Sitsky, *The Classical Reproducing Piano Roll*, vol. 1 pp. xvii–xviii, for a resumé of Welte's probably sanitized account of how master rolls were made. From the editorial point of view it's fortunate that Welte appears to have avoided correcting performers' fluffs (see ibid., p. xliii n1), as Debussy's, Fauré's and Ravel's Welte rolls all suggest.

27. Actual track timing: the Condon CD label misprints it as 5′57″.
28. Other factors that affect speed are the reciprocal drag of the supply spool (necessary for good contact with the suction bar) and the diameter of paper round it, along with any sudden change of dynamics that diverts air or vacuum pressure from the spool drive.
29. See note 2 to Appendix 3.
30. Nichols, *Debussy Remembered*, p. 162.
31. Since Welte rolls were all intended for a uniform playback setting, the most plausible explanation would seem that the information (perforations) somehow became compressed on the 1913 production master roll. Caswell's realization of the *Children's Corner* roll on Pierian 001 (all LP or CD recordings so far published have been made from the 1913 'red roll' version) solves the pneumatic-mechanical problems by skilful instrument adjustment; even so the particular vulnerability of just this roll to the problem underscores the point. Over-slow playback conversely causes pedal smudging and dynamic ballooning, problems tellingly absent from the 1920s reissue of the *Children's Corner* roll.
32. In conversation, after a lecture given by myself under the auspices of EPTA (the European Piano Teachers Association) in February 1987. Regarding Langrish see Roberts, *Images*, pp. 258–61.
33. See Delage, *Emmanuel Chabrier*, pp. 294–5.
34. Cortot, *La musique française de piano*, vol. 1 p. 202. Among many close collaborations, Cortot and Risler premièred Fauré's *Dolly* suite in 1897.
35. Delage, *Emmanuel Chabrier*, p. 285.
36. Ibid., p. 252.
37. Ibid., pp. 267–8.
38. Ibid., p. 114.
39. Myers, *Emmanuel Chabrier and his Circle*, p. 29.
40. Delage, *Emmanuel Chabrier*, p. 598.
41. Elder, *Pianists at Play*, pp. 33, 73 and 75.
42. Priest, *Louis Laloy*, p. 249.
43. Nichols, *Ravel Remembered*, p. 41.
44. *A Ravel Reader*, p. 219.
45. Quoted in Milon et al., *Maurice Ravel à Montfort l'Amaury*, p. 30.
46. On the Fichman–Weinstein film *Ravel* Harry Adaskin relates that after his quartet played Ravel's Quartet to the composer in 1928 Ravel replied, 'That's not how I conceived the Quartet . . . But you play it with such conviction that I wouldn't dream of touching it. Just leave it the way it is. Let's go and have lunch.' Gérard Poulet (booklet for Arion CD 63610) quotes Debussy's similar response after hearing his Quartet played in 1916 by the Poulet Quartet. Similar stories concern George Copeland playing 'Reflets dans l'eau' (Nichols, *Debussy Remembered*, pp. 164–5) and Paul Paray conducting *La valse* (*A Ravel Reader*, p. 580: 'that's not it at all, but it's magnificent').
47. 'He never did this at rehearsal!' was all Szigeti was capable of panting as he went offstage; recounted by Adaskin (who was turning Ravel's pages) in the Fichman–Weinstein film *Ravel*. The plausible tempi of the remaining *valses* on Ravel's Welte roll suggest that it reliably reproduces his tempi, complete with some rushing of the right-hand arpeggios from bars 39 and 131 in the seventh *valse*.
48. Regarding the much-debated tempo of this piece see Roger Nichols's preface to the London Peters Edition, also *A Ravel Reader*, p. 536. Of eighteen recordings of the *Pavane* listed by Angela Turner from the years 1922–93 (*Maurice Ravel's Performances of his Own Piano Compositions*, Appendix C), Ravel's roll emerges as the second fastest (5′05″ on Denis Condon's CD realization), outpaced only by Ravel's colleague Marcelle Meyer (4′52″ in a 1952 audio recording); the slowest performances run to almost 7′. (Kenneth Caswell's CD realization of Ravel's roll takes 5′45″, while Roger Nichols's Peters Edition preface estimates its correct timing at the instructed settings as 4′52″.)

49. Nectoux, *Gabriel Fauré: A Musical Life*, pp. 42–4.
50. *Marguerite de Saint-Marceaux: Journal*, p. 468 (entry for 12 January 1907).
51. Fauré-Fremiet, *Gabriel Fauré: lettres intimes*, p. 186, *Claude Debussy: correspondance*, p. 1471, *Emmanuel Chabrier: correspondance*, p. 113, and *A Ravel Reader*, p. 38.

APPENDIX 1

1. For these phrases of Chopin's see Eigeldinger, *Chopin, Pianist and Teacher*, pp. 29–30.
2. These metronome indications appear in Chabrier's two-piano version of *España*.
3. Orenstein, *Ravel, Man and Musician*, p. 127.

APPENDIX 2

1. See Carbou, *La leçon d'interprétation d'Yvonne Lefébure*, p. 137; also Thierry et al., *Au cœur de l'impressionisme*, p. 68, for a photo of Yvonne Lerolle-Rouart around 1900 – just before Debussy dedicated the Sarabande of *Pour le piano* to her – dancing in long silk robes borrowed from Loïe Fuller. Varèse's recollection came via Paul Jacobs (liner notes for his 1978 Nonesuch recording of Debussy's Preludes), who possibly heard it from Varèse. Roger-Ducasse regarded the title as referring to boat sails, reportedly on the word of Emma Debussy (*Roger-Ducasse: lettres à Nadia Boulanger*, p. 81). Perhaps Debussy was happy to leave the ambiguity.

APPENDIX 3

1. For more details see Diane Enget, 'Debussy in Jersey': Enget clears up some confusion by establishing that Debussy acquired it in Eastbourne in 1905, not Jersey in 1904 or Bournemouth as recounted respectively by Mme de Tinan and Maurice Dumesnil (Nichols, *Debussy Remembered*, pp. 158 and 199). The piano reached Brive via Debussy's stepson Raoul Bardac, who moved to the region in 1940.
2. According to Smith and Howe, *The Welte-Mignon: Its Music and Musicians*, p. 215, the serial numbers 2532–2777 were certainly recorded in 1912, probably along with some numbers on either side. This could just include Ravel's, unless Welte took his equipment back to Paris again in 1913 (conceivably in November 1913 when Debussy heard the production masters: see p. 317). In a 1958 interview Edwin Welte confirmed that he had recorded both Debussy and Ravel in Paris (*A Ravel Reader*, p. 532).
3. On a much-circulated later Telefunken LP realization *D'un cahier d'esquisses* ends with a spattering of wrong notes, the result of technical malfunction or a damaged roll.
4. These appear to be the subject of a letter from Debussy to Georges Jean-Aubry of 3 March 1917, referring to the Orchestrelle Company's wish to buy them from Aeolian – unless, as Denis Herlin surmises, Debussy has confused them with his Welte recordings (see *Claude Debussy: correspondance*, p. 2081 and nn3–4).

BIBLIOGRAPHY

BOOKS, DISSERTATIONS, ARTICLES, CATALOGUES AND CONFERENCE PAPERS

Abbate, Carolyn: '*Tristan* in the composition of *Pelléas*', *19th-Century Music* 5:2 (Fall 1981), pp. 117–41

Abraham, Gerald: *On Russian Music*. New York and London: Reeves, 1939

Abraham, Hélène: *Un art de l'interprétation: Claire Croiza – Les cahiers d'une auditrice*. Paris: Office de centralisation d'ouvrages, 1954

d'Almendra, Julia: 'Debussy et mouvement modal dans la musique du XXe siècle', in *Debussy et l'évolution de la musique au XXe siècle*, ed. Edith Weber. Paris: Centre national de la recherche scientifique, 1965, pp. 109–26

Antokoletz, Elliott: *The Music of Béla Bartók*. Berkeley: University of California Press, 1984

Argüelles, José A.: *Charles Henry and the Formation of a Psychophysical Aesthetic*. Chicago and London: University of Chicago Press, 1972

Auclert, Pierre: 'La Ballade op. 19 de Fauré dans le souvenir de Madame Hasselmans', *Association des amis de Gabriel Fauré*, Bulletins 15 (1978), pp. 3–11, and 16 (1979), p. 19.

Austin, William (ed.): *Debussy, Prélude à l'après-midi d'un faune: An Authoritative Score, Historical Background, Analysis, Views and Comments*. New York: Norton Critical Scores, 1970

Bailly, Edmond: *Le son dans la nature*. Paris: Librairie de l'Art indépendant, 1900

Bannerman, Betty (ed. and trans.): *The Singer as Interpreter: Claire Croiza's Master Classes*. London: Gollancz, 1989

Banowetz, Joseph: *The Pianist's Guide to Pedaling*. Bloomington: Indiana UP, 1985

Bardac, Dolly [Mme Gaston de Tinan]: 'Memories of Debussy and his circle', *Recorded Sound* 50–51 (April–July 1973), pp. 158–63; transcription of a lecture given on 18 December 1972 at the British Institute of Recorded Sound (now the National Sound Archive), London

Bartók Remembered, see Gillies.

Bathori, Jane: *On the Interpretation of the Mélodies of Claude Debussy*, ed. and trans. Linda Laurent. Stuyvesant, NY: Pendragon, 1998

Baur, Steven: 'Ravel's "Russian" period: octatonicism in his early works, 1893–1908', *Journal of the American Musicological Society* 52:3 (1999), pp. 531–92

de Beaupuy, Anne, with Claude Gay and Damien Top: *René de Castéra (1873–1955): un compositeur landais au cœur de la musique française*. Paris: Séguier, 2004

Becker-Derex, Christiane: *Louis Diémer et le clavecin en France à la fin du XIXe siècle.* [Paris]: Zurfluh (*Le temps musical*), 2001

Blanche, Jacques-Émile: 'Souvenirs sur Manet et Debussy', *Le Figaro*, 22 June 1932

[Bodin, Thierry]: *Les Autographes*, monthly sale catalogue (numbers as specified in the text), Paris: Piasa

Bosch, Ineke: 'Fauré, Ravel, Perlemuter', *Piano Bulletin* (Netherlands) 19:1 (2001), pp. 24–31

Botstein, Leon: 'Beyond the illusions of realism: painting and Debussy's break with tradition', in Fulcher (ed.), *Debussy and his World*, pp. 141–79

Boyd, Anne: 'Debussy and the Javanese gamelan', paper delivered at the conference *Europe and the Exotic*, Humanities Research Centre at the Australian National University, Canberra, 10 July 1987

Bretell, Richard R.: *Impressionism: Painting Quickly in France, 1860–1890.* New Haven and London: Yale UP, 2000

Briscoe, James R. (ed.): *Debussy in Performance.* New Haven and London: Yale UP, 1999

Brody, Elaine: *Paris: The Musical Kaleidoscope, 1870–1925.* London: Robson, 1984

— 'The Russians in Paris, 1889–1914', in *Russian and Soviet Music: Essays for Boris Schwarz*, ed. Malcolm Hamrick Brown. Ann Arbor, Mich.: UMI Research Press (Russian music studies 11), 1984, pp. 157–83

— 'Viñes in Paris: new light on twentieth-century performance practice', in *A Musical Offering: Essays in Honor of Martin Bernstein*, ed. E. Clinkscale and C. Brook. New York: Pendragon, 1977, pp. 45–62.

Bromfield, David: 'Japanese art, Monet, and the formation of Impressionism', in Gerstle and Milner (eds), *Recovering the Orient*, pp. 7–43

Brown, Dan: *The Da Vinci Code.* London: Random House, 2003

Bruyr, José: *Maurice Ravel, ou le lyrisme et les sortilèges.* Paris: Plon, 1950

Burkhart, Charles: 'Debussy plays "La Cathédrale engloutie" and solves metrical mystery', *Piano Quarterly* 65 (Autumn 1968), pp. 14–16

Busser, Henri: *De Pelléas aux Indes galantes . . . de la flûte au tambour.* Paris: Fayard, 1955

Caballero, Carlo: *Fauré and French Musical Aesthetics.* Cambridge: CUP, 2001

Callias, Hélène de: *Magie sonore.* Paris: Véga, 1938

Carbou, Yvette: *La leçon de musique d'Yvonne Lefébure.* Paris: Van de Velde, 1995

Emmanuel Chabrier: correspondance, see Delage

Chimènes, Myriam et al. (eds): *Marguerite de Saint-Marceaux: Journal, 1894–1927*, preface by Michelle Perrot. Paris: Fayard, 2007

Christoforidis, Michael: 'Manuel de Falla, Debussy and *La vida breve*', *Musicology Australia* 18 (1995), pp. 3–12. French version: 'De la composition d'un opéra: les conseils de Claude Debussy à Manuel de Falla', *Cahiers Debussy* 19 (1995), pp. 69–76

— 'The Moor's last sigh: Paris, symbolism and the Alhambra', paper delivered at the Annual Meeting of the American Musicological Society, Seattle, November 2004

Church, A. H.: *On the Relation of Phyllotaxis to Mechanical Laws.* London: Williams and Norgate, 1904

Clark, Walter A.: *Isaac Albéniz: A Guide to Research.* New York and London: Garland, 1998

Cobb, Margaret G. (ed.): *Debussy's Letters to Inghelbrecht: The Story of a Musical Friendship*, translations by Richard Miller. Rochester, NY: University of Rochester Press, 2005

Colette et al., *Maurice Ravel par quelques-uns de ses familiers.* Paris: Tambourinaire, 1939

Colman, Samuel and Coan, C. A.: *Nature's Harmonic Unity: A Treatise on its Relation to Proportional Form.* New York: G. P. Putnam's Sons, 1912

— *Proportional Form: Further Studies in the Science of Beauty.* New York: G. P. Putnam's Sons, 1920

Cook, Theodore A.: *The Curves of Life.* London: Constable, 1914

— *Spirals in Nature and Art.* London: John Murray, 1903

Cooke, Mervyn: *Britten and the Far East*. Woodbridge (Suffolk): Boydell (Aldeburgh Studies in Music 4), 1998

Copeland, George: 'Debussy, the man I knew', *Atlantic Monthly*, January 1955, pp. 34–8

Cortot, Alfred: *Aspects de Chopin*. Paris: Albin Michel, 1949

— *La musique française de piano*, 4 vols. Paris: Rieder, 1930

— see also under Thieffry

Crisp, Deborah: 'Between the sublime and the terrible: moments of transfiguration in Chopin and Delacroix', in *Verwandlungsmusik*, vol. 48 of *Studien zur Wertungsforschung*, ed. Andreas Dorschel. Vienna, London, New York: Universal, 2007, pp. 190–215

Cui, César: *La musique en Russie*, Paris: Fischbacher, 1880; first published as articles in *Revue et gazette musicale* between 12 May 1878 and 5 October 1880

Claude Debussy: Correspondance, see Lesure

Claude Debussy: Étude retrouvée (alternative version of 'Pour les arpèges composés'), facsimile reproduction with preface and performing realization by Roy Howat. Bryn Mawr, PA: Theodore Presser, 1980

Claude Debussy: Études pour le piano, fac-similé des esquisses autographes (1915), introduction by Roy Howat. Geneva: Minkoff, 1989

Claude Debussy, Images, première serie, collection de fac-similés de manuscrits de Claude Debussy, préface générale de Pierre Boulez. Paris: Centre de documentation Claude Debussy, 2008

Claude Debussy, Images, deuxième serie, collection de fac-similés de manuscrits de Claude Debussy, préface générale de Pierre Boulez. Paris: Centre de documentation Claude Debussy, 2008

Claude Debussy: lettres à deux amis, see Jean-Aubry

Claude Debussy: Monsieur Croche et autres écrits, ed. François Lesure. Paris: Gallimard, 1987 (revised edition)

Claude Debussy: Preludes Book 1, the autograph score [in facsimile], introduction by Roy Howat. New York: Dover, 1987

Debussy Letters, see Lesure

Debussy on Music: The Critical Writings of the Great French Composer, ed. F. Lesure, trans. R. Langham Smith. London and New York: Secker and Warburg, 1977

Debussy Remembered, see Nichols

Delage, Roger: 'Debussy et Chabrier', *Cahiers Debussy* 17–18 (1993–4), pp. 57–64

— *Emmanuel Chabrier*. Paris: Fayard, 1999

— (ed.): *Chabrier*. Paris: Minkoff-Lattès (Iconographie musicale 6), 1982

— with Frans Durif and Thierry Bodin (eds): *Emmanuel Chabrier: correspondance*. Paris: Klincksieck, 1994

Demarquez, Suzanne: *Manuel de Falla*. Paris: Flammarion, 1963

DeVoto, Mark: *Debussy and the Veil of Tonality: Essays on his Music*. Hillsdale, NY: Pendragon, 2004

— 'The Russian submediant in the nineteenth century', *Current Musicology* 59 (1995), pp. 48–76

Devriès, Anik: 'Les musiques d'extrême-orient à l'Exposition Universelle de 1889', *Cahiers Debussy* new series 1 (1977), pp. 25–37

Dietschy, Marcel: *A Portrait of Claude Debussy*, ed. and trans. William Ashbrook and Margaret G. Cobb. Oxford: OUP, 1990

[Dukas, Paul:] *Les écrits de Paul Dukas sur la musique*, preface by G. Samazeuilh. Paris: Société d'éditions françaises et internationales, 1948

Durand, Jacques: *Quelques souvenirs d'un éditeur de musique* [1re série, 1865–1909]. Paris: Durand, 1924

van Eck, Ton: 'César Franck's metronome markings reconsidered', *The American Organist* (February 2002), pp. 52–5

Eigeldinger, Jean-Jacques: 'Chopin and "la note bleue": An interpretation of the Prelude op. 45', *Music & Letters* 78:2 (May 1997), pp. 233–53 (also in French in *L'univers musical de Chopin*, pp. 169–90)

— *Chopin, Pianist and Teacher*, trans. Naomi Shohet, Krysia Osostowicz and Roy Howat, ed. Roy Howat. Cambridge: CUP, 1986

— 'Debussy et l'idée d'arabesque musicale', *Cahiers Debussy* 12–13 (1988–9), pp. 5–14

— 'Twenty-four Preludes op. 28: genre, structure, significance', in Samson (ed.), *Chopin Studies*, pp. 167–93 (also in French in *L'univers musical de Chopin*, pp. 137–54)

— *L'univers musical de Chopin*. Paris: Fayard, 2000

Elder, Dean: 'Gieseking's pedaling in Debussy and Ravel', in Banowetz, *The Pianist's Guide to Pedaling*, pp. 230–87 and 293–4

— *Pianists at Play*. Evanston: The Instrumentalist Company, 1982

Ellis, Katharine: *Interpreting the Musical Past: Early Music in Nineteenth-century France*. New York: OUP, 2005

Falkenberg, Georges: *Les pédales du piano*. Paris: Heugel, 1892

Falla, Manuel de: *On Music and Musicians*, ed. Federico Sopeña, trans. D. Urman and J. M. Thomson. London and Boston: Marion Boyars, 1979

Faret, Le Sieur: *L'Honneste-Homme, ou, l'Art de plaire à la court*. Paris: Du Bray, 1630

Fauquet, Joël-Marie, *César Franck*. Paris: Fayard, 1999

— (ed.): *César Franck: correspondance*. Liège: Mardaga, 1999

Faure, Henriette: *Mon maître Maurice Ravel*. Paris: A.T.P., 1978

Gabriel Fauré: A Life in Letters, see Jones

Gabriel Fauré: His Life through his Letters, see Nectoux

Gabriel Fauré: lettres intimes, see Fauré-Fremiet

Fauré, Gabriel: 'Souvenirs', *La revue musicale* 4:11 (special Fauré number, 1 November 1922), pp. 3–9

Fauré-Fremiet, Philippe: *Gabriel Fauré*. Paris: Albin Michel, 1957

— (ed.): *Gabriel Fauré: lettres intimes*. Paris: Grasset, 1951

Fauser, Annegret: *Musical Encounters at the 1889 Paris World's Fair*. Rochester, NY: University of Rochester Press, 2005

Fechner, Gustav: *Vorschule der Aesthetik*, 2 vols. Leipzig: Breitkopf & Härtel, 1876

Ferroud, Pierre-Octave: 'Moussorgski et Chabrier', *Latinité* 10 (December 1929), p. 309

Février, Jacques: 'Les exigences de Ravel', *La revue internationale de musique* 5–6 (1939), pp. 892–4

Fontana, Eszter (ed.): *Namhafte Pianisten im Aufnahmesalon Hupfeld*. Halle an der Saale: Stekovics, 2000

Françaix, Jean: *De la musique et des musiciens*. Paris: Fondation Polignac, 1999

César Franck: correspondance, see Fauquet

Fulcher, Jane (ed.): *Debussy and his World*. Princeton: Princeton UP, 2001

Garden, Edward: 'Balakirev's influence on Musorgsky', in *Musorgsky in memoriam 1881–1981*, ed. Malcolm Hamrick Brown. Ann Arbor, Mich.: UMI Research Press (Russian music studies 3), 1982, pp. 11–27

Garden, Mary and Biancolli, Louis: *The Mary Garden Story*. London: Michael Joseph, 1952

Gerstle, C. Andrew and Milner, Anthony (eds): *Recovering the Orient: Artists, Scholars, Appropriations*. Chur: Harwood, 1994

Gervaise, Françoise: *Etude comparée des langages harmoniques de Fauré et de Debussy*, 2 vols. *La revue musicale*, special numbers 272–3 (1971)

Ghyka, Matila: *Esthétique des proportions dans la nature et dans les arts*. Paris: Gallimard, 1927

— *The Geometry of Art and Life*. New York: Sheed & Ward, 1946 (repr. New York: Dover, 1979)

— *Le nombre d'or*, 2 vols. Paris: Gallimard, 1931

— *Philosophie et mystique du nombre*. Paris: Payot, 1952

Gil-Marchex, Henri: 'La technique du piano', *La revue musicale* 6:6 (special Ravel number, 1 April 1925), pp. 38–45

Gillies, Malcolm (ed.): *Bartók Remembered*. London: Faber, 1990

Giraud, Pierre (ed.): *Paul Loyonnet (1889–1988), un pianiste et son temps: souvenirs réunis et présentés par Pierre Giraud*. Paris: Champion, 2003

Grayson, David: 'Bilitis and Tanagra: afternoons with nude women', in Fulcher (ed.), *Debussy and his World*, pp. 117–33

Grier, James: *The Critical Editing of Music: History, Method, and Practice*. Cambridge: CUP, 1996

Gubisch, Nina: 'La vie musicale à Paris entre 1887 et 1914 à travers le journal de R. Viñes', *Revue internationale de la musique française*, 1:2 (June 1980), pp. 154–248

— (ed.): *Le journal de Ricardo Viñes* [provisional title]. Montreal: Presses universitaires de Montréal, forthcoming (2009)

Hall, Denis: 'The player piano on record: a discography', *Pianola Journal* 3 (1990), pp. 25–39

— 'The reproducing piano: what can it really do?', *Pianola Journal* 14 (2001), pp. 3–26

Hambidge, Jay: *Dynamic Symmetry: The Greek Vase*. New Haven: Yale UP, 1920

— *The Elements of Dynamic Symmetry*. New Haven: Yale UP, 1948

— *The Parthenon and Other Greek Temples: Their Dynamic Symmetry*. New Haven: Yale UP, 1924

Harper, Nancy Lee: *Manuel de Falla: His Life and Music*. Lanham, Md., and Oxford: Scarecrow Press, 2005

Hartmann, Arthur: '*Claude Debussy as I Knew him*' and Other Writings by Arthur Hartmann, ed. Samuel Hsu, Sidney Grolnic and Mark Peters, foreword by David Grayson. Rochester, NY: University of Rochester Press, 2003

Hedley, Arthur (ed.): *Selected Correspondence of Fryderyk Chopin*. London: Heinemann, 1962

Herlin, Denis: 'Une œuvre inachevée: *La Saulaie*', *Cahiers Debussy* 20 (1996), pp. 3–23

— see also under Kaufmann and under Lesure

Heyde, Neil James: *Claude Debussy, rhétoricien français: The Three Sonatas (1915–17)*. PhD thesis, King's College London, 2003

Holloway, Robin: *Debussy and Wagner*. London: Eulenburg, 1979

Homer, William Innes: *Seurat and the Science of Painting*. Cambridge, Mass.: MIT Press, 1964

Howat, Roy: 'Architecture as drama in late Schubert', in *Schubert Studies*, ed. Brian Newbould. Aldershot: Ashgate, 1998, pp. 168–92

— 'Bartók, Lendvai and the principles of proportional analysis', *Music Analysis* 2:1 (March 1983), pp. 69–95

— 'Chabrier "par" Debussy', *Cahiers Debussy* 19 (1995), pp. 79–91

— 'Debussy and the Orient', in Gerstle and Milner (eds), *Recovering the Orient*, pp. 45–81

— 'Debussy et le piano', in Kaufmann et al., *Claude Debussy: textes*, pp. 35–47

— *Debussy in Proportion*. Cambridge: CUP, 1983

— 'Dramatic shape and form in "Jeux de vagues", and its relation to *Pelléas*, *Jeux* and other scores', *Cahiers Debussy* 7 (1983), pp. 7–23

— 'En route for *L'isle joyeuse*: the restoration of a triptych', *Cahiers Debussy* 19 (1995), pp. 37–52

— 'Modes and semitones in Debussy's Preludes and elsewhere', *Studies in Music* (Perth, Australia) 22 (1988), pp. 81–104

— 'Ravel and the piano', in Mawer (ed.), *The Cambridge Companion to Ravel*, pp. 71–96 and 271–3

— 'Reading between the lines of tempo and rhythm in the B-flat Sonata, D. 960', in *Schubert the Progressive*, ed. Brian Newbould. Aldershot: Ashgate, 2003, pp. 117–37

— '"Un tas de petites choses" et de petits mystères pour quatre mains', in *André Caplet, compositeur et chef d'orchestre*, ed. Denis Herlin. Paris: Éditions Symétrie, in press (2009)

— see also under Samson

Inghelbrecht, D.-E.: *Mouvement contraire: souvenirs d'un musicien*. Paris: Domat, 1947

James, Burnett: *Ravel*. London: Omnibus, 1987

Jankélévitch, Vladimir: *Debussy et le mystère*. Neuchâtel: La Baconnière, 1949

Jean-Aubry, G. and Godet, Robert (eds): *Claude Debussy: lettres à deux amis: soixante-dix-huit lettres inédites à Robert Godet et G. Jean-Aubry*. Paris: José Corti, 1942

Joly-Segalen, Annie and Schaeffner, André: *Segalen et Debussy*. Monaco: Éditions du Rocher, 1962

Jones, J. Barrie (trans. and ed.): *Gabriel Fauré: A Life in Letters*. London: Batsford, 1988

de Jong-Keesing, Elisabeth: *Inayat Khan: A Biography*. The Hague: East-West Publication Fonds, 1974

Jourdan-Morhange, Hélène: *Mes amis musiciens*. Paris: Les Éditeurs français réunis, 1955

— 'Ravel à Montfort-l'Amaury', in Colette et al., *Maurice Ravel par quelques-uns de ses familiers*, pp. 163–9

— see also under Perlemuter

Kahan, Sylvia: *Music's Modern Muse: A Life of Winnaretta Singer, Princesse de Polignac*. Rochester, NY: University of Rochester, 2003

— '"Rien de la tonalité usuelle": Edmond de Polignac and the octatonic scale in nineteenth century France', *19th-Century Music* 29:2 (Fall 2005), pp. 97–120

Kasztelan, Helen: 'Debussy's *Estampes*: a new approach to Salzerian interpretations', unpublished seminar paper delivered at University of Melbourne, 15 September 1986

Kaufmann, Martine, with Denis Herlin and Jean-Michel Nectoux (eds): *Claude Debussy: textes*. Paris: Radio France; Van Dieren, 1999

Kelly, Barbara L.: 'History and homage', in Mawer (ed.), *The Cambridge Companion to Ravel*, pp. 7–26

— and Murphy, Kerry (eds): *Berlioz and Debussy: Sources, Contexts and Legacies: Essays in honour of François Lesure*. Aldershot: Ashgate, 2007

Khan, Inayat: *Music*. Farnham: Sufi Publishing Co., 1962

Khan, Musharaff: *Pages in the Life of a Sufi*. Farnham: Sufi Publishing Co., 1971

Koechlin, Charles: *Gabriel Fauré (1845–1924)*, trans. Leslie Orr[e]y. London: Dobson, 1946

Korevaar, David and Sampsel, Laurie J.: 'The Ricardo Viñes Piano Music Collection at the University of Colorado at Boulder', *Notes* 61:2 (December 2004), pp. 361–400

LaFarge, John: 'An Essay on Japanese Art', in R. Pumpelly, *Across Asia and America: Notes of a Five Year's Journey around the World*, pp. 195–202. New York: Leypoldt and Holt, 1870 (3rd edition)

Laforgue, Jules: 'Impressionist art' (English translation), in Bretell, *Impressionism*, pp. 233–5

de La Grange, Henri-Louis: *Gustav Mahler: chronique d'une vie*, vol. 3: *Le génie foudroyé*. Paris: Fayard, 1984

Laloy, Louis: *Debussy*. Paris: Aux armes de France (J. Dumoulin), 1944

— *La musique chinoise*. Paris: Laurens, 1910

— *La musique retrouvée, 1902–1927*. Paris: Les Petits-fils de Plon et Nourrit, 1928

— *Rameau*. Paris: Alcan, 1908

— see also under Priest

Lambert, Constant: *Music ho! A Study of Music in Decline*. London: Faber, 1966 (3rd edition)

Lawson, Rex: 'On the roll', *Pianola Journal* 5 (1993), pp. 30–9

Le Bordays, Christiane: 'L'Espagne ravélienne', *Cahiers Ravel* 2 (1986), pp. 44–61

Lendvai, Ernő: *Béla Bartók: An Analysis of his Music*. London: Kahn & Averill, 1971

— *The Workshop of Bartók and Kodály*. Budapest: Editia Musico Budapest, 1983

Lépine, Jean: *La vie de Claude Debussy*. Paris: Albin Michel, 1930

Lesure, François: *Claude Debussy: biographie critique, suivie de Catalogue de l'œuvre*. Paris: Fayard, 2003 (revised edition)

— (ed.): *Claude Debussy*. Geneva: Minkoff (Iconographie musicale 4), 1975 (re-edition: Paris: Minkoff & Lattès, 1980)

— and Nichols, Roger (eds): *Debussy Letters*, ed. F. Lesure and R. Nichols, trans. R. Nichols. London: Faber, 1987

— and Herlin, Denis (eds): *Claude Debussy: correspondance (1872–1918)*, annotated by François Lesure, Denis Herlin and Georges Liébert. Paris: Gallimard, 2005

Levey, Michael: 'The real theme of Watteau's *Embarkation for Cythera*', *Burlington Magazine* 8 (May 1961), pp. 180–5

Lockspeiser, Edward: *Debussy: His Life and Mind*, 2 vols. London: Cassell, 1962 and 1965 (repr. Cambridge: CUP, 1978)

— *Music and Painting*. London: Cassell, 1973

Long, Marguerite: *Au piano avec Claude Debussy*. Paris: Julliard, 1960 [in English: *At the Piano with Debussy*, trans. Olive Senior-Ellis. London: Dent, 1972]

— *Au piano avec Gabriel Fauré*. Paris: Julliard, 1963 [in English: *At the Piano with Fauré*, trans. Olive Senior-Ellis. London: Kahn & Averill, 1981]

— *Au piano avec Maurice Ravel*, ed. Pierre Laumonier. Paris: Julliard, 1971 [in English: *At the Piano with Ravel*, trans. Olive Senior-Ellis. London: Dent, 1973]

McFarland, Mark: 'Debussy and Stravinsky: another look at their musical relationship', *Cahiers Debussy* 24 (2000), pp. 79–112

— 'Transpositional combination and aggregate formation in Debussy', *Music Theory Spectrum* 27:2 (October 2005), pp. 187–220

McManus, I. C.: 'The aesthetics of simple figures', *British Journal of Psychology*, 71:4 (November 1980), pp. 505–24

Marmontel, Antoine: *Les pianistes célèbres*. Paris: Heugel, 1878

Marnat, Marcel: *Maurice Ravel*. Paris: Fayard, 1986

— (ed.): *Ravel: souvenirs de Manuel Rosenthal, recueillis par Marcel Marnat*. Paris: Hazan, 1995

Mawer, Deborah: *The Ballets of Maurice Ravel*. Aldershot: Ashgate, 2006

— (ed.): *The Cambridge Companion to Ravel*. Cambridge: CUP, 2000

Max-Anély [pseud. of Victor Segalen]: 'Voix mortes: musiques maori', *Mercure musical et Bulletin français de la S.I.M.* 3:10 (15 October 1907), pp. 1005–27

Mercier, Alain: *Les sources ésotériques et occultes de la poésie symboliste*. Paris: A.-G. Nizet, 1969

Merlet, Dominique: 'Conseils pour interpréter Ravel', ed. Christian Lorandin, *Piano 20* (special annual number, 2006–2007, of *La lettre du musicien*), pp. 89–91

Messiaen, Olivier and Loriod, Yvonne: *Analyse des œuvres pour piano de Maurice Ravel*. Paris: Durand, 2003

Messing, Scott: *Neoclassicism in Music: From the Genesis of the Concept through the Schoenberg / Stravinsky Polemic*. Ann Arbor, Mich.: UMI Research Press, 1988

Michelet, Victor-Émile: *Les compagnons de la hiérophanie*. Paris: Dorbon, 1937

Milon, Yves et al.: *Maurice Ravel à Montfort l'Amaury*, preface by Manuel Rosenthal, texts by Yves Milon, captions by Claude Moreau, photographs by Thomas Renaut. Paris: Éditions ASA [1996]

Moldenhauer, Hans: 'From the library of a forgotten pioneer [Ricardo Viñes]', n.d. Unpublished typescript, Paul Nettl Papers, William and Gayle Cook Music Library, Indiana University

Mueller, Richard: 'Javanese influence on Debussy's *Fantaisie* and beyond', *19th Century Music* 10:2 (Autumn 1986), pp. 157–86

Myers, Rollo: *Emmanuel Chabrier and his Circle*. London: Dent, 1969

Nagy, Dénes: 'Golden section(ism): from mathematics to the theory of art and musicology', *Symmetry: Culture and Science*, 7:4 (1996), pp. 413–41, and 8:1 (1997), pp. 74–112

Narbaïtz, Pierre: *Maurice Ravel: un orfèvre basque*. Anglet (Côte basque): L'Académie internationale Maurice Ravel, 1975

[Nectoux, Jean-Michel:] 'Entretien avec Emmanuel Fauré-Fremiet, propos recueillis par Jean-Michel Nectoux les 14 janvier et 11 février 1971', *Association des amis de Gabriel Fauré*, Bulletin 9 (1972), pp. 12–17

Nectoux, Jean-Michel: 'Debussy et Fauré', *Cahiers Debussy* new series 3 (1979), pp. 13–30
— *Fauré.* Paris: Seuil, 1972 (revised edition 1995)
— *Gabriel Fauré: A Musical Life*, trans. Roger Nichols. Cambridge: CUP, 1991. Revised French edition: *Gabriel Fauré: les voix du clair-obscur.* Paris: Fayard, 2008
— *Harmonie en bleu et or: Debussy, la musique et les arts.* Paris: Fayard, 2005
— 'Maurice Ravel et sa bibliothèque musicale', *Cahiers Ravel* 3 (1987), pp. 53–63
— (ed.): 'Albéniz et Fauré (correspondance inédite)', *Travaux de l'Institut d'études ibériques et latino-américaines* (Strasbourg), XVIᵉ–XVIIᵉ année (1977), pp. 159–86
— *Camille Saint-Saëns & Gabriel Fauré: correspondance (1862–1920).* Paris: Klincksieck, 1994
— *Gabriel Fauré: correspondance.* Paris: Flammarion, 1980
— *Gabriel Fauré: His Life through his Letters*, trans. J. A. Underwood [from the above volume]. London: Marion Boyars, 1984
— see also under Kaufmann
Neuhaus, Heinrich: *The Art of Piano Playing*, trans. K. A. Leibovitch. London: Barrie & Jenkins, 1973
Newbould, Brian: 'Ravel's *Pantoum*', *Musical Times* 116:1585 (March 1975), pp. 228–31
Nichols, Roger: *Maurice Ravel: A Biography* [provisional title]. New Haven: Yale UP, in press
— 'The prosaic Debussy', in Trezise (ed.), *The Cambridge Companion to Debussy*, pp. 84–100
— (ed.): *Debussy Remembered.* London: Faber, 1992
— *Ravel Remembered.* London: Faber, 1987
Nijinska, Bronislav: *Bronislav Nijinska: Early Memoirs.* New York: Holt, Rinehart and Winston, 1981
Okamoto, Kimiko: *Between the Ancient and the Modern: A Study of Danses à Deux in Duple-metre within Changing Aesthetics in France 1700–1733.* PhD dissertation, School of Arts, Roehampton University, London, 2005
Orenstein, Arbie: *Ravel, Man and Musician.* New York: Columbia UP, 1975 (revised edition: New York: Dover, 1991)
— (ed.): *A Ravel Reader: Correspondence, Articles, Interviews.* New York: Columbia UP, 1990. French edition, *Maurice Ravel: lettres, écrits, entretiens.* Paris: Flammarion, 1989
Orledge, Robert: *Debussy and the Theatre.* Cambridge: Cambridge UP, 1982
Oudin, Bernard: *Aristide Briand: la paix: une idée neuve en Europe.* Paris: Laffont, 1987
Pahissa, Jaime: *Manuel de Falla: His Life and Works*, trans. Jean Wagstaff. London: Museum Press, 1954 (repr. Westport, Conn.: Hyperion, 1979)
Perlemuter, Vlado and Jourdan-Morhange, Hélène: *Ravel d'après Ravel: les œuvres pour piano.* Lausanne: Éditions du Cervin, 1970. [Augmented re-edition: *Ravel d'après Ravel, suivi de Rencontres avec Vlado Perlemuter par Jean Roy.* Aix-en-Provence: Alinéa, 1989]
— *Ravel according to Ravel*, trans. Frances Tanner [from the above 1970 volume], ed. Harold Taylor. London: Kahn & Averill, 1990
Persia, Jorge de et al.: *Manuel de Falla: His Life and Works.* Madrid: Ministerio de Cultura, 1996
Peter, René: *Claude Debussy.* Paris: Gallimard, 1944 (10ᵗʰ edition)
Philip, Robert: *Early Recordings and Musical Style.* Cambridge: CUP, 1992
— *Performing Music in the Age of Recording.* New Haven: Yale UP, 2004
Phillips, Edward: *Gabriel Fauré: A Guide to Research.* New York and London: Garland, 2000
Phillips, John A.: 'Viennese fundamental bass tradition in the late nineteenth century', in *Music Research: New Directions for a New Century*, ed. Michael Ewens, Rosalind Halton and John A. Philips. London: Cambridge Scholars Press, 2004
Pierné, Gabriel and Paul Vidal: 'Souvenirs d'Achille Debussy', *La revue musicale* 7:7 (special number, *La jeunesse de Claude Debussy*, 1 May 1926), pp. 10–16
Platt, Peter: 'Debussy and the harmonic series', in *Essays in honour of David Evatt Tunley*, ed. Frank Callaway. Perth, Australia: Callaway International Resource Centre for Music Education 1995, pp. 35–59

Poulenc, Francis: *Emmanuel Chabrier*. Geneva: La Palatine, 1961 (English edition, trans. Cynthia Jolly, London: Dobson, 1981)
— *Entretiens avec Claude Rostard*. Paris: Julliard, 1954
Priest, Deborah (ed. and trans.): *Louis Laloy (1874–1944) on Debussy, Ravel and Stravinsky*. Aldershot: Ashgate, 1999
Rao, B. Subba: *Rāganidhi: A Comparative Study of Hindustani and Karnatak Rāgas*, vol. 4. Madras: Music Academy, 1966
Ravel Remembered, see Nichols
A Ravel Reader, see Orenstein
Régnier, Henri de: 'Souvenirs sur Debussy', *La revue musicale* 7:7 (special number, *La jeunesse de Claude Debussy*, 1 May 1926), pp. 89–91
Roberts, Paul: *Images: The Piano Music of Claude Debussy*. Portland, Ore.: Amadeus Press, 1996
Robinson, Lucy: 'Forqueray *Pièces de viole* (Paris 1747): an enigma of authorship between father and son', *Early Music* 34:2 (May 2006), pp. 259–76
Roger-Ducasse: lettres à Nadia Boulanger, ed. Jacques Depaulis. Liège: Mardaga, 1999
— see also below under **Historic Editions**, Fauré
Roland-Manuel, *Maurice Ravel*, trans. Cynthia Jolly. London: Dobson, 1947 (repr. New York: Dover, 1972). French edition: *Ravel*. Paris: Nouvelle Revue Critique, 1938
Rolf, Marie: 'Debussy, Gautier, and "Les papillons"', in Fulcher (ed.), *Debussy and his World*, pp. 99–115
— 'Symbolism as compositional agent in Act IV, Scene 4 of Debussy's *Pelléas et Mélisande*', in Kelly and Murphy (eds), *Berlioz and Debussy*, pp. 117–48
Romilly, Mme Gérard de: 'Debussy professeur, par une de ses élèves (1898–1908)', *Cahiers Debussy* new series 2 (1978), pp. 3–10; also (with an introduction by François Lesure) in Kaufmann et al., *Claude Debussy: textes*, pp. 11–23
Rosen, Charles: 'Where Ravel ends and Debussy begins', *Cahiers Debussy* new series 3 (1979), pp. 32–3 (originally in *High Fidelity* magazine, May 1959)
Rosenblum, Sandra P.: 'Some enigmas of Chopin's pedal indications: what do the sources tell us?', *Journal of Musicological Research* 16:1 (1996), pp. 41–61
Rosenthal, Manuel: *Musique adorable*. Paris: Hexicorde, 1994
— see also under Marnat
Rousseau-Plotto, Étienne: *Ravel: portraits basques*. Paris: Séguier, 2004
Routley, Nicholas: 'Debussy and Baudelaire's *Harmonie du soir*', *Musicology Australia* 15 (1992), pp. 77–82
— '*Des pas sur la neige*: Debussy in Bilitis's footsteps', *Musicology Australia* 16 (1993), pp. 19–27
Rutter, John: *The Sonata Principle*, Open University Course A241, Elements of Music. Milton Keynes: Open University, 1975
de Saint-Marceaux, Marguerite, see Chimènes
Saint-Saëns, Camille: 'Quelques mots sur l'exécution des œuvres de Chopin', *Le courrier musical* 13:10 (1910), pp. 386–7
Samson, Jim (ed.): *Chopin Studies*. Cambridge: CUP, 1988
— et al.: *Falla–Chopin: la música más pura: estudios de Jim Samson, Roy Howat, Paolo Pinamonti and Víctor Estapé*, ed. and trans. Luis Gago. Granada: Archivo Manuel de Falla), 1999
Samuel, Claude: *Entretiens avec Olivier Messiaen*. Paris: Éditions Pierre Belfond, 1967
Schaeffner, André: 'Debussy et ses rapports avec la musique russe', in Schaeffner, *Essais de musicologie et autres fantaisies*. Paris: Le Sycomore, 1980, pp. 157–206; first published as 'Debussy et la musique russe' in *Musique russe*, vol. 1, ed. Pierre Souvtchinsky. Paris: Presses universitaires de France, 1953
— see also under Joly-Segalen

Schmidt, Carl B.: *The Music of Francis Poulenc (1899–1963): A Catalogue*. Oxford: OUP, 1995

Schmitz, E. Robert: *The Piano Works of Claude Debussy*. New York: Duell, Sloane and Pearce, 1950 (repr. New York: Dover, 1966)

— 'A plea for the real Debussy', *The Etude* 55:12 (December 1937), pp. 781–2

Scott, Cyril: *Bone of Contention*. New York: Arco, 1969

— *My Years of Indiscretion*. London: Mills & Boon, 1924

Segalen, see Max-Anély, also Joly-Segalen

Shah, Idries: *The Sufis*. London: Allen, 1964 (repr. New York: Doubleday, 1971)

Siegele, Ulrich: *Bachs theologischer Formbegriff und das Duett F-dur*. Neuhausen and Stuttgart: Hänssler, 1978

Simeone, Nigel: 'Debussy and expression', in Trezise (ed.), *The Cambridge Companion to Debussy*, pp. 101–16

Sitsky, Larry: *The Classical Reproducing Piano Roll: A Catalogue-index*, 2 vols. New York and London: Greenwood Press Music Reference Collection no. 23, 1990

Smith, Charles Davis and Howe, Richard James: *The Welte-Mignon: Its Music and Musicians*. Vestal NY: Vestal Press, 1994

Sorrell, Neil: *A Guide to the Gamelan*. London: Faber, 1990

Stravinsky, Igor: *An Autobiography*. New York: Norton, 1936

— and Robert Craft: *Conversations with Igor Stravinsky*. London: Faber, 1959

Stuckenschmidt, Hans-Heinz: 'Debussy or Berg? The mystery of a chord progression', *Musical Quarterly* 51:3 (July 1965), pp. 453–9

— *Maurice Ravel: Variations on his Life and Work*, trans. S. R. Rosenbaum. London: Calder & Boyars, 1969

Suares, André: 'Pour Ravel', *La revue musicale* 6:6 (special Ravel number, 1 April 1925), pp. 3–8

Suschitzky, Anya: 'Debussy's Rameau: French music and its Others', *Musical Quarterly* 86:3 (Fall 2002), pp. 398–448

Tait, Robin: *The Musical Language of Gabriel Fauré*. New York and London: Garland, 1989

Taruskin, Richard: 'Chernomor to Kashchei: harmonic sorcery; or, Stravinsky's "angle"', *Journal of the American Musicological Society* 38:1 (Spring 1985), pp. 72–142

— '"Entoiling the Falconet": Russian musical orientalism in context', *Cambridge Opera Journal* 4:3 (1992), pp. 253–80

Thieffry, Jeanne (ed.): *Alfred Cortot: cours d'interprétation, recueilli et rédigé par Jeanne Thieffry*. Paris: Legouix, 1934

Thierry, Solange et al.: *Au cœur de l'impressionnisme: la famille Rouart*. Paris: Association Paris Musées, 2004 (issued for the 2004 Rouart exhibition at the Musée de la vie romantique)

Thompson, D'Arcy Wentworth: *On Growth and Form*. Cambridge: CUP, 1917

Timbrell, Charles: *French Pianism*. London: Kahn & Averill, 1999 (2nd edition)

— *Prince of virtuosos: A Life of Walter Rummel, American Pianist*. Lanham, Md.: Scarecrow Press, 2005

Trezise, Simon (ed.): *The Cambridge Companion to Debussy*. Cambridge: CUP, 2003

Tunley, David: 'The union of words and music in seventeenth-century French song: the long and the short of it', *Australian Journal of French Studies* 3 (1984), pp. 281–308

— *François Couperin and 'The Perfection of Music'*. Aldershot: Ashgate, 2004

Vallas, Léon: *Claude Debussy et son temps*. Paris: Albin Michel, 1958 (revised edition)

Vanhulst, Henri: 'L'éditeur bruxellois Schott frères et *D'un cahier d'esquisses* de Claude Debussy', *Cahiers Debussy* 26 (2002), pp. 3–13

Visser, Peter: 'Een muzikale Oost-West-ontmoeting in de Haagse Kunstkring', *Mens en melodie* 87:9 (1987), pp. 401–8

Walker, Alan: *Franz Liszt: The Final Years, 1861–1886*. Ithaca, NY: Cornell UP, 1996

Wallace, Hannah: *Nationalism and Identity in the Solo Piano Music of Gabriel Fauré and Isaac Albéniz.* BA Honours thesis, University of York, 2008

Walsh, Stephen: *Stravinsky: A Creative Spring: Russia and France, 1882–1934.* New York: Knopf, 1999

Watson, Derek: *Bruckner.* London: Dent (The Master Musicians), 1975

Wenk, Arthur B.: *Claude Debussy and the Poets.* Berkeley: University of California Press, 1976

Whitehead, William: 'New perspectives in Franck studies', *Royal College of Organists Year Book* 2003–4, pp. 53–60

Whittall, Arnold: 'Tonality and the whole-tone scale in the music of Debussy', *Music Review* 36 (November 1975), pp. 261–71

Williams, Graham: *The Theories of Olivier Messiaen: Their Origins and their Application in his Piano Music,* 2 vols. PhD thesis, University of Adelaide, 1978

Youens, Susan: 'Debussy's setting of Verlaine's "Colloque sentimentale": from the past to the present', *Studies in Music* (Perth, Australia) 15 (1981), pp. 93–105

Zank, Stephen: *Maurice Ravel: A Guide to Research.* New York and London: Routledge, 2005

Zeising, Adolf: *Der Goldene Schnitt.* Halle: Engelmann, 1884

— *Neue Lehre von Proportionen des menschlichen Körpers.* Leipzig: Weigel, 1854

Encyclopedias and Dictionaries

The New Grove Dictionary of Music and Musicians, 2nd edition, ed. Stanley Sadie and John Tyrrell. London: Macmillan, 2001, 29 vols

Liner notes for recordings

Caswell, Kenneth: to Pierian CD 0001 (2000), *Claude Debussy: The Composer as Pianist: All his Known Recordings.* The Caswell Collection, vol. 1

— to Pierian CD 0013 (2002), *Maurice Ravel: The Composer as Pianist and Conductor: All of his Known Recordings.* The Caswell Collection, vol. 4

Hudry, François: to Claves CD 50–9102 (1997), Dukas Symphony in C and Fauré *Pelléas et Mélisande,* Orchestre philharmonique de Monte-Carlo, conducted by Lawrence Foster

Jacobs, Paul: to Nonesuch double LP HB-73031 (1978), *Claude Debussy (1862–1918): Preludes for Piano, Books I & II,* performed by Paul Jacobs

Lerner, Bennett: to Bridge Records CD Bridge 9186 (2006), *Claude Debussy: The Complete Piano Music vol. 1,* performed by Bennett Lerner

Poulet, Gérard: to Arion CD ARN68228 (1994), violin sonatas by Debussy, Ravel and Pierné, performed by Gérard Poulet and Noël Lee

Historic editions

Debussy, Claude (ed.): *J.-S. Bach, 6 Sonates [pour] violon et piano,* révision par Claude Debussy. Paris: Durand, 1917

— (ed.): *Chopin, Œuvres complètes pour piano,* révision par Claude Debussy. Paris: Durand, 1915–17

Diémer, Louis (ed.): *Les clavecinistes français du XVIIIe siècle: Couperin–Daquin–Rameau: 20 pièces choisies, transcrites par Louis Diémer.* Paris: Durand & Schoenewerk, 1887. Vol. 2 (works by Dagincourt, Dandrieu, Daquin and Lully). Paris: Durand, 1896

Fauré, Gabriel (ed.): *J.-S. Bach, Le clavecin [sic] bien tempéré,* révision par Gabriel Fauré [fingering by Marguerite Long]. Paris: Durand, 1915

— (ed.): *J.-S. Bach, Œuvres complètes pour orgue*, révision par Gabriel Fauré [with Joseph Bonnet and Eugène Gigout]. Paris: Durand, 1917–20

— (ed.): *Schumann, Œuvres complètes pour piano*. Paris: Durand, 1915–24

— *Huit nocturnes* [1–8]. Paris: Hamelle [1924, re-edition], preface by Roger-Ducasse [with the assistance of André Lambinet]

Ravel, Maurice (ed.): *Mendelssohn, Œuvres complètes pour piano, révision par Maurice Ravel*. Durand, 1915–18

CD-ROMs

Turner, Angela M.: *Maurice Ravel's Performances of his Own Piano Compositions, as Evidenced by the Piano Rolls*. BMus Honours dissertation, Queensland Conservatorium of Music, Griffith University, 2000

FILMS

Ravel, directed by Niv Fichman and Larry Weinstein, Rhombus Media, Toronto (for the Canadian Broadcasting Corporation), 1987

INTERNET

Antoine, Laurent: 'Andalousie au temps des Maures', in *Exposition Universelle Paris 1900* (February 2006), http://lemog.fr/lemog_expo_v2/thumbnails.php?album=152 (accessed 27 December 2008)

Enget, Diane: 'Debussy in Jersey', *Litart* (Spring 2004, updated October 2005), www.litart.co.uk (accessed 27 December 2008)

INDEX

Page numbers in bold indicate music examples. Listing of surnames beginning with the prefixes 'de', 'van', 'von', etc., varies according to accepted usage (e.g. 'van Gogh, Vincent' but 'Beethoven, Ludwig van').

CPSIA information can be obtained
at www.ICGtesting.com
Printed in the USA
BVHW040921071218
535024BV00009B/394/P